––––– THE POWER OF –––––
THE STEEL-TIPPED PEN

THE POWER OF
THE STEEL-TIPPED PEN
Reconstructing Native Hawaiian Intellectual History

NOENOE K. SILVA

With a foreword by Ngũgĩ wa Thiong'o

Duke University Press · Durham and London · 2017

© 2017 DUKE UNIVERSITY PRESS
All rights reserved

Designed by Courtney Leigh Baker
Typeset in Trade Gothic and Arno Pro by Westchester Publishing Services
Library of Congress Cataloging-in-Publication Data
Names: Silva, Noenoe K., [date] author. |
Ngūgī wa Thiong'o, [date] writer of foreword.
Title: The power of the steel-tipped pen : reconstructing native
Hawaiian intellectual history / Noenoe K. Silva ;
with a foreword by Ngūgī wa Thiong'o.
Description: Durham : Duke University Press, 2017. |
Includes bibliographical references and index.
Identifiers: LCCN 2016046670 (print) |
LCCN 2016049127 (ebook)
ISBN 9780822363521 (hardcover : alk. paper)
ISBN 9780822363682 (pbk. : alk. paper)
ISBN 9780822373131 (ebook)
Subjects: LCSH: Kānepuʻu, Joseph Hoʻonaʻauao, 1824–approximately 1886—
Influence. | Poepoe, Joseph Mokuʻōhai, 1852–1913— Influence. | Hawaii— Intellectual
life—19th century—Sources. | Hawaiian newspapers—History—19th century. |
Hawaiian literature—19th century—History and criticism. | Hawaii—
History—19th century—Sources. | Hawaiian language—Social aspects. |
Hawaiian philosophy. | Hawaiians—Songs and music.
Classification: LCC DU624.5 .S48 2017 (print) |
LCC DU624.5 (ebook) | DDC 996.9/027—dc23
LC record available at https://lccn.loc.gov/2016046670

COVER ART: Haley Kailiehu, *Moʻokūʻauhau*. Courtesy of the artist.

For Sam L. Noʻeau Warner and
Haunani-Kay Trask

———

Contents

Foreword by Ngũgĩ wa Thiong'o · ix

Acknowledgments · xi

"Ke Au Hawai'i" by Larry Kauanoe Kimura · xiii

Introduction · 1

PART I
JOSEPH HOʻONAʻAUAO KĀNEPUʻU

—— 1 ——

Joseph Hoʻonaʻauao Kānepuʻu · 21

—— 2 ——

Selected Literary Works of Joseph Kānepuʻu · 53

—— 3 ——

Kanaka Geography and Aloha ʻĀina · 82

PART II
JOSEPH MOKUʻŌHAI POEPOE

—— 4 ——

Joseph Mokuʻōhai Poepoe · 105

—— 5 ——

Singing (to) the ʻĀina · 150

—— 6 ——

Moʻolelo Hawaiʻi Kahiko · 174

Conclusion · 211

Appendix A: Kānepuʻu Selected Bibliography · 215
Appendix B: Poepoe Selected Bibliography · 217
Notes · 221
Glossary · 241
Bibliography · 247
Index · 263

Foreword

NGŪGĪ WA THIONG'O

The popular African proverb that until the lions have their storytellers, the story of the hunt will always glorify the hunter, applies to the two connected binaries of the colonizer and the colonized, the oppressor and the oppressed. Telling tales is part of the whole realm of a people, any people, naming the world. To name is also to claim a particular relationship to the named. Language is a vast system of naming the world, which expresses that community's total relationship to their environment, their economic activities, their political and social relations, and ultimately their view of themselves in the world.

Oppressors and their oppressing system understand that it is not enough for them to seize people's land, impose their rule, but they go further and control the culture and the value system of the conquered. Economic and political control are incomplete without cultural control. The entire edifice of economic, political, and cultural control remains shaky without control of the mind of the conquered. Hence, in history, the conqueror has always felt it imperative to control the mind of the conquered. The easiest route to that conquest is language. Colonization of a people's naming system is an integral part of an oppressing system.

The story of Hawaiian is the struggle of many marginalized languages in the world today, which have been buried under or sidelined by conscious laws and education programs. Prior to conquest and annexation, Hawaiian had been the root center of Hawaiian being. But from 1898 to 1978, it was pushed to the margins through laws banning it and educational programs that forcibly put English at the center. But Hawaiian orature survived the onslaught: so also some of the writings in the language.

Resistance to oppression includes reclaiming a people's land, politics, and culture, for economic and political liberation can never be complete without the cultural. The struggle for their own language is central to the entire enterprise. And once again the fight-back spirit of the Hawaiian culture has ensured the survival and even renaissance of the language. The excavation of the intellectual history produced in the language is an integral part of the struggle for its continued being.

One of the ways in which suppressed languages are marginalized is by convincing its users that it is not an adequate basis for intellectual production. Hence the importance of this work: *The Power of the Steel-Tipped Pen*. The two Josephs, Kānepuʻu and Poepoe, produced ideas in Hawaiian. This book ensures that the young generation has something concrete to help them feel connected to a rich intellectual ancestry.

But the work as a whole has a resonance that goes well beyond Hawaiʻi to other areas in the world where a people are still struggling to decolonize their minds. It is a welcome addition to the global movement for the decolonization of languages and the minds.

When the dispossessed finally get their storytellers and their own workers in ideas, then the story of the struggle will finally glorify the people's heroism and their resistance spirit. Their language becomes the center from which to connect with other languages and cultures.

NGŨGĨ WA THIONGʻO is Distinguished Professor of English and Comparative Literature at the University of California, Irvine. His 1984 book, *Decolonizing the Mind*, has become a standard text in decolonial studies and theory.

Acknowledgments

I am very grateful for support from the School of Advanced Research in Santa Fe, New Mexico, and from the Department of Political Science at the University of Hawaiʻi at Mānoa.

I can never repay the generosity of Jonathan Goldberg-Hiller, who read every page, many multiple times, and cheerfully discussed every idea. Many ideas and articulations in this book would never have come to be without his patience and intellect.

Palena ʻole kuʻu mahalo i ka hui heluhelu Hāmanalau a inu waina, ʻo ia hoʻi ʻo Leilani Basham, Uʻilani Bobbitt, Kahikina de Silva, a me Maya Kawailana Saffery. Ua waiwai loa ko ʻoukou mau manaʻo a waiwai pū nā kamaʻilio leʻaleʻa.

Jodi Byrd, kuʻualoha hoʻomanawanui, J. Kēhaulani Kauanui, and Brandy Nālani McDougall read drafts and participated in many conversations over the years that assisted in the writing of the book. Mahalo nui e nā hoa wahine mana. Many thanks as well to Hokulani Aikau, Marie Alohalani Brown, John Charlot, Noelani Goodyear-Kaʻōpua, Craig Howes, Sankaran Krishna, and Albert J. Schütz for reading and commenting on the manuscript or parts of it. I am also grateful to all of the above friends for many bits of information and research directions to follow, not to mention the stalwart support through thick and thin. I am also indebted to Ronald Williams Jr. and Sāhoa Fukushima for much information gleaned from the Hawaiian papers and to David Chang, Laiana Wong and Kaleomanuʻiwa Wong for helpful conversations.

My ability to conduct the research depended on the smarts, skills, and generosity of many librarians and archivists, among them Joan Hori and Dore Minatodani of the Hawaiian collection in Hamilton Library at the University of Hawaiʻi, Mānoa; Jason Kapena Achiu, Luella Kurkjian, Gina

Vergara-Bautista, Ju Sun Yi, and the other archivists and staff at the Hawai‘i State Archives; DeSoto Brown, Leah Pualaha‘ole Caldeira, Tia Reber, B. J. Short, and the other staff at the Bishop Museum Library and Archives; Barbara Dunn and Jennifer Higa of the Hawaiian Historical Society Library and Archives; and Carol White and John Barker of the Mission Houses Archives. If I have inadvertently forgotten anyone, I apologize for the faulty memory; please know that I am ever grateful.

To Joseph Moku‘ōhai Poepoe's descendants, I cannot thank you enough. Sybil Pruett provided the photograph of Mr. Poepoe as well as a genealogy. Mahalo nui e ku‘u tita. George Kaleionamokuokalani Muneoka shared a photo and the site where Mr. Poepoe is buried. To George, his daughter Shelley Muneoka, and the rest of the ‘ohana, thank you for your support and enthusiasm for the project.

Many thanks to Marie Alohalani Brown for formatting the genealogy table and providing much technical help, and to Charles "Kale" Langlas for use of the map of the Kalapana region. Mahalo a nui loa iā Larry Kauanoe Kimura i ka ‘ae ‘ana mai i ke mele "Ke Au Hawai‘i"; he mele ho‘oulu a ho‘olana i ka na‘au a me ka ‘uhane pū.

I extend my thanks to the many students who have discussed the rationales and research methods with me over the years.

To Ken Wissoker, it is impossible to express just how grateful I am for your continued enthusiasm and belief in this book though it has taken so long. Your reassurances over the years have helped me to persevere to the end!

I am grateful as well to Courtney Berger at Duke University Press for her support, to Jade Brooks and Lisa Bintrim for the editorial assistance, and to Christine Dahlin, the copy editor, for her patience and talent.

KE AU HAWAIʻI

Auē nā aliʻi ē	O my chiefs
O ke au i hala	Of times past, I feel your presence even more now
E nānā mai iā mākou	To see and observe us
Nā pulapula o nei au e holo nei	The sons and daughters of this current time
E ala mai kākou e nā kini, mamo o ka ʻāina aloha	Let us rise up, o multitudes, descendants of the beloved ʻāina
Aloha wale ia ʻāina, ko kākou kahua	I am moved deeply with concern for the ʻāina, our true foundation
Auē ka ʻiliʻili ē i ka hoʻopuehu ʻia nei	We grieve the little stones that are being scattered
E paepae hou ʻia ka pōhaku i paʻa maila ke kahua hale hou	The large stones must be reset in place so that a new house foundation is completed
No kākou e nā pua e hoʻolulu ai	For us, the children, to find security in
E ala e ka ʻĪ, ka Mahi, ka Palena	Rise up, families of the ʻĪ, the Mahi, the Palena
I mua a loaʻa ka lei o ka lanakila.	Go forward until we gain the lei of victory.

—Larry Kauanoe Kimura

Introduction

> We, as Native Hawaiians, must continue to unveil the knowledge of our ancestors. Let us interpret for ourselves who our ancestors are, how they thought, and why they made certain decisions. In the process, we treat them with honor, dignity, love, and respect.
>
> PUALANI KANAKAʻOLE KANAHELE

The main purpose of this book is to further the project of mapping Kanaka Hawaiʻi (Native Hawaiian) intellectual history. How can we know that our ancestors were (are) intellectual beings, and know more specifically in whose path we are now following? Fortunately, our ancestors took great pains to write down our moʻolelo; lyric, epic, and other forms of poetry; political and economic analyses of their times; interpretations of *their* ancestors' philosophies, histories, and oral literatures; and so on.

As we read what they wrote, which is overwhelmingly in their native language, ʻōlelo Hawaiʻi, we inevitably gain an appreciation of the depth of their thought and their artistic genius. As Pualani Kanahele articulates in the epigraph, when we do this work of interpretation, we honor and respect our ancestors. We are also then able to consciously continue distinctive Kanaka thought and intellectual production. This book, then, mainly consists of reading the works of our ancestors, concentrating on the writing careers of two men. The first, Joseph Hoʻonaʻauao Kānepuʻu, was a schoolteacher from Kalawao, Molokai, who lived his adult life on Oʻahu and contributed a wide variety of writing to Hawaiian-language newspapers. He was a strong advocate for the newspapers, the native language, and native ontologies and epistemologies. He published between about 1856 and 1883. The second is Joseph Mokuʻōhai Poepoe, who was an attorney, writer, editor, and politician from Kohala, Hawaiʻi, who also lived his adult life in the capital of Honolulu. He published in the Hawaiian-language newspapers, starting with translations of European tales, from about 1870 to 1913.

The study of these authors—a concentrated reading of their works—forms part of the resurgence of a Hawaiian world, working toward a hegemony of Hawaiian ways in Hawai'i nei. What I mean by resurgence is our creation of a world in which we speak, write, and compose in our native language; take care of our 'āina (land) and waters; reinvoke and appreciate our native deities; and live (at least mentally) free from the destructive settler colonialism in which we now find ourselves. This is inspired by Taiaiake Alfred's work on Onkwehonwe (Mohawk): "It is time for our people to live again. [This means] a living commitment to meaningful change in our lives and to transforming society by recreating our existences, regenerating our cultures, and surging against the forces that keep us bound to our colonial past."[1]

Thousands of people are creating or regenerating a more Hawaiian world for us and our descendants to live in. Hawaiians all over Hawai'i (and other places to a lesser extent) are opening or reopening lo'i and planting kalo with other native plants, using diverse cropping as our ancestors did; learning, speaking, and teaching 'ōlelo Hawai'i; creating master's and PhD programs in Hawaiian language and Hawaiian studies; writing master's theses, dissertations, books, and newspaper columns in 'ōlelo Hawai'i; composing Kanaka language- and culture-based music; broadcasting Hawaiian music shows with all commentary in 'ōlelo Hawai'i; broadcasting news in 'ōlelo Hawai'i; building, consecrating, and voyaging on wa'a (vessels often misnamed canoes) that are inspired by ancient forms; founding, administering, teaching in, or attending native Hawaiian culture–based charter schools; rebuilding our ancestors' fishponds; making and using fishing nets in the styles of our ancestors; learning, dancing, and teaching hula and all the art forms associated with hula; participating in makahiki and other ceremonies and festivals; and so on. Separately, these are coincidental initiatives that satisfy various desires to make life better for specific segments of our lāhui (people; nation); together they function as a network of significant sites in which to live native lives: to be educated, work, speak, have a spiritual life, be an artist, grow one's food, sail the oceans, be entertained, contribute politically, and so forth, in native rather than the foreign hegemonic ways that have been imposed on us for too long. A child can conceivably now receive an education from a Hawaiian immersion preschool in Pūnana Leo to a PhD in programs conducted in Hawaiian or which are Hawaiian-centered, and spend her spare time in voyaging, loʻi farming, hula, or other Hawaiian arts, and, thus, while still surrounded by a hegemonic American culture, live a life that is substantially based in Hawaiian culture.

This book is my contribution to this resurgence: it is intended to demonstrate the full and dynamic intellectual lives that our recent ancestors (ca. 1856 to 1913) lived, many as public intellectuals, producing and engaging literature and politics in their own native language. It is crucial that in addition to reestablishing our self-sufficiency, spirituality, and art forms, we reclaim our history of intellectual efforts and accomplishment. We must do the hard work of both reading our ancestors' writing in our heritage language and also analyzing our ancestors' places in our history.

The method that I used to do this began with collecting everything I could that each of these authors wrote. The thousands of pages of Hawaiian-language newspapers have never been indexed, and at the time I began the research, only a portion of them had been digitized, and a much smaller portion had been OCR'd so that they were searchable. Thus, it was necessary to first determine which newspapers each author worked for and published in, then go through those page by page to pull out the news reports, histories, geographies, mele (songs and poetry), moʻolelo (narratives), and letters they contributed. From that collection, I compiled bibliographies and, from there, I read. In order to understand what I was reading, I also read the works around them, the day-to-day politics of each paper, the debates and outright fights between editors and writers at different papers, and the treasures their fellow contributors published. I researched the editors and publishers of each of the papers to get a sense of the political and cultural landscape of the time.

Both of the authors studied in this book were committed to recording and interpreting not only the wisdom of their ancestors, but also their own political and cultural circumstances. They needed to set down in print their engagement with the intellectual traditions of ancestors of previous eras and they needed to analyze their world, and thereby not only describe what Hawaiian intellectual life is or was, but to live it. Our intellectual engagement is part of our specifically Hawaiian ontology, our way of being in the world. This ontology is not and has never been static but is constantly formed in relation to our ʻāina and our ancestors.

The two very different men in this study wrote within different contexts. Nevertheless, I found some similarities in their motivations for writing and publishing and commonalities in their philosophies. First is a deeply ingrained commitment to our people and land: aloha ʻāina; second, acceptance of the kuleana to teach through writing and publishing; and, third, an ethic and orientation to the world I am calling moʻokūʻauhau consciousness. I will now briefly describe these terms.

Aloha ʻāina is a central ideology for our ancestors that is striking in the works of both Kānepuʻu and Poepoe and also in our current movement(s) of resurgence. Aloha ʻāina is a complex concept that includes recognizing that we are an integral part of the ʻāina and the ʻāina is an integral part of us. Part of that is a regenerated belief in our ancestors' cosmogonies, which include moʻolelo, moʻokūʻauhau (genealogies), and mele koʻihonua (genealogical chants) that tell us that the earth is Papahānaumoku, the expanse of the sky is Wākea, and that among their children and descendants are the kalo, Hāloa, and his younger brother Hāloa, the first human being. Within this idea of aloha ʻāina is the concept of kino lau, or multiple physical bodies of spirits. Such spirits may include that of individual humans; ʻaumākua, ancestors whose spirits were transformed into specific animals or elements; and akua (deities or other spirits), who may manifest in animals, plants, or elements such as rain, rainbows, clouds, volcanic fire, and so on. Our familial relationships to these beings are part of our feeling and our ethic of aloha ʻāina.

Kekuewa Kikiloi summarizes the importance of aloha ʻāina to the well-being of the lāhui Hawaiʻi:

> Hawaiian well-being is tied first and foremost to a strong sense of cultural identity that links people to their homeland. At the core of this profound connection is the deep and enduring sentiment of aloha ʻāina, or love for the land.... The ʻāina sustains our identity, continuity, and well-being as a people.... Place names are important cultural signatures etched into the Hawaiian landscape and are embedded with traditional histories and stories that document how our ancestors felt about a particular area, its features, or phenomena. They help to transform once-empty geographic spaces into cultural places enriched with meaning and significance.... The concept of aloha ʻāina is one of great antiquity that originates from the ancient traditions concerning the genealogy and formation of the Hawaiian Archipelago.[2]

Aloha ʻāina, moreover, is an important political concept. It includes the kuleana to mālama or care for the ʻāina. Kuleana encompasses right, authority, and responsibility, and it suggests a familial relationship.[3] Because we are not in charge of our own lands today, we are forced to struggle politically on many fronts: we must defend our ʻāina from further encroachment; try to win back ʻāina lost in the past; regain and protect our fresh and ocean waters; stop the desecration of places like Mauna a Wākea (Mauna Kea); and protect our ancestral remains. Working for the independence of Hawaiʻi from US control is one way this has been expressed in recent years.

Aloha ʻāina is a concept that must be taught. Just as our ancestors felt that ʻōpio (youth) of their day needed to be taught aloha ʻāina, we must continue to teach it. It is neither an instinctive knowledge nor an essentialist quality. On January 6, 1893, one week before the overthrow of Liliʻuokalani's government by a conspiracy of missionary sons and the US Consul, in the preface to the moʻolelo of Hiʻiakaikapoliopele, John E. Bush wrote,

> Aole he loihi o ka noho ana o ka lahui a nalo aku mai ke ao, ke hoomaloka a hoopoina lakou i ka hiipoi ana me na ohohia nui i na moolelo a me na mele o na ano a pau, a kamailio mau imua o ka poe opio i kumu e mau ai na hooipo a me na liʻa ana o ka naau o ke kanaka i ke aloha aina mamuli o ka hooni ana o na moolelo a me na mele e pili ana i kona one hanau, na wahi pana, a me na hana kaulana a kona mau kupuna.[4]
>
> ———
>
> It is not long before a people will disappear from sight should they disbelieve and forget to cherish with enthusiasm the moʻolelo and mele of every kind, and discuss them in the presence of young people as a foundation to perpetuate the love and desire of people for aloha ʻāina based on the stirring nature of the moʻolelo and mele about their birth sands, the storied places, and the famous deeds of their ancestors.

Bush thus explicitly describes aloha ʻāina as something to be cultivated in young people for our continuation and, I would add, resurgence as a lāhui. It is through literature that Bush (and Paʻaluhi, his coauthor) decided to perpetuate the love and desire for ʻāina that is aloha ʻāina. While some, perhaps many, stories were being told in homes and enacted in hula performances, published literature provided an additional vehicle for aloha ʻāina, one that assisted in teaching and perpetuating it in a different and differently enduring way.

In the analyses of literature in this book, aloha ʻāina is apparent in such literary devices as ʻōlelo noʻeau (proverbs and poetical sayings), where many, if not most, poetical sayings draw upon characteristics of the land, its plants, animals, elements, and place names to cleverly mask and reveal multiple meanings. The Kanaka geographer Kapā Oliveira explains, "Because place names are so closely tied to our kūpuna and the ʻāina, place names play a significant role in narrating our identity."[5] She goes on to explain that "place names are the words of our ancestors. Each time we recite a place name, we are quoting our kūpuna. Those things that our kūpuna did not tell us while they were alive are embedded in the place names, orature and physical presence of the land."[6]

Kānepuʻu and Poepoe, along with Bush and Paʻaluhi and the other ancestors in our intellectual history, saw themselves as teachers. They took opportunities within their narratives to provide information about the ʻāina, such as place names, and to explain ʻōlelo noʻeau, history, and geography. They also taught through their works how to unravel kaona (discussed below), how to read ancient mele, and so forth. Poepoe was also committed to teaching the law to those who were monolingual in Hawaiian.

These commitments characterize a certain mode of thought and action that I am calling moʻokūʻauhau (genealogical) consciousness. Kānepuʻu and Poepoe (among many others) thought about the Kanaka descendants of the twenty-first century, and they wrote with us in mind. They drew on their ancestral knowledge and accepted and carried out the kuleana to record it so that Kānaka in their own time(s) as well as in the distant future would benefit from it. Here I build on much recent work that highlights the importance of moʻokūʻauhau for our lāhui. In her groundbreaking 1992 book, Lilikalā Kameʻeleihiwa analyzed moʻokūʻauhau as one of the defining concepts for ruling aliʻi in Hawaiʻi throughout the nineteenth century.[7] More recently, to give several examples, kuʻualoha hoʻomanawanui uses the concept of moʻokūʻauhau to analyze the various iterations of the Pele and Hiʻiaka literature and thus sets up the idea of an intellectual genealogy in our literature. Also, perhaps more important, hoʻomanawanui emphasizes the idea of Kanaka intellectual history throughout her book.[8] Oliveira introduces her book on Kanaka geographies with a chapter on mele koʻihonua, the poetic cosmogonic form of moʻokūʻauhau because they "illuminat[e] the genealogical connection that Kānaka share with the ʻāina . . . are crucial to understanding a Kanaka worldview, and [because] through these cosmogonic genealogies we learn of the formation of the ʻāina, the first living organisms, and the birth of the akua (gods) and the people."[9] Pualani Kanakaʻole Kanahele also begins her book on "the unwrapping of the epic tale of Pele" with moʻokūʻauhau, which in that context she explains as "a literary introduction to a family lineage. The family line may include humans, elements of nature, sharks, or other forms of life."[10] Furthermore, Marie Alohalani Brown astutely explains that "in terms of intellectual endeavors, moʻokūʻauhau refers to the worldview we have inherited as ʻŌiwi, which informs how we conceive, reason about, and understand thought and artistic production."[11]

Although "moʻokūʻauhau" gets translated as "genealogy" in English, moʻokūʻauhau consciousness should not be confused with contemporary theoretical strands called genealogical, as in the works of Nietzsche, Foucault, and others. While, as ʻUmi Perkins has pointed out, the two are not necessarily inherently contradictory, what I am describing here is a specifically Hawaiian orientation to the world (that shares some aspects with other Oceanians).[12]

Throughout this book, we see the ways that our intellectual kūpuna of the nineteenth and early twentieth centuries used moʻokūʻauhau consciousness to perpetuate our language, moʻolelo, mele, and so on. They positioned themselves within the moʻokūʻauhau of our lāhui; that is, they greatly valued the narrative and poetic traditions of *their* kūpuna and used their talents to record them for their descendants. In the twenty-first century, we are who they foresaw: descendants whose primary language is now that of the colonizer, but who need and are benefiting from their efforts to write in Hawaiian. Many of us are similarly building on their foundations—or as Larry Kauanoe Kimura put it, re-laying the large stones of the foundation—to have a Kanaka house in which we and our descendants can live.[13]

Joseph Kānepuʻu exemplified moʻokūʻauhau consciousness when in 1862 he wrote a letter to the editor protesting the shortening of chants in Kapihenui's "Moolelo o Hiiakaikapoliopele":

> Ua ike au, ua hakina ka moolelo o Hiiakaikapoliopele, ua hakina kona mau mele e pili ana i na "huli," a pehea la anei e loaa ai na koena i na hanauna hope o kakou, ke makemake lakou e nana, aole no e loaa, e hele ana kakou i ka nalowale, e hele ana o Kau ka makuahine o M. G. Kapihenui [mea kakau moolelo Hiiakaikapoliopele] i ka nalowale. E makemake ana ka hanauna Hawaii o na la A.D. 1870, a me A.D. 1880, a me A.D. 1890, a me A.D. 1990.[14]

———

> I see that the moʻolelo of Hiʻiakaikapoliopele has been broken off, its mele about the "huli" or volcanic upheavals, have been cut off; and how will the generations after us obtain the remainder when they want to see them; they won't be able to get them [because] we

are disappearing, Kau, the mother of the author, Kapihenui, will be gone. Generations of Hawaiians in 1870, 1880, 1890, and 1990 are going to want [these moʻolelo and mele].

While Kānepuʻu obviously was worried about Kanaka Hawaiʻi and our ancestral knowledge disappearing, his response to that was to foresee future generations and to work to ensure that that knowledge was preserved in print so that we might know who we are, who and where we come from, in order that our lāhui continues to thrive in our specifically Kanaka ways.

I hope this work on these two authors will encourage similar studies. The idea is that as we gather the bibliographies of each author, study the works, and put them into political, cultural, and historical context, we can map our intellectual history. We will then have a far more detailed picture of who our intellectual ancestors are, and not only what each of them wrote, but who influenced whom and in what ways. These are the writers who influenced the various mōʻī and aliʻi nui, who were determining how their country and islands were governed, how the economy developed in their times, and how everyday life was conducted. How will our picture of Hawaiian history, them, and ourselves change when we know their names, their politics, and the extent of their written philosophies, literature, and so forth? I envision a future bookshelf of studies of how these ancestors' philosophies and theories developed, genealogical studies of who responded to whom with new ideas. In order to get there, I suggest we compile the bibliographies, read and contextualize them, with a view to whom each writer was responding, and whom they inspired. These will also be acts of moʻokūʻauhau consciousness as we lay down foundations for more study by our descendants.

Besides the themes just outlined, it is helpful to align this work with recent theoretical developments in American Indian and indigenous studies, especially Robert Allen Warrior's work on intellectual sovereignty, which has been built upon by a number of other scholars, and Alfred's concept of indigenous resurgence, discussed earlier.[15]

Warrior argues that "a process-centered understanding of sovereignty provides a way of envisioning the work Native scholars do," and he examines "the role of American Indian intellectuals in the struggle for sovereignty."[16] He "contend[s] that it is now critical for American Indian intellectuals committed to sovereignty to realize that we too must struggle for sovereignty, *intellectual sovereignty*, and allow the definition and articulation of what that means to emerge as we critically reflect on that struggle."[17]

In other words, our intellectual work is necessarily bound to our sovereignty struggles. Warrior notes, "[Vine] Deloria believed that the key to an American Indian future was the return to Native ceremonies and traditions within a framework of asserting sovereignty."[18] Although Deloria worried about the strategies of the American Indian sovereignty movement and its mistakes, he noted approvingly that "the militants gravitated with ease toward traditional spiritual leaders very early on, asserting that a truly liberative American Indian politics would have at its center an affirmation of culture, spirituality, and tradition."[19]

Using these ideas, I posit that both writers in this book can be seen as asserting and exercising native intellectual sovereignty. That is, they were committed to writing moʻolelo, moʻokūʻauhau, mele, and other works in ʻōlelo Hawaiʻi, and to perpetuating our ancestral knowledge, including spiritual, geographical, cultural, astronomical, and other knowledge. The work to honor our ancestors is part of the resurgence of our native ontology.

Our ancestral knowledge includes close relationships with people in the pō (the realm from which we come and to which we return at death; therefore the realm where our deceased kūpuna continue to exist). Joseph Kānepuʻu, in a slightly fictionalized autobiography, writes that it was predicted at birth that his alter ego would learn the art of kilokilo, or reading signs (hōʻailona) in weather phenomena, not from a physical teacher but "e aoao mai no na aumakua o ka po ia, i loaa ai ia ike" (the ʻaumākua of the pō would teach him so that he would receive that knowledge).[20] This ability to receive knowledge from the spirit world is a persistent belief and practice among Kanaka Hawaiʻi to this day. In the novel *Waimea Summer* (1976), John Dominis Holt writes of life in rural Waimea: "People don't *believe* in spirits here. . . . They *live* with them."[21] Manulani Meyer found that dreams play an active role in contemporary Hawaiian epistemology. She writes, "Many mentors used their dream states to connect with past relatives, create a composition, receive a name for a child, or simply as a vehicle for learning."[22] Similarly, as Kikiloi writes in the preface to his groundbreaking article in native archaeological methodology, "As Native Hawaiians, each of us has the ability to tap into a preconscious reservoir of past experiences and to access all that exists in a storehouse of knowledge called ancestral memories."[23] He credits the idea of ancestral memories to Pualani Kanahele, who writes that her book, *Ka Honua Ola*, is a portal to the expanse of ancestral memory. Ancestral memories offer us many lifetimes of experience, love, pain, belief, understanding and wisdom. They come to our lāhui as a gift and we can decide how this gift is used. . . . The primary source for all Hawaiian knowledge, including the mele in *Ka Honua Ola*, is the kūpuna, the ancestors and keepers of Native Hawaiian intellect from time immemorial. Often the channels are open, and information flows freely through dreams, thoughts, and participation in hula and other aspects of daily Hawaiian living. Written records by various compilers capture some of this collective intelligence.[24]

I see here, along with moʻokūʻauhau consciousness, an unabashed commitment to Kanaka ontology and epistemology, which also can be called practicing intellectual sovereignty. Here intellectual sovereignty means that we are not ceding ground to empiricist or other haole ideas of what counts as knowledge. It is important that we describe our reality, as did Joseph Kānepuʻu, despite opening ourselves to possible ridicule as superstitious primitives or primitivists by the hegemonic culture. Further, this is not so far from Deloria's work in his final book, *The World We Used to Live In: Remembering the Powers of the Medicine Men*, itself a project of intellectual sovereignty.

Kānepuʻu and Poepoe shared a penchant for using Hawaiian systems of knowledge and organization, such as telling time and counting using the Hawaiian monthly moon night names and special numbers for fours, among other linguistic forms that were receding in Kānepuʻu's day and had nearly disappeared during Poepoe's. By Kānepuʻu's time, American weekday names had nearly replaced the indigenous names of the moon nights; counting in the American style was also on the ascendant. Fishers and farmers continued to use the old systems, but they were in the minority. Poepoe and Kānepuʻu, among many, strove to keep this knowledge alive in their writings, which might be seen as acts of intellectual sovereignty.

Kaona

Kaona is one of the most common and most intriguing features of Hawaiian speech, prose, and poetry and thus requires discussion here. This integral characteristic of the Hawaiian language recurs in many places in this book. In "Songs (Meles) of Old Kaʻu, Hawaii," Mary Kawena Pukui defines kaona as the hidden meanings in songs. That is, kaona is a story, a critique, or another kind of message discernible to the recipient of the message, those who know the people involved, or whomever the composer might inform.²⁵ The message is made up of a series of metaphors, allusions, connotations, and evocations associated with words and place names. As Brandy Nālani McDougall notes, Pukui warns against imputing or reading kaona into songs when one is not knowledgeable about the composer or whatever situation the song is about. McDougall correctly goes on to assert that this should not discourage us from our important work of interpretation.²⁶ McDougall, with her coauthor, Georganne Nordstrom, notes that in prose as well as mele many layers of kaona are expected: "there is the literal meaning; references to the ancient through myths, events, gods, and chiefs; the intertextual use of chants and proverbs; and finally, [that other] possible layer" of a hidden story that Pukui described. McDougall and Nordstrom elaborate:

> The composer is expected by Hawaiian audiences to employ kaona, and they know to look for kaona as they hear or read a composition. Kaona demands both an in-depth knowledge of the subject in terms of the audience as well as poetic acumen so as to appeal to the audience's sense of aesthetic. The kaona the composer employs is thus a direct reflection of his or her knowledge of the targeted audience(s) and a reflection of his or her level of rhetorical skill. The complexity involved in creating and deciphering kaona has resulted in it being traditionally regarded as a "skill to be honored at the highest level and an indication of one's intelligence" . . . that is at once both aesthetic and rhetorical.²⁷

Further, Kekeha Solis notes how valued figurative speech in Hawaiian was among early twentieth-century speakers and writers, some of whom bemoaned a diminishing ability to produce kaona. Solis quotes a pseudonymous writer from 1928:

> O ka olelo Hawaii me ke kaona o kona manao, ka pookela o na olelo i waena o na lahui o ka honua nei, ma na hua mele a na kupuna e ike ia ai ka u'i, ka maikai o ke kaona o ka manao, aole hoi e like me ko keia au e nee nei, he hoopuka maoli mai no i ka manao me ka hoonalonalo ole iho i ke kaona.²⁸
>
> ———
>
> The Hawaiian language with the kaona of its meanings is the finest of all languages among the peoples on earth; the beauty and the excellence

of the kaona is seen in the song lyrics of its ancestors; not like it is today, where the meaning is just said with no hiding of the kaona.

One can see that this writer did not refer to kaona only as specific hidden stories within mele; rather she or he uses the word "kaona" to refer to figurative speech more broadly. Thus as readers and listeners, it is our kuleana as well as our delight to consider all possible implications of each word and phrase, to unspool the threads of connotations and allusions, and to let our minds run with composers' metaphors and other wordplay. In this book I attend to these webs of associations, allusions, and connotations, and to the Hawaiian propensity for metaphor and figurative speech, including the tendency to eschew direct, easily understood prose. I use the word "kaona" in this extended way: beyond just a specific, hidden story within a mele, to describe the rich and layered nature of Hawaiian writing. I note as well here that writing and print allowed for more kaona even than speech and spoken poetry, as words that may have been easily distinguishable to the ear became homographs in print. The words "pua," "puʻa," and "pūʻā" serve as examples; before the use of the macron to distinguish them from each other, they were homographs, that is, they looked identical on the page. "Pua" can refer to a blossom, a child, the young of a fish, or the act of issuing or emerging, among other meanings; "puʻa" can be a whistle or to excrete; and "pūʻā," a herd or flock, a sheaf or bundle, to pass food from mouth to mouth, and more.[29] The possibilities for punning and allusion using this one collection of letters in its unmarked form are endless.

A preponderance of kaona is drawn from the ʻāina (including the ocean) and its elements, reflecting the depth of aloha ʻāina in the culture. Place names are a favorite in mele as well as in ʻōlelo noʻeau. Pukui, Elbert, and Mookini write in the preface to *Place Names of Hawaiʻi* "an important element—one virtually unknown in Euro-American culture—that added zest to the use of place names and encouraged their proliferation is the pleasure they provided the poet and the jokester."[30] They note the pervasive expression of aloha ʻāina in the language, especially in proverbial or poetic sayings:

> Like most Polynesians, Hawaiians are fond of proverbial sayings that are memorized verbatim and are used less for didactic purposes than as displays of wit and as praise of the land. They differ from Euro-American proverbial sayings in that they rely heavily on place names.... Many sayings that use place names describe emotional states or important

events, but the largest proportion show aloha ʻāi-na [sic] "love for the land and the people of the land."³¹

According to George Kanahele, 40 percent of the ʻōlelo noʻeau in Pukui's book mention place names.³² Oliveira suggests that in addition, many, many more concern the ʻāina; each of her chapters is illustrated with a plethora of ʻōlelo noʻeau about ʻāina and human relationships to it.³³

Why Joseph Kānepuʻu and Joseph Poepoe?

Joseph H. Kānepuʻu first came to my attention during a seminar on Hawaiian religion taught by John Charlot. Charlot presented the class with Kānepuʻu's 1862 protest letter (described earlier). I next saw Kānepuʻu's name within other letters published in the first Kanaka-oriented newspaper, *Ka Hoku o ka Pakipika*, which led me to understand that he was one of the group of Kānaka who established that paper. A further impetus to my choice was his very long letter detailing the history of Kanaka-oriented newspapers that appeared on the front page of *Ko Hawaii Pae Aina* in 1878. As I read more of his letters and other publications, I came to see that he loved the Hawaiian papers and understood their importance for his lāhui. His exhortations to readers to have their copies bound so that they might return to them in later years may have had a significant impact on our ability to read the papers now. He likely was not alone in this practice; rather, he was a reporter who reflected sentiments of the intelligentsia in the islands.

Furthermore, Charlot used Kānepuʻu's fictionalized autobiography liberally in his analysis of traditional Kanaka educational practices.³⁴ Solis also chose Kānepuʻu for his graduate course on Mea Kākau (authors), the other being the very well-known Samuel M. Kamakau.³⁵

Kānepuʻu is an intriguing writer, born on Molokai before the arrival of missionaries there, so it is likely that his frames of reference included much Hawaiian orature. His formal schooling consisted only of the primary missionary school in Kaluaʻaha, Molokai. Thereafter he seems to have been self-taught. He never wavered from his love of Hawaiian language and literature, although he was interested in learning English, and he wanted to offer that opportunity to his daughter as well. As important, Kānepuʻu is of the first generation of Kanaka writers to offer written forms of moʻolelo kuʻuna (traditional, hereditary histories/stories/literature) for publication in the nūpepa.

More than twenty years ago, Rubellite Kawena Johnson, in a class on Hawaiian literature, assigned me the task of writing a short biography of Joseph Mokuʻōhai Poepoe, and she suggested to me that a larger biography of him was warranted. All these years later, here is the result of that suggestion. Why had she suggested this? He was the author of long versions of the moʻolelo of Hiʻiakaikapoliopele and Kawelo and was closely associated with Hoʻoulumāhiehie, which is likely a pseudonym that either he used on his own or he used with other writers.

Poepoe is of a later generation and had much more formal education than Kānepuʻu, born into a world in which American-style education was the norm. He learned several languages and began his illustrious career as a translator of tales from English into Hawaiian. He is much more well known among Hawaiian-language and Hawaiian studies scholars than Kānepuʻu. Some of his work, under the pseudonym Hoʻoulumāhiehie, is the subject of recent and forthcoming translations.[36] Poepoe, very much like Kānepuʻu, also never wavered from his love of Hawaiian language and literature, and he advocated for the perpetuation of both in times much harder for our language and culture. He did this primarily through writing and editing Hawaiian-language newspapers.

Background on Nūpepa (Hawaiian-Language Newspapers)

Calvinist missionaries, as an integral part of their project to Christianize Kanaka, developed an orthography for Hawaiian and began the work to establish literacy in the islands.[37] Soon afterward, according to Kamakau,

> learning to read became popular. The chiefs saw the value of education and of observance of the Sabbath. . . . Teachers were sent all about the country districts. Every chief's household had a teacher, some of them women. There were as many as forty such schools in Honolulu and an equal number at Waikiki, and education spread widely in those years. . . . The wish of the king [the young Kamehameha III], his sister, and his guardians acted upon the people like a lightning flash stimulating all hearts. . . . The spread of knowledge was very rapid in Hawaii.[38]

In 1834 at the first missionary secondary academy, Lorrin Andrews instituted the first newspaper in Hawai'i, *Ka Lama Hawaii*, as curriculum for the students. As he wrote in a letter, he did so,

> First, to give the scholars of the High School the idea of a newspaper—to show them how information of various kinds was circulated through the medium of a periodical. Secondly, to communicate to them ideas on many objects.... Thirdly, it was designed as a channel through which the scholars might communicate their own opinions freely on any subject they chose.[39]

Ka Lama Hawaii lasted less than a year, but it can be considered a success, because it set the foundation for more than a century of Hawaiian-language newspapers. Later the same year the mission headquarters in Honolulu started its own newspaper, *Ke Kumu Hawaii*, which lasted five years. In contrast to *Ka Lama* it had a much expanded readership. It seems to have reached all of the most populated islands, judging from the letters sent to it. The content of *Ke Kumu* was mainly evangelizing by missionaries, with some letters from students and community members.

In 1841, the slightly less evangelical and more newspaperlike *Ka Nonanona* appeared. This paper, however, was still edited by a missionary, Richard Armstrong, called Limaikaika (Strongarm) in Hawaiian. *Ka Nonanona* published news and opinions of the ali'i in Honolulu as well as letters by residents from various islands.

Ka Elele Hawaii followed *Ka Nonanona* and was even less evangelical; it published not only news from the capital, but also the treaties that Hawai'i negotiated with other countries, and laws that went into effect. It continued the practice of publishing letters from people around the archipelago.[40]

In 1861, the first Kanaka-centered newspaper emerged, *Ka Hoku o ka Pakipika*, and from that time until World War II, Kānaka wrote in, edited, and published a fairly wide variety of newspapers, including church, government-sponsored, and independent papers. There they published, along with international and local news, their political opinions, literature, works of geography, many kinds of mele, and so on.

Structure of the Book

In this book, I demonstrate our intellectual ancestors' dedication to aloha ʻāina, use of kaona, and Hawaiian epistemological frames as practices of intellectual sovereignty and moʻokūʻauhau consciousness. I examine in detail works of literature drawn from the oral tradition and other writings by both authors. The book is in two parts.

Part I begins with a literary biography of Joseph Hoʻonaʻauao Kānepuʻu, concentrating most of all on his published works and his fulfillment of his perceived kuleana as a public intellectual and schoolteacher. It includes his role in establishing and supporting various newspapers, as well as the criticism he received from other Kanaka writers, notably Samuel M. Kamakau.

Chapter 2 is a reading of Kānepuʻu's works of literature. This chapter concentrates on his most important full-length works of moʻolelo kuʻuna. One is the longest version of a moʻolelo that has been found and another is the only version. This chapter discusses his mastery and use of many specifically Kanaka literary devices.

Chapter 3 is a review and analysis of Kānepuʻu's works of geography. His longest work is called "Ka Honua Nei: a me na Mea a Pau maluna iho," a Kanaka rewriting of a world geography text used in the public schools. Perhaps his most valuable is a geography of his home island of Molokai, a five-part series of which only three parts have survived.

Part II similarly begins with a literary biography of Joseph Mokuʻōhai Poepoe. Poepoe was highly educated and multilingual, an attorney qualified to litigate in all courts in the country, and a translator to and from English. The chapter includes a discussion of his role in politics, both as a newspaper editor and as a candidate for office.

Chapter 5 is a reading of Poepoe's moʻolelo of Hiʻiakaikapoliopele, focusing on the various mele that commemorate the ʻāina. It would take an entire book to analyze the whole epic moʻolelo, and these mele demonstrate his dedication to aloha ʻāina, as well as his role in teaching readers of his day and today how to read and interpret the mele.

Chapter 6 is an analysis of Poepoe's "Ka Moolelo Hawaii Kahiko" (Ancient Hawaiian history). This post-annexation work is probably the longest of the genre of "moʻolelo Hawaiʻi kahiko," which comprises cosmogonic genealogies, and the important moʻolelo contained in them or attached to or inspired by them. This work is characteristic of and demonstrates Poepoe's unfailing commitment to our native language and the expression of our ancestors' philosophies. He wrote it out of and in moʻokūʻauhau consciousness, fully aware of the accelerating shift to English that was happening before his eyes and ears.

In chapter 7 are concluding thoughts reviewing the purposes of the book, how the two authors exemplify the need for a Kanaka intellectual history, and the current shift to valuing Kanaka thought and language in new ways. How do we embody moʻokūʻauhau consciousness and aloha ʻāina ourselves? What do we leave for our descendants in the current era of indigenous resurgence and intellectual sovereignty?

PART I
Joseph Hoʻonaʻauao Kānepuʻu

1

Joseph Hoʻonaʻauao Kānepuʻu

He mea maikai ma ka hoiliili ana i ka *Hae Hawaii,* mai ka helu 1 a hiki i ka pau ana o na pepa 52, a e lawe aku ma ka Hale paipalapala ma Kawaiahao ia Samuela Russell nana e hana a paa. . . . Makehewa ka poe lawe a hoolei, a haehae, a kiola, ua like ia me ka mea lalau i kana dala iloko o ka pakeke, a hoolei kuleana ole, me he pupule la.

Ina i paa i ka humuia ka *Hae Hawaii* a me ka *Elele Hawaii* paha, a hiki i ka wa e hoihoi ai oe e heluhelu, e kamailio pu no oe me ko hoa aloha au i ike ole ai e noho ana ma kahi loihi aku mai ou aku la, me he mea la e no[ho] pu ana olua ia wa.

In gathering the copies of Ka Hae Hawaii, *from the first issue, number one, to the end at fifty-two, it is good to take them to the printer Samuel Russell at Kawaiahaʻo who will bind them . . . People who take the paper and toss it, tear it up, and dispose of it are like people who grab the money in their pocket, and throw it with no reason, as if they were crazy.*

If the copies of Ka Hae Hawaii *and* Ka Elele Hawaii *are bound, when you return to read them, it will be as if you are conversing with a friend you haven't seen who lives far away from you, as if you were both in the same place at that time.*

JOSEPH H. KĀNEPUʻU, "E Malama i ka Nupepa"

Joseph Hoʻonaʻauao Kānepuʻu was born around 1824 in Kalawao on the Kalaupapa Peninsula of Molokai. His father was Aberahama Kaʻalihi, but no other names in his moʻokūʻauhau are known.[1] It is known, however, that sometime in Kānepuʻu's childhood, his family moved to Hālawa, Molokai. Kānepuʻu first entered school at the age of twelve at the mission school at Kaluaʻaha, near Hālawa. Several of his classmates went on to the Lahainaluna secondary school on Maui, but he was not among them.² As an adult, he moved to Oʻahu, where, as he describes it, he received a teacher's certification in December 1853 "mamuli o ka hoopii ana o na makua o Maunalua, e lilo au i kumukula malaila" (because the parents in Maunalua [Oʻahu] petitioned that I become a schoolteacher there).³

From the 1850s until the 1880s, Kānepuʻu was a regular contributor to the Hawaiian-language newspapers and one of the most ferocious and consistent defenders of the papers and of Hawaiian language, culture, and indigenous knowledge. He was a complex personality who also defended Christianity and wrote that Hawaiʻi's people needed education and that some native practices were of "ke ano pouli" or a "dark" or "unenlightened" nature.⁴ He was active as a schoolteacher and occasional political commentator, and he was the mea kākau (writer) of Molokai versions of important moʻolelo and mele.

Kānepuʻu chronicled the establishment of and struggle over the first Kānaka Maoli–controlled newspaper, *Ka Hoku o ka Pakipika* (1861–1863). He also criticized the editors of that paper for cutting short the mele in Kapihenui's "He Mooolelo no Hiiakaikapoliopele," as mentioned in the introduction. His dedication to the value of the moʻolelo of our ancestors and to the generations of Kanaka Hawaiʻi in the future is striking. It was as if Kānepuʻu looked directly into the future, into the next century, anticipating my own and younger generations of Hawaiian scholars and our enduring interest in and need for both the literature produced by his generation and the orature from all the generations before him. This orientation to the world and to his writing is what I have come to call moʻokūʻauhau consciousness. He was among the first generation to take the oral traditions and create literature from them. His care for future generations extended beyond writing; he also foresaw that print copies of nūpepa needed to be preserved, or the carefully written and printed words could still disappear. In the same letter in which he advised his readers to have their copies bound, he wrote,

> No ka mea, eia iaʼu kekahi olelo paa, "o na nupepa a pau i pai ia ma ka olelo Hawaii, a i lawe ia e aʼu mai loko mai o na aoao a pau, e hiki no iaʼu ke humu Buke, a e hooili ia no, no na hooilina. Aole au e haalele i kela nupepa, keia nupepa olelo Hawaii, a hiki i koʼu la e make ai."⁵

Because, I have taken this vow: "all the newspapers published in the Hawaiian language, which I have subscribed to from all sides [political and/or religious], I can take and bind into books, and they will be bequeathed to heirs. I will not quit any Hawaiian-language newspaper until the day I die."

It is because of Kānepuʻu's and others' commitment to the newspapers and their preservation that we are able to recover thoughts and themes from the literature of our ancestors. We are, in a sense, just continuing the work that he envisioned so long ago. He made sure that the connection to his ancestors and descendants (heirs) was made on his part, and other scholars and I are attempting to ensure a connection between his generation and our descendants. In this way, this work is a genealogy, a moʻokūʻauhau of writing and scholarship.[6] It seems crucial that the generations of Hawaiians following my own know that they have a long intellectual tradition.

Moʻokūʻauhau consciousness also means a connection to ʻāina and implies both aloha ʻāina and mālama ʻāina (see the introduction). Kānepuʻu exemplifies moʻokūʻauhau consciousness in this way as well, as he documents indigenous Hawaiian geography, uses indigenous Hawaiian time markers such as month and moon night names, and incorporates place names as well as natural forms in his metaphors.

Some of Kānepuʻu's writings are significant and others are perhaps less so.[7] In this chapter, I review some of his more significant writings with as much context as seems appropriate. His more significant writings can be grouped into the following categories: journalistic reporting; advice and opinions, including two long serialized essays, entitled "Ke Ano o ka Wa Ui o ke Kanaka a me na Mea a Pau e Hiki mai ana ia Ia mahope Ona" (The nature of young adulthood and all the things that will happen to a person afterward) and "Ka Hana Kupono e Ao aku ai na Makua i ka Lakou Poe Keiki" (The proper behavior that parents should teach their children); history, especially the history of the Hawaiian newspapers; geography; kaʻao (legends) and mele; and short essays on various topics, such as the decrease of numbers of Kānaka and the value of using the indigenous counting system.[8]

In these letters, essays, and moʻolelo, Kānepuʻu promoted the teaching of Hawaiian language, literature, and indigenous knowledge along with the imported curriculum of the schools. The project of schooling, at least in part, was meant to "civilize" natives by replacing indigenous knowledge with what the missionaries and others believed to be the superior knowledge and values of Europe and the haole United States.[9] Kānepuʻu's intent to promote the value of indigenous knowledge is especially evident in the mele, the geographies, the short essay on counting in Hawaiian, his fictionalized autobiography, the two kaʻao from the oral tradition, and some of his unpublished essays for the Board of Education. Moreover, Kānepuʻu served as a reporter of makaʻāinana concerns and as a recorder of particular Molokai traditions. The following review of his works is organized by the newspapers in which they appeared and in roughly chronological order.

Ka Hae Hawaii (The Hawaiian Flag), 1856–1861

Kānepuʻu made several important contributions to the newspaper *Ka Hae Hawaii*, published between 1856 and December 1861. *Ka Hae Hawaii* was the government newspaper under the direction and serving the purposes of the Papa Hoʻonaʻauao (the Department of Public Instruction). Richard Armstrong (Limaikaika), a former Calvinist missionary, was head of the department. According to Helen Chapin, author of *Shaping History: The Role of Newspapers in Hawaiʻi*, Armstrong controlled the content of the newspaper.[10] James Fuller, also affiliated with the Calvinist mission or the ʻAhahui ʻEuanelio Hawaiʻi (AEH, Hawaiian Evangelical Association), served as the editor.[11] Until just before Limaikaika's death in September 1860, the paper was filled with laws, farming news, information about the value of farming, advice to parents, puritanical admonitions concerning everyday behavior, and some evangelizing. In addition, subscribers from all over the islands sent in news and opinions, kanikau (mourning and condolence mele), and lists of names of varieties of kalo and other Hawaiian-language terms. Kanaka missionaries in Nukuhiva, Fatuhiva, and Micronesia contributed accounts of their travels and work.

As Limaikaika's death approached, the number of mele in the paper greatly increased, and the first moʻolelo kaʻao and shorter moʻolelo appeared. The first two moʻolelo kuʻuna were very short renditions of part of the Hiʻiakaikapoliopele cycle by B. Kalaihauola (a.k.a. B. K. Hauola).[12] Traditional mele were sent in by Samuel Kamakau, B. R. Kalama, L. S. Kalama, and others, including Kānepuʻu. Solomona Kawailiʻulā (usually published as S. K.) Kuapuʻu contributed three short moʻolelo that were explanations of the names of various lands.[13] Kuapuʻu shortly thereafter wrote the first long moʻolelo, the story of Pākaʻa and Kūapākaʻa, serialized in ten parts (and much later made famous by Moses Nakuina and eventually translated into English as *The Wind Gourd of Laʻamaomao*).[14] As soon as the moʻolelo by Kalaihauola was finished, *Ka Hae Hawaii* began publishing "He Moolelo no Kamapuaa" by G. W. Kahiolo, the first full-length moʻolelo kuʻuna.[15] Thus, *Ka Hae Hawaii*, just before its demise, became a rich site for the publication of traditional knowledge. All of the moʻolelo just mentioned are replete with expressions of aloha ʻāina; place, wind, and rain names; and ʻōlelo noʻeau. Armstrong's son Samuel (also working at the paper) ran an ad in July 1860 asking for people to send in mele "no ka pae ana mai o Papa ma . . . a me na mele no ke Kaiakahinalii, a me na Mele e hoike i ka manao o na kanaka kahiko no ka La, a me ka Mahina, a me na Hoku" (about the arrival of Papa and family . . . mele concerning Kaiakahinaliʻi [Pele's mother and maker of tsunamis], and mele that show the ideas of the people of old concerning the sun, moon, and stars).[16]

The publication of these moʻolelo at that time is perhaps indicative of a loosening of the grip of missionary prohibition on Hawaiian knowledge, although missionaries continued to decry any such loosening.[17] Many if not most schoolteachers by this time were Hawaiian, and they expressed interest in collecting the moʻolelo, mele, and other forms of knowledge from the oral traditions. In July 1860, J. Kaʻelemakule wrote an account of a four-day-long meeting of teachers in Hilo that was held in a church and open to the public. The teachers shared their knowledge of science and other subjects, and the major topic seemed to be moʻolelo kuʻuna. Kaʻelemakule reported that Hewahewa told the story of Kana; Naia told a Māui story; Makuakāne recounted the names of the nights of the month (moon phases); and others told of the ʻai kapu (restricted eating system), the voyaging vessels of old, and so on. At the end, Kaʻelemakule wrote,

> Ua maikai keia mau mooolelo i haiia, i mea e maopopo ai ka oiaio, a me ka oiaio ole. He hana maikai keia i hapaiia e ka Luna Hoomalu, i mea e paaʻi ka mooolelo kahiko o Hawaii nei, i ka poe hou.[18]

> These moʻolelo that were told were good, as a way to understand what is true and what is not. This was a good thing taken up by the President, in order to preserve the traditional moʻolelo of Hawaiʻi for new people [younger Kanaka].

Kānepuʻu was part of this first cadre of writers who took the traditional knowledge and transformed it into written mele and moʻolelo in *Ka Hae Hawaii*. The following section details his contributions, which are particularly significant because he was born and raised on Molokai.

Both of Kānepuʻu's early mele, published in *Ka Hae Hawaii*, are associated with the moʻolelo of Kana and Nīheu, which he himself did not write until seven years later. They are "He Mele no ke Kauo ana i na Waa o Kana ia Kauwelieli ma" (A mele about the hauling of the double-hulled waʻa of Kana, named Kauwelieli) and "Ka Moeuhane a Moi" (Moi's dream).[19] It is evident from these mele that Kānepuʻu must have been raised as one who was entrusted with the oral traditions. It is likely that he had memorized these mele and the moʻolelo of Kana. Although he does not say specifically who taught him the moʻolelo, someone must have taught him because there are no other printed versions of the moʻolelo or these mele prior to his, except a very short moʻolelo in response to one of his mele, and the later versions differ significantly.[20]

Mary Kawena Pukui, the twentieth century's foremost scholar of Hawaiian language and culture and coauthor of the *Hawaiian Dictionary*, explains how moʻolelo were taught and how their teaching was restricted:

> Hawaiians regarded the lore of their ancestors as sacred and guarded it jealously. Such subjects were not talked about lightly nor too freely. Those who were versed in poetry (mele), storytelling (haʻi kaao), genealogy (mookuauhau) and oratory (kakaolelo) found themselves in the courts of the chiefs. Before tellers of stories would relate the tales of the gods or of the chiefs who ranked next to the gods in sacredness, they first took note of whom they were relating the stories to and the significance of the occasion. A person who was likely to repeat all he heard was not trusted and so he did not learn very much.
>
> Grandparents who were versed in the lore of their people and their homeland picked out the grandchildren with the most retentive minds to teach. Should a young person wish to learn from an old one other than his own grandparent, he asked permission to become a pupil and if accepted, became a member of that household. There had to be quiet during the story telling period so that the mind would not be distracted. Strict attention had to be paid to every word of the narrative. No unnecessary movement was permitted except to change the sitting position when uncomfortable. The call of nature must be attended to before the story telling began, for it was kapu to attend to

such matters in the middle of a tale. Tales learned were not repeated casually without thinking to whom and where one spoke.[21]

Perhaps Kānepuʻu learned his mele and moʻolelo in similar conditions. Kānepuʻu's illustrious contemporary, Samuel Mānaiakalani Kamakau, was trained at Lahainaluna in interviewing and in writing history but since Kānepuʻu was not, it is more likely that Kānepuʻu drew on his own knowledge from his ʻohana's (family's) traditions for his moʻolelo and mele. The most well-known versions of the Kana story, to which these mele belong, appear in Abraham Fornander's collection (published much later by the Bishop Museum), and they are substantially different from Kānepuʻu's versions.[22]

Kānepuʻu provided this introduction summarizing the context for the mele:

> Eia malalo iho ke Mele (oia hoi ka pule ma ka olelo Hawaii) no ke kauo ana i na waa o Kana, oia hoi kekahi kanaka kaulana o ka wa kahiko. He waa e kii ai i ka makuahine o lakou ia Hinalealua, ka wahine manuahi a Hakalanileo, a ka makuakane o lakou. Lawe ia hoi e ke ʻlii o kekahi puu kaulana ma Molokai, oia hoi o "Haupukele." O Kapepekauila [sic] ke koa o ia puu ikaika [a] o Keolewa ke Alii. A ma ia lawe ana, uwe kanikau ko lakou makuakane, a hele e ninau i na keiki a pau, aole nae lakou i aa e hele e kaua me Kapepeekauila, o Niheukolohe ke keiki hope loa ka mea i aa e hele e kaua. A no ka pono ole o ka hana ana, kokua pu kona kupunawahine o Uli, a makaukau na mea a pau, a no ka hiki ole ke kauo i kai, hapai ae la o Kana i keia Mele.[23]

> Below is the Mele (called a prayer in Hawaiian) about the hauling of the waʻa [voyaging vessels] of Kana, a famous person of the past. This was a waʻa for the purpose of fetching their mother, Hinalealua, the second spouse of Hakalanileo, their father. She had been taken by the aliʻi of a famous hill called Hāʻupukele. Kapepeʻekauila was the warrior of that strongly held hill and Keolewa was the aliʻi. When she was taken, their father wept in grief, and went to ask all the children, but they would not dare to go to war with Kapepeʻekauila; Nīheukolohe, the youngest child, was the one who dared to go to war. And because his attempt was not pono [complete or correct or right], his grandmother Uli assisted, until everything was prepared, and when the waʻa could not be hauled to the sea, Kana took up this Mele.

Kānepuʻu does not explain that though Kana is also a child of Hakalanileo, he was not known to the family, because he was born as a kaula (cord or rope) and raised by Uli in the uplands, away from the family. He became a kupua, a sort of magical being who could stretch his body like a rope to great heights. Kānepuʻu must have assumed that most readers were somewhat familiar with the story and thus knew who Kana was.

As Kānepuʻu explained, the mele is a prayer. It mentions many of the deities associated with waʻa construction and sailing, including Lea (Laea), Kūmokuhāliʻi, Kūpulupulu, Kūolonowao, Kūpepeiaoloa, Kupaikee (Kūpaʻaikeʻe), Kanealuka (probably Kāneʻāluka), and others.[24] Some of these names will be familiar to many readers who know the often-heard rousing chant called "I Kū Mau Mau." In fact the first two lines of this pule are "O Ikuwa ka honua ilalo, O Ikumaumau ai ka lani," which is very much like the current chant that begins with "I Kū Mau Mau, I Kū Wā."[25]

The prayer refers to the many koʻi (adzes) used to carve the waʻa as well as the offerings the kāhuna made to the deities before the felling of the tree. The mele then names the waʻa Kaumelielie, although in the title the name is Kauwelieli, and in the Fornander version it is given as Kaumaielieli. The mele goes on to give names to each piece of the waʻa, including the hulls, the keels, the boom, the sails, the seats, the spreaders that keep the hulls from collapsing inward, and the lashings. The mele later gives names to the various malo (loincloths) that its aliʻi, Nīheu, will wear at sea. It then names the navigator, the paddlers, the astronomer, and the kahuna on board. It ends with a prediction that Kapepeʻekauila and Keolewa will die and that control over the mountain Hāʻupukele will be lost.

This mele is similar in many parts to a version given in the "Kaao No Kana a Me Niheu" in Fornander.[26] Kānepuʻu's version can provide some clarity to the translation in Fornander. In Fornander, for example, several lines appear this way, with translations by W. D. Alexander:

O ka waa kapipi mai i ka lai,
O ka waa ekepue i ka lai . . .

[The canoe that is sprinkled in the calm,
The canoe that jumps playfully in the calm . . .][27]

Similar lines in the Kānepuʻu version appear this way, with my translation:

Ka waa a kapipi ma—ia la i kalai,
Ka waa a Koi-iki la i kalai . . .

[The waʻa that Kapipimaia carved,
The waʻa that Koʻi-iki [small adze] carved . . .]²⁸

This interpretation, based on Kānepuʻu's spelling, fits in better with the sense of the mele, not to mention that the phrase "sprinkled in the calm" is nearly nonsensical. The main difference is in the spelling of "kalai," which Alexander interpreted as two words, "ka lai" (the calm), while Kānepuʻu rendered it as the single word "kalai" (carved).

A more striking example is found in these lines in Fornander (again with a translation by Alexander), which are mystifying unless one compares them to the similar lines in Kānepuʻu's version.

O Kanaloa i luna o ka pola,
E hei ana i ka heana . . .

[Kanaloa is on the platform,
Playing at cat's cradle with the dead . . .]²⁹

Here are the Kānepuʻu lines, with my translation:

O Mooaiku ke kahuna,
E hai ana i ka heana . . .

[Mooaiku is the kahuna,
Calling out . . .]

The nonsensical interpretations by Alexander are perhaps the result of poor transcription as well as ignorance of other versions to assist with the translation. The transcription of Kānepuʻu's version that enabled it to be printed in the paper, is much clearer. The strange interpretation may also indicate Alexander's and the publisher's (Thomas Thrum's) ideas about Hawaiians and Hawaiian religion—that Kanaloa, a major deity of the sea, might play with the dead as a cat does with a piece of string, or play the string game of cat's cradle with dead people.

At the end of the mele, Kānepuʻu says that following the mele, he would write down "ka inoa a Moi, a ke kahuna mana, oia hoi ka hihio i loaa ia ia mamua iho o ko Kana hele ana mai, he kahuna o Moi no Keolewa na ke alii o Haupukele, a me Kapepeekauila, ke koa ikaika" (the name song of Moi, the powerful kahuna, being the dream that he received before Kana's arrival; Moi was a kahuna of Keolewa, the aliʻi of Hāʻupukele [the mountain mentioned earlier], and Kapepeʻekauila, the strong warrior).³⁰ In the moʻolelo, the aliʻi Keoloewa (the same as Keolewa) asked Moi to verify that no kupua (supernatural beings) would be able to approach Hāʻupu and defeat Kapepeʻekauila and Keoloewa. When Moi dreamed, his dream instead revealed that Hāʻupu would fall. The dream does not speak of Kana by name, but, instead, the beginning implies that someone from Hawaiʻi Island would arrive there. The mele starts like this:

> No Puna la e, no Puna,
> No Kau, no Haili, no Makakalo, no Oo,
> No ka Haupoiakane, no Waipapa.[31]

> Of Puna, of Puna,
> Of Kaʻū, of Haili, of Makakalo, of Oo,
> Of the Haupoiakane, of Waipapa.

Puna, Kaʻū, and Haili are well-known place names in the eastern and southern parts of Hawaiʻi, where Kana and Nīheu are from, and the island of Hawaiʻi is sometimes known as "ka houpo o Kāne," similar to "Haupoiakane."[32] There are other unidentifiable place names (Maea-iki and others starting with Maea), then the following:

> No Nuuhiwa, no Nu-o,
> No Waiake'kua,
> He mau akua ke lele nei,
> He kuli [huli]au i ka moana,
> No Hawaii nui ke-i,
> No Hawaii nui ke-pane.[33]

> From Nuʻuhiwa, from Nuʻo,
> From Waiaakeakua,
> Are some deities that are flying/jumping,
> A current in the ocean, an overturning in the ocean,
> From Hawaiʻi nui is the word,
> From Hawaiʻi nui the response.

In the moʻolelo, Nuʻuhiwa is a place where Kana's kūpuna (ancestors) reside; in other mele and moʻolelo, Nuʻuhiwa is a legendary place, like Kuaihelani. The name is undoubtedly related to a real place named Nukuhiva, in what are now called the Marquesas Islands (in Hawaiian, this archipelago is called ka pae ʻāina o Nuʻuhiwa, or Nā Hiwa). The rest of this excerpt predicts that a supernatural (akua) force will arrive and says again that the word about this comes from Hawai'i Island. The end of the mele gives an explicit prophecy:

> He alii e pane mai, e hemo kona aina,
> He kanaka e pane mai, e make ia,
> O ka puu, ua hee, o ka aina, ua lilo.
>
> An ali'i will respond, his land will be undone/taken from his control,
> A person will respond, he will die,
> The hill [Hā'upu], is defeated, the land is lost.

The last line of this mele, "Au—e, alia—e, e hee keia mau—na" (Oh no, before long, this mountain will be defeated), is almost identical to the penultimate line of the wa'a-hauling mele of Kana discussed earlier.

Kānepu'u's publication of these two mele prompted a response from Keawekolohe of Kāhilipali, Kona 'Ākau, Hawai'i Island.[34] Keawekolohe submitted a very short version of the mo'olelo of Kana and Nīheu, accompanied by a version of the wa'a-hauling mele of Kana. Interestingly, he or she attributes the differences in the mo'olelo and mele to the differences in the way the story was preserved: "he like ole ka malama ana o ka poe kahiko, aole hoi paanaau, a pela no na mele" (the preservation is not like that of the people of old, it is not memorized, and the same is true for the mele). Keawekolohe's version of the mo'olelo is indeed different, with Hakalanileo's wahine's name given as Hoahoaikalani; also, she was not kidnapped by Kapepe'ekauila, but while visiting Molokai, "lilo o Hoahoaikalani ia Kapepeekauila," which implies that she left Hakalanileo for Kapepe'ekauila of her own volition. Further, Keolewa does not exist in this version. The wa'a-hauling mele of Kana is similar to Kānepu'u's version but is much shorter; Keawekolohe's is 48 lines, while Kānepu'u's is 149. Just before the mele, Keawekolohe again attributes the differences to the way the mele is passed on: "aole like loa me ka mea i haiia ma ka Helu 6, Buke 5, aoao 26. No ka paanaau ole i ka poe nana i malama keia hemahema" (it is not exactly like the one told in volume 5, number 6, page 26 [i.e., Kānepu'u's]; this defect probably occurred because the mele was not memorized by the people who kept it). Because Keawekolohe's version is so much shorter, it is unclear which version he means is defective: Kānepu'u's or his own. This opinion also conflicts with the haole idea, expressed in the early *Mooolelo Hawaii*, that traditions are unreliable because they are memorized rather than written down. The 'ōlelo ho'ākāka (preface) of *Mooolelo Hawaii*, written by students of Lahainaluna under the direction of their teacher, Reverend Sheldon Dibble, and edited by Dibble, begins in this way:

> Aole paha i pololei loa na mea a pau i paiia iloko o keia buke. He pololei a he oiaio paha ka nui, aka, ma kau wahi ua kekee iki paha, no ka mea, o kekahi mau olelo, he mau olelo kahiko loa, a ma ka naau o na kanaka i paa ai, aole ma ka pepa, nolaila ua paa kapekepeke, aole i pololei loa.[35]
>
> ———
>
> It is likely that not everything in this book is absolutely correct. Most of it is correct and true; however, in some places, it may be slightly distorted because these stories are very old, and were preserved in the minds of people rather than on paper, and therefore, preserved incompletely, not absolutely correctly.

It seems that Keawekolohe is asserting that the oral tradition is actually more accurate. Both of these positions perhaps fail to take into account at least two pertinent circumstances: first, writers obviously select certain things to be included, leave others out, and interpret events and text in certain ways. And, second, orature is similar in that the specific ancestors chosen for any given moʻokūʻauhau, for example, are chosen for certain reasons, often to maximize an aliʻi's prestige.[36] Further, and more pertinent perhaps, Walter Mignolo has analyzed literacy's development along with the colonization of the so-called New World. Alphabetic literacy distinguished the civilized from the savage. He explains that

> writing came into the picture when the consolidation of vernacular languages, whose classical legacies placed them next to nonbarbarian languages, needed the letter to tame the voice and grammar to control the mobility of the flow of speech. Writing was then [considered to be] the end result of an evolutionary process, one of the highest achievements of human intelligence.[37]

The exchange between Kānepuʻu and Keawekolohe reveals several other points: various versions of moʻolelo and mele in different traditions were handed down in ʻohana and communities, and from region to region, and writers did not always agree with each other. Historian Noelani Arista observes that "writers who published in the newspapers would routinely solicit more information on a subject from their readers. . . . Multiple versions of the same story, chant, or history were passed down through families belonging to different places in the island chain."³⁸

Writers from different traditions sometimes welcomed each other's contrasting versions, but also contested them, sometimes politely and sometimes with scathing language and contempt. We will see some further examples of this in Kānepuʻu's career later on in the chapter.

Ka Hoku o ka Pakipika (Star of the Pacific), 1861–1863

In September 1861, just three months before the demise of *Ka Hae Hawaii*, a new and unprecedented kind of Hawaiian newspaper appeared called *Ka Hoku o ka Pakipika*. It was published by a collective of Hawaiian writers and editors, Ka ʻAhahui Hoʻopuka Nūpepa, who wanted more and better outlets for their writing. Joseph Kānepuʻu was a founding member of the collective. He and others had tried to get *Ka Hae Hawaii* to expand into more pages, but it ceased publication instead. They had also tried unsuccessfully to get Henry Whitney, the publisher of the English-language *Pacific Commercial Advertiser*, to publish a paper in Hawaiian. So the hui put their money and talents together and created their own paper. Among the hui was David Kalākaua, who later became Mōʻī. One of the ways that we have knowledge of the hui and the struggle over the existence of the paper is because Kānepuʻu wrote an account of the whole struggle, which was published in *Ka Hoku o ka Pakipika*.³⁹

Ka Hoku o ka Pakipika was far richer in traditional lore than *Ka Hae Hawaii*. Its inaugural issue ran the first written version of "Ka Mooolelo no Kawelo," by S. K. Kawailiʻulā.⁴⁰ The newspaper published moʻolelo in nearly every issue for its entire existence of a too-short twenty months: twenty-two moʻolelo from the oral tradition (or similar to those from the oral tradition) by authors including S. N. Haleʻole, famous for writing *Lāʻieikawai*.⁴¹ These important moʻolelo include the first written version of the moʻolelo of Hiʻiakaikapoliopele, by Kapihenui.⁴² Most of the moʻolelo were published weekly as serials. In addition to the ancestral lore, *Hoku* published tales from the *Arabian Nights* (the tales were translated by Ke Aliʻi Simeona K. Kaʻai, a member of the House of Nobles), three short histories of Kamehameha I, and a story of Esther, presumably from the Bible.⁴³ The paper was also rich in both ancestral and contemporary mele, kanikau, and mele inoa (name songs), some of which were composed in honor of the paper itself.

Kānepuʻu did not contribute mele or moʻolelo to *Hoku*, but he was active in the life of the paper. Besides the account of the struggle over the paper, he wrote a three-part political essay regarding voting and methods of taxation.[44] In addition, he wrote an important critique of the selective deployment of British history by the Congregational missionary Artemas Bishop. At that time, the Mōʻī Kamehameha IV (A. Liholiho) and Emma were bringing in the Anglican Church, a move the Congregationalists were vehemently opposed to. Bishop had translated some stories from British history, but only about Henry VIII, whose invention of the Anglican Church was seen as quite evil. Kānepuʻu unmasked this use of history and advocated for wider teaching of English, including in schools for adults, so that people could read about other events from British history if they chose.[45]

Ka Nupepa Kuokoa and the Establishment of *Ke Au Okoa*, 1863–1864

Kānepuʻu began to flower as a mea kākau at the next newspaper that was edited by Kānaka Maoli, *Ke Au Okoa* (The Different Time/Current). *Ka Hoku o ka Pakipika* ceased publication without warning in May 1863, and the Hawaiian-reading public was left only with *Ka Nupepa Kuokoa* until April 1865. During this time, the young Mōʻī Kamehameha IV (Alexander Liholiho) died suddenly. His last years were marked with violence and sorrow, after a short but much-loved reign. He and his Mōʻīwahine Emma had, among other things, founded Queen's Hospital to care for the poor. In 1859, the Mōʻī had shot and critically injured his secretary, who was a good friend of his. The historian Ralph Kuykendall says the unfortunate incident began this way: "The king's mind had been poisoned against Neilson [his secretary] by some means—idle or malicious gossip—and he was led to believe that his secretary had abused his confidence; the queen's name was somehow involved."[46] The Mōʻī tried to make amends, became depressed, and even meant to abdicate the throne, according to Kuykendall.[47] He was persuaded to continue on and worked on getting the Anglican Church established in Hawaiʻi nei as an alternative to the oppressive Congregational institution.[48]

But fewer than three years later, the little Haku o Hawai'i (Prince of Hawai'i), the Mō'ī's four-year-old son, died; he was the only living heir from the Kamehameha line of the next generation. The Haku o Hawai'i was an important symbol of hope to the lāhui Hawai'i, because so many of the Mō'ī's family had died and no one else had children to carry on the monarchy. Newspapers of the day continually expressed worry and blame about the decrease in the population, as well as much worry about the lack of ali'i to rule the country. Many ali'i had died from infectious diseases and others suffered from infertility.[49] Kānepu'u wrote an essay on this problem, "Ke Emi ana o na Kanaka" (The decrease of the people), as did many others.[50] Kānepu'u documented the reduction in numbers of people living in the large district of Maunalua, which in ten years' time went from 310 to 140. He attributed the causes to people having no place to plant their sweet potatoes because the land was being used for animals. He reported that many people died and many others left.

Alexander Liholiho was unable to recover from the loss of his son and died on November 30, 1863. He was succeeded by his brother, also a grandson of Kamehameha I. Lota Kapuāiwa took the throne as Kamehameha V and ushered in an era of upheaval for the government.

Kapuāiwa did not take the usual oath to uphold the constitution. He wanted to make several controversial changes, including instituting a property qualification for both voters and for representatives in the Hale 'Aha'ōlelo Maka'āinana (the lower legislative house); eliminating the Kuhina Nui (premier or regent), an office usually held by an ali'i wahine (woman) who cosigned all laws and proclamations with the Mō'ī; removing the 'Aha Kūkā Malū (Privy Council), a council of ali'i nui advisers who might exert restraint on his executive powers; and changing the bicameral to a unicameral legislature.[51]

During the heated controversies that characterized the year of 1864, Wini's (Henry Whitney's) paper, *Ka Nupepa Kuokoa*, opposed all the changes that the new Mō'ī tried to effect, especially the ways in which he effected them. First, the Mō'ī called for an 'Ahahui 'Elele (convention) of ali'i and maka'āinana to come and discuss a new kumukānāwai (constitution) with him. Wini opposed this, as did many others, saying that there had recently been an election, and the elected representatives were the proper ones to deliberate with the Mō'ī. The Mō'ī instead held new elections for delegates and called a constitutional convention. All went well until the assembly had to decide on the property qualification for voters and Luna Makaʻāinana (representatives to the lower house of the legislature). Almost all the ʻElele (delegates) opposed any property qualification, while the ʻAha Kuhina (cabinet) and the Mōʻī stubbornly held out for it. The ʻElele represented the common working people, and the Kuhina (cabinet ministers) represented the landed and monied aliʻi and haole. No matter how low a property qualification was proposed (at one point it went down to $25), the ʻElele held firm. Finally, after several days, the Mōʻī adjourned the convention and announced the suspension of the existing kumukānāwai. He went into meetings with the Kuhina and drafted a new kumukānāwai without any input from the ʻElele.[52]

These actions incensed Wini, most of the missionaries, and many Kānaka Maoli as well. *Nupepa Kuokoa* continuously ran editorials that insulted the Kuhina and, by extension, the Mōʻī, although the paper did not insult the Mōʻī directly. In an editorial the day before the election of the delegates, for example, *Kuokoa* asserted that there was a secret agenda for the constitutional changes and that the government (by implication, the Kuhina) wanted the public to elect uninformed delegates so that the agenda could proceed without resistance. An excerpt from this editorial follows:

> E hiki koke mai ana io kakou nei ka wa a kakou e hoouna aku ai i poe nana e hilo ke kaula, a nana e kaawe i ko kakou ola iho, ma ka hoouna ana'ku i ka poe naaupo i Elele no kakou e hui ai me ke Alii, a me na ʼLii iloko o ka Ahaolelo Kuka Elele e hiki mai ana ...
>
> ... he maunu nae kai hookauia mai, a ina e ai ka lehulehu, alaila o ke oki no ia, a o ka hoi hou no ia o Hawaii e noho iloko o ka luameki ona i kauoia mai ai. "Pehea la e ai ai ka lehulehu i ka ma[u]nu?" wahi a ka mea ninau. Penei no e ai ai ka lehulehu i ka maunu, ma ke koho ana i ka poe naaupo, ka poe e pahee ana na alelo i ke kamailio me ka ike ole i na Kumukanawai a me na Kanawai.[53]

> The time is fast approaching when we will send people who will braid the rope by which we will strangle ourselves, by sending uninformed or uneducated people to confer with the Aliʻi [the Mōʻī] and the Aliʻi [plural] in the coming [constitutional] convention ...
>
> ... bait is being dangled, and if the public eats it, then, that is the end, and Hawaiʻi will return to live inside the pit it has been dragged

into. "How would the public eat the bait?" asks the questioner. This is how the public would eat the bait, by electing the uninformed/uneducated/uncivilized people whose tongues will slide in conversation while knowing nothing about Constitutions or Laws.

Kuokoa printed letters, as well, that were highly critical of these actions. For example, immediately after the Mōʻī's call for the election of ʻElele to the constitutional convention, two letters or essays in *Kuokoa* suggested that the Mōʻī's cabinet was leading him in the wrong direction. The writers J. Dowsett (Kimo Pelekane), T. Metcalf (Meka), Gerrit P. Judd (Kauka), and W. N. Pualewa wrote that the cabinet composed the call for ʻElele and "i alakai hewa ai hoi i ko kakou Moi Lokomaikai, a kakau ai oia i kona inoa ma ka Olelo Hoolaha Alii" (wrongly led our goodhearted Mōʻī to sign his name to the Aliʻi's announcement). They further asserted,

> He mea hilahila loa keia hoihope ana o na Kuhina o ka Moi o Hawaii nei, a i ka wa e loheiaʻi o keia mau hana imua o na aupuni e o ka honua, he mea maopopo e akaaka ia, a e *heneheneia* mai ana no hoi ko kakou nei mau Kuhina.[54]

This regression or step backward of the Mōʻī's Cabinet ministers is something very embarrassing, and when these acts are heard of among the foreign nations of the world, it is understood, they will be laughed at, and our Ministers will be ridiculed.

Kuokoa was culturally quite American; it always mentioned celebrations of American holidays, such as Thanksgiving, Washington's birthday, and July 4th. Detailed news from the United States generally took up most of one page. The US Civil War was going on at this time and *Kuokoa* provided the latest news of each battle. *Kuokoa* was also dedicated to promoting American cultural, political, and economic ways. Chapin notes that *Kuokoa* angered the editor of *Ka Hoku o ka Pakipika* because of its "continuous promotion of American institutions and culture."[55] Chapin also highlights Wini's "fervent pro-Americanism."[56] More serious was Wini's "contempt for Hawaiians," reflected in his editorials. Chapin quotes from one of his editorials in the *Pacific Commercial Advertiser* that gave his opinion of Kanaka Maoli: "Though inferior in every respect to their European or American brethren, they are not to be . . . wholly despised. . . . They are destined to be laborers in developing the capital of the country."[57] The Kanaka intellectuals, including the writers described so far in this book, whose occupations included schoolteacher, church minister, attorney, politician, physician, and so forth, certainly did not agree that they or their descendants were inferior in *any* respect, nor were they destined to be poor laborers under wealthy plantation owners. Creating *Ka Hoku o ka Pakipika*, a newspaper by and for Kanaka, was one way to fight this battle over how they were being represented in print.

Ka Nupepa Kuokoa also served as a site for exchange of information among Kānaka Maoli, and there must have been Kānaka on the staff. But although Kānepu'u reported later that Bila Auwana was an editor and Joseph U. Kawainui was an assistant editor, neither name appears on any article, nor are they ever addressed by name within a letter.[58] Occasionally, *Kuokoa* printed moʻokūʻauhau and mele kahiko, but not often. In late 1864, someone using a pseudonym asked people to send in their knowledge of the ways of old, especially the hoʻomana kahiko, or the old (pre-Christian) religion.[59] In response perhaps, the following month *Kuokoa* began a series called "Ka Hoomana Kahiko" (The ancient religion).

Despite these Hawaiian cultural forms, for all of these reasons, Kānepu'u and others, especially perhaps the Mōʻī, ardently desired another newspaper that would be more reflective of themselves, their language, and their culture, that would celebrate rather than defame their history, literature, and ancestors. These needs became even more urgent in November 1864, when Wini announced that he had sold *Kuokoa* to Luther Halsey Gulick, who would be the editor and who would have Henry Hodges Parker as an assistant editor.[60] Gulick was a missionary and a physician, born in Honolulu of missionary parents who were in the third company to come to Hawaiʻi.[61] Parker was also a son of missionaries to Hawaiʻi, Benjamin and Mary Parker; he was a theologian "known as an orator who always expounded God's word in Hawaiian."[62] Having Gulick and Parker take over *Kuokoa* was alarming because, although Wini was the son of missionaries, and socially he was in the missionary quarter, he was not interested in evangelizing through the newspaper, and he tried to keep it from being the voice of the ʻAhahui ʻEuanelio Hawaiʻi, and the AEH still had its own newspaper, *Ka Hoku Loa*.[63] *Kuokoa* was now sure to become more evangelical and more supportive of the AEH and critical of other denominations because both Gulick and Parker were active AEH missionaries.

Some readers wrote in their suggestions for the new editors of *Kuokoa*, including urging them to make the paper more puritanical, as in this letter from J. W. Kupakee of Kona Hema, who had been designated by a meeting of luna ekalesia, or church leaders, to write to Gulick with their ideas. His letter says in part,

> Aole he kupono ke Pai ia na "mele" Hawaii ma ka Nupepa. Ua manao lakou, o ke Paiia ana o na mele ma ka Nupepa, he mea ia e alakai ana i ka lahui opiopio i ko lakou ano kahiko.[64]

> It is not appropriate that Hawaiian "mele" be published in the Newspaper. They [the church leaders] think that the publication of the mele in the Newspaper is something that leads the young people to their old ways.

As *Kuokoa* became more of a voice for the AEH, often devoting page 4 to Bible lessons and short morality stories, many Kānaka expressed dissatisfaction with it. As J. W. Kahiamoe put it,

> Ua ohumu io no kakou i keia Nupepa [Kuokoa] i keia wa, no ke aha la? eia no ka haina, no ke kohu ole, aole hoi e like me ka wa ia H. M. Wini, aole no hoi i lawa ka makemake o keia lahui ili ulaula, i ka lakou puni, oia hoi na mele, na kaao, na nu hou, na kanikau, a ia mea aku ia mea aku.[65]

> We have earnestly complained about this Newspaper at this time, why? Here is the answer, because of its unattractiveness, it's not like the time of Wini; it does not satisfy the desire of this red/brown-skinned people for their favorite things, the mele, kaʻao, news, kanikau, and other things.

Readers were also unhappy with *Kuokoa's* new policy of printing some news in English. This was expressed by D. K. Kahoʻohalahala:

> He hoohalahala! He hoohalahala! E i mai paha auanei oe he aha ia Manao Hoohalahala o oukou e o'u mau makua aloha.
> Eia no ia o ko makou makemake ole e kau puia na hua haole me na hua Hawaii iloko o na moolelo a me na nu hou o ko na aina e mai e like me ke Kuokoa e namu nei.[66]

> A criticism! A criticism! Perhaps you are saying, what is this critical opinion of yours, my beloved parents.

It is this—we do not want to see foreign [i.e., English] words put together with the Hawaiian words in the stories and in the news of foreign lands as the Kuokoa is doing, printing gibberish/English.

For all of these reasons, Kānepu'u and his contemporaries welcomed the new newspaper, *Ke Au Okoa*. The paper was established by Lota Kapuāiwa's government primarily to promote the government's views, explain policies, and publish political and governmental news. According to Chapin, the sole editor of this important paper was John Makini Kapena. Mookini, however, says that *Ke Au Okoa* was edited by Kapena during its last three years only. Mookini notes that Kapena had held high government positions; he was a member of the Privy Council and the House of Nobles; governor of Maui; Minister of Foreign Affairs; and Special Envoy and Minister Plenipotentiary to Japan. He was considered a Kanaka scholar of marked ability and a diligent student of Kanaka literature.[67]

In the paper itself, however, the name of the editor was not printed until March 10, 1870, so for the first few years, it is not clear who edited the paper. However, the paper was meant mainly to be the voice of the government. This is an excerpt from the first editorial:

> Ua akaka lea paha i ka nui o na makamaka heluhelu nupepa Hawaii i na kumu kuoo i loohia'i e ke Aupuni ka manao e pai mau i ka nupepa.... A he mea pono loa no ia, no ka mea, ua nui no ka poe kue mai iloko o na aupuni a pau, mamuli o ka naaupo a me ke kuhihewa o kekahi poe, a mamuli hoi o ka manao pakuikui wale, ka opu ino a me ka hookekee maoli o kekahi. A no ka hoohuli ana a me ka halihali olelo ana o ka poe o ia ano, ua nemanemaia ka inoa maikai o na Kuhina, ua kailiia ka manao o na mea puni wale, a ua kapekepeke a kanalua hoi ka hilinai ana o na kanaka mamuli o ke aupuni, me he mea la he mau pono okoa ko na Kuhina, a he pono okoa hoi ko na kanaka; a no laila, aole no i holo pono na hana i manaoia e pomaikai ai na aoao a pau mai na 'lii a i na makaainana, a ua anoninoni lolii ole ka noho ana.[68]

It is likely quite clear to the majority of Hawaiian-language newspaper readers the serious reasons why the idea to continually publish a newspaper has fallen to the Government.... And it is pono because there are many oppositional people within every government, because of the ignorance or erroneous suppositions of some people, or because of contrariness, bad intentions, or true crookedness. Because some of those are influencing others and gossiping, the good names of the Cabinet Ministers have been belittled, and the trust of the people for the government has become uncertain and doubted, as if the Ministers had different interests from the people; and so the work planned to be beneficial to all sides, the aliʻi and makaʻāinana alike has not succeeded, and our lives have thus been made perplexed and ill-at-ease.

Ke Au Okoa's goal, then, was to explain the policies of Kamehameha V's government to the people. It intentionally served as a place to debate issues and to publish government reports, laws, treaties, Supreme Court decisions, members of juries selected, and so forth. At the same time, it served as a lively site where people from the different islands could express their opinions on any topic, argue different viewpoints, and share news of their communities. It also served as an outlet for a considerable amount of creative writing, moʻolelo, mele, and moʻokūʻauhau, and especially for kanikau, or songs honoring those who had recently died. In the first year of publication, *Ke Au Okoa* published "He Moolelo no Lonoikamakahiki," an eight-part serial from the oral tradition, written by B. L. Koko.[69] At the same time, the paper continued to publish stories translated from English and from Arabic.[70] These were great favorites of readers, along with the moʻolelo Hawaiʻi.

Haleʻole wrote in the first edition that the members of the ʻAhahui that had published *Ka Hoku o ka Pakipika* were still regretting the loss of it and that they would subscribe to *Ke Au Okoa* without having to be persuaded, as he saw it fulfilling the same need and desires.[71]

Kānepuʻu did the bulk of his most important work in this period (1866–1868) and mainly in the pages of *Ke Au Okoa*. He wrote two significant geographies: one is a rather short description of the valley of Pālolo, Oʻahu, and the other is a five-part series on the island of Molokai, called "Kaahele ma Molokai." In these, Kānepuʻu argues for the value of a native approach to geography and against a US-centric geography curriculum in the schools. These arguments, as well as the rich linguistic and cultural information in these geographies, are discussed in chapter 3.

Kānepuʻu expressed his concern for the loss of native knowledge within another article of this period, "Ka Helu Hawaii" (Hawaiian counting). Here is how it begins:

Ma ka helu kahiko o Hawaii nei, oia hoi, 4 kahi, hookahi ia kauna, a mahope aku oia, e pii paumi ana na huahelu 4, me na inoa pakahi, e like me keia.

4	kahi, hookahi ia kauna		....	4
10	kauna,	"	kaau..	40
10	kaau,	"	lau	400
10	lau	"	mano....................................	4,000
10	mano	"	kini	40,000
10	kini	"	lehu	400,000
10	lehu	"	poina...............................	4,000,000
10	poina	"	nalowale........................	40,000,000

In the old counting system of Hawaiʻi, a group of four (four ones) make one "kāuna," and afterward raising by tens the "4" numbers are this way, with each of their names.

4 ones make one kāuna.	4.
10 kāuna make one kaʻau,	40.
10 kaʻau make one lau,	400.
10 lau make one mano,	4,000.
10 mano make one kini,	40,000.
10 kini make one lehu,	400,000.
10 lehu make one poina,	4,000,000.
10 poina make one nalowale, ...	40,000,000.[72]

Kānepuʻu goes on to observe that at the fish market at Ulakoheo in Honolulu, most of the men, women, and children use this indigenous counting system, since the fishers use it and will teach it to newcomers to the profession. He then cites two instances of having to translate between this system and the haole system, and he records a conversation with an aliʻi who says he warned Limaikaika not to abandon the Hawaiian language. Kānepuʻu says that because people are not using these words while shopping and during other activities, he wanted the article to explain it to the public.

His concern about native language and knowledge extended to his writing down three elaborated versions of famous legends. I describe and comment on these briefly here, but there is a fuller discussion and analysis of these moʻolelo in chapter 2. The first to be published was "He Moolelo no Pakaa," which appeared in *Ke Au Okoa* in serial form from October 24 to December 5 or 12, 1867.[73] This is seven years after the first moʻolelo from the oral tradition began to appear in print, and that first one happened to be a different version of this same moʻolelo, written by S. K. Kuapuʻu (as mentioned earlier). In these seven years, many moʻolelo had been written and published, especially in *Ka Hoku o ka Pakipika*. This period represents the first blooming of Hawaiian moʻolelo as written literature, and Kānepuʻu both helped to create the conditions for its possibility and also contributed several important written works. Kānepuʻu followed "He Moolelo no Pakaa" with "He Moolelo no Kana, ka Hanai a Uli," which is the longest and most elaborate version of this moʻolelo known so far.

Ka Nupepa Kuokoa and *Ke Au Okoa*, 1868

Although Kānepuʻu published regularly in *Ke Au Okoa* at this time, he chose to submit his version of "He Moolelo no Hamanalau, Hanai a Hawea" to *Ka Nupepa Kuokoa*, which was still being edited by Luther Gulick. Joseph Kawainui was an assistant editor, and other Hawaiians were listed as writing for the paper at this time, including Kamakau, Reverend Moses Kuaea, and David Malo (not to be confused with Davida Malo of the previous generation). Three haole men associated with the AEH were also listed as writers for the paper: Curtis Jere Laiana (Lyons); the son of the Reverend Laiana, also listed; and Reverend Claudius Buchanan Anelu (Andrews).[74] Kānepuʻu himself was listed in the paper as a "luna," or the person who would distribute the paper within his valley of Pālolo. Although he was closely associated with the rival paper *Ke Au Okoa*, Kānepuʻu obviously didn't scorn *Kuokoa*, but he appreciated and supported it, as he did all the Hawaiian-language papers. And *Kuokoa*, while still evangelizing on page 4, was also publishing a lot of Hawaiian moʻolelo. At the time, Kamakau's long-running history of the Kamehameha dynasty, "Ka Moolelo o Kamehameha I," ran on the front page right next to "Hamanalau."

Kānepuʻu's long moʻolelo kahiko is titled "He Moolelo no Hamanalau, Hanai a Hawea" (*A* story [not *the* story] of Hāmanalau, Hānai of Hawea). Kānepuʻu never claims to be the sole authority for any moʻolelo kahiko; indeed, he, like other mea kākau Hawaiʻi, invites others to contribute more knowledge.⁷⁵ This particular moʻolelo, while certainly a moʻolelo kuʻuna, that is, a story originating in the oral tradition (as attested to by letters to the newspaper, an issue we will return to later), does not seem to have been published before or after Kānepuʻu's version. (Research in the newspapers and archives is never complete, however, and it is possible that another, possibly previous, published rendition will eventually surface.) What this means, now, is that we have a full, elaborated, well-written moʻolelo kuʻuna that so far has not been republished, and it has not been well documented or studied.

Here I take the opportunity to discuss a conflict that arose over the moʻolelo, which gives us some insight into the critical debates our ancestors engaged in over our literature as it was first written and published. "He Moolelo o Hamanalau" was criticized in three letters to *Nupepa Kuokoa*. The first, written by J. D. Kūlanakauhalealiʻi of Kunawai, Honolulu, asks six questions about Kānepuʻu's version of the moʻolelo. Kūlanakauhalealiʻi questions the name of Hāmanalau's kāne hoʻāo (male partner),⁷⁶ the place her daughter was born, the place Hāmanalau herself was born, and the place she died.⁷⁷ Kānepuʻu responded that "Ua hoolaha aku au e like me koʻu lohe mai i ka poe lohe mua" (I have published it the way I heard it from people who heard it before me). He goes on: "E ke hoa malama Kaao a moolelo hoi, he kuhi koʻu aia a pau kaʻu, alaila kalai mai oe i kau" (My fellow keeper of kaʻao and moʻolelo, I expect that when my version is done, you will formulate yours). And he ends his response with "Ua lohe no kakou i ka olelo a ka poe kahiko, 'he lehulehu na mana o Kamapuaa'"⁷⁸ (We have all heard the saying of the old folks, "There are many versions of [the story of] Kamapuaʻa").

Kamakau followed with a longer, much more detailed questioning of all three moʻolelo about Pākaʻa, Kana, and Hāmanalau by Kānepuʻu. This was more devastating because Kamakau was from the land where the moʻolelo of Hāmanalau takes place, Waialua (Mokulēʻia specifically), and he was firmly established as a distinguished intellectual and historian. Kamakau begins by asserting that Kānepuʻu (without, however, ever mentioning his name) had made many errors in the moʻolelo of Kana. He then goes on to say that the same is true of the story of Hāmanalau, whose genealogy belongs to Oʻahu. He is not more specific than that. He then makes a similar criticism of Kānepuʻu's story of Pākaʻa, saying,

> He pono i ka poe kakau i ke kaao e hooponopono mua i ka mookuauhau a me ka moolelo Hawaii a maopopo kahi e alakai aku ai i ka Lahui

i ka ike a me ka oiaio. O ke kakau moolelo a kaao, he kanaka oia i manao nui i ka moolelo Hawaii, i na mookuauhau, a me na mookaao kahiko o Hawaii nei.[79]

People writing kaʻao should first correct the genealogy and the Hawaiian moʻolelo and understand that the place they are leading the Lāhui to is knowledge and truth. The moʻolelo and kaʻao writer is a person who has thought a great deal about moʻolelo Hawaiʻi, the genealogies, and the ancient stories of Hawaiʻi.

Kamakau's main criticisms are about an apparent lack of knowledge of moʻokūʻauhau. At Lahainaluna he had conducted research among kūpuna, gathering stories, and apparently learning the moʻokūʻauhau of many aliʻi lines. Kānepuʻu, in contrast, lacked a secondary education and, it seems, was self-taught in the writing of moʻolelo and kaʻao. It is not clear whether or not he was trained in moʻokūʻauhau at all, and, even if he had been, moʻokūʻauhau also come from different sources of knowledge. A common ʻōlelo noʻeau says "ʻAʻole pau ka ʻike i ka hālau hoʻokahi" (Not all knowledge is from one school). Kamakau's criticism is quite harsh and does not allow for the possibility that Kānepuʻu's story comes from a different tradition, but he also suggests that this writer (Kānepuʻu) join with other intellectuals to write Hawaiian moʻolelo (history and literature) books. Kānepuʻu writes that he set down the moʻolelo as it was told to him. He uses his imagination, however, like any other writer, which left him open to a charge of anachronism, a trivial concern, in the third letter that critiqued Hāmanalau.

Kānepuʻu does not respond to the criticism (printed on January 25 and February 15, 1868) until the April 18 issue. He had pulled the story from publication because he did not want *Kuokoa* to lose readers because they did not like his stories. In his response, he addresses his critics as kaikuaʻana, older brothers, and then suggests the difference in his version of the moʻolelo may be because it is about a different woman named Hāmanalau.

His response includes a lengthy answer to the letter that had criticized the anachronistic detail in the Kānewailani story. Kānepuʻu quotes at length from the mele of Kūaliʻi, which celebrates the uniqueness of that aliʻi, in effect implying that there is no one like him, and thus metaphorically asserting the value of his own stories, which are not like other versions. He ends with a pun regarding part of a mele from his story of Hāmanalau: "Hamau la—e hamau/Hamau la e keiki" (Hush, hush/Hush, child), suggesting that his critics quiet down.

On July 11, the Hāmanalau story resumes after having been suspended since March 28. Kānepuʻu introduces it, explaining that he had withheld it after all the criticism, being called "kuhikee" (a blunderer), and had released the story to people "kuhikee ole" (who didn't blunder), but they had not written it and the editors wanted him to finish it. He did finish it, but unfortunately, it seems he took these criticisms to heart and, as far as I can tell, never published another kaʻao or moʻolelo. This ended his association with both *Ke Au Okoa* and *Nupepa Kuokoa*, with the exception of a three-part series about a trip to Kauaʻi.[80]

Following Kānepuʻu's departure, neither paper had as many moʻolelo kaʻao or moʻolelo Hawaiʻi for some time. In 1871, the celebrated writer Mose Manu (author of the recently reprinted and translated "He Moolelo Kaao no Keaomelemele") became a staff writer for *Ke Au Okoa*, but he produced only translations during this period, no moʻolelo kahiko or moʻolelo kaʻao.[81] Kānepuʻu either withdrew or was asked to stop contributing to the papers. This is regrettable, especially since Kānepuʻu was so productive of unique versions of moʻolelo, and he was conscientious and prescient in providing details of lifeways, including words and sayings, that were disappearing.

We might pause to consider whether Kānepuʻu did not know the moʻokūʻauhau of the people in his moʻolelo. Did he perhaps know different versions because he came from Kalawao and Hālawa on Molokai? Because Kānepuʻu's own moʻokūʻauhau apparently is not extant, it is possible he came from a makaʻāinana family who, like most, did not keep or stress moʻokūʻauhau. I don't have definite answers to these questions, but they should be researched further. More important to ask, perhaps, is, how did Kamakau's assertion that writers should know moʻokūʻauhau before they put their moʻolelo out to the public affect the development of Hawaiian literature? We see these moʻolelo as somewhat fabulous and mythical today, but they also have factual elements. Kānepuʻu's moʻolelo have value even though they lack the details of moʻokūʻauhau. It seems they may also include details based on the oral traditions of Molokai that were not shared by Kamakau. Kamakau's criticism may have prompted young scholars to study the moʻokūʻauhau and become better historians, but it also seems to have contributed to discouraging Kānepuʻu from further efforts at writing moʻolelo.

"He Moolelo No Kanewailani"

Overlapping in time with "Hamanalau" was Kānepuʻu's "He Moolelo No Kanewailani, ke Keiki a Maoloha." "Hamanalau" ran in *Nupepa Kuokoa* while "Kanewailani" appeared in its rival, *Ke Au Okoa*. In a preface to the first installment, Kānepuʻu says that "Kanewailani" is "unuhiia mailoko mai o na Moolelo kahiko o Hawaii nei" (taken from the old moʻolelo of Hawaiʻi).[82] It quickly becomes apparent, however, that it is fictionalized. He sets the story in a pae ʻāina (archipelago) he calls "Kanehunapegana," and he puts the arrival of missionaries a hundred years prior to their actual appearance. The name "Kanehunapegana" is reminiscent of Kānehunamoku, a legendary place. The name has been translated as "hidden land of Kāne." It could, however, be interpreted as Kānehūnāmoku, which could be glossed as "Kāne who hides islands." Kānehūnāpegana might then be "Kāne who hides pagans."

At the end of the moʻolelo in April 1868, a letter runs in *Ke Au Okoa* from "Molokainuiahina," a probable pseudonym. Molokai nui a Hina, or great Molokai of Hina, is an epithet for the island, based on its birth story as the offspring of Hina and Wākea. This letter explains that the character Kānewailani is none other than Kānepuʻu, thinly fictionalized. Molokainuiahina says that Kānewailani's sister Luʻukia (Kapāʻūoluʻukia in the moʻolelo) "e ola mai ia no i Kuliouou, he kane aku kona hope, a o ua J. K. [sic] Kanepuu nei e ho[o]nalonalo nei me ka nalo ole" (is now living in Kuliʻouʻou, the child following her being a boy, J. K. Kānepuʻu, who is concealing this without it actually being concealed). He or she goes on to say that Kānepuʻu has written that Kānewailani was born in 1724; if one replaces the 7 with an 8, that is the year of Kānepuʻu's birth. Molokainuiahina obviously is a person who knows Kānepuʻu and his family and who is also from the island of Molokai; this person does not find the autobiography entertaining and wishes for an actual kaʻao.[83] What we have here, then, is not a moʻolelo kaʻao but a fictionalized autobiography. It is just as valuable and interesting but for different reasons. Kānepuʻu was given the space to fill as he liked; he wrote that he had planned to write a version of Kamapuaʻa, but "no ka pakuwa," or due to the overfamiliarity of that moʻolelo he was trying something new.[84] Further discussion of this moʻolelo follows in chapter 2.

Ka Lahui Hawaii, Ko Hawaii Pae Aina, and *Ka Elele Poakolu*, 1877–1885

In 1877, Kānepuʻu wrote a twenty-part weekly serial called "Ka Honua nei: A me na Mea a Pau maluna iho" (This world and everything on it), a Hawaiian-centered world geography with a political-economic critique; its content is analyzed in chapter 3 and its import is more deeply analyzed in David Chang's book, *The World and All the Things upon It*.

It was published in the newspaper called *Ka Lahui Hawaii*, which was run by the Protestant Mission and edited by Henry Parker, the same missionary who had been responsible for the wane in *Kuokoa*'s popularity.[85] *Ka Lahui Hawaii* was like its mission-paper predecessors; it published news of the Kingdom, news of the AEH, Christian songs, and occasionally a translated story. It ran from January 1875 through December 1877, which was early in Kalākaua's reign.

Lota Kapuāiwa (Kamehameha V) died in 1872 without naming an heir. The obvious choice for Mōʻī was the Kamehameha descendant Lunalilo, who, however, insisted on an election to be sure of his subjects' collective support. He only reigned for one year before passing on, also without naming an heir. This resulted in another election in which Kalākaua campaigned against Mōʻīwahine Emma, the widow of Alexander Liholiho (Kamehameha IV) and herself a Kamehameha descendant. The election of Kalākaua by the legislature ended in a riot by Emma's supporters.[86] The Kingdom of Hawaiʻi was on the defensive against attempts by the United States to limit its sovereignty and control its waters and ports, especially Pearl Harbor. Kalākaua, while supported by US representatives, who hoped that he might capitulate and give them the exclusive lease to Pearl Harbor in exchange for tariff-free sugar sales, actually stubbornly refused to do so and set out to strengthen Hawaiʻi's sovereignty in a number of ways.[87] He expanded Kamehameha IV and V's commitment to Hawaiian language and culture through bringing hula into public performance; founding a new version of the Hale Nauā as well as the Papa Kūʻauhau Aliʻi to collect moʻokūʻauhau, mele, and moʻolelo; and, most pertinent here perhaps, establishing and supporting Hawaiian-language newspapers.[88] Kalākaua had been involved in establishing *Ka Hoku o ka Pakipika* in 1861. In the 1880s, he established *Ke Koo o Hawaii* (1883), and his administration supported *Ka Elele Poakolu* (1880–1881) and *Ka Elele Poaono* (1885), both edited by Walter Murray Gibson, Kalākaua's prime minister, friend, and a very controversial character.[89]

One of the most historically valuable articles that Kānepuʻu wrote was "Ahe! He Nupepa Hou Ka!!" (Yes! A new newspaper!!), published in February 1878.[90] It is a long letter to Joseph Kawainui, the editor of the newly established *Ko Hawaii Pae Aina*, which contained congratulations and advice and appeared on that paper's front page. In it, Kānepuʻu recounts the establishment of both *Hoku o ka Pakipika* and *Ka Nupepa Kuokoa* in more detail than anywhere else, except in the pages of *Hoku o ka Pakipika* itself. This account provides the names of people who were in the associations that founded those important newspapers, which were not in those previous accounts. He writes also that *Ke Au Okoa* was a successor to *Hoku o ka Pakipika*, and he makes the point that the lāhui should not live with just one newspaper, because it will only provide a limited range of opinion and other content. He puts it this way:

> Aole au e ae e ai wale no au i ka ai, a hala ka makahiki hookahi, me koʻu ai ole i ka i-a; aole no hoi au e aahu wale no i ke kapa e mehana ai ke kino, me ka uhi ole iho o ka malumalu o ka hale. Aole paha e ae wale mai ka poe puni nupepa o keia pae aina, e lalau ole mai i ko lakou mau lima, a kukulu ae i nupepa hou, me ke kokua pu ana mai i ke ola oia nupepa hou &c.

———

> I would not agree to eat only kalo for a year without eating fish or meat; and I would not agree to cover myself in kapa to warm the body without the shelter of a house. The newspaper-loving people of this archipelago would not just agree to not take in their hands and build a new newspaper, helping [instead] the life of that new paper, etc.

Kānepuʻu also stressed that the editor and publisher should remain independent. This is a big issue for Kānaka because the first forty years of publishing had been controlled by the Congregational churches.

When Kānepuʻu offers advice to Kawainui, he begins in this way:

> E pono paha e hoomanao pu kaua i ke aloha, a me ka mahalo pu ana aku i ko kaua poe hiki mua, no ka hoonioni ana i keia mea he nupepa, a e kukulu hoi i mau nupepa nui e like me keia nupepa e hele nei.

———

> We should remember the aloha and also be grateful to those who came before us, for the stirring up of this thing, a newspaper, to build big newspapers like this one running now.

He goes on to suggest that all Kanaka were indebted to those first writers, editors, and supporters. After giving their names, he writes,

> Nolaila, ua aie ka lahui naauao o Hawaii nei ia lakou, no ka paipai a hoolaha ana i keia mea he nupepa akea, e kuokoa akea ai ka manao o ke kanaka, e like me ke alakai ana a kona lunaikehala iho.
>
> ———
>
> Therefore the educated people of Hawai'i are indebted to them, for the support and spread of this thing, a public newspaper, in order that independent opinions of Kanaka can be published, in accordance with the leadership of their own consciences.

This same idea is hugely important to us today. Without the hard work from Kanaka ʻŌiwi of organizing, writing, editing, and standing up to would-be censors, we would be left with only the colonizing narratives of narrow-minded censors. Kānepuʻu recounts the story of the opposition to *Hoku o ka Pakipika* briefly here too. Because he was moved to write this, we now have the names of the people and a bit more of the history of those who made it possible for us to begin to understand our ancestors in their own idioms and ontologies. This is another instance we can interpret as demonstrating his moʻokūʻauhau consciousness: he saw the need to document the processes and actors that resulted in a tradition of newspapers, which in turn recorded literature, events, opinions, and many forms of indigenous knowledge so that those could be passed to us and our descendants.

In 1881, Kānepuʻu published several short essays in *Ka Elele Poakolu*. One of those short essays was the story of the hero of Molokai, Kaohele (perhaps Kaʻōhele). In the time of the interisland wars, before Kamehameha conquered the main islands, Peleiōhōlani of Oʻahu invaded Molokai, and Kaohele was famed for warding off the attacks. He was equally revered for his ability to run long distances quickly and jump incredibly long distances. His most famous leap, Kānepuʻu says, was over a stream in Nīheukawa, a distance of twenty-one feet and a height of twenty-two feet. Kānepuʻu ends the article by saying that Kaohele's story inspired his own father's name, Kaʻalihi, for Kaʻalihi koa o/ʻo Kaohele, or the warrior-strategist (of) Kaohele.[91]

During this period, Kānepuʻu was a dues-paying member of Kalākaua's Hale Nauā, an organization named after the moʻokūʻauhau and knowledge-seeking institution of the time of Kamehameha I and prior. Kalākaua's Hale Nauā was modeled in part on Masonic societies as well. Members conducted research into Hawaiian knowledge and presented lectures to each other; nonmembers with research of interest were invited to lecture to the group as well. Kānepuʻu was also employed by Kalākaua's Papa Kūʻauhau Aliʻi, a government-sponsored organization that collected moʻokūʻauhau aliʻi, moʻolelo, mele, and other genres of Hawaiian knowledge. Kānepuʻu and a few others were hired for the purpose of "hoakaka ana i na moolelo kahiko" (clarifying or explaining the ancient moʻolelo) that the group had collected between 1880 and 1882.[92] Kānepuʻu also assisted Kalākaua's office when the printers of the 1883 coronation program were arrested and put on trial for creating a public nuisance. For the coronation, Kalākaua invited several accomplished kumu hula to perform publicly. The names of the kumu and the titles of the hula were printed in a program that the Mōʻī's political enemies used to try to harass him, alleging that the titles were lewd or obscene and thus a public nuisance. Kānepuʻu was called upon to give expert testimony in the Kanaka printer's (William Auld's) defense regarding the meanings of Hawaiian words.[93]

The last known work of Kānepuʻu's that was published is a letter of condolence to his longtime friend, the editor Joseph U. Kawainui, on the death of his younger brother, Benjamin W. Kekapa Kawainui. Kānepuʻu expresses gratitude for the younger Kawainui's assistance in the publication of his lengthy series on world geography.[94] Perhaps Kānepuʻu felt that his geography series might not have been published without Benjamin Kawainui's advocating for it (see chapter 3). If so, Kānepuʻu's last-known publication reflects his intermittent struggles with editors and critics over his works, some of which were perceived as so different from those of others from Oʻahu or Hawaiʻi Island.

Conclusion

For thirty years, during a crucial time in the history of our nation and the development of writing in Hawaiian, Joseph Kānepuʻu contributed writing in various genres to the newspapers in our native tongue. His stories, essays, and letters show the range of his intellect, which was developed through his own study after primary school. He consistently expressed his love for our language, orature, and literature, as well as our ʻāina. He was a committed teacher of the young people in his own era, as well as in today's and tomorrow's, which he foresaw and planned for. He dedicated himself very early on to preserving the Hawaiian-language newspapers because he recognized the value of the indigenous knowledge being published in his lifetime, and he saw that, if not preserved, it might be difficult or impossible to retrieve by later generations of Kanaka ʻŌiwi. In the following chapters, I examine his literary artistry as well as his expression of aloha ʻāina in specific works of geography.

2

Selected Literary Works of Joseph Kānepuʻu

> Ua lohe no kakou i ka olelo a ka poe kahiko, "he lehulehu na mana o Kamapuaa."
>
> We have all heard the saying of the people of
> the past, "There are many versions of [the story of] Kamapuaʻa."
>
> J. H. KĀNEPUʻU, "Pane i ka Poe Loiloi"

Joseph H. Kānepuʻu penned four serialized works that can be described as literary, all published between October 1867 and August 1868. Three of them, "He Moolelo no Pakaa," "He Moolelo no Kana, ka Hanai a Uli," and "He Moolelo no Hamanalau, Hanai a Hawea," are moʻolelo kuʻuna, taken from the oral tradition. The fourth, "He Moolelo no Kanewailani, ke Keiki a Maoloha," is a fictionalized autobiography modeled on that oral tradition. In these works, all springing from his moʻokūʻauhau consciousness, we see that Kānepuʻu is fully displaying his talents as a writer, that his kuleana as a teacher extended to the public sphere, and that he is committed to native language and epistemology. He intentionally positions himself to act as a bridge spanning the divide between the world of thought and practice of his ancestors and us, his descendants. He, along with many of his contemporaries, observes an ever-accelerating shift to English along with the loss of ʻāina, and he foresees the Kanaka of future generations and our deep need to remain connected to his generation and those before. In this chapter I give short analyses of these works and the context within which they were published. I follow these with a reading of "He Moolelo no Hamanalau, Hanai a Hawea," as an example of the riches of Hawaiian-language literature, including a synopsis of the moʻolelo and an examination of the literary devices that Kānepuʻu employs.

Contexts

"Pakaa," "Kana," and "Kanewailani" were all published in *Ke Au Okoa*, the newspaper of Lota Kapuāiwa's (Kamehameha V's) government and the perceived successor to the first newspaper that was Kānaka-centered, owned, and edited, *Ka Hoku o ka Pakipika* (see chapter 1). "He Moolelo no Hamanalau" was published in *Nupepa Kuokoa*, the rival newspaper to *Ke Au Okoa*. *Nupepa Kuokoa* was at this time published and edited by Luther Gulick and Henry Hodges Parker, both sons of missionaries who had followed in their parents' footsteps. They also employed the Kanaka Joseph U. Kawainui as an assistant editor. *Ke Au Okoa*, on the other hand, was published by the more secular government.[1] In some ways *Ka Nupepa Kuokoa* was an unlikely venue for Kānepuʻu. He had helped to found *Ka Hoku o ka Pakipika* and had supported *Ke Au Okoa*, both of which had struggled against missionary influence. Kānepuʻu, however, had more than once expressed his support for all newspapers that were published in the mother tongue. He also served as a carrier for *Kuokoa* in Pālolo Valley where he lived at the time.[2]

Gulick, Parker, and Kawainui, moreover, did not eschew Hawaiian literary and cultural works; in fact, they seem to have cultivated them. *Ka Nupepa Kuokoa* was where Kamakau's important history of the times of Kamehameha II and III were published. Many mele, including mele koʻihonua (cosmogonical chants that link the aliʻi to the divine and thus justify their rule) for important aliʻi, were also published alongside Kamakau's and Kānepuʻu's moʻolelo.[3] While supporting the aliʻi was antithetical to the mission's objectives, that is, persuading Kanaka to abandon their beliefs in favor of Christianity and "civilization," Gulick and Kawainui continually published such mele and moʻolelo.

"He Moolelo no Pakaa"

Although Kānepuʻu's name is not on any of the installments that we have of "He Moolelo no Pakaa," there is no doubt that he wrote this serial because at the place in the story where the winds of Maui and Molokai would have been printed, the author says that before he knew he would be writing the moʻolelo of Pākaʻa, he had written this wind chant down in his geography of Molokai (see chapter 3) and that it would be boring to reprint it, because it had been in the paper just the previous month.[4]

It is clear, as well, that Kānepuʻu did not simply rework the previous version of this moʻolelo (published by S. K. Kuapuʻu), although he had read it. In the preface, Kānepuʻu writes, "Aole nae hoi i kulike loa kaʻu me kana, a ua kulike no ma kekahi wahi" (My version is not exactly like his, though it is alike in some places).[5]

The preface also contains Kānepuʻu's strong expression of the importance of these moʻolelo, and he recounts how it is that they are no longer as well known as they were before the missionary arrivals.

> Ua huli nui hoi na kanaka ma ka pono, a o ke Kuhina Nui hoi kekahi i oi aku ka ikaika ma ka hoolaha ana i ka pono, oia hoi o Elisabeta Kaahumanu, a mai a ia ia [*sic*] mai kekahi mau olelo alii a koikoi hoi, e papa ana i na Kaao lapuwale o ka wa kahiko, a me na pule anaana, a me ia mea aku, a ia mea aku o ka wa kahiko. A mamuli oia olelo, ua ano weliweli na kanaka, no ke ao ana i na Kaao, na Moolelo, a me na Mele, a ua koe kakou ka poe hemahema.
>
> ———
>
> Many people converted to pono [Christianity], and the Kuhina Nui, that is, Elizabeth Kaʻahumanu, was the one who was the strongest in spreading the ideas of pono, and it was from her that some aliʻi commands and orders came, forbidding the useless Kaʻao of olden times, and pule ʻanāʻanā [sorcery] and many other things of olden times. Because of this word [command], people were somewhat terrified of teaching the Kaʻao, Moʻolelo, and Mele, and now we are left, a people deprived or left unprepared.

Here, Kānepuʻu is referring to Kaʻahumanu, who was the most powerful aliʻi in Hawaiʻi after the death of Kamehameha. She and two other aliʻiwahine, all high-ranking wāhine of Kamehameha, forced the end of the ʻai kapu, the sacred eating system at the heart of the institutionalized religion. Kaʻahumanu proclaimed herself a coruler with Kamehameha II when he became Mōʻī. Shortly afterward, the US missionaries arrived and it didn't take long before Kaʻahumanu became their most powerful convert and advocate.[6] Kānepuʻu tells us here that one effect of Kaʻahumanu's devotion to the religion was harmful to the lāhui; the turning away from our own people's moʻolelo created a serious deprivation. His moʻolelo was a contribution to a remedy for that deprivation (which, by the way, is still harming us: knowledge of our important orature and literature is still not common among the lāhui Hawaiʻi).

Kānepuʻu's "He Moolelo no Pakaa" uses the same plot lines in Kuapuʻu's, recounting the same events, except possibly for the ending. Briefly, it tells the story of Pākaʻa, a talented and loyal servant to Keawenuiaʻumi, the aliʻi nui of Hawaiʻi Island. Pākaʻa inherits a gourd from his mother that contains the bones of his female ancestor, Laʻamaomao. The possessor of the gourd, if trained in the wind names and their chants, has the ability to call forth or calm the winds. Pākaʻa overcomes his enemies and ensures the life and prosperity of his son through the use of the gourd. Kuapuʻu (and, later, Moses Nakuina) ends the moʻolelo with Pākaʻa being restored to his former position, his lands restored, and his son Kūapākaʻa entering the court of Keawenuiaʻumi in the same capacity as his father. Kānepuʻu, however, may have written another ending that takes place on Oʻahu and results in Kūapākaʻa ruling over part of that island. Since the last installment of the story in *Ke Au Okoa* is not available because certain issues have not been preserved, it is not known whether this ending appeared in the paper or not. It appears in a manuscript and typescript version of the story in Bishop Museum, which appears to have been copied from the newspaper.[7] Still, without the issue itself it is impossible to say what actually was published.

Kānepuʻu's version deserves to be read and studied not just because of the possible alternative ending, but because a significant portion of the moʻolelo takes place on Molokai, where he was born and raised, thus giving us a different view of the moʻolelo from that of Kuapuʻu of Kauaʻi and Nakuina of Oʻahu.

"He Moolelo no Kana, ka Hanai a Uli"

As soon as Kānepuʻu's "He Moolelo no Pakaa" ended, "He Moolelo no Kana, ka Hanai a Uli" began. This is the most elaborate version of the moʻolelo of Kana known so far. Abraham Fornander's versions of this moʻolelo are short, and no others in Hawaiian are extant. David Kalākaua wrote an English-language version in *The Legends and Myths of Hawaii*.[8] William Hyde Rice also wrote an English-language version.[9] Both of these differ substantially from Kānepuʻu's, especially in their lack of Hawaiian literary features: the mele of the waʻa hauling of Kana and Moi's dream (discussed in chapter 1) are absent, replaced by short narrations. According to kuʻualoha hoʻomanawanui, Rice and possibly Kalākaua as well, writing as he was for an English-speaking audience, are "'translating' culture as much as language for a western audience; leaving the chant(s) and genealogies out is a way to focus on plot and avoid 'unnecessary' details that would annoy, distract, or confuse western readers." hoʻomanawanui also suspects that authors like Rice might have been "intentionally redacting things (to use Charlot's term) to justify colonialism by 'dumbing down' the traditions from sophisticated stories to quaint folktales."[10] Perhaps it is no accident that these mele are among our lāhui's oral and literary treasures, showing off as they do our kūpuna's knowledge and artistry and providing us names of both deities and important objects, as well as an engagement with their thought world(s).

Kānepuʻu, writing for his audience of Kānaka who were literate in Hawaiian, characteristically takes the opportunity to enrich the story with Kanaka poetics and language, following in the footsteps of his kūpuna. He uses, for example, the names of the nights of the moon to describe when events took place. I have no doubt that he does so because the use of these terms was becoming increasingly rare as Westernization progressed in Hawaiʻi. He also puns on the words "kaula" (cord) and "kāula" (seer), which can only happen in Hawaiian. He has Uli, Kana's grandmother, explain the signs that he will be born as a kaula/kāula. A kaula, as a rope or cord, is long by nature. Uli says,

> He kaula keia keiki, ua ike no kakou i na ia hookauhua o keia keiki, he mau ia loloa wale no, he loihi ke Auau, he loihi ke Aha, a pela ka Puhi, ke Auki, &c.[11]
>
> ———
>
> This child is a kaula/kāula; we have seen the pregnancy cravings of this child, they are only long fish, the aʻuaʻu [swordfish] is long, the ʻaha [needlefish] is long, and so are the puhi [eel] and the aʻukī [marlin], etc.

In this recitation, Kānepuʻu not only enlivens the story with cultural knowledge—grandmothers and kāhuna being able to tell a baby's nature by the cravings of pregnancy—but also educates the public in a traditional Hawaiian way, that is, through the means of a memorized list of things that belong to a category, in this case, long-bodied fish. In his study of classical Hawaiian education, John Charlot quotes Beckwith: "The Hawaiian . . . composer, who would become a successful competitor in the fields of poetry, oratory, or disputation must store up in his memory the rather long series of names for persons, places, objects, or phases of nature which constitute the learning of the aspirant for mastery in the art of expression." Charlot goes on to note that "the most basic means of such organization [of words, names, etc.] is the formation of lists. . . . Such lists were used to assist memory, but were also intellectual tools and elements of literary aesthetics; they shared in the power of the word, being used in or even as prayers and charms." He observes as well that "lists and especially list chants . . . were of obvious importance in Hawaiian education as devices for learning and memorization."[12] Thus, Kānepuʻu here and elsewhere in these moʻolelo is educating his readers as well as showing off his own knowledge and literary and poetic talents.

Unfortunately, in one place, after describing many kupua of the sea, he says, "He nui no na kupua i koe o ka moana, a no koʻu manao e hooluhi wale aku ia oukou i ka heluhelu ana, nolaila, ke hoopokole nei au i ka olelo ana maanei" (There are many more kupua of the sea, but because I think that I might tire you reading [them all], I have shortened my narrative here).[13] If he had heeded his own exhortation of 1862—that people should write down their traditional knowledge—we might have a fuller list.

In addition, while Kānepuʻu's version has many more mele and pule than any other, Kānepuʻu believes there may be more of these than he knows. After telling all of Moi's dreams that he knows, he writes,

> Na mele ae la no ia o ka moe a Mo-i i loaa iaʻu, na kekahi poe o kakou e hoopiha mai, na ka poe i oi aku ke akamai a me ka lohe ana i ka poe kahiko, he mea kahe no ka hoi, no ka hou o ka lae.[14]
>
> ———
>
> These are the mele of the dream(s) of Moi that I have, it is up to some other people among us to fill in more; it is up to the people who are smarter and who listened to the old folk; this is work that causes the sweat of the brow to flow.

The comment about "smarter people" might also be a sarcastic jab at and/or an invitation to Keawekolohe, the letter writer who intimated that

Kānepuʻu's version of one of the mele might have been distorted (see chapter 1).

In other places in the moʻolelo, Kānepuʻu describes important cultural information, such as the various kuleana that the aliʻi, the kāhuna, and the ʻalihikaua (war leader) each have.[15] It is important to note also, and this is not specific to Kānepuʻu's version, that men in the story often rely on women for knowledge, advice, and wisdom. Nīheu, for example, does not know how to go about making his waʻa properly until his grandmother Uli (who is also an akua, i.e., a deity) teaches him the protocols of making offerings to his ancestors.[16] Similarly, when Moi's life is in danger for reporting his dream prophecies, he must turn to Nuʻakea, his sister, to save him.[17] Moreover, although originally the women in the story are captured when Kapepeʻekauila wages war against Hakalanileo, they later exercise their own agency by refusing to return to Hakalanileo—they apparently fall in love with Keolewa.[18] (This could be interpreted another way, however, as a male storyteller's fantasy of women loving their captors.)

This moʻolelo, then, is extremely rich in cultural and literary treasures. Despite the unfortunate loss of one installment (and, most unfortunately, it is the one in which Kana and Nīheu "rescue" their mother), this moʻolelo is among Kānepuʻu's best work.

"He Moolelo no Hamanalau"

"Hamanalau," for some months, was published on the front page of the paper right next to Kamakau's "Ka Moolelo o na Kamehameha" (moʻolelo of the Kamehamehas [II and III]). This prestigious location signals the editors' regard for Kānepuʻu and the quality of his moʻolelo. The front page of the Hawaiian papers in those years usually attracted readers not by printing important news, but by offering intriguing mele and moʻolelo, both historical and literary, as exemplified here.

SYNOPSIS

This moʻolelo is the coming-of-age story of Hāmanalau, the granddaughter and hānai (adopted child) of Hāwea, who raises her at her home at the summit of Kaʻala, the highest peak on the island of Oʻahu.[19] Hāwea is a kahuna kilokilo who can read as well as send hōʻailona (signs and omens) using clouds, rainbows, and other weather phenomena. She also speaks

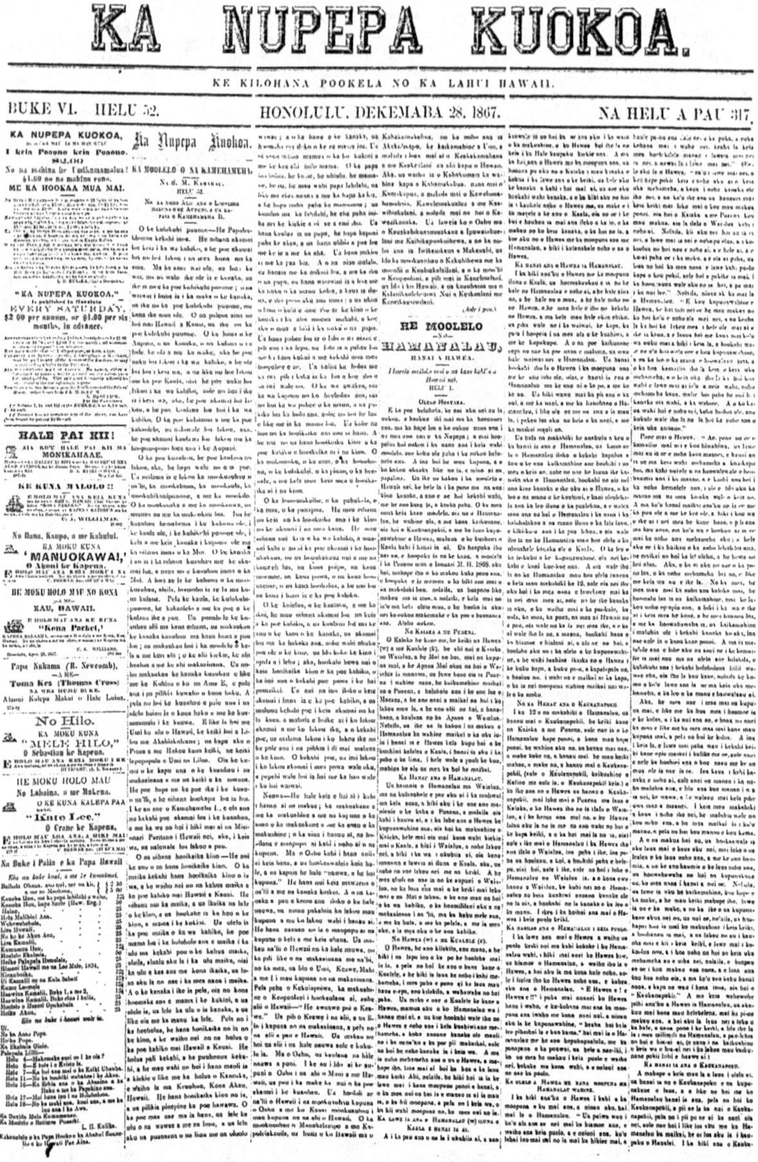

KA NUPEPA KUOKOA.

KE KILOHANA POOKELA NO KA LAHUI HAWAII.

BUKE VI. HELU 52. HONOLULU, DEKEMABA 28, 1867. NA HELU A PAU 317.

KA NUPEPA KUOKOA,

Ka Nupepa Kuokoa.

KA MOOLELO O NA KAMEHAMEHA.

HE MOOLELO

—NO—

HAMANALAU,

HALE PAI KII!

"KA NUPEPA KUOKOA."

EVERY SATURDAY.

'MANUOKAWAI,'

No Hilo.

"MELE HILO,"

FIGURE 2.1

Kānepuʻu's "He Moolelo no Hamanalau" on the front page of *Ka Nupepa Kuokoa,* next to S. M. Kamakau's "Ka Moolelo o na Kamehameha," December 28, 1867.

regularly with the "kupunakane o ka po," her deceased husband and male ancestors of the pō—the realm from which humans come and to which we return at death. Hāwea's son Kaiaka and his wahine, Puaʻena, who are Hāmanalau's parents, are the ruling aliʻi of the moku of Waialua (one of the six large districts of Oʻahu).

Hāwea raises Hāmanalau under strict kapu. No one is allowed to see her and she is not allowed to visit anyone else. Hāwea cares for her as an extra-special child. The only ones Hāmanalau speaks with are Hāwea, the kūpuna o ka pō, and the birds.[20]

After a few years, Hāwea also takes Hāmanalau's younger brother, Kaukanapōkiʻi, as a hānai, but he is not raised under kapu. As a child he develops a love for waʻa (sailing vessels) but does not have a parent to make a toy waʻa for him. He contents himself with fetching the waʻa of other children at the Waialua beach.

One night, Hāmanalau, in a dream state, travels to the island of Hawaiʻi, where she meets a young, handsome aliʻi, Kaihuʻauwaʻalua. They fall in love in the dream, and she tells him her name and where she lives. He too is enamored of waʻa, but of the real thing: he builds and sails voyaging waʻa. He sails to Oʻahu, where he meets Kaukanapōkiʻi and arranges a trade: Kaukanapōkiʻi is to kidnap his sister while she sleeps and deliver her to Kaihuʻauwaʻalua and in return he will be allowed to sail to Hawaiʻi on Kaihuʻauwaʻalua's waʻa kaulua (double-hulled waʻa).[21]

On Hawaiʻi, Hāmanalau remains with Kaihuʻauwaʻalua, who soon grows indifferent to her presence. She follows him to the top of Waipiʻo, where he is felling trees to make new waʻa. When he and his men return to the shore area, she cannot follow because she is pregnant and about to give birth. They abandon her and for a while Kaihuʻauwaʻalua sends food up to her, which, however, she doesn't receive because the messengers do not want to climb all the way up. Her brother joins her and works to supply them with the little food available in the forest. She grows weak and after giving birth to a healthy baby girl, Kūkona, she announces that she is going to die, but she intends to visit Hāwea in spirit form in the hope of being revived. She explains that she was weakened by both the lack of food and the lack of communication with the kūpuna o ka pō. She often spoke with them in her dreams while living on Kaʻala, but not while at Waipiʻo. This familial spiritual connection is thus an integral element of her life and crucial to her survival. Hāmanalau tells her brother that if he takes good care of her when she returns, she will live, but if he takes care of her poorly, she will die. She leaves Kaukanapōkiʻi with the baby, whom he nurses with ʻōpuʻu maiʻa (buds of the banana plant), and other forest foods. Soon, some birdcatchers discover him with the baby, and he takes the baby down to the shore to live with her father's family. Kaukanapōkiʻi then returns to the upland to wait for Hāmanalau's return.[22]

Meanwhile on Oʻahu, Hāwea places Hāmanalau's spirit in a bird, an ʻiʻiwi maka pōlena (scarlet Hawaiian honey creeper with yellow-rimmed eyes [*Vestiaria coccinea*]). Hāmanalau then flies in this bird body back to Waipiʻo, where Kaukanapōkiʻi places her spirit back into her real body.[23] When she is well, they go to tell Kaihuʻauwaʻalua that they are returning to Oʻahu, leaving Kūkona with him to raise. But when they arrive near his residence, Hāmanalau gets frightened, just as a bird does, and flees into the forest. Kaihuʻauwaʻalua engages a kahuna named Ka-Makāula, who has people construct a structure like a giant birdcage, which they fill with forest plants, live birds, and food. When Hāmanalau enters the structure, they drop sheets of kapa across the whole thing, blocking her exit. After a few days, she calms down and is able to go and talk with Kaihuʻauwaʻalua. Kaihuʻauwaʻalua asks Hāmanalau to come back to him, but instead she relates to him all the damage he has done by abandoning her, and she then leaves for Oʻahu with her brother.[24]

On the way, she and her brother first stop at Keʻanae on Maui, where they meet and make friends with a young woman named Luʻukiakaʻahalanalana (Luʻukia) and others.[25] They make another stop at Hālawa, Molokai (where Kānepuʻu was raised). Kaukanapōkiʻi makes a friend there, a young man named Kaili.[26] These friends sail with them to Oʻahu, where they all meet Hāmanalau and Kaukanapōkiʻi's birth parents for the first time.[27]

At this time, Kaukanapōkiʻi appears to have passed a crucial test by reviving Hāmanalau, despite his earlier immature and disastrous act of kidnapping her. Because of this and because he was not haumia (having violated a kapu), as Hāmanalau was, Hāwea trains him in the art of kilokilo. This takes about a year, and for that year he lives under strict kapu and is not allowed to cut his hair.[28]

After that year, he and Luʻukia are joined in a hoʻāo ceremony that is very elaborate, analogous to a wedding. Two of their friends are also joined to each other during the same ceremony.[29]

Not long afterward, Hāwea's husband, Kualele, comes to her and tells her to have Kaukanapōkiʻi read the signs of the day. When she does, Kaukanapōkiʻi predicts the weather and then also sees, via the actions of certain clouds, that there is a young man who has been raised under kapu at the top of Wahiawā, in Oʻahunui, by Kualele's relatives and is of an age to be joined in hoʻāo. He seems to be a perfect life partner for Hāmanalau. Kaukanapōkiʻi proposes that a delegation be sent to talk to those relatives about joining the young man, Hinahelelani, with Hāmanalau. This is arranged, despite Hāmanalau having had a previous relationship and a child. In having read the cosmic signs correctly, Kaukanapōkiʻi has passed another test and we now see him acting as an adult and a community leader, a role he continues in for the remainder of the moʻolelo.[30]

In preparation for the hoʻāo ceremony, Hāmanalau bathes in order to be cleansed of her prior experiences. Afterward, turtles and birds carry her down to the shore for the ceremonies. Hinahelelani, in contrast, spends the night before the ceremonies being prepared by spirit helpers. He has a series of visitors in the night who come to prepare his hair; make his breath sweet, make his eyes, shoulders, chest, torso, thighs, and knees beautiful; and make his poli (the shoulder and chest area where one cradles a child) full of kindness only and free of anger or crankiness. The hoʻāo ceremony joining Hāmanalau to Hinahelelani is even more elaborate than the one for Kaukanapōkiʻi and Luʻukia. Afterward, Hāmanalau happily goes to live at Oʻahunui with Hinahelelani.[31]

When Kūkona is a teen, she, her father, and hānai mother (who is raising her) visit Hāmanalau and Kaukanapōkiʻi. Kūkona decides to remain on Oʻahu with them, and Kaukanapōkiʻi arranges a hoʻāo for her as well, with a young man from Kuaihelani (likely in what we now call Papahānaumokuākea, or the Northwest Hawaiian Islands),[32] whose delegation has come to Oʻahu to seek a suitable young woman for him.[33]

The moʻolelo ends with Kūkona's hoʻāo ceremony and an account of each of the main characters, including how long they lived, where they died, and how many children they had. In a final note, Kānepuʻu reminds readers about the previous criticism of this moʻolelo (see chapter 1) and asks other writers to submit their own renditions for publication.[34]

One unusual feature of this moʻolelo is that it has two coming-of-age stories within it: a woman's (Hāmanalau's) and a man's (Kaukanapōkiʻi's). More well-known moʻolelo seem to concentrate on one or the other, as "Hiʻiakaikapoliopele" is a woman's tale and "Kawelo" is a man's tale.[35] Those two are very concentrated on either women or men in the central roles. While Hāmanalau is the title character of Kānepuʻu's moʻolelo, Kaukanapōkiʻi is as much a main character as she is.

LITERARY FEATURES

This moʻolelo beautifully shows how Kānepuʻu enjoyed the language play characteristic of Hawaiian. Kānepuʻu employs both familiar and unusual literary devices. Among the well-known Hawaiian literary devices are ʻōlelo noʻeau; repeated sounds or assonance; allusion to other moʻolelo, both Hawaiian and foreign; and kaona, or layers of meaning. In addition, he demonstrates his knowledge and love of the ʻāina in various ways. Kānepuʻu uses all of these devices as well as one that has been less commented upon in previous scholarship: repetition of imagery. Part of what makes reading moʻolelo an almost endlessly repeatable experience is puzzling out the figurative sayings and allusions. Many of the figurative sayings and allusions Kānepuʻu makes to other moʻolelo and mele are understandable, provided the reader does some sleuthing, but others seem almost impossible and remain there as a challenge to readers' further study and puzzle-solving abilities.

BIRD IMAGERY

I would first like to examine the repetition of bird and feather imagery. In this moʻolelo, it is striking how closely associated with birds Hāmanalau is. While she is growing up, she is said to have only Hāwea, her kūpuna o ka pō, and the birds to talk to.

> Aohe no nae he launa ike kanaka aku o Hamanalau, hookahi no aia nei ano kino kanaka e ike aku ai o Hawea, o ka leo o na manu o ke kuahiwi, e kani oleolehala ana ka leo iluna o ka pualehua, a e walea mau ana no hoi o Hamanalau i ka nana i ka halahalakau a na manu iluna o ka lala laau, e kiki-ko-u ana i ka pua lehua, a oia wale iho la no ko Hamanalau mau hoa olelo o ka ulunahele kanaka ole o Kaala.[36]

> Hāmanalau had never met another person; the only person she had ever seen in the flesh was Hāwea; the voices of the birds of the mountain singing were the only voices on the lehua flowers, and Hāmanalau was always at ease watching the birds perched on the tree branches, chirping [while] on the lehua flowers, and they were Hāmanalau's only conversation companions in the uninhabited forest of Kaʻala.

When Hāmanalau has been abandoned at the top of Waipiʻo, a bit later in the moʻolelo, Kānepuʻu writes,

> Lawe ia ka anei a ke kuahiwi haalele ia, nolaila, aole e pono ke olelo e, he hoa noho no kauhale kane, he hoa noho no no kauhale a ka leo o ka manu.[37]

> [She] was brought to the mountain and abandoned, therefore it isn't correct to say she is a living companion of the man's houses;[38] rather she is a living companion of the houses of the voices of the birds.

As mentioned earlier, Hāwea puts Hāmanalau's spirit into an ʻiʻiwi bird. When the bird arrives on Hawaiʻi, Kānepuʻu uses further bird imagery, as in this example:

> A i ka loaa ana ae la o ua manu uhane nei, o ko ia nei hoihoi no ia a loko o kekahi ipu pu-uli-uli,[39] a waiho paa loa malaila e u-u ai.[40]

> When the spirit bird was gotten [trapped], [Kaukanapōkiʻi] put her inside of a small gourd and left her there to complain.

Kānepuʻu could choose any other kind of container, but he chooses the pūʻulīʻulī type of small gourd used to make feathered gourd rattles. Note here also that the word he chooses to represent the sounds Hāmanalau makes while her spirit is in the bird contains a bit of kaona. Rather than one of the several words for chirping or bird singing, he chooses "ʻūʻū," to stutter or stammer. It is also a reduplication of "ʻū," to complain, mourn, or grieve.[41] The latter two remind the reader that Hāmanalau has actually died and Kaukanapōkiʻi is faced with the task of bringing her back to life. This word describes their emotions of potential future grief and mourning should Kaukanapōkiʻi's efforts fail, which, fortunately, does not come to pass.

In another example, where Kaukanapōkiʻi gathers bananas for their food, Kānepuʻu inserts birds as well:

> Kii aku la keia i ka maia e-a o ke kuahiwi, kaa wale ae la no ma ka haka e kokoke ana i ka hale o lakou nei. A i ka pala ana o ka maia, ike aku la keia i ka pohai puni ana mai i ua mea he manu, makena no nae hoi ua mea he manu o kela ano manu, keia ano manu.[42]

> [Kaukanapōkiʻi] gathered the mountain bananas, set them aside on a shelf near their house. And when the bananas were ripe, he saw them encircled by birds, many birds of every kind.

Kānepuʻu uses kaona in this passage also. The word he chooses for "many" is "mākena," pronounced differently, but which, before diacriticals were introduced, was spelled the same way as "makena," "mourning, wailing, lamentation; to wail, lament."[43] Kānepuʻu takes advantage of the ambiguity created in the print version to evoke this double sense of the word.

When Hāmanalau runs away from Kaihuʻauwaʻalua after returning from the top of Waipiʻo, Kānepuʻu describes her flight this way:

> Ae mai no ka Ma-kaula. "Ae, ua ola no o Hamanalau, mamuli o ke ano kupua o ko wahine, ua ola no ia, a ma ia ano no, ua ula-ia hou ko wahine, ua holo i ka nahelehele, ua ahiu, ua maka-pa."[44]
>
> ———
>
> The seer agreed. "Yes, Hāmanalau is alive, because of the magical nature of your wahine [Hāmanalau], she survived, and in that same nature, she has again become deranged, she has run into the forest, become wild, wild like a bird."

Again, Kānepuʻu could choose any number of other words or descriptions, but here he specifically chooses "makapā," "shy, wild, as a bird."[45] When Hāmanalau enters the forest house built to trap her and approaches the food put there for her, Kānepuʻu writes, "O ka hele hoonenene mai la no ia o ua o ino o Hamanalau a hiki i kahi papa-aina"[46] (Then this damaged Hāmanalau went, flutteringly, to where the food table was). This translation sounds odd because Kānepuʻu chooses the word "hoʻonenene" to describe Hāmanalau's hesitant approach to the food. Pukui and Elbert translate "nenene" as "fluttering the wings" and also note it as a reduplication of "nene," "to stir, show animation, move, as a fledgling."[47] Kānepuʻu describes her as eating like a bird too: "Ai oe [o ia] la me ke ano mu-ka mu-ka, aohe nei o ka ai o ka pono, he okoa no hoi ka ai a ka ulaia, ke ai la, a ke hoolei la ka nui"[48] (She ate in a gobbling way, not in the proper way of eating; the deranged eat differently, [and] while eating, most of the food was tossed around). This creates an image of a bird pecking at food in a messy way and scattering seed around the plate or ground.

While Hāmanalau and her companions are living atop Kaʻala, Kānepuʻu refers to them several times as ʻiwa (frigate birds).[49] Pukui and Elbert note that the ʻiwa is used figuratively for a handsome person, or one dressed in finery. The ʻiwa flies and glides high up in the sky and is rather huge, having a wingspan of more than two meters. The sight of an ʻiwa portends wind. Because of their size, effortless gliding on high winds, and distinctive shape, they are fascinating to watch. Pukui and Elbert note this ʻōlelo noʻeau: "Kīkaha ka ʻiwa, he lā makani, poises the frigate bird, a windy day (of a handsome person who draws attention, as does the *ʻiwa* bird poised aloft)."[50]

Kānepuʻu continues to use bird imagery in the descriptions of Hinahelelani, the young man to be joined to Hāmanalau, and of his grandparents' first sight of him after he had been groomed for the hoʻāo:

> Ia wa no hoi i hiki aku ai ua mau kupuna, a i nana aku ko laua nei hana, he aiwaiwa loa aku ka hoi ua mea he nani a me ka maikai o keia wa i oi ae mamu[a] o ka wa i hala, oia no ka hoi oe i ka moho-ea la, ua mea he onaona o na maka, aohe wahi nani ole i ka laua nana aku. Ina he eheu ko laua, i na la paha ua like me ka manu, a ma ko laua nei paulehia, aohe o laua nei pane leo aku ia Hinahelelani a loihi wale, me he mea la ua maule, a o ke kunou poo wale aku no ka laua imua o ua moopuna me he kolea la.[51]

> At this time, [Hinahelelani's] kūpuna arrived, and when they looked at him, it was very mysterious how beautiful and good he looked now, much better than in the past; like a mohoea bird, his eyes (or facial features) were lovely, and there was nothing not beautiful that they could see. If they had had wings, they would have been like birds; in their complete fascination, they had no voices with which to speak to Hinahelelani for a long time, as if they had fainted, so they just bowed their heads before the grandson like a kōlea bird.

In this passage, Kānepuʻu first compares Hinahelelani to a mohoea bird, a flightless bird often used as a metaphor for a tenacious person[52] but used here to describe his beauty. He follows this with two more bird references, one of which is to the kōlea, whose bobbing action is used as a simile to describe the bowing of the grandparents' heads.

Finally, in the hoʻāo ceremony, birds are the helpers that dry Hāmanalau's body after her bath of purification, and they accompany her from the top of Kaʻala to the shore area where the ceremony takes place.[53]

The overall effect of this continual allusion to birds and feathers is to remind the reader of how close Hāmanalau is to the birds. Birds and their feathers are symbols of aliʻi and their (semi-)divine nature. Hāmanalau, Kaukanapōkiʻi, their parents, and especially their grandmother Hāwea are the aliʻi nui family as well as the kāhuna of Waialua. Their home atop Kaʻala is the closest point to the heavens that humans can attain on the island of

Oʻahu. Birds are the only creatures that can go higher. Featherwork in Hawaiʻi was brought to a high art and aliʻi nui often wore feather cloaks, helmets, and lei, and they or their attendants or both carried feather standards called kāhili.[54] Two of the birds that Kānepuʻu emphasizes in the moʻolelo—the ʻiʻiwi and the ʻiwa—provided special feathers for these garments and kāhili.[55] Hāmanalau's spirit in the ʻiʻiwi also alludes to the idea of kino lau, in which deities and ʻaumakua live in the bodies of various animals, plants, and other natural elements. Although she doesn't include the term "kino lau," Lilikalā Kameʻeleihiwa gives us an excellent illustration of it:

> Kamapuaʻa, the Hawaiian Pig-God . . . is that *Akua* who changes his body form at will; now a beautiful and virile youth, tempting women, and then a giant boar ruthlessly devouring his terrified enemies. Sometimes he is a *nukunuku-ā-puaʻa* fish cowering in the sea, fleeing the burning wrath of Pele's lava, and then he becomes a *kukui* tree or a clump of *ʻuhaloa* grass, silently hiding from his enemies in the forest.[56]

Hāmanalau is not an akua like Kamapuaʻa, but the allusion to kino lau evokes for the reader the close association of animals, other natural elements, and the spirit world that was characteristic of our kupuna's world, represented by Hāmanalau's kupuna, Hāwea.

ʻŌLELO NOʻEAU

Now we turn to some of the many ʻōlelo noʻeau that Kānepuʻu employs. Many of these are similar to examples collected by Mary Kawena Pukui and published in *ʻŌlelo Noʻeau* in 1983. But others are not found in that work and it falls to the reader to puzzle out what they refer to. This illustrates that while Pukui's book contains nearly three thousand such sayings, many, many more can be found in our literature. For that collection, she drew from her own memory, fieldwork, and reading in the Hawaiian-language papers.[57] It would have been impossible for her or any one person to read every moʻolelo and mele in the newspapers and manuscripts, despite her access to the Bishop Museum library and archives. It is the same with words in the existing dictionaries and place names in current reference works. None of those works are as comprehensive as one might suppose, and new reference works should be created to supplement all of them. Kānepuʻu's Hāmanalau is exemplary of nearly all moʻolelo in its use of ʻōlelo noʻeau, words, and place names that cannot be found in contemporary reference works.

ʻŌlelo noʻeau are important in how they reflect the worldviews of our kupuna. While all languages are inherently metaphorical, Hawaiian is characterized by its proliferation of these figurative sayings, as well as the practice of kaona of which they often form a part, both of which suggest that directly representational forms of speech or writing are less valued than poetic utterances.[58] Rather, play in language is highly valued. In the most extended study of ʻōlelo noʻeau, Kekeha Solis quotes a writer from 1928 who explains this well in a lament on its decline:

> O ka olelo Hawaii me ke kaona o kona manao, ka pookela o na olelo i waena o na lahui o ka honua nei, ma na hua mele a na kupuna e ike ia ai ka uʻi, ka maikai o ke kaona o ka manao, aole hoi e like me ko keia au e nee nei, he hoopuka maoli mai no i ka manao me ka hoonalonalo ole iho i ke kaona.[59]
>
> ———
>
> The Hawaiian language with its idea of kaona is the most excellent of the languages among the peoples of this earth, in the song lyrics of the ancestors in which its beauty is seen, the beauty of the kaona of its thought, which is not like today's, [where people] just tell the thought or idea without concealing the kaona.

Along with the bragging, this writer tells us that the presence of kaona in song lyrics and elsewhere is considered beautiful, and also that he or she does not appreciate artless writing or composition. The reason for the decline of the use of kaona in speech, story, and even lyrics is no doubt related to the rise of English and its attendant valuing of clarity and directness.

Solis also points out that understanding the play in the language of our kupuna often requires work. Utterances, whether spoken or written, are reflections and products of their contexts, so it may take research to understand sayings that may have been rather more obvious at the time they were published. Another aspect of kaona enters in here too, and that is that some uses of kaona are never meant to be understood by everyone but are aimed at specific persons who will get the meaning or at least its drift.[60] Moreover, Solis asks, "He pili ke kuanaʻike o nā kūpuna i ko lākou nohona o ka wā i hala. He aha ka waiwai o ka paʻa ʻana o ia kuanaʻike iā kākou, i ka poʻe e noho nei i kēia au hou?"[61] (The worldview[s] of the kūpuna are related to their lives of the past. What is the value of learning that worldview to us, people living in this current day?) He answers this by pointing out how colonialism has devalued so much of our kupuna's knowledge, refused to include any of it in our schooling, and used it to create representations of our kupuna as primitive. The project of decolonization and rebuilding our Kanaka world therefore requires a foundation, and these ʻōlelo noʻeau form an integral part of that foundation, which is understanding our ancestors' epistemologies. For this, Solis uses a well-known ʻōlelo noʻeau himself: "ʻO ke kahua ma mua, ma hope ke kūkulu"[62] (The foundation comes first, then the building).

The first example of Kānepuʻu's ʻōlelo noʻeau is one that is reflected in Pukui: "Eia no ka i Hikauhi," when explaining how Kaihuʻauwaʻalua's people supposedly took food to Hāmanalau but did not climb all the way up to where she was. She therefore had no idea where it was and never received it. Pukui's version is "I Hikauhi, i Kaumanamana" (At Hikauhi, at Kaumanamana), for which she gives the following explanation:

> A man and his wife lived at Kaunakakai, Molokaʻi. While he was gone fishing one day, she felt the beginning of labor pains and went to her mother's home in another village. When the husband arrived home and his wife was not there, he began to search for her. After he had searched fruitlessly for several days, his wife returned with their baby daughter, whom they named Hikauhi. Ever since that day, hikauhi has meant "in vain," and when a person loses something and goes in search, one says, "I Hikauhi, i Kaumanamana."[63]

Kānepuʻu's usage differs a little from Pukui's; he doesn't include Kaumanamana, and he extends it to something that can't be found but that isn't searched for either. This is typical of the flexibility of ʻōlelo noʻeau; what is given in Pukui's book is not the only explanation for these sayings.

An example of an ʻōlelo noʻeau in this moʻolelo that has no corollary in *ʻŌlelo Noʻeau* is "aohe wahi hemahema iki o Hopoikeau," which I might translate roughly as "there are no flaws in Hopoikeau"—meaning everything is perfect. This is a play on the word "hopo," to worry. Kānepuʻu uses this saying in describing the preparations for the many visitors coming from Kuaihelani for the hoʻāo ceremony of Kūkona with their aliʻi, Hoomaileanue. Even though many visitors were coming and needed to be fed and housed, Kaukanapōkiʻi had organized everyone in the region to supply everything that might be needed, so there was no need to worry.[64]

These are just two examples of the many ʻōlelo noʻeau that Kānepuʻu includes—some are reflected in Pukui's collection and others not. Like the other accomplished writers in Hawaiian, Kānepuʻu drew on the wisdom and artistry of his ancestors and contemporaries to make his moʻolelo worth reading; the ʻōlelo noʻeau are an integral part of what makes it worthy.

ALLUSION

Kānepuʻu, like other Hawaiian-language writers, delights in showing off his knowledge of literature, history, and religion through allusion. In this section, I describe a few examples in "Hamanalau." This first example alludes to a moʻolelo that I have been unable to find: "A eia no o Hamanalau me kana huakai nui e pohai hele aku nei, me he mea la o Luanuu ma ka hele a luhe i ke alanui, i hikiwawe aku no la hoi i ka lio"[65] (There was Hāmanalau with her big traveling party encircling [her] wherever they went, as if it were Luanuʻu traveling until he or she withered on the road, and whose [travel] was speeded up by horses). It seems obvious that the reference to Luanuʻu alludes to a moʻolelo that his readers were familiar with, meant to bring a certain image to mind.

In a second example, Kānepuʻu alludes to a mele maʻi that was composed originally for Kīnaʻu, a son of the aliʻi nui Keʻelikōlani (according to one source), and which was later dedicated to Liliʻuokalani.[66] At the time of the publication of "Hamanalau," Liliʻu was not yet Mōʻīwahine, but the mele was likely already in circulation. Kānepuʻu makes two references to it, close together, in the section where supernatural persons prepare Hinahelelani for his hoʻāo ceremony to Hāmanalau. Group after group of these magical people enter his house and groom different parts of his body. In the section about his ʻōiwi, the upper part of his body,[67] Kānepuʻu has them say, "Kai no hoi o kahi oiwi o Hinahelelani, oia no oe i kahi kii milimili la, kupololei lua kahi oiwi, pouli ke kua mahina ke alo" (One would think Hinahelelani's body would be like a beloved doll; his trunk standing straight [or doubly straight], the back being dark, and the front bright like the moon).[68] Although I have translated "kii milimili" here as "beloved doll," following Pukui, it really evokes a beloved child or favorite little one. It is worth noting here as well that Kānepuʻu offers a variation on the well-known ʻōlelo noʻeau for beauty: "pali ke kua, mahina ke alo" (the back is straight like a cliff, the front [face] bright like the moon).[69] He uses "pouli" instead of "pali," bringing in dark skin (perhaps) as an element of beauty.

Shortly thereafter, magical people (poʻe ʻeʻepa) come to make Hinahelelani's knees beautiful. They say

O makou keia o Nukumoi, o Ihumoi, o Moilii, o Nukuiki, i hoounaia mai nei makou e ko makou alii e lawe mai i na mea nani a hoomaikai a hoohui pu aku me na kuli o Hinahelelani.[70]

———

We are Nukumoi, Ihumoi, Moiliʻi, and Nukuiki; we have been sent by our aliʻi to bring the things to beautify, improve, and put together with the knees of Hinahelelani.

Both "kii milimili" and "nuku moi (Nukumoi)" are descriptors of the aliʻi child in the mele best known as "E Liliʻu ē," a song for Liliʻu Kamakaʻeha, who grew up to become Liliʻuokalani, the last monarch of Hawaiʻi. The first verse of the mele describes the child's body as doll-like and loved:

E Liliʻu ē
Noho nani mai
Kō kino ē
Kiʻi milimili

Liliʻu
Sitting pretty
Your little body
Like a beloved doll[71]

The mele goes on to describe different parts of the child's body, including the knees:

Kō kuli ē
Nuku moi ʻoe
Kō wāwae
Pahu aʻe i luna

Your little knees
Like the snout of the threadfish
Your little feet
Pushing upward[72]

The reference to "nuku moi," the snout of the threadfish, evokes the image of dimples in a child's knees. The word "moi," moreover, is spelled the same way in Kānepuʻu's time as "mōʻī," ruler of an island or the archipelago. Hāmanalau and Hinahelelani are aliʻi nui, with the potential to become mōʻī. The further kaona is that the song is a mele maʻi, and Hinahelelani is being groomed for a conjugal partnership.

In the next example, Kānepuʻu shows his knowledge of both the moʻolelo of Kamapuaʻa, the important pig deity, and Hawaiian history. The translation is rough because the passage is a bit difficult to decipher. It describes Hinahelelaniʻs clothing and his residence filled with treasures:

> Ua lako pono no hoi ko Hinahelelani mau kahiko kino, aohe hua holo i Kahiki i-o Koea la i ua mea hoi he eueu o keia keiki kuawaa o ka uka waokele a ka laau ala i noho ai, he loaa ole paha ia Poki ma a me ka poe kua laau ala i ka wa iho nei o Kaahumanu ma.[73]

Hinahelelaniʻs bodily adornments had been completely supplied, there was no hua that sailed to Kahiki to Koea, to this energetic activity of this kuawaʻa child of the upland forest region where sandalwood grows, which was not acquired by Boki and the other people who cut down sandalwood in the time of Kaʻahumanu.

The word kuawaʻa is somewhat difficult to clearly understand; it is not in any of the dictionaries, and a search in the papakilo database only returns personal names. However we can see that Kānepuʻu is referring to the moʻolelo of Kamapuaʻa in his reference to Koea of Kahiki, who was the father of Kamapuaʻaʻs wāhine in Kahiki.[74] Kuawaʻa could refer to a back (kua) like a waʻa, which would be an allusion to Kamapuaʻaʻs carving a waʻa shape into the cliff named Kaliuwaʻa (the water in the waʻa bilge).[75] He alludes as well to Boki, an aliʻi nui who was involved in the sandalwood trade during the time when Hawaiʻi was virtually ruled by Kaʻahumanu. He says the sandalwood was "not acquired" by Boki, a further reference to Bokiʻs need for more sandalwood than he could obtain in Hawaiʻi, which led him to sail in search of other lands in Oceania where he might find more. He was lost on that journey and never returned. The "hua" mentioned is likely an allusion to another set of ʻōlelo noʻeau concerning the migrating bird, the kōlea. One of the ʻōlelo noʻeau is "ʻO ka hua o ke kōlea aia i Kahiki" (The egg of the kōlea is in Kahiki). This refers to foreigners who come to Hawaiʻi and amass wealth and then return with it to foreign lands.[76] The hua (the egg), or products of their work, go somewhere else to benefit others. Here it seems Kānepuʻu is using it to emphasize that the wealth was there for Hinahelelani; none of it went to Kahiki.

The final example of allusion is to the Bible. Most Hawaiians of Kānepuʻu's time were very knowledgeable of the Bible and used its passages in argumentation and allusions. The following sentence describes the arrival of the magical people who groomed Hinahelelani: "I ke ano ana iho o ke aumoe, kamumu ana o waho o ka hale, a iku-wa ana ka leo o ka poe e-epa o ka aina o Apoluona ma" (When night arrived, there was a sound of footsteps outside the house, and the voices of the magical people of the land of Apollyon resounded).⁷⁷ Kānepuʻu metaphorically links these poʻe ʻeʻepa to the devil named in Revelation 9:11. The King James version of the passage reads: "And they had a king over them, *which is* the angel of the bottomless pit, whose name in the Hebrew tongue *is* Abaddon, but in the Greek tongue hath *his* name Apollyon."⁷⁸ He thus acknowledges the missionary teaching that everything in the Hawaiian religion was the work of the devil, but only in this one, odd reference. Everything in that section is actually presented as positive and delightful.

KAONA VIA ASSONANCE

Many times, Kānepuʻu (and many other writers) use similarity in sound (assonance) to create kaona. For example, when the magical people come to prepare Hina's poli, Kānepuʻu takes advantage of the double meanings of the word "pēpē":

> Kai no hoi o kahi poli o Hinahelelani, oia no oe i ka hele a polinahe la, lahilahi lua kahi poli ke hala aku, aohe hoi he nui ino e opu keke ai, a hookuolo, aohe hoi he wiwi ino, e lao-lao ai, laalaau, eha ke hoouka ia mai; o keia hoi, nolunolu pepe i ka lomia e ka [I]nuwai.⁷⁹
>
> ———
>
> One would think the poli of Hinahelelani, would have become polinahe (soft and gentle but also slim-waisted and broad-shouldered), a poli that is light and fragile as one passes, it is not too big to cause complaint, or cause a trembling, neither is it too thin, to be uncomfortable, like sticks, and hurt when it is touched; this one, rather, is softly fragrant, crushed by the Inuwai [water-drinking] wind.

This passage is obviously highly poetic, so the translation I give here must be regarded as a loose interpretation, provided only to orient the reader. The phrase at the end, "nolunolu pepe i ka lomia," is reminiscent of both the phrase "nolu pē," softly fragrant, and "pēpē lomia," crushed, both found in Pukui and Elbert, in separate entries.⁸⁰ Thus the word "pēpē" does double duty here: it denotes fragrance and also being crushed by the wind called the Inuwai. This seems to describe how love can feel sweet but also heavy in the chest, the poli. Kānepuʻu also artfully repeats the sound "poli" in the word "polinahe," and again later in the sentence.

In another example, Kānepuʻu refers to young couples being joined in hoʻāo as ʻōmalemale. The first use refers to Kaukanapōkiʻi and Luʻukia and another couple: "A o ua mau omalemale nei hoi a kakou" (And as for these ʻōmalemale of ours).[81] The second refers to Hāmanalau and Hinahelelani, after their ceremony: "Aohe no he hoi kauhale aku o kekahi poe, o kahi iho la no ia e noho mau ai a lu-a wale iho hoi ka noho ana iho o ua mau poe omalemale nei"[82] (Some people did not go back to their homes; they continued living in this place until the lives of the ʻōmalemale people were old and shabby). The word "ʻōmalemale" refers to a young uhu (parrotfish). According to Pukui and Elbert, "The colors of this fish are so pretty that it is sometimes compared to a sweetheart: Momomi wale kuʻu ʻono i ka uhu māʻalo, my craving makes my mouth water for the parrotfish passing before my eyes."[83] Kānepuʻu chooses this word to reinforce the youth and beauty of the couples in the story. And there is further kaona because the word "male" is a Hawaiianization of the English word "marry."

These are just two of perhaps hundreds of instances of kaona in this moʻolelo. It is up to the astute and studious reader to find and enjoy them all.

OTHER METAPHORS

Kānepuʻu uses colorful and concrete metaphors to create pleasurable images in the minds of his readers. In one example from the many in the text, Kaukanapōkiʻi is meeting with Kaihuʻauwaʻalua after the long absence in which Hāmanalau's baby was born and she herself died (or was in a death-like physical state). The two greet each other in the old Kanaka way, crying upon their reunion:

> A i ka hiki ana aku o Kaukanapokii, he oi aku ke aloha iwaena o Kaihuauwaalua a me Kaukanapokii, o ke olo ae la no ia o ka makena mai o a o, o ke alo-alii o Kaihuauwaalua. A pau ko lakou hookolokolo ana i na kuaua mua o ko lakou mau kii onohi, e hoaleale ana iluna o Hihimanu, a akakuu mai la hoi na paka wai ua a ke kehau.[84]

Upon Kaukanapōkiʻi's arrival, the aloha was greater between Kaihuʻauwaʻalua and Kaukanapōkiʻi. The wails of grief resounded from one end of Kaihuʻauwaʻalua's aliʻi living complex to the other. Then their questioning each other in the first sudden rain coming from their eyes, which was agitating atop Hīhīmanu, was finished, and the rain drops of dew cleared.

Here Kānepuʻu uses rain as a metaphor for tears, an unsurprising choice, but he adds a place name to make it more interesting. Hīhīmanu is a peak in the Hanalei district of Kauaʻi, famous for its drenching rains, and a peak there would be the rainiest of all.

Another example is one that is typical of ordinary speech in Hawaiian. When Hāmanalau, Kaukanapōkiʻi, and their friends arrive back in Waialua after their journey, they are feasted by their parents' community. Kānepuʻu writes, "O ka hoopiha ia iho la no ia o ka lua o ko lakou inaina a piha i neia mea he ai"[85] (They filled the pit of their anger until it was filled with food). The "pit of anger" is a metaphor for hunger that is relatively common in Hawaiian texts. Hundreds of these kinds of metaphors are found not only in Kānepuʻu's works, but also in the works of even modestly talented writers in Hawaiian.

REDACTION OF LOCAL MOʻOLELO

Kānepuʻu takes or creates the opportunity to redact local moʻolelo into this moʻolelo when Hāmanalau and company stop at Hālawa, Molokai, on their way back to Oʻahu. John Charlot explains that Hawaiian writers of moʻolelo kaʻao used redaction to add local episodes to moʻolelo.[86] Hālawa is where Kānepuʻu grew up and he is sure to have known many moʻolelo of that area, which is amply demonstrated in his other works. In this short moʻolelo, the young folks are at a hula performance when Kaukanapōkiʻi notices a woman who looks strange, like a kupua, a supernatural person. Soon the woman, Kaluanou, and her kāne leave the place, her stomach distends, and she then vomits up water filled with freshwater creatures. Because of this, the muliwai of Hālawa, the brackish water part of the river where it flows into the sea, is very deep. This event caused the place where the guardian shark Kauhuhu lives to become blocked so that he had to break it open to enter. Kānepuʻu writes that the place where this happened and the house where the woman lived were still there at the time he wrote.[87] In this way, Kānepuʻu teaches us more about his ʻāina than is contained in our reference works. While Kauhuhu, the guardian shark, is fairly well known, the story of Kaluanou is not in Beckwith's *Hawaiian Mythology* or in Summers's *Molokai: A Site Survey*. This leads us into the examination of how Kānepuʻu uses wahi pana, or storied places, in his moʻolelo.

WAHI PANA, ʻIKE ʻĀINA, AND ALOHA ʻĀINA

While Hāmanalau is not replete with mele ʻāina like the Hiʻiaka sagas or others, Kānepuʻu does demonstrate his knowledge and love of the ʻāina through the select use of wahi pana, wind and rain names, and other devices. For example, in the scene where they sail by Hālawa, Molokai, and decide to stop, Kānepuʻu takes the opportunity to give us several place names:

> A ke hai ia mai la e na hookele, o Halawa keia, o ka lae o Kauhuhu, o ke one o Kamaalaea kela, o ke one o Kaawili keia, o ka pali o Puupa, a me ke oinaina [*sic:* ʻoiʻoina? nānaina?] pali o Hikiaupea, o Halawaiki, o ka lae o Hinalenale aku, o ka wailele o Moaula.[88]

> They were being told by the navigators, this is Hālawa, the cape of Kauhuhu [the guardian shark], that is the sand of Kamāʻalaea, this is the sand of Kaʻawili, the cliff of Puʻupā, and the lookout point of the cliff of Hikiaupea, Hālawaiki [Hālawa Iki], the cape of Hīnalenale, and Moaʻula waterfall.

Two of these are not in our available place-name references: the beach called Kaʻawili and the cliff Hikiaupea. In addition, Kamāʻalaea is only known as Māʻalaea and is in only one place-name source, John R. K. Clark's *Hawaiʻi Place Names*.[89] Kānepuʻu here documents and thus enriches our knowledge of Molokai place names.

A bit later in the moʻolelo, when the young people pass by Hauʻula on Oʻahu, Kānepuʻu gives us a short moʻolelo that is not in *Sites of Oahu:*

> I ka hiki ana aku o lakou nei i Hauula, ua ikeia ke ino mamua iho oia aina, he aina maikai o Hauula mamua, a no ka pepehi ia ana o ka Hilu malaila, i hei i ka upena kahe, a pau i ka ai ia e ko laila kamaaina. Nolaila, ua hoohalahala ke kaikuaana no ka make ana o ke kaikaina, a pii a mauka o na pali hookui, a hoopiha i ka wai malaila, a kuu ia mai i kai, a lilo ai ia aina i aina ino i keia manawa e noho nei (aole paha kakou e kamailio loihi loa no ia Hilu moe kahawai, a ina he manawa kupono, e hiki no ia kakou ke kaao nona).[90]

When they arrived at Hauʻula, the poverty before that land was seen; Hauʻula was good land previously, and because of the killing of the hilu [a fish], which were caught in nets that captured whole schools of fish, they were eaten by the local people until there were no more. Therefore the older sibling criticized [others] for the death of the younger sibling, climbed up to the top of the joined cliffs, filled the area with water, released it down toward the ocean, and that land became a poor land and still is (we will not perhaps speak too long about the stream-reposing hilu, and if there is an appropriate time [in the future], we can tell the story about him/her).

This story explains why there is a dearth of the hilu fish in Hauʻula's streams. It tells us something about the ʻāina there and is also an environmental caution not to take too much of any one resource. Kānepuʻu reminds us also that we, people and fish, can be viewed as family when he says that the older sibling, here the people, criticized those who caused the death of the younger, the hilu.

In the following passages, Kānepuʻu shows his aloha for the ʻāina of Kaʻala and its awe-inspiring landscape. When Kaihuʻauwaʻalua's men go with Kaukanapōkiʻi to abduct Hāmanalau, they are astonished by the forest of Kaʻala:

> I nana aku ka hana o ua poe malihini nei ia luna o Kaala, hewa i ka wai ua mea he maikai, a kohu hoohihi maoli no, o ka hele mai no a ka moa, ua hele a wili kakala, o ka noho mai no a ka ilio, ua hele a kio ka wai ia luna o ke kua, . . . o ka puaa keia, ua hele ka niho a na maka, i ua mea he wili kekee o ka niho, [a] o ka wai auau o Hamanalau, ua ninini ia a maikai, e ku ana na kumu lehua ma na kapa, ua hele a luluu na lala i loko o ka wai, e haiamu ana na lehua apane, i hooluluu ia e na manu, e kani oleolehala ana i ko lakou mau leo hoolealea.[91]

When the strangers looked at the summit of Kaʻala, it was amazingly beautiful, really enrapturing; chickens were walking around with their curled combs; and dogs were sitting, water flowing on their backs [wet from the constant mist perhaps] . . . here was a boar whose tusks had grown all the way back to its face, a curling of the tusk, and the bathing water of Hāmanalau had poured down well [forming a pool], with lehua trees on the banks [of the pool], the branches hung down into the water, the dark-red flowered lehua crowded around, drooping because of all the birds who were calling out in their cheerful voices.

As they approached the houses, the malihini (visitors) could not stop staring at the sights in the unusual landscape:

> Ua hele ka maia a pala ku iluna o ka pumaia, he ai na na manu, o ke kalo keia, ua hele a poho-a, hele a oo kahi, ua hele a hakahaka i ka ai ia e ka moa, o ke ko keia, ua hele a hilala ilalo, a ala mai a hina hou—a ala mai, o ke keiki keia o ke ko e pili la ma ka puna-ko, ua like no me ke kumu, ua hina no hoi a ala mai, o ka awa keia, ua hele a nunui ka hakai me he kumu kukui la, e pipii ka umi kanaka iluna o ka hakai, aole e haki, ke aloalo wale la ka maka o ka poe malihini mao, a maanei o ke alanui hele.[92]

———

> Bananas had ripened on the trees as food for the birds; there was kalo, which had become pitted, grown mature, full of holes because of being eaten by the chickens; there was sugar, grown until it tilted over, rose up again and fell over again, this was the young sugarcane growing on the side of the cane joints, and just like the older, main cane stalk, fell and grew up again; here was ʻawa, its stalk having grown as big as a kukui tree—ten people could climb on top of its stalk and it wouldn't break; the eyes of the visitors kept looking from one side of the path to the other [in amazement].

Today the landscape atop Kaʻala is still wonder-inducing, although it is marred now by invasive foreign plant and animal species and the presence of the US military. It is still a place where many varieties of ʻōhiʻa lehua in various colors, the medicinal herb koʻokoʻolau, and the fragrant maile all grow.

Kānepuʻu's aloha ʻāina includes descriptions of how abundant the land of Waialua was, as in this example:

> Ua ike aela hoi o Kaihuauwaalua me ke kane hou a Hamanalau, a ua lokahi pu ka manao o lakou a pau, a hookahi no aina o Waialua e noho ai, o ka poi nui ae no ko uka, o ka ia nui mai no ko loko o ke kai, a o na a-holehole momona ae no ko Ukoa, a me Lokoea.[93]

———

> Kaihuʻauwaʻalua met with Hāmanalau's new man, and all of their [the people of the area's] thoughts were united together, and there was

just one single land of Waialua to live on: the uplands had a great deal of poi, there was an abundance of fish in the sea, and the fishponds of ʻUkoʻa and Lokoea had fat, sweet āholehole fish.

ʻUkoʻa, according to the archaeologist J. Gilbert McAllister, is a "long narrow fresh-water [fish]pond, approximately a mile in length."[94] Lokoea is a smaller pond in the same ahupuaʻa of Kawailoa in Waialua.[95] In McAllister's time, the 1930s, both of these fishponds were still in use and they are being restored today.

Several times, Kānepuʻu uses the names of winds for illustration, as in this exposition of Hāmanalau's emotional state. At age eighteen she is beginning to long for close companionship beyond that of her brother and grandmother:

> Ua hiamoe iho oia i kekahi po i ka wa ana i hoopau ai i ka hoolohe ana i ke kikikoʻu mai a ka leo o na manu iluna o ka laau, i ka wa hoi a ka Waikoloa i hoomeha iho ai i kona lawe ana mai i ke ala o ke kupukupu, a e hoolai malie mai ana hoi ke kehau i kona hooluhelelei ana mai i na lau laau, a e hooneoneo mai ana hoi ka ho-uwi ana a ka makani i ka huinahookuipili o na laau.[96]

> She slept one night at the time that she had ceased to listen to the chirping of the birds on the branches, at the time that the Waikōloa wind had made [the place seem] lonely as it brought the fragrance of the kupukupu fern and the dew was calming in its cool dripping from the leaves of the trees, and the whistling of the wind through the entangled branches made [everything seem] desolate.

Here he uses the wind called Waikōloa to visualize the scene of her loneliness. Waikōloa brings in not only the fragrance of the kupukupu, but also the dew that weighs down the branches of the trees, and the eerie whistling of the wind through the trees that emphasizes the isolation of the place. The place seems cold, heavy, and lonely. This prepares the reader to understand why Hāmanalau later chose to engage in the love affair with Kaihuʻauwaʻalua, even though it was brought about by her kidnapping.

These are but a few examples of Kānepuʻu's aloha for the ʻāina, knowledge of the ʻāina, and clever use of that knowledge to illustrate his moʻolelo. Thus, while this moʻolelo is not overly abundant in descriptions of ʻāina, it has much to offer readers to increase our understanding of our language and our places.

Conclusion

Joseph Kānepuʻu wrote several serialized moʻolelo. In doing so, he consciously made himself a conduit for the ancient thought, speech, artistry, and practices of his ancestors for us, his descendants. He believed in the importance of these moʻolelo for the young people of his day, and he foresaw how important they would be for us today. As Solis says of the ʻōlelo noʻeau, the moʻolelo also form an integral part of the kahua upon which we are building our Kanaka world.

3

Kanaka Geography and Aloha ʻĀina

Kīhei de Silva, a composer, teacher, and eminent interpreter of Hawaiian texts, writes,

> We live in a time of un-naming, in a time when old names for the land—names given in honor, happiness, and sorrow—have been set aside for marketing jingles that commemorate little more than a desire for sales. . . . We who learn and love these old names are, therefore, people of two worlds, residents of rival geographies. We lead our lives on the congoleum, concrete, and tiff-green crust of Hawaiʻi's Bay Views, Crest Views, Soda Creeks, and Enchanted Lakes. But when our souls wither and thirst, we seek nourishment in that other, deeper geography.[1]

De Silva's eloquent lament, written in 1993, articulates for many Kānaka today our deep desire to connect to our ancestors, understand how they saw the world—their epistemological frameworks—and create works that celebrate the love of our ʻāina and all its natural features. But how is it that we have become "people of two worlds, residents of rival geographies"? Although de Silva's phrase "when our souls wither and thirst" seems to imply an occasional event, the constantly accelerating transformation of our ʻāina into concrete and asphalt roads and platforms holding up structures that pollute and otherwise harm the land and fresh and ocean waters means that the "when" is every moment of every day.

The processes of settler colonialism disrupt our connection to our kupuna and our ʻāina. No less important, those same processes have disrupted our ability to understand our kupuna's ontologies and epistemologies. Not only do we live in a land of congoleum and concrete, we live in a land of English where most people cannot pronounce our most common place names, let alone understand their significance. Kānepuʻu was an observant eyewitness and a talented critic of his era of settler colonialism, which is, according to Patrick Wolfe, a structure, not an event.² Kānepuʻu watched and warned as Kānaka ʻŌiwi lost their land and saw their ancestral wisdom marginalized within schools. Kānepuʻu's works of geography continue to bring light to these settler-colonial processes, many decades after he wrote them. His aloha ʻāina—expressed in his vast knowledge of the land and its place names—necessarily includes aloha for his lāhui.

Over the past thirty or so years, increasingly, Kānaka have been learning the language of our ancestors and revitalizing their arts of open-ocean star navigation, kalo farming, fishpond technologies, weaving, dance, martial arts, lyrical composition, and so forth. Our souls thirst and our entire beings crave not only the names of places buried by concrete and time, but also a connection to and understanding of them, the stories they come from, and the songs associated with them. We look at our ʻāina and our lāhui with aloha and thus work to understand and revive life—human and nonhuman, animate and inanimate (in haole terms)—on this ʻāina. To these ends, much new Kanaka-centered scholarship has been and continues to be produced. Several of these works are concerned with describing and revitalizing a specifically Kanaka geography. The purpose of this chapter is to describe and analyze two of Kānepuʻu's important works of geography in the hope of contributing to this scholarly endeavor. I hope that this study will show how Kanaka geography in any era of colonialism—his or ours—is necessarily a political project that must include critiques of the processes that are harming our people and our ʻāina.

Recent Works in Kanaka Geography

In 1992, Lilikalā Kameʻeleihiwa made clear the relationship between moʻokūʻauhau and ʻāina in *Native Land and Foreign Desires*.³ This work changed forever how Hawaiians understood themselves in relation to our ancestors and our ʻāina, by reminding us of important stories and moʻokūʻauhau. The essence of her insight is that the Kumulipo and other moʻokūʻauhau and mele koʻihonua trace lineages of people, both aliʻi and makaʻāinana, to the same original parents of the ʻāina itself, usually Papahānaumoku (the woman Papa who gives birth to islands) and Wākea (the man who manifests as the expanse of the sky, among other forms). One of the most powerful stories in the Papa and Wākea complex is that of Hāloanaka (a.k.a. Hāloalaukapalili), the kalo, and Hāloa, his younger brother. Hāloanaka is the offspring of Wākea with his daughter, Hoʻohōkūkalani. At birth he resembled a cord rather than a child so they buried him near one of their houses. From the spot grew the first kalo, whom they named Hāloanaka. The second child from this pair was a human male, whom they named Hāloa after the first offspring. Based on this moʻolelo, Kameʻeleihiwa explains one of the central metaphors in aliʻi (and makaʻāinana) behavior toward ʻāina. Hāloanaka represents the ʻāina and Hāloa represents human beings; it is the kuleana of the older sibling to feed the younger, which the ʻāina does with kalo. It is the younger sibling's kuleana to care for the older, which humans do through mālama ʻāina, or caring for and making productive the ʻāina. Kameʻeleihiwa puts it this way:

> The relationship is [hereby] further defined: it is the *ʻĀina*, the *kalo*, and the *Aliʻi Nui* who are to feed, clothe, and shelter their younger brothers and sisters, the Hawaiian people. So long as younger Hawaiians love, serve, and honor their elders, the elders will continue to do the same for them, as well as to provide for all their physical needs. . . . [I]t is [thus] the duty of Hawaiians to *Mālama ʻĀina*, and as a result of this proper behavior, the *ʻĀina* will *mālama* Hawaiians.[4]

This sense of relationship to the ʻāina continued in practice by many Kānaka throughout the twentieth century even though we lost some of the knowledge and understanding of the moʻokūʻauhau and mele koʻihonua because of the coerced shift to English.

In more recent works, Kanaka geographers have described the salient characteristics of specifically Kanaka geography. Each of these has focused research on specific regions. Carlos Andrade concentrates his study on the ahupuaʻa of Hāʻena on the island of Kauaʻi; Katrina-Ann Kapāʻanaokalāokeola Oliveira provides a substantial introduction to Kanaka geography as a whole, focusing on Maui; and Renee Pualani Louis's forthcoming book examines the Kona coast of the island of Hawaiʻi, and analyzing indigenous performance cartography.[5] Following Kameʻeleihiwa, all of them begin with the cosmogonic moʻokūʻauhau as the starting place for understanding Kanaka geography.

In *Hāʻena: Through the Eyes of the Ancestors,* Andrade includes the older moʻolelo and moʻokūʻauhau like the Kumulipo, place names, familial relationships to the land, an explanation of Hawaiian land divisions, songs about the area, the processes of change to private property and dispossession, the ways that Kānaka banded together to purchase their land back, and portraits of the kūpuna who are the contemporary transmitters of the knowledge.[6] He says of this work and the place, Hāʻena, Kauaʻi, that

> Hāʻena is only one place in an archipelago filled with storied places.... Examples of the perspectives of the indigenous people of Hāʻena can be found in their oral traditions (*mele, ʻoli* [sic]*, kaʻao, moʻolelo*), in their dances, and in the meanings of names affixed to the land. These names are attached to rocks, waters, and reefs. They are found in forests, on the peaks of the uplands, in the hollows of the lowlands, far out on the wind-swept sea, and out into the universe of stars overhead.[7]

Andrade points out here that Kanaka have a different relationship to the ʻāina based on their long association and perceived kuleana, which is based on their conception of ʻāina as kin.

Andrade notes the specific importance of place names in past as well as contemporary Hawaiian culture, as noted earlier. He elaborates:

> Like traveling in a time machine, a study of places and their names can be one of the best methods available for looking at our world through the eyes of the ancestors.... Despite over two hundred years of occupation by those from other lands, a great number of the names have survived—on maps, in land deeds, on street signs, and in the shared experiences of those *kūpuna* who continue to cherish the treasures passed on by their forebears. Place names are an important ingredient of indigenous prose and poetry and continue to be celebrated in songs composed by the Native people today.[8]

In *Ancestral Places,* Oliveira charts more fully than any previous source the elements of Kanaka geography. She begins with moʻokūʻauhau, specifically with the cosmogonic genealogies, including the Kumulipo and others. She explains that "moʻolelo (historical accounts), especially those cosmogonic in nature, form the foundation for a Kanaka (Native Hawaiian) geography, illuminating the genealogical connection that Kānaka (Native Hawaiians) share with the ʻāina (land; that which feeds)."[9] She analyzes Kanaka geography as performance cartography, giving many specific examples. She devotes an entire chapter to the sensual nature of Hawaiian geography, demonstrating some of the ways that "Kānaka developed keen intellectual perceptions informed by our interactions with our environment and our kūpuna. Our deep consciousness and appreciation for the natural environment are reflected in the many 'sense abilities' that Kānaka have refined over time."[10] Like Andrade, Oliveira focuses attention on the importance of place names, giving us many examples from ʻōlelo noʻeau and other forms of orature and literature.

In a forthcoming book, Renee Pualani Louis notes the importance of the ʻāina in Hawaiian orature and literature, including moʻokūʻauhau. In a journal article, she, like Oliveira, explains that Hawaiian-performance cartography is striking in its sensual aspects: "From a Hawaiian point of view, place is a part of a larger order of a living Earth. Each place is alive and made up of distinctive sights, sounds, smells, sensations, and essences."[11]

She also focuses on place names as especially important in Hawaiian geography.

> Many Hawaiian place names performed in daily rituals were a conscious act of reimplacing genealogical connections, recreating cultural landscapes, and regenerating cultural mores. They constitute a critically important body of Hawaiian cultural knowledge and are used in all forms of Hawaiian cartographies. Hawaiian cartographies are interactive presentations of place as "experienced space." They situate mapping in the landscape and encode spatial knowledge into bodily memory via repetitive recitations and habitual performances.[12]

She goes further, however, observing how place names are not just alive in bodily memory or recitations. They connect us to our ancestors who are still present in metaphysical senses. She notes,

> Hawaiian place names are more than just identification tags for the features and/or phenomena of the physical world. They are also powerful cognitive mechanisms that unfold the richness of the Hawaiian cultural landscape, revealing as much about Hawaiian perceptions of the metaphysical world (their beliefs about their gods, their interac-

tions with nature, and their cultural practices) as they do about the places and times to which they refer.[13]

Similarly, Aileen Moreton-Robinson articulates a difference in the indigenous peoples' relationship to land in Australia, where it is understood that ancestral beings created the land. This difference is inherently incommensurable. She writes,

> Our ontological relationship to land, the ways that country is constitutive of us, and therefore the inalienable nature of our relation to land, marks a radical, indeed incommensurable, difference between us and the non-Indigenous. This ontological relation to land constitutes a subject position that we do not share, and which cannot be shared, with the postcolonial subject whose sense of belonging in this place is tied to migrancy.[14]

She explains that this is based on the continuity of belief:

> Because the ancestral spirits gave birth to humans, they share a common life force, which emphasizes the unity of humans with the earth rather than their separation. The ontological relationship occurs through the inter-substantiation of ancestral beings, humans and land; it is a form of embodiment. As the descendants and reincarnation of these ancestral beings, Indigenous people derive their sense of belonging to country through and from them. . . . This ontological relationship to country was not destroyed by colonization.[15]

Her description is strikingly similar to the indigenous Hawaiian situation.

These Kanaka scholars have identified, described, and analyzed some significant aspects of specifically Kanaka geographical thought and practices. What I hope is that the following examination of a scholar's geographical works from an earlier era in this moʻokūʻauhau of scholarship adds another substantial layer, one that is, like earlier layers, firmly grounded in native language, epistemology, and ontology.

"Kaahele ma Molokai"

In 1867 *Ke Au Okoa,* the newspaper of Kamehameha V's office and the perceived successor to *Ka Hoku o ka Pakipika,* the first Kanaka-centered newspaper, published "Kaahele ma Molokai." Kānepuʻu structures this geography as a report about a tour around the island. He begins his geographical descriptions at Hālawa in the northeast corner of the island. From there he describes the ʻāina in a clockwise order, proceeding southwest along the coast. In the first two installments, he covers the island from Hālawa to Keawanui, which is only about one-third the way along the southern coast. Most unfortunately, the third and fourth installments were in issues that have not been preserved. In these, Kānepuʻu presumably continued this clockwise virtual journey around the island, covering the remainder of the southern coast, the west end, and the north, which would include the Kalawao, Kalaupapa, and Makanalua Peninsula where he was born, as well as Hāʻupu, the storied place so prominent in his Kana moʻolelo (see chapter 2).

In these first two installments, Kānepuʻu describes features of the landscape with their specific names, including capes, waterfalls, fishponds (the native system of aquaculture), streams, kaupapaloʻi (wetland kalo gardens), and so forth. He includes historical and cultural information, such as noting the place where the famed warrior and runner Kaohele leaped over a twenty-foot-wide gap in the cliffs, high above a running stream.[16] He mentions as well the place Pākaikai, where Kamehamehanui (the aliʻi nui of Maui, not to be confused with Kamehameha I) was raised eating the special lūʻau, or tender kalo leaves, and where his bones were hidden and cared for after his death.[17] The story of Kamehamehanui being fed lūʻau in place of fish is the origin of an enduring ʻōlelo noʻeau, "Ka iʻa i nui ai ʻo Kamehameha"[18] (The fish on which Kamehameha was raised).

Kaupapaloʻi are a constant feature of the descriptions of ʻāina, maybe because certain areas of Molokai are extremely wet and conducive to irrigated kalo farming, while other areas are extremely dry. The people of Molokai, over centuries, engineered systems of ʻauwai that fostered highly productive kalo farms. Hālawa, where Kānepuʻu grew up, is one of those places, and he notes that almost all of the kalo for the island comes from Hālawa and is taken atop animals (horses or mules most likely) to the dry areas like Kaunakakai and Pālāʻau. He also notes that kaupapaloʻi covered the ʻāina from Pōniuohua to Kawela along the dry leeward coast, a stretch of more than twenty miles, a circumstance only possible with sophisticated irrigation engineering.[19] He describes how the farmers made the land even more productive by constructing mounds between the kalo paddies in which they planted banana, sugarcane, sweet potato, onion, and so on.

In these installments, Kānepuʻu notes where important historical figures were born, raised, and lived, among them Abner Pākī, an aliʻi nui, a grandson of the aforementioned Kamehamehanui, and the hānai father of Liliʻuokalani.[20]

Kānepuʻu carefully details many place names in each installment, including the last one in which he gives the wind names mele (chant) from the moʻolelo of Pākaʻa, which he wrote and published in the paper immediately following this geography (see chapter 2). The insistence on recording place names, including those for specific fishponds and kaupapaloʻi, supports the conclusions of today's Kanaka geographers that our place names and wahi pana (storied places) are important links in our collective moʻokūʻauhau, reflecting enduring feelings of aloha ʻāina. The phrase "wahi pana" denotes a celebrated, noted, or legendary place, but the word "pana" also evokes its other meanings, including heartbeat, pulse, throb, and the beat in music. In this way, a wahi pana is like a pulse or heartbeat of the living ʻāina, in which we are prompted to bring to mind the mele and/or moʻolelo with which it is associated. It is perhaps for this reason that Hawaiian moʻolelo are often brimming with bits of song and take detours to explain moʻolelo associated with specific spots. For example, Kānepuʻu includes the place named Nīheukawa, named for the brother of Kana who rescued their mother in the epic written down by Kānepuʻu and others. The same place name evokes the history of Kaohele, as mentioned above. The importance of place names and the richness of Kānepuʻu's contribution can be seen in the sheer numbers of names he provides. In the first and second installments, which cover only about a third of the island, he mentions sixty-one place names. In the fifth installment he gives twenty-eight more for Molokai, as well as a number for Maui and Lānaʻi. Of these eighty-nine names for Molokai, six or seven are not in current reference works, and others could be used to correct spelling errors in reference works and on maps.

In the fifth and last installment, Kānepuʻu makes more general observations, beginning with a report about newspaper subscriptions. The newspapers are always on Kānepuʻu's mind, it seems, because he is concerned with the preservation and perpetuation of indigenous Kanaka knowledge. Because the rural areas were somewhat sparsely populated, people did not get the papers regularly. It was a long journey into the one town on the island and the newspaper luna (head person) wasn't remunerated enough to bother delivering to out-of-the-way places. Kānepuʻu suggests to his Molokai readers that they band together in groups and go get their papers. He then tells a story about an elderly man on Oʻahu who didn't know how to read, but Kānepuʻu began reading the paper to him. The man then subscribed to every Hawaiian-language paper and would walk around the neighborhood getting people to read parts of the papers to him.

Another issue on everyone's mind at the time was the dwindling number of Kānaka. Kānepuʻu reported on couples he met on Molokai who had many children and urged his readers to follow their example.

He follows this with a section on Molokai's climate and the mele of wind names mentioned above. Before the mele, he writes,

> He aina makani o Molokai, e pa mau ana mai ka Hikina, a mai ka Hikina Akau mai, he malihini ka la malie no Molokai, he lai nae ma Kaunakakai ma, a hiki [i] Punakou ma, oia hoi ka lai a ke Kioea, he Kaao, aia no nae i ke ahiahi a me ke kakahiaka, he makani ikaika ko ke awakea, he Moae.[21]

> Molokai is an ʻāina of wind, which blows continuously from the East and from the Northeast; a calm day is a stranger to Molokai, although it is calm from Kaunakakai to the Punakou area, which is called the laʻi [peace, calm, or stillness] of the Kioea; a Kāʻao wind is there, however, in the evenings and mornings, and the middle of the day has a strong wind, a Moaʻe.

This passage is of interest not only because it details when certain winds blow and from which direction, which is more information than we get from the mele of wind names, but also because it provides an epithet for the less windy stretch of the leeward (southern) side from Kaunakakai to Punakou, "ka laʻi o ke Kioea" (the peace, quiet, calm, or stillness of the kioea bird). The kioea (a bird) is noted for its cry, "lawekeō" or "lawelawekeō."[22] This same phrase is in an ʻōlelo noʻeau that advises us to carry our food along on a very windy day, or figuratively, "When one doesn't know what to expect, it is better to be prepared."[23] This is an instance of kaona that Kānepuʻu slips into this narrative about climate and wind, no doubt for the enjoyment of his readers who can figure it out.

In *Ancestral Places*, Oliveira quotes part of Kānepuʻu's mele of wind names. She observes:

> Together this moʻolelo and the mele that accompany it epitomize performative cartography.... The mele ... reflects the depth of knowledge that Kānaka had about their places. Each place had its own winds and rains—all were named. The name of each wind and rain revealed

its nature; some were gently blowing winds, while others were destructive rains. Through mele such as this, the names, physical locations on the landscape, and characteristics of winds and rains were mapped.[24]

I would add to this a little. First, such mele do epitomize performance cartography in part because of the ephemeral nature of wind. European-derived cartography, which seeks to describe and inscribe lands in two dimensions (usually) on paper, does not include winds. Winds are a part of the sensual nature of Hawaiian geography that Oliveira and Louis both point out. We feel them and smell the fragrances or odors they carry with them. Winds affect crops, fishing, sailing, surfing, and the comfort or lack of comfort of houses and other buildings, so Kānaka were and are aware of their effects. (Unfortunately, today, builders in Hawai'i are not mindful of where and how the winds in each place blow and thus do not take advantage of that in the architecture of buildings or their placement.) This kind of performance cartography is based on actually living in a place and observing the actions of winds and rains (among other things) and then, so important here, transmitting that knowledge from one generation to another.

To put this knowledge into a mele allows it to serve as a mnemonic device or, as Joseph Poepoe put it, endows it with a "kulana panoonoo," or remembering function.[25] Songs and chants are easier to remember than simple lists or unorganized facts. Memorizing the mele would keep the names of places as well as winds in the memorizer's mind, available as a sort of map if one were traveling around the island and as basic geographical knowledge for any educated person. One must not, however, take the idea of a map too literally here. The composer has given us a selection of places and the names of their winds. They follow various orders around the islands (here Maui and Molokai), sometimes clockwise, sometimes counterclockwise, but they are not complete or consistently in one particular order.

Kānepu'u then enumerates some mountains, flat lands, and places where women used to make kapa. In the "manao hope," or final thoughts, he exhorts others, especially schoolteachers, to write similar articles for the newspapers:

> Alaila, he waiwai nui no ia i ka poe naauao, ke kuhikuhi nei kakou, a ke ao nei hoi i na haumana i ke ano o na aina haole, a kakou i ike ole aku ai. A pehea la ka hoi kakou e hoomaauea ai, i ke ao ana i na haumana, i ke ano o ko kakou mau aina, na lae, na kuahiwi, na papu, na luapele, na kai kuono, na makani, na pohaku o kane, na heiau, na wahi noho mau a na 'lii, na wai puna, na muliwai, na anemoku, na

puali, na wahi pana, na wahi e Kaao ia nei, na mahina ko nui i keia manawa, na wai lele.[26]

And then that will be of great value to educated people; we are directing or pointing out and teaching students the nature of foreign lands that we have not seen. And how is it that we are lazy about (or we disregard) teaching the students the nature of our own lands, the promontories (capes), mountains, forts, volcanic craters, bays, winds, stones of Kāne, heiau, places that the aliʻi customarily lived, spring waters, rivers, peninsulas, isthmuses, legendary places, wahi pana, the sugar plantations of our time, the waterfalls.

This extraordinary list reveals that Kānepuʻu is working within a Hawaiian epistemological framework. What should be included in a Kanaka geography? Besides describing features such as mountains or rivers that a haole geographer would include, Kānepuʻu lists wind names, the stones of Kāne (still existing from times before the decline of the indigenous religion), and sacred and storied places. He goes on to suggest that if other teachers were to write their knowledge of their places, they could collect them together and "loaa no he Hoikehonua hou no ka pae aina Hawaii, e pakui hou iho ana maluna o ka Hoikehonua a na kumu Purikano o Amerika i hoolaha uuku mai ai"[27] (and would then have a new geography of the Hawaiian Islands, that would be attached atop the geography that the Puritan teachers of America have scarcely distributed). It may be significant that he uses "maluna o" (atop) instead of "after" or "onto": "atop" gives the Kanaka work primacy as opposed to a more ignorable appendix.

Ka Honua Nei

Ten years later, when Kānepuʻu writes "Ka Honua Nei," the political-economic landscape has changed and his concerns along with it. In 1867, he had focused both on including Hawaiian knowledge in the public school curriculum and on the dwindling native population. Now in 1877, three years into the reign of Kalākaua, who had been elected after the possible Kamehameha descendants had been exhausted (see chapter 1), Kānepuʻu observes how Kānaka ʻŌiwi are being dispossessed of land and impoverished by the increasingly plantation-friendly policies of the Kingdom government. This series is often oriented to the monetary value it may be possible to extract from rivers, waterfalls, and other natural features in the land in Hawaiʻi and in other places around the world. Kānepuʻu, however, as always, writes from a Kanaka standpoint, centered in Kanaka ontology and epistemology. Kānepuʻu takes his title from textbooks that had been translated from English and taught in Hawaiʻi's schools.[28] This publication, it seems to me, was a partial fulfillment of his desire to have Hawaiʻi's, and specifically Hawaiian, geography taught to students in the schools, as well as to the general public via the newspaper.

Kānepuʻu, however, cannot simply describe the ʻāina without exposing what he thinks were unfair practices in the process of the Māhele (change from indigenous to capitalist land tenure) that began in 1848 and the Kuleana Act of 1850, which brought permanent and extreme changes to the ʻāina and its people. Both the Māhele and the Kuleana Act were meant to convert the native land tenure system to one of private property in a fair distribution among the Crown (lands for the government and separate lands for the Mōʻī, to be the property of whoever held the office); other aliʻi who derived their living as konohiki, or land overseers or managers; and the makaʻāinana, who lived on, farmed, and otherwise labored on the land and waters (including forest and fishpond maintenance).[29] Kānepuʻu, a keenly observant eyewitness to these processes, asserts that, on average, based on the total number of acres divided by the number of Kānaka, each person should have about seventy-seven acres of land. He writes,

> Aka, ma ko kakou ike ana i ka palapala hooko o na Luna Hoona, he oleloa malalo iho o ka mailuilu. Nawai lilo ole i ka haole, ua keakea ae kela haole ma ke anapuni o waho o ka aina konohiki, a aina aupuni paha me ka hookaumaha, a pani ae paha i na alanui o mua, a lilo iho la ke kanaka me heaha la la.[30]

> However, when we see the executive documents of the Commissioners to Quiet Titles, there is less than nothing, under a pittance. Who did not lose to the haole, since that haole obstructed [the work] by surveying outside of the konohiki land and government land perhaps, and in the process laying down burdens, and blocking the roads forward, and thus the Kanaka becomes I don't know what.

I interpret this passage as Kānepuʻu saying that the government surveyors, who were haole and included W. D. Alexander, whom he named, worked to deprive people of land and also assisted in creating tax burdens, which then blocked possible avenues to viable lives for the Kānaka who were pushed off their lands. The following week he estimates how little land the makaʻāinana actually ended up with out of the more than four million acres of land in the islands:

> Ina paha e huiia na eka aina, o na kanaka a pau i loaa ko lakou mana hooko, a alodio paha, aole no paha e hiki i ka hookahi haneri tausani eka, ke kuhihewa ole au; a ina hoi, e huiia me na wahi aina kuai, hiki paha i ka elua haneri tausani; aole au e olelo ana no na alii aina nui.[31]

> If all the acres of land for all the kānaka were added together acquired from their grants and allodial titles, it would not amount to a hundred thousand acres, if I am not mistaken; and if that were added together with lands that were purchased, it might amount to two hundred thousand acres, and I am not talking about the aliʻi who have a lot of land.

Kānepuʻu is particularly concerned that this lack of land in the hands of makaʻāinana is reducing the amount of kalo being farmed, and thus available to eat, no doubt because both land and water are being taken for sugar production (an ongoing issue). He is also worried about the spread of epidemics and leprosy. He decries the proliferation of sugar plantations and how a few plantation owners are becoming wealthy. Beginning with a view of the land as producing the valuable commodity, sugar, he asks, "Owai la ka poe pomaikai no keia mau miliona dala . . . [?] Eia no ka poe pomaikai, 1 ka poe mea aina; 2 ka poe mea dala"[32] (Who benefits from these millions of dollars? These are the people who benefit: (1) the people with land; (2) the people with money). He observes that as more land is used to grow sugar, fewer people are able to continue planting kalo, and famine is a result. Most Kānaka have only two or three loʻi to sustain themselves, which is not enough to grow any surplus crops to sell for cash; if they were to take any of the food and sell it, their families would suffer. Because of this,

> A no kekahi mau ulia e ae paha, ua hoopau a kipaku ia mai ka mea e mahi ana, a nele iho la ka makaainana aina ole, hoopili wale paha, a auwana hele aku la ma kahi e ae, me ka hoowahawaha ia, a lilo aku la ia aina no ka nahelehele a me ke poho.[33]

> And because of other accidents perhaps, the farmer is kicked out, and the makaʻāinana without land is impoverished and must wander

to some other place and attach themselves to someone else [for food], while being disparaged, and then their land turns into forest and bog.

Kānepuʻu doesn't say so here, but we know that the result of this scenario is that plantations took over the lands of those farmers forced out economically through legal processes, such as adverse possession.[34] Kānepuʻu blames Mōʻī Kalākaua for this situation as much as the planters themselves. He writes,

> Eia kekahi kuhihewa, ua kuai aenei ko kakou Moi Kalakaua me kekahi poe mea hui o lakou, a manao kuhihewa ʻe nei, e ola na iwi o ka poe ilihune aina ole, o ka ke alii la ke kuai i ka aina, o ka poe mea aina ole la e hoi lakou ilala [ilaila?] e mahiai ai malalo o ke alii . . . a i ka loaa ana o ke kanaka i ka poe kepa, o ke alakai iaʻku la no ia ma kahi o ka poe luna kepa, a hoohoihoi me ka pelo ia.[35]

Here is another mistake, our Mōʻī Kalākaua has done business with some of those people (planters), wrongly thinking, the poor landless can live, the aliʻi would be the one to buy the land, and the landless would return and farm under the aliʻi. . . . [But] when the person is gotten by the contract labor people, he is led to the bosses' place, and induced with lies [to work for them].

The result of the increase in the number of sugar plantations is the scarcity of ʻai (kalo) and of poi, the staple food that comes from it. Kānepuʻu asserts that while the people with land are profiting, "pii mai hoi ke kumukuai o ka ai, a pela hoi ka ia, kahi e noho ai, a me ia mea aku ia mea aku"[36] (the price of kalo rises, along with fish, places to live, and everything else). This scarcity of kalo along with the terrible conditions on the plantations were contributing to poor health among Kānaka. Kānepuʻu writes,

> A ua loaa hoi kekahi mai na hoounauna ino mai a na haku mahiko, i ka hana iloko o ka ua a me ka la ino, ke anu o ke kehau huihui o ke kakahiaka nui molehulehu wale, nolaila, inoino ke koko, paakuku, oiai, aohe mea nana e lomilomi, e opaopa, e hahi, a ua like no hoi ka poe kumakahiki me ka poe i loaa i ka mai pake.[37]

Other illnesses are from the sugar plantation bosses wickedly sending workers to work in the rain and on stormy days, in the cold of the freezing dew of the dark early morning, and therefore, the blood becomes bad and clots, since there is no one there to lomilomi [massage], and the people on yearly contracts are just like people with leprosy.

Here Kānepuʻu is saying the people working contract labor are like the people with leprosy in two ways: one is that they are becoming ill because of bad working and living conditions; second, they are similarly exiled, living in work camps without their families who might provide comfort and the native massage treatment for their ailments.

Kānepuʻu then, in an act of moʻokūʻauhau consciousness—that is, in a way that an advisor to aliʻi in previous eras would have done—reminds his readers, including the Mōʻī and his advisors, of how similar situations were handled in the past:

> Ua oleloia i ka wa kahiko, ina e loaa ke aupuni i ka pilikia no ka wi, ke ahulau a me na mai o kela a me keia ano; na ka Moi e olelo pu me na kahuna i ke kumu e pau ai ka pilikia; a ua pau io no, a hoolaupai hou ka lahui, a ulu hou na mea kanu, a pae wale mai na ia o ke kai, a ola no ka lahui; a i keia wa hoi, o ke emi o ka lahui ka mea e ikeia nei, a o ka holo aku imua he mea ole hoi ia; . . . eha hoomana Kristiano e noho nei ma ko kakou Paeaina. Aka, ke hoole nei lakou, aole e ola; ae, oia no ka mea nui, o ka hoomaemae mua i ka lahuikanaka, a mahope ka huli waiwai ana.[38]

> It is said that in the old days, if the aupuni [the nation/government] was troubled by famine, epidemics, or illness of any kind, the Mōʻī would consult with the kāhuna [experts, priests, medicinal healers] about how to end the trouble; and then it would end, the number of people would increase again, the crops would grow again, fish of the sea would just land on shore, and the lāhui would live; now we are seeing the lāhui diminish, and there is no progress. . . . There are four denominations of Christianity in our islands. But they refuse or deny [that they are able to help, saying], you will not live; instead agreeing that what is important is first purifying the lāhui, and then seeking wealth.

Kānepuʻu critiques the priorities of the Christian churches here from his standpoint and ontology as a Kanaka; the churches are more interested in saving souls by getting people to conform to their puritanical mores while

Kanaka traditions tell of how to save actual lives and create thriving communities. He observes also that Christianity is a religion whose adherents are wealth seekers. Kānepuʻu goes on from there to criticize even more strongly his fellow Kānaka whom he sees as having abandoned the ways of their ancestors and subsequently forgotten their vows to their churches too:

> Ua hehi i na mea i maa mai na kupuna mai, ua hoohiki hewa imua o na kahunapule no ka papakema ana, ua hoi hope, ua poina, ua haalele i ka hoohiki.[39]

> They have trampled upon the customs from the ancestors, then wrongly took vows before ministers to be baptized, then regressed, forgot, and abandoned the vows.

The following week, the editors of this paper, *Ka Lahui Hawaii*, chastised Kānepuʻu in an editorial. They misrepresented what he was criticizing, saying that he wrote that being sent to work in the cold and dark on the plantation was a cause of leprosy, rather than what he actually wrote, which was that working on the plantations in those conditions caused other illnesses and having to live in a work camp without family was like being quarantined for leprosy. They blamed this on his supposed ignorance and framed their criticism by bemoaning "ka pau ole ana o ke koena kuhihewa iwaena o kekahi poe o kakou i manao ia he poe naauao"[40] (the continuation of the wrong idea among some of us who are thought to be educated [or enlightened or civilized] people). The "wrong idea" that hasn't ended no doubt refers to Christian missionary evangelizing and "civilizing" of the Kānaka, and perhaps also to the rejection of the same by many Kānaka. This is part of the common discourse of savagery and civilization that circulated (and still circulates), based on the presumed superiority of the white American Christians over their Kanaka brethren in the same churches or in the same communities, and the same country.[41] The editors began with other examples of ignorance, including the wrong interpretation of a Bible passage and someone confusing an ant with a bee. This framing is meant to embarrass Kānepuʻu as a Kanaka who is educated but apparently still dim-witted or very ignorant.

Two weeks later, Kānepuʻu, in a couple of paragraphs embedded in "Ka Honua Nei," responds to this criticism. He frames his response as a "moe ʻuhane," a dream.[42] He refuses to be shamed or embarrassed; rather, he writes,

> Eia no ka'u olelo ia oukou, e hele no i ka mahiai ko, ke makemake oukou, mai kanalua oukou no ka'u mau wehewehe ano olelo laula. . . . Aole au e kunana wale aku i ka pilikia e hanaia ana pela i ko'u lahui kanaka Hawaii ponoi, ina nae ua hana io ia, ina aole i hanaia pela e na haku hana, a e na luna paha o lakou, mai ka wa i hoomaka ia ai keia mea he mahiai ko ma Hawaii nei a hiki i keia la, ina aole ma ka la, ma ka hora paha, ma ka minute, alaila e hoihoi hou no wau i ka'u olelo me ka mihi aku imua o ke akea.[43]

> This is what I say to you folks, go ahead and work on the sugar plantation if you like, do not be doubtful [just] because of my public analysis. . . . [But] I will not just stand and look at the harm being done to my own Hawaiian people if it has really been done; if [harm] has not been done by the bosses and foremen from the time sugar planting started here in Hawai'i until today, if not each day, each hour, each minute, then I will retract what I said with a public apology.

He definitely did not retract what he said and did not apologize. It seems to me that although this episode was painful—in his "moe uhane" he quotes the speech of David in Psalms 41:9, "Yea, mine own familiar friend, in whom I trusted, which did eat of my bread, hath lifted up his heel against me"—he felt that his kuleana as a public intellectual demanded that he speak for those who were being exploited and harmed by the burgeoning plantation system.[44] Noelani Goodyear-Ka'ōpua writes that "the notion of kuleana . . . is oriented toward relational obligations as shaped by genealogy and land."[45] In this case, Kānepu'u seems to feel a kuleana to his "lahui-kanaka Hawaii ponoi," his own Hawaiian people with whom he shares this land. Goodyear-Ka'ōpua further explains that "kuleana is also tied to the wellbeing of the 'ohana or learning community."[46] Kānepu'u is teaching the public about both world and Hawaiian geography in this series, and he expresses concern for the well-being of his people. His kuleana is based in part on a sense of responsibility that derives from his position of privilege as an intellectual, a teacher, and a published writer. I read his response as saying that he cannot refrain from criticizing the expanding sugar industry as long as it is hurting his "'ohana or learning community."

I also see this as an instance of what Foucault calls parrhesia, truthful and fearless speech. Kānepu'u is saying something that he knows to be true and that he could predict would not be agreeable to some of the editors or publishers of *Ka Lahui Hawaii*, since among the planters he is admonishing are descendants of the missionaries, like the publisher and editor, Henry Hodges Parker (see chapter 1). Foucault notes, "Someone is said to use *parrhesia* and merits consideration as a *parrhesiastes* only if there is a risk or danger for him in telling the truth," and he explains that "this risk is not always a risk of life."[47] What Kānepuʻu risked was censure, which he suffered, and the possible loss of his series, which, fortunately, he did not. He also risked and incurred shaming from those he considered friends. In his response, however, Kānepuʻu does not lump all the editorial staff together; rather, he is careful to single out and thank W. B. Kekapa Kawainui (a.k.a. Benjamin W. Kekapa Kawainui), the Kanaka assistant editor, for putting his series on page 1 of the paper. In doing this publicly, we can discern as did his readers that he supposed that Parker, the missionary, and not Kawainui, wrote the condescending and shaming editorial. When Kawainui died years later, Kānepuʻu again thanked him within a published condolence letter.[48]

Kānepuʻu's series gives us more than this overtly fearless speech, however. As he detailed important features of the ʻāina like puʻu (hills), waterfalls, streams, and so on, he paid a good deal of attention to the place names, providing us with many that are not in our current reference sources and maps. He thus worked to perpetuate these names and their mele and moʻolelo, another kind of fearless speech perhaps, as it is anticolonial in nature. Today's scholars and activists can pick up his work and use it in reclaiming our ʻāina and restoring their names, along with some of the links in our moʻokūʻauhau.

Like other writers, Kānepuʻu quotes mele for some ʻāina that link certain place names together like a map, as in the following example for the area from Kualoa to Kahana in the moku of Koʻolauloa on Oʻahu:

> Hoolalau ana ke aloha i Kualoa,
> Pii ana iluna o Kanehoalani,
> Iho ana ma kela aoao o Kaaawa,
> Hele ana o [sic] ke kaha o Makaua,
> Auau i ka wai o Kahana &c.[49]

> Aloha grasps at or wanders to Kualoa,
> Climbs up Kānehoalani,
> Descends on the other side of Kaʻaʻawa,
> Down to the shore of Makaua,
> Swimming in the fresh water of Kahana, etc.

This mele works as a kind of map, because it names places from the southwest to northeast in order, from the boundary line of the moku of Koʻolauloa, which is Kualoa. This is a lovely example of performance cartography, as aloha for the ʻāina is the character in the mele: aloha first wanders to Kualoa or takes hold of Kualoa—the word might be "hoʻolalau" (to wander or cause to wander) or "hoʻolālau" (to take hold of). This aloha then climbs up Kānehoalani, reminding us that it is a mountain peak; it descends on the northern side near the village of Kaʻaʻawa; traverses the beach of Makaua, still moving north; and bathes in the fresh water of Kahana, thus calling to mind for us the bodily experiences we would have if we were to similarly travel that ʻāina.

He also peppers the descriptions with moʻolelo, both ancient and recent (for him). One example is in his descriptions of peaks, hills, and mountains. For Kahana, he tells this brief moʻolelo about Kana, the kupua who could stretch his body as tall as cliffs:

> Ua olelo ia, ua ku aku o Kana ma ka aoao maanei o Kahana, a kiei ma o o Punaluu, a kahea aku la i na kanaka e apoapo loi ana, "aia ae ka lalani kekee a olua, hoopololei hou ae." Ke aloalo wale la laua la, i nana ae ka hana, e kiei iho ana keia kanaka maluna o ka pali.[50]

> It is said that Kana stood on this side of Kahana, and peered over [the ridge] to Punaluʻu, and called out to some folks who were building up the banks of the loʻi, "You have some crooked lines there, you should re-straighten them." The two looked around, and when they looked up, there was a person peering over the cliff.

In addition to these much-needed descriptions of ʻāina in Hawaiʻi, Kānepuʻu provided the public with the names of rivers, mountains, and other geographical features in Europe, China, and many other places. He thus fulfilled his kuleana as a Kanaka public intellectual, teacher, and critic.

Conclusion

Taken together, Kānepuʻu's various geographical works illustrate to us the commitment of our kūpuna to education and to perpetuating indigenous linguistic, literary, and practical forms of knowledge. These works are prime examples of his aloha for the ʻāina and his moʻokūʻauhau consciousness, as he perpetuated the knowledge of his ancestors in the newspapers where that knowledge had a fighting chance of making it through the ravages of time and colonialism to us, their mamo (descendants). We can now use these to deepen our understanding of Kanaka geography, epistemology, and ontology.

In the following chapters, I examine the life and works of another extraordinary person, Joseph Mokuʻōhai Poepoe, who belonged to the generation just after Joseph Hoʻonaʻauao Kānepuʻu and followed in his footsteps.

PART II
Joseph Mokuʻōhai Poepoe

4

Joseph Mokuʻōhai Poepoe

> O ke aloha i ka hae, aole hiki ia mea ke holoiia mai ka puuwai aku o ke kanaka Hawaii i hanau i Hawaii nei. Aole—aole.
>
> Love for the flag, this cannot be erased from the heart of the Kanaka Hawaiʻi born in Hawaiʻi nei. No—no.
>
> "KA HAE HAWAII," 2

In Hawaiian language and Hawaiian studies more broadly, Joseph Mokuʻōhai Poepoe is likely the most-respected writer and newspaper editor of the late nineteenth and early twentieth centuries. He was multilingual and a talented translator of works in English and other languages into Hawaiian, and of a handful from Hawaiian into English. Most important, however, is his acting on his kuleana as an educator, legal advocate, editor, writer, political activist, and thinker from a position of moʻokūʻauhau consciousness. In his times of struggle for the pono of the lāhui, which he saw as springing from our native language, literature, and knowledge, times that were sometimes dangerous to his life, he fearlessly put forward our ancestral knowledge. He did this in books and newspapers, many times weekly and even daily, with

FIGURE 4.1
Joseph Mokuʻōhai Poepoe.

his thoughts on the Kanaka youth of his day and using foresight into our times and times to come. He had faith that the lāhui Kanaka would not disappear, even after the US language and culture started to become hegemonic before his eyes.

In this chapter, I provide an overview of his written works, contextualized within the political and economic times in which they emerged. As with chapter 1 about Kānepuʻu, I organize this overview in sections corresponding to the newspapers that he was publishing in and/or editing.

Poepoe was born in Honomakaʻu, Kohala, on the island of Hawaiʻi, in March 1852.[1] His mother was Keawehiku, and his father was G. W. Poepoe, also known as G. W. Kahiolo, a teacher and an assistant principal. Kahiolo was the author of the first full-length Hawaiian moʻolelo published in the newspapers, "He Moolelo no Kamapuaa."[2] Joseph M. Poepoe was a grandchild of Kalanikaapau, who was the daughter of Piʻipiʻi and Hewahewanui, Kamehameha I's premier kahuna. Through Piʻipiʻi, Joseph Poepoe was a descendant of many illustrious ancestors and was also a cousin to Samuel Parker, the wealthy Kanaka owner of Parker Ranch.[3] Poepoe's middle name, Mokuʻōhai, perhaps refers to Kamehameha's final victorious battle for the island of Hawaiʻi.[4]

By the time that Poepoe was of school age, the family had moved to the capital of Honolulu on Oʻahu. He attended public schools in Kalihi and Kalauao in ʻEwa, and afterward he attended Kahēhuna (now the Royal School), which in an earlier era was called Kula Aliʻi and had educated the mōʻī and other aliʻi nui.[5] He completed his secondary school education at ʻĀhuimanu, a Roman Catholic school now called St. Louis.[6] He was a native Hawaiian speaker and an accomplished speaker and writer in English, and he knew French, Latin, and Hebrew.[7]

Following his secondary education, Poepoe returned to Kohala where he worked as a schoolteacher, and he established the first school that taught English there. Apparently unsatisfied with teaching as a career, he began his study of law in Kohala, under the tutelage of Judge P. Kamakaia. He returned to Honolulu to further his study of law with W. R. Castle, Sanford Dole, and the firm Davidson and Lukela. He became an attorney licensed to practice in all Hawaiʻi courts.[8]

At around the same time that Poepoe began practicing law, he also began to publish in newspapers. These simultaneous careers started in the late 1870s, while Mōʻī Kalākaua reigned. The sugar plantation economy was firmly rooted, and the mostly haole plantation owners, many of them missionary descendants, aggressively demanded a say in the government. They had counterparts who served as politicians in the Kingdom's legislature, as judges, and as heads of government departments like health and education.

At this same time, the cultural influence of the Congregationalists continued to wane. Kamehameha IV, Alexander Liholiho, (1854–1863) and his Mōʻīwahine, Emma, had successfully established a branch of the Anglican Church in Honolulu, the Mormon faith had gained a foothold, and Roman Catholicism continued to spread among the population. Like Kamehameha IV and V, Kalākaua regularly and publicly violated the puritanical codes of behavior that the Congregationalists had previously somewhat successfully promoted among Kānaka. Thus, the struggles for hegemony that developed in the 1860s intensified in the 1870s and 1880s, with the cultural, political, and economic fronts of battle hardly distinguishable from each other.[9]

Ko Hawaii Pae Aina, 1878–1880

Poepoe's first two publications were works of translation. Both were serialized in *Ko Hawaii Pae Aina*, the newspaper founded by Joseph U. Kawainui in 1878 and celebrated by Kānepuʻu (see chapter 1). The Kanaka reading public was interested in literature of all genres from foreign lands; history, fiction, and poetry were commonly translated and reproduced in the Hawaiian papers. Tales of knights and courts, like Malory's *Le Morte d'Arthur*, were especially popular.[10]

Poepoe's first moʻolelo was "He Moolelo Kaao no ka Naita Rokekila Hinedu" (A fanciful story of the knight Rokekila Hinedu). It was very long, running weekly from June 1878 through December 1881.[11] The first installment notes, "Unuhiia e ka peni manawalea a Joseph Poepoe no ka Hiwahiwa a ka Lahui" (translated by the charitable pen of Joseph Poepoe for the Precious One of the Lāhui [i.e., the newspaper]). It appears that the first story in this epic is "The Dragon-Giant and His Stone Steed," attributed to O. L. B. Wolff, translated from Russian into English in *Fairy Tales from All Nations* by Anthony Reubens Montalba, and published in 1849.[12] The original name from which "Rokekila Hinedu" was Hawaiianized remains unknown. In the Montalba volume, the same character is named Dobrünä Mikilitsch.[13] In this work, Poepoe draws on Hawaiian sayings and imagery, sometimes inserting ʻōlelo noʻeau, as in the November 16, 1878, installment in which he describes a character in the forest searching in vain for someone: "Ua puhalahio ke aloha/Aia me ke Kalukaluokewa" (Love has whizzed by/It is with Kekalukaluokēwā, or the Kalukalu of Kēwā). Kekalukaluokēwā is a famous character in moʻolelo kuʻuna and Kēwā is a place on Kauaʻi, famous for its kalukalu grass. The phrase "ke kalukalu o Kēwā" (the kalukalu grass of Kēwā) is common in songs referring to that area. But true to Hawaiian poetics, the kaona, or connotations of these few words, add to the story: kalukalu also refers to a "fine gauze-like tapa made on Kauaʻi, reserved for chiefs,"[14] a way of describing how cherished the lost person is. The word "kēwā" refers to both "anticipation" and a "far-off place inhabited by spirits," like a forest.[15] Just this one example tells us that Poepoe was not merely translating words or phrases from English, but also carefully crafting a story in Hawaiian that his erudite readers would enjoy.

His second serialized translation is "He Moolelo Kaao no ke Keiki Alii Otto! Ka Naita Opio o Geremania"[16] (A fanciful story of Prince Otto! The young knight of Germany). In a short foreword, Poepoe says that it is "ano like . . . me ko Rokekila ma kekahi mau mea" (somewhat similar to Rokekila in some ways). It is a translation of *The Magic Ring* by La Motte-Fouqué, a German author of fairy tales and romances perhaps best known for *Undine* (Ondine).[17] An English translation from the German was published in 1876, which it appears Poepoe translated into Hawaiian, as the first line demonstrates: "Ma ka aina kaulana o na Suabia, e kokoke ana hoi ma na kapa wai uliuli o ka muliwai Danuba, e waiho molaelae maikai ana kekahi kula manu nani" (In the favored land of the Suabians, hard by the banks of the Danube, lies a beautiful mead.)[18] Although the series stops before reaching its conclusion, most of this long tale was translated and published; it ran from January 17 to October 23, 1880, when it stopped without explanation. (This is fairly common, unfortunately, for moʻolelo in the newspapers.)

Ka Hoku o ke Kai, 1883–1884

After publishing these courtly tales in translation, Poepoe began his career as an editor while also working as an attorney and involving himself in politics. In 1883, the year that Mōʻī Kalākaua held a coronation ceremony and the new ʻIolani Palace was completed, Poepoe founded *Ka Hoku o ke Kai*, a monthly magazine on newsprint. His magazine published many translations of European tales, including a continuation of the Rokekila Hinedu and other courtly and fairy tales, but also more contemporary popular works like a translation of a Jules Verne story ("He Moolelo no Kapena Nimo"; A story of Captain Nemo) and mysteries ("Ka Moolelo o ka Elemakule Haze: Ka Makai Kiu Kaulana o Nu Ioka"; The story of Old Man Haze: The famous detective of New York).[19] The great majority of these works did not include the names of the original authors or the translators; exceptions include works by L. J. Nahora Hipa, Sam Kaeo, Thos. N. Kaiaikawaha, and Tao Se, who translated an Arabic story, perhaps from the *Arabian Nights*.[20]

We also see in *Ka Hoku o ke Kai* the first indication of Poepoe's interest in moʻolelo kaʻao Hawaiʻi. Only four moʻolelo Hawaiʻi were published there but, importantly, they include a complete, though short, version of the story of the riddling child, Kalapana.[21] Many years later, Moses Nakuina wrote a much longer and much-loved version of this moʻolelo, which is missing the ending, likely because the volume in which it appeared has not yet surfaced in any library or archive. This version in Poepoe's magazine is one of the sources by which we know the ending of the story.

Poepoe also published columns and articles in this magazine. In *Ka Hoku o ke Kai* Poepoe first advocated for the perpetuation of the native language. One editorial, for example, was "E Nalowale ana Paha ka Olelo Hawaii" (The Hawaiian language may be disappearing).[22] The topic of another column was which language, Hawaiian or English, could be trusted when laws were published in both.[23] This advocacy of Hawaiian would appear in every paper he edited until the end of his life. Among these columns and articles we see Poepoe's sense of kuleana and commitment to educating the lay Kanaka public about the law and politics. One column in the magazine was called "Ke Kanawai" (The law), another "Na Kumu Mua o ke Kanawai" (The original sources of the law), and in December 1883 and January 1884, he published the decisions of the Supreme Court.[24] He ran a news article about the representatives in the Kingdom legislature and another about the millionaire Claus Spreckels, whose activities were affecting politics in the Kingdom.[25]

Ka Hoku o ke Kai ceased publication in December 1884. Despite its short life of twenty-four months, the magazine is extraordinarily rich in its offerings of literature in translation as well as its snapshot of the legal, cultural, and political issues of those two crucial years in Kalākaua's administration. In some ways, the magazine mirrored Kalākaua's mix of culture and politics. Just as Kalākaua brought hula performance to the public once again and fostered the publication of the Kumulipo and genealogical and literary research, Poepoe's *Hoku o ke Kai* also offered a mix of Hawaiian and foreign literature along with its news and political and legal commentary.

Ke Alakai o Hawaii and Opposition to the Bayonet Constitution

In June 1887, missionary descendants, wealthy planters, and their business associates carried out the coup known as the Bayonet Constitution. The Bayonet mandated that the Mōʻī could make no decisions without Cabinet approval. Citizens of Asian descent became disenfranchised and "extremely high property qualifications [were] placed on both candidates and their electors that for all intents and purposes eliminated Natives from either running or voting for these seats."[26] Poepoe was among the leaders of the native opposition to the Bayonet. He gave two speeches in July 1887 as part of organizing an opposition slate for the special election of 1887: one on

July 19, and another on July 25. Unfortunately the text of these speeches in Hawaiian is not available. Jonathan Osorio quotes the account of the July 19th speech from the *Pacific Commercial Advertiser*, the paper supporting the Bayonet perpetrators. Poepoe sounded this warning: "The Americans have no respect for royalty, for they have no king. Therefore, they want to exercise the same power here as they do in their own country. They are doing it little by little, and it will not be long before Hawaii becomes an entire republic. We who cherish our King ought not to allow this to be done."[27]

A week later, Poepoe spoke again, and the *Nupepa Elele*, edited by a pro-Kanaka writer, Daniel Lyons, called his speech "kaulana a waiwai" (famed and valued) and promised to publish it in full. Issues of the paper in the following weeks, unfortunately, seem not to have been preserved.

This anti-Bayonet group held another meeting on August 19 at Kaumakapili church, and its minister, Reverend Waiamau, chaired the meeting. (A few years later Waiamau was ousted by his congregation for supporting annexation.)[28] Those participating in this meeting included Antone Rosa, D. W. Pua, S. K. Kane (Kāne), and others. The *Pacific Commercial Advertiser* approved of the meeting but not without some racist condescension to Hawaiians: "It had been said that native Hawaiians could not conduct an orderly meeting, but the result of this meeting showed the fallacy of such a statement."[29]

The group elected a slate of candidates to run for office in the September election and Joseph Poepoe was among those selected—he became a candidate for Lunamakaʻāinana (the lower house) for Honolulu. On August 31, 1887, *Ke Alakai o Hawaii* ran the names of the full slate just after a statement of the platform upon which the newspaper was founded. The names of those running for the Hale Aliʻi (House of Nobles) appear under the headline "Ka Balota Alii Aloha Moi, Makee Aina a me na Makaainana, a e Hoomaemae ana hoi i ke Kumukan[a]wai" (The ballot of Aliʻi who have aloha for the Mōʻī, value the ʻĀina and the Makaʻāinana [common people], and who will reform the constitution). The headline over the candidates for Lunamakaʻāinana was very similar. At the end of the slate of names is this statement:

> No Hawaii lakou i keia la! No Hawaii lakou i ka la apopo!! No Hawaii lakou i na la a pau. A e paio ana lakou no ka hoonipaa ia ana o ka Nohoalii o Hawaii, ka hoomau ana i ke kuokoa o ke Aupuni Moi, a me ka Pono Kaulike o ka lahuikanaka o ka aina.
> "Imua a Lanakila"

―――――

They are for Hawaiʻi today! They are for Hawaiʻi tomorrow!! They are for Hawaiʻi every day. And they will fight for the security of the Monarchy of Hawaiʻi, the continued independence of the Monarchical Government, and Equal Rights of the people of the land.
"Forward to Victory"

The Bayonet Constitution, however, was successful in its intent to wrest political power away from Kānaka Hawaiʻi and hand it to the moneyed class who were mostly haole. In Osorio's words, "The turnabout between the dominance of the king's party and the dominance of the haole party was abrupt and demonstrated the swift transformation of electoral power generated by the new constitution."[30] Ralph Kuykendall proposes that, although "the opposition . . . candidates in Honolulu and in all but one of the rural Oahu districts received more votes than their counterparts[,] . . . [i]t was the votes of foreigners including the Portuguese, enfranchised by the new constitution, that gave the Reform [haole] Party its decisive victory."[31] No one from the slate of opposition candidates was elected.

Ke Alakai o Hawaii published a platform for the paper, which was, no doubt, identical with the platform of this political group. One of the first statements in the platform is "E kakoo mau ana keia nupepa i na hana a pau e hoonipaa loa ia ai ke kulana Aupuni Moi o Hawaii, malalo o ke Kumukanawai"[32] (This newspaper will always support all actions to secure firmly the Monarchical system of government under the Constitution). The wording here is almost identical to that in the paragraph following the slate of names. Furthermore, "E kakoo mau ana na kalaimanao ana o keia pepa i na hoakaka ana no na pono kivila o na kanaka Hawaii a me na lahui mai na aina e mai" (This paper will always support discussions or analyses that clarify or explain the civil rights of Hawaiians and peoples from foreign lands), and "O ke ola o ka lahui he mea nui ia iloko o na mea i hiipoi ia e keia pepa" (The life of the lāhui is very important among the things that are cherished by this paper).

Enoka Johnson was the editor of *Ke Alakai o Hawaii* until at least October 1887, and according to Esther Mookini, Poepoe took over editing the paper in 1888.[33] His name as the editor was never printed in the paper itself, however. During 1888, *Ke Alakai* remained primarily political, printing editorials criticizing the government and the laws enacted by the new legislature. According to Kuykendall, Poepoe worked with Robert Wilcox, who had been sent by Kalākaua for an education in Europe and summarily recalled after the Bayonet, and Edward Kekoa, a staunch aloha 'āina, to form a committee to speak to Kalākaua about the defects in the constitution.[34] This came to nothing, because Wilcox left soon afterward for San Francisco. *Ke Alakai* kept a close watch on everything the legislature did, printing reports in every issue during the legislative season in a column titled "Ahaolelo o 1888."[35] Like most other Hawaiian-language papers, it ran a significant number of moʻolelo, mainly translations, including a serialized mermaid story called "He Moolelo Kaao no Roumiana Ho!," translated by Ben Kalana.[36]

The following year, 1889, Wilikoki (Robert Wilcox) returned from California and led an armed insurrection against Kalākaua's Bayonet Constitution government. Poepoe participated in the planning meetings.[37] On July 30, Wilikoki led a small army through the streets to ʻIolani Palace where he hoped they would meet with the Mōʻī. In the course of the day, this army exchanged gunfire with the government troops. Seven of Wilikoki's men were killed. Although Poepoe does not seem to have been among those who participated in the battle, he was arrested and held in jail for over two months.[38] On October 7, Poepoe pled guilty to conspiracy and the following day the attorney general declined to indict him for treason and released him. He was fined four hundred dollars, a huge sum at that time.[39] The list of others arrested includes several other newspapermen: John K. Kaunamano, who had also been a member of Kalākaua's Privy Council, Thomas P. Spencer, John Sheldon (a.k.a. Kahikina Kelekona), and John Edwin "Ailuene" Bush. This would not be the last time that newspapermen were rounded up for defying the haole who were bent on taking over rule of Hawaiʻi.[40]

According to Kuykendall, of the seventy men arrested, only three were put on trial. A dual jury system was in place at the time: a native jury judged the Kānaka, and a haole jury judged the haole. Kuykendall writes, "Wilcox, who was to be tried by a native jury, was at first indicted for treason, but it became clear that, whatever the evidence, no native jury would convict him of that crime. The treason charge was dropped and he was brought to trial on an indictment for conspiracy. The native jury, by a vote of 9 to 3, found him not guilty. From a strictly legal standpoint, the outcome was unquestionably a miscarriage of justice.... [But] [b]y the time he came to trial, Wilcox had become a hero to the native Hawaiians."[41] This passage highlights a constant conflict between what is considered legal and what is pono. The Bayonet Constitution that set these events in motion was not accomplished by any legal means, nor was it ratified by the populace, and it was certainly not considered pono. Kuykendall's phrasing—"from a strictly legal standpoint"—asks us to suspend the knowledge of the illegality of the constitution in place, which should invalidate its laws and law enforcement regime. It asks us to, or assumes we will, accept the fiction that the constitution was agreed to by the populace and that an armed insurrection against those in power in order to obtain a more democratic constitution was thus obviously, unquestionably, against the law. Furthermore, Kuykendall posits that with some passage of time, Wilikoki became a folk hero, but he doesn't give the reason, which is that Wilikoki, in taking such rash action, expressed the outrage and frustration of the lāhui at having their civil rights curtailed, their Mōʻī humiliated, and the power over their lives taken by capitalists who cared for profits only. Thomas Nakanaela describes the popular reaction to Wilikoki after his arrest:

> Haku ia ae la na mele hauoli o kela a me keia ano nona; a ua ku'i aku la ka lono ma na Mokupuni no keia mau hana hookalakupua a ke koa Italia. Pai ia iho la kona mau kii e na hale pai kii o keia kulanakauhale o Honolulu, a ua lilo i ke kuai ia he mau tausani kii ma na wahi a pau o ka Paeaina.[42]

> Joyful songs of every kind were composed for him; and the news resounded on the islands about the extraordinary deeds of the Italian soldier. Pictures of him were printed by photography studios in this city of Honolulu, and thousands of these photos were sold in places all over the islands.

Nakanaela includes twenty of these songs in his biography of Wilikoki; in her master's thesis, Leilani Basham describes and analyzes many of them.[43]

Death of Kalākaua, Support for Liliʻuokalani, Two Books, and *Hawaii Holomua*, 1891–1892

A year after this attempted countercoup, in November 1890, the virtually deposed Kalākaua traveled to San Francisco, desiring a vacation in a cool climate because his health had been deteriorating.[44] After traveling around California a bit, Kalākaua became very ill and died in his room at the Palace

Hotel in San Francisco on January 20, 1891.[45] His lāhui in Hawaiʻi only learned of his death as the ship carrying his body came into view in Honolulu Harbor. Poepoe writes,

> Aia i ka hiki ana i ka hora 9, ua hoike ia mai la ka lono e na hae laweolelo o ua Kaletona nei i ka mokukaua Mohican, a kau hapa ia iho la ka hae o ia moku, a o ka manawa ia i hiki ole ke kanalua iho—ua make o Kalani! O na uwapo o ka aekai, ua piha u aku la i na makaainana, a i ka wa a ke Kaletona e hookomo malie mai ana i ka nuku o Mamala, me ka uhipaa ia me na kahanahana [sic] kanikau, aia hoi, ua haehae aela na leo kumakena o ka lehulehu i na eheu ea o ka lewa.[46]

> At nine [in the morning], the news was brought by flags of the *Charleston* [the ship carrying the Mōʻī's body] communicating to the warship *Mohican*, and the flag of that ship was lowered to half-mast, and that was when one could no longer doubt—Kalani [the Mōʻī] was dead! The wharves on shore were filled with makaʻāinana, and when the *Charleston* slowly entered Māmala Bay, covered in the drapery of mourning, suddenly, the grieving voices of the people tore the airy wings of the sky.

Poepoe immediately wrote a book honoring the beloved Mōʻī. His short preface reads as follows:

> Iloko o na la eono wale no i hoomakaukauia ai keia moolelo me ka awiwi nui, a nolaila, ke nonoi nei ka mea kakau moolelo i ko ka mea heluhelu kala ana mai ke ike oia he mau kinaunau maloko o keia buke.
>
> Ke haawi nei au i koʻu mahalo kiekie i ke Keena o ke Kuhina o ko na Aina E, no ke kokua i loaa mai no kekahi mea e pono ai keia buke. Pela no hoi ia Mr. J. G. M. Sheldon a me kahi mau makamaka no na kokua ana e makaukau ai keia moolelo.[47]

> This moʻolelo was prepared with great haste in just six days, and, therefore, the author asks the reader's forgiveness should they see any errors in this book.
>
> I give my highest form of gratitude to the office of the Minister of Foreign Affairs for the assistance received for this book. And the same to Mr. J. G. M. Sheldon and other friends for help in preparing this moʻolelo.

This short book of about ninety pages might best be characterized as a eulogistic biography.[48] It narrates the story of Kalākaua's life in the most glowing terms possible, while also expressing deep mourning. Poepoe describes Kalākaua's trip around the world, including some of the Mōʻī's mele for his queen, Kapiʻolani. He skips over all the trouble with the haole who deposed Kalākaua, saying,

> He mea makehewa no ka mea Kakau Moolelo ke kuekaa ana i na mea a pau i hanaia a i ikeia iloko o kona hookele ana i ka Waa Aupuni o Hawaii nei, oiai, ua kamaaina ka hapanui o ia mau mea i kona mau makaainana e noho nei me ke kumakena nona.[49]
>
> ———
>
> It would be useless for the Author to search out everything that was done and seen in his navigating the Ship of Hawaiʻi, since most of these things are familiar to his makaʻāinana now in mourning for him.

He continues, "He oiaio nae ua hookele oia i kona Aupuni me ka noiau kamahao loa i mahalo nuiia e na Aupuni holo mua e ae o ka poepoe honua" (It is nevertheless true that he steered his Government with amazing skill that was greatly appreciated by the other progressive Governments of the earthly sphere). He then goes on to describe Kalākaua's travel to San Francisco, his death there, and the return of his body home. The volume ends with a timeline of the important events in Kalākaua's life, the plan of the funeral march, some prayers to be read at the funeral, and two hymns.

Poepoe's next publication was a legal handbook for the lay public, also published in 1891. For this volume, he translated Supreme Court decisions, rules of the various courts, and laws into Hawaiian. Poepoe, despite his conviction for conspiracy less than two years earlier, was still an attorney in good standing, able to litigate in all courts. In the introduction to the book, he thanks the Chief Justice, A. Francis Judd, for his assistance in providing him with the text of many of the decisions.[50] Apparently, many important decisions, rules, and so on were being published only in English, and Poepoe felt compelled to bring this important information to the Hawaiian-speaking public, a majority of whom lived their lives using the Hawaiian language only. The entire Supreme Court was haole, and English had become the preferred language should there be a conflict between the Hawaiian and English versions of any law.[51] Poepoe not only translated a huge amount of legal information for the public, but also provided more access. He writes,

O kekahi mea maikai i hookomoia, oia na olelo hoakaka malalo o kekahi mau aoao o ka buke e hoakaka ana i ke ano a me ka manao o kekahi mau huaolelo Kanawai ma ka olelo malihini i ke Kanaka Hawaii.[52]

Something good that is included are the explanations at the bottom of some pages of the nature and meaning of legal terms that are in language unfamiliar to Hawaiians.

The scope of this chapter precludes detailed analysis of the contents of *Ke Alakai o ke Kanaka*, but I can give highlights of each section here. In the first section, "Na Olelo Hooholo o ka Aha Kiekie" (Decisions of the Supreme Court), the final "decision" is actually the text of instructions to the jury during the trial for treason of Albert Loomens for his participation in Wilikoki's 1889 armed attempt to reverse the Bayonet Constitution. Why would jury instructions merit inclusion among Supreme Court decisions? First, Chief Justice Judd delivered those instructions personally to the jury. Second, they contain explanations of various points of law, the most important perhaps being the rationale for considering the Bayonet Constitution a legal one.[53] It also brings up contradictions in the law as well as the political situation. The jury was being asked to consider whether the Mōʻī himself was implicated as part of the conspiracy to overthrow the government in these actions meant to reverse the Bayonet Constitution. This is rather confounding because that would mean Kalākaua would have been trying to overthrow his own government, and charges would have then been brought against him under his own name. I hope that other scholars agree that further study of this section of Poepoe's book is warranted. Why did Poepoe choose these specific cases? What issues did they contend with, and what effect did those decisions have on law and life in Hawaiʻi?

The second section of the book concerns the rules of the three main courts in Hawaiʻi's system: the Supreme Court, the circuit courts, and the district courts. These rules were important for everyone who got into legal trouble, whether civil or criminal, and must have been a handy guide for attorneys who litigated in Hawaiian. Poepoe writes in the introduction, "Ua like ko lakou koikoi me ko na kanawai maoli o ka aina" (They are as important as the actual laws of the land). Poepoe also says that the rules are crucial for both judges and attorneys to know.[54]

The first pages of this section contain many terms in Hawaiian with their English equivalents, including "na *palapala noi* a pau (petitions), na *olelo pane* (answers), na *olelo pale pili laula ole* (pleas), na *koi* (claims), a me na *noi kuikawa* (special motions)."[55] These can be useful to many scholars today who might study this text and wish to understand legal cases and the commentary about them written in our native tongue.

The third and final section is titled "Ke Kanawai, oia hoi ka Hoakaka Kanawai i Kakau Mua ia ai e ka Mea Hanohano A. F. Judd, Lunakanawai Kiekie a Kaulike o ke Aupuni, a i Hooponopono a Hoomahuahua Hou ia aku e ka Mea Nana i Hoomakaukau i keia Buke" (The law, that is, legal explanations first written by the Honorable A. F. Judd, chief justice of the government, edited and newly expanded by the person who prepared this book). This section contains explanations of many legal terms and the complicated details of many specific crimes and laws governing marriage, adultery, homosexuality, married women's wealth, and real estate. These explanations often include the English terms and thus are also still useful today.

Overall, this book, *Ke Alakai o ke Kanaka Hawaii*, is an extraordinarily valuable contribution that deserves to be studied in detail. Poepoe demonstrates here his sense of kuleana to his fellow Kānaka who were not bilingual yet were at the mercy of the law, and he simultaneously bequeaths to us (and our descendants) a rich resource for understanding the law and legal issues of his time, as well as furthering our understanding of our native language.

In addition to these two books, 1891 was the year that Poepoe began to edit *Hawaii Holomua*, a newspaper that continued the opposition to the unworkable and anti-Kanaka Bayonet Constitution and that supported Liliʻuokalani, who took the throne after the death of Kalākaua, her brother. In its first issue, its editorial says that it stands independent of the two major political divisions in the country and hopes to bring unity and end the disagreements within the lāhui. According to Kuykendall, the two major political groups dominated by Kānaka at the time were the Liberal Party, whose leaders included John E. Bush, Wilikoki, and Joseph Nāwahī, and the National Reform Party, which "had the blessing of the queen."[56] Bush and Wilikoki were vociferous in their opposition to many policies of Liliʻuokalani, and consequently, she considered them enemies during this time.[57] Despite these painful divisions, it seems both parties presented the Mōʻī with petitions for a new constitution, and she actually met with William White and Joseph Nāwahī.[58]

Elections for the Hale Aliʻi and Lunamakaʻāinana were held in February 1892. *Hawaii Holomua* expressed firm opinions on a range of issues, but Poepoe remained uncommitted to any party at this time. On January 23, 1892, the paper ran an editorial laying out the party terrain and articulating the paper's position. The main parties were the Hui Kālaiʻāina and Mechanics' Union, the Liberal Party, and a new party called Na Keiki Oiwi o Hawaii, (Native Sons of Hawaiʻi). The editorial says that all the parties had leaders, candidates, and members who are "Hawaii maoli" (Native Hawaiian), and all were "ma ke alahele e imi a e naʻi ana no ka pomaikai o ka aina, ka lahui, ka nohoalii a me ka hooni paa loa ia ana o ke Kuokoa o Hawaii" (on the path seeking and striving for the best for the ʻāina, the lāhui, the throne, and continued secure independence of Hawaiʻi). The paper, therefore, did not choose among these parties. Rather, it stood for any party supporting the lāhui Hawaiʻi:

> Aia makou ma ka aoao o ka lahui, pela no makou e hooia aku nei i keia wa, me ke ku ana hoi e kue aku ma na mea a pau e alakai aku ana ia kakou e komo iloko o ke kulana Aupuni Repubalika. E kumau aku ana makou ma ia aoao me ka paio ana no ka pono kaulike o ka lahui, ka aina a me ka nohoalii.[59]

We are on the side of the lāhui; which is what we are affirming now, standing in opposition to everyone or everything that is leading us to enter a Republican form of government. We always stand on the side that is struggling for equal rights or equal pono for the lāhui, the ʻāina, and the throne.

On January 30, 1892, Poepoe ran an editorial in *Hawaii Holomua* that gives us further insight into his political thinking at the time. It is titled "Ke Kumukanawai Hou" (A new constitution) and it questions the wisdom of putting all the lāhui's energy into trying to replace the Bayonet, since that is what had been done for the last several years without success. Kalākaua had not responded to the many petitions for a new constitution and neither had the Cabinet. Poepoe doesn't, however, offer any solid suggestions for what to do instead.[60] A guest editorial in the same issue makes a strong appeal for supporting the constitutional monarchy and the Mōʻī Liliʻuokalani.[61] What is clear in all of these is that Poepoe supported Mōʻī Liliʻuokalani, the continuation of the constitutional monarchy, and pono for the ʻāina and the lāhui Hawaiʻi.

Hawaii Holomua, like his other publications, offered a mix of news, moʻolelo Hawaiʻi, and translations of European and American tales. Only one issue from 1891 seems to have been preserved and it includes the start of a seemingly unique version of "He Moolelo no Pakaa a me Kuapakaa," which the reader may remember from the discussion of Kānepuʻu's version (chapter 2), as well as the first installment of a translation of *The Count of Monte Cristo*. Neither includes the name of the author or translator.[62]

Overthrow of Liliʻuokalani's Government, 1893–1896

In February 1892, Poepoe apparently resigned as the editor of the *Holomua* and returned to his law practice.[63] Kahikina Kelekona took over as editor and Thomas Nakanaela stayed on as secretary. Poepoe doesn't explain this action, at least not in any of the issues of the paper that survive, so it isn't known whether or not this was a political decision. He seems to remain out of the newspaper business during the turbulent years of 1893 to 1895. During that time, the haole businessmen who had perpetrated the Bayonet Constitution conspired with the US minister, John L. Stevens, to depose Liliʻuokalani after she attempted promulgating a new constitution. Shortly afterward, Nāwahī, Bush, and others founded the Hui Aloha ʻĀina, and together with the Hui Kālaiʻāina they tried many strategies and tactics to recover native rule over the country.[64] In December 1894, the haole Republic government rounded up many newspaper editors, including Nāwahī, Bush, and Kelekona, and charged them with conspiracy and sedition. The following month brought the attempted armed countercoup, which Wilikoki led. After a disastrous engagement with the heavily armed Republic and a manhunt through Oʻahu's mountains, Wilikoki was captured. Republic forces arrested Mōʻī Liliʻuokalani and two hundred or so others. Liliʻu was coerced to abdicate the throne and then held under house arrest until December 1896.[65] Nāwahī, Bush, and Kelekona were eventually released, after which Nāwahī founded the newspaper *Ke Aloha Aina* and continued to lead the Hui Aloha ʻĀina as its president. Bush returned to editing *Ka Leo o ka Lahui* but was never again as outspoken as he had been before his arrest.

Shortly after the failed armed uprising, Poepoe publicly announced in the English-language papers that he was supporting annexation. He and some associates formed an organization called the Hawaiian Annexation League; its membership was made up of Kānaka only. Because the country was under martial law, a committee of five drafted a letter requesting permission from the government to form a new political group. Members of the committee were John F. Colburn, C. L. Hopkins, Enoch Johnson, J. H. Hoʻokano, and Poepoe. This letter and the reply of the Republic government were printed in the *Pacific Commercial Advertiser*.[66]

Despite this surprising political turn, Poepoe served on the team, along with James Kaulia and J. M. Kaneakua, that defended Joseph Nāwahī and John Bush at their trial for conspiracy. He also defended at least one other aloha ʻāina charged in the countercoup.[67]

Ka Nupepa Kuokoa, 1896–1900

In January 1896 Poepoe returned to public life as the editor of the pro-Republic, pro-annexation, anti-Liliʻuokalani *Nupepa Kuokoa*. In this role, he appears to fully support the Republic and the project of annexation to the United States. This was as perplexing to some at the time as it seems to us today. In June 1896, *Ke Aloha Aina*, Nāwahī's paper and the paper of the Hui Aloha ʻĀina, ran a guest editorial signed with the pseudonym "Kanilehua," which signifies a person from Hilo.[68] This column expresses sadness and dismay that a person of Poepoe's caliber should virtually defect to the other side of the political struggle. The title of the column is "He Lolelua Maopopo Io No" (Understood to be a turncoat or fickle). It begins,

> He minamina au i ka hoopili aku i na olelo o kela ano ae la maluna, i kekahi hoa a mau hoa kanaka maoli i hoonaauao ponoia, a i loaa hoi na ike hohonu o ke kulana kalaiaina e hoopomaikai mai ai i ka Lahui Hawaii.[69]

> I am sorry to attach words of the above sort to friends and fellow Kānaka Maoli who are well educated, and who have acquired deep knowledge of the political position that would benefit the Lāhui Hawaiʻi.

It then goes on to detail Poepoe's many excellent qualities and intellectual skills:

> . . . o J. M. Poepoe Esq., kekahi kanaka ma ke kulana helu ekahi o ka naauao me ka makaukau nui, he akamai olelo, he noeau kalaimanao,

he loea unuhi olelo a hooponopono buke pili kanawai, he alelo olelo like ole, he noonoo mohala a malaelae, a pela wale aku.⁷⁰

. . . J. M. Poepoe, Esq., is a person of the first order of education and great skill; he is articulate, wise in discussions, an expert translator and legal book editor, a speaker of various tongues, a clear and developed thinker, and so forth.

But despite all these fine qualities and his previous work, "A o kona kulana, a me kona ano a me kana e hana nei i keia wa, aia ma ka aoao o ka poe e anai nei e make loa ka Lahui Hawaii. Aloha no!" (His position, character, and actions at this time are on the side of the people grinding down the Lāhui Hawaiʻi to the death. How sad!).⁷¹ Kanilehua then goes on to remind readers and, we presume, Poepoe himself of his previous stance on the monarchy and independence of the country, by quoting these words from a campaign flyer from 1887:

E na makamaka, e hoomanao i ka'u hoohiki. No Hawaii au i keia la! No Hawaii au i ka la apopo!! No Hawaii au i na la a pau!!! A e paio ana au i ka paio maikai no ka hoonipaaia o ka Nohoalii o Hawaii nei. O ke Kuokoa oiaio ko'u kulana, a o ke kaulike ke kahua o ko'u Kuokoa. Aole o na kanaka ko'u enemi, aka, o na hana e poino ai ka Nohoalii, a e pau ai ke Kuokoa o ke Aupuni, a e hahaoia ai ka Lahui holookoa iloko o ka moana kupikipiki-o . . . o ko'u mau enemiia [enemi ia].⁷²

My friends, remember my vow. I am for Hawaiʻi today! I am for Hawaiʻi tomorrow!! I am for Hawaiʻi every day!!! And I will fight the good fight for the security of the Throne of Hawaiʻi. True Independence is my position, and equality/equity/fairness (kaulike) is the foundation of my Independence. People/Hawaiians (kanaka) are not my enemy, however, acts that harm the Throne and end the Independence of the Government, and put the entire Lāhui into the rough ocean . . . are my enemies.

At the end, Kanilehua again expresses sadness and a wish that Poepoe be forgiven for this political lapse. He or she writes, "Minamina wale! Aka, e kala aku iaia, aole hoi e hoomauhala mau loa"⁷³ (That is too bad! But forgive him; do not hold a grudge forever).

Poepoe doesn't answer this directly in *Nupepa Kuokoa*, and he never explains his political turn in that paper. Twelve years later, around the ten-year anniversary of the annexation, he does justify his decision. In a four-part essay in his paper *Kuokoa Home Rula*, he explains that when Grover Cleveland attempted to support the restoration of Queen Liliʻuokalani at the end of 1893 and his effort was mishandled by her and her advisors, he understood that the monarchy would never return, and at that point he decided to work for annexation. He based his understanding of the mishandling on the account by US minister Albert Willis (subsequently refuted by the Queen). He writes,

> Ma ka noho mana ana o ke Aupuni Repubalika o 1894 o Hawaii nei, ua kuio iho la ia ma ke ano *de facto* ame *de jure* (ma ka oiaio a ma ka mana). Aia a loaa he mana nana e kulai a lilo i mea ole, oia wale no ka mea e hiolo ai ia Aupuni. A oiai, aole hiki i na Roialiti ke hoohiolo ia aupuni, nolaila, ua lilo ua aupuni nei i Aupuni Mana; a ma ia ano, ua hiki ole ia'u ke alo ae i ke komo kino ana e kakoo i ke kumuhana, hoohui aina maoli (annexation) aole hoi i ke kulana aupuni *protectorate* (hoomalu).[74]

> The Government of the Republic was in power de facto and de jure (in fact and in power). Only if a greater power overthrew it would it come down. Since the Royalists could not bring it down, therefore, it became an empowered Government, and in that case, I could not help but personally enter into supporting the project of annexation, but not [the other option of becoming] a protectorate.

It is worth noting that Poepoe uses the terms "de facto" and "de jure," which are generally understood to mean "in actuality" and "legally," respectively, but he does not explain them that way; rather, he says "ma ka oiaio a ma ka mana" (in fact and in power), replacing the expected "kānāwai" (law) with "mana." I interpret this as his implying that although the Republic created itself illegally, its leaders have enough power that they are in control of the law and all of its apparatuses. This is a bending of the use of the term meaning "legal," perhaps meant to alert his readers to the reality that whoever holds power wields the law, whether they came into power legally or not.

He then explains that he supported annexation so that Hawaiians would get American citizenship and live in a democracy with broad suffrage. This status might provide access to more legal resources that could lead to broader civil rights and courts that are not controlled by a local oligarchy. He writes here that he did not support but actively opposed the Republic's (and previous governments') property requirements for the right to vote.[75] His opposition to the Republic in *Nupepa Kuokoa* on specific issues was not evident at the time, however.

In 1896, for example, the Republic legislature passed a law ending Hawaiian as a medium of instruction in all public and private schools in the country. In May of that year, Poepoe ran an editorial approving of the Board of Education's report to the legislature, which included a recommendation to close the remaining Hawaiian-language schools. The board reported that only three schools remained that were teaching in Hawaiian. The board claimed to have received petitions from parents asking that these schools teach in English. Poepoe's editorial did not express any alarm over this, nor did any other editorial when the law was passed. Today that law is recognized as one of the signposts of major loss for Hawaiians in the struggle for hegemony.[76] Earlier that year, Poepoe advocated for higher education in Hawaiian, publishing an editorial asking for government funding for a private seminary that promised to teach some courses in Hawaiian. The students there would be better prepared for their roles in the ministry if they learned Hawaiian grammar and rhetoric.[77] He argued that although such a proposal seemed unconstitutional since the government should not fund any one religion in any way, the exception was warranted in order to keep education in the native language alive.[78] One can only wonder at the contradiction in these two positions.

As the editor of *Kuokoa*, Poepoe demonstrates a much-increased interest in Hawaiian knowledge. In his first issue, he promotes the book *Buke Mele Lahui*, which celebrated the acts of the poʻe aloha ʻāina who attempted the armed coup a year earlier. Although Poepoe was politically opposed to the book's view at this time, he endorses the book because of the two hundred mele it contained (which he valued), and he notes the editor's name as F(riend) Joseph Testa, who was also the editor of an opposition paper, the *Makaainana*.[79] Testa's first name was not Friend (it was Francisco)—Poepoe was playing with his initial in a gesture of approval. In this same issue, he published a schedule of monthly lectures for a group called Hui Hoonaauao Hawaii Opio (Association to Educate Hawaiian Youth).[80] The speakers delivered lectures that were also given to the participants as written essays. Poepoe was scheduled to give two lectures, and among the other speakers were some of Poepoe's political opponents, including Kaulia, an officer in the Hui Aloha ʻĀina. Poepoe lectured on the origins of the islands and the origins of the Hawaiian people and Kaulia on the profession of kahuna.

Poepoe published a written version of his lecture for the ʻAhahui ʻŌpio Hawaiʻi in two parts on July 24 and 31, 1896.[81] It is a very detailed argument of approximately ten thousand words, organized into four parts. The first part comprises the ideas or theories of Hawaiʻi's ancient people concerning how the universe (or in his terms the sky and the earth) was made; the second part contains other theories of the ancient people of Hawaiʻi about the origins of the archipelago; the third section discusses theories of scientists that there was a continent in the Pacific in ancient times; and the fourth compares the idea of an ancient Pacific continent with Hawaiian moʻolelo and biblical passages that suggest changes to the earth after the Flood. In the first, second, and fourth parts, Poepoe draws upon mele, moʻokūʻauhau, and moʻolelo from his own knowledge and archives; the writings of Kamakau; and Abraham Fornander's *An Account of the Polynesian Race*. The main argument that Poepoe threads throughout the essay is that some of the ancient Hawaiians conceived of a trinity of deities that corresponds to the biblical trinity of the Father, Son, and Holy Spirit. Furthermore, the stories of global floods in the Bible correspond with Hawaiian lore and explain how the Pacific islands are the high peaks of a continent that had been flooded.

This seems to be an attempt to reconcile Poepoe's and many others' belief in the Christian Bible with their own histories and with contemporary scientific theories. What is interesting today is not the argument itself, which a hundred years later predictably seems antiquated, but the wealth of Kanaka knowledge that Poepoe brings to the project, as well as his insistence that such knowledge is no less valid than that of any information from University of California scientists or the Bible. He also brought to the reading public of 1896 a reminder of the worth of Kamakau's writings from thirty years earlier. This is important because Kamakau's work had been serialized in newspapers; there was no book that students of Poepoe's time could pick up to read and learn from (and, in fact, such books did not exist until 1996).[82] Poepoe's work kept Kamakau's memory alive, and those fortunate enough to have access to preserved copies of the newspapers could look up his work. Similarly, Poepoe brought a bit of Fornander's research to the public; Fornander's books were published in English only and were thus inaccessible to those who were monolingual in

Hawaiian. In addition to the main argument, then, the Hui ʻŌpio Hawaiʻi, the readers of Poepoe's newspaper in 1896, and Poepoe's readers today have been given the text of several ancient mele, as well as glimpses of moʻokūʻauhau and moʻolelo kahiko from the perspective of a highly educated Kanaka. Poepoe's deep respect for the wisdom and artistry of our ancestors—his moʻokūʻauhau consciousness—is evident when he writes here of his regret that he doesn't have more time for study:

> He nui na mele i koe i pau ole iaʻu i ka huli ia, aʻu nae i hoomaopopo ai he mau mea waiwai nui ia no keia kumumanao; aka, o ka haiki o ka manawa ka mea nana i keakea mai i ka mahuahua ana aku o na noii ana ma ia mau mele, oiai, he mau waiwai ahiu a laka ole ka hapanui o lakou i keia wa, aneane hiki ole no paha ke loaa.[83]

There are many more mele that I have not researched but which I know are very valuable for this topic; however, time limits restrict the growth of the research on these mele, since the majority of these are wild and untamed treasures; one almost cannot catch them.

Poepoe also published Kaulia's lecture on the ʻOihana Kahuna, or the professions of kahuna, the professional class of aliʻi that included priests, waʻa-builders, physicians, and so on. These acts—promoting Testa's *Buke Mele Lahui*, and working with political opponents to educate Kanaka youth—demonstrate the commitment of all these Kānaka to the well-being of the lāhui. Their dedication to the lāhui exceeds governmental politics: annexation or not, a Republican form of government versus the monarchy. These men drew on Kanaka intellectual traditions to work together to leave a written legacy for future generations, proceeding from moʻokūʻauhau consciousness. These same intellectual traditions must have informed their politics, but their actions were not limited by those politics.

A further demonstration of Poepoe's and his opponents' willingness to work together at times for the good of the lāhui can be seen later that year when Joseph Nāwahī died. Nāwahī had been the founder and president of Hui Hawaiʻi Aloha ʻĀina, established after the 1893 overthrow to support the restoration of the native government and prevent annexation. In December 1894, Nāwahī had been arrested and imprisoned for three months for planning to overthrow the Republic, and, when freed, he established *Ke Aloha Aina* newspaper. He died after contracting tuberculosis during his imprisonment. The news article in Poepoe's paper expresses genuine sadness and aloha for Nāwahī, his wife, and children. It begins with "Ua loaa mai ka lono eehaeha [ehaeha] ma ka Poaha nei . . . ua haalele mai la i keia ola ana ko makou hoa o ka makapeni Joseph Nawahi"[84] (We received the painful news on Thursday . . . that our companion of the pen Joseph Nāwahī has departed this life). The following week, Poepoe published an account of Nāwahī's Honolulu funeral, noting many touching details of the expressions of mourning. Notable is the list of the pallbearers and the comment about it:

> Na poe hapai pahu oia o J. O. Carter (Keo Kaaka), Charles Creighton, David Dayton, R. W. Wilcox, W. C. Achi, S. K. Ka-ne, J. L. Kaulukou, F. J. Testa, E. K. Lilikalani, S. M. Kaaukai, J. K. Kaunam[a]no ame W. P. Kanealii.
>
> Hui na poe Repubalika me ka poe Repubalika ole, hookahi no manao nui o ka hoike ana i na manao aloha hiwahiwa i ka mea i hala aku ma kela aoao.
>
> ---
>
> The pallbearers were J. O. Carter (Keo Kaaka), Charles Creighton, David Dayton, R. W. Wilcox, W. C. Achi, S. K. Ka-ne, J. L. Kaulukou, F. J. Testa, E. K. Lilikalani, S. M. Kaaukai, J. K. Kaunamano and W. P. Kanealii.
>
> Republic people and non-Republic people met together, with one main idea, to show their esteem and aloha for the one who passed to other side.

In this list we see members of Hui Aloha 'Āina: John Kaunamano, Samuel Kaaukai, and Kanealii. Along with them are anti-annexationists who were not members of Hui Aloha 'Āina: Francisco Testa, the editor of the anti-annexationist paper *Ka Makaainana* and Robert Wilcox; and the pro-Republic and pro-annexation politicians William C. Achi and John Lota Kaulukou.[85]

After this moment of collective bereavement, however, partisan politics resumed. William McKinley, an expansionist, was elected to the US presidency in November, scheduled to take office in March 1897. In February 1897, Achi, Kaulukou, C. L. Hopkins, and Poepoe put forth an argument in favor of annexation, based on economic fears. They argued that Japanese immigration was keeping wages low and that a treaty with Japan prevented the government from stemming the tide. They also argued that previous US Congresses had supported the Reciprocity Treaty that allowed tariff-free

Hawaiian sugar, but that had changed because of an increase in sugar beet production in the United States. Without the Reciprocity Treaty the plantations would go out of business, the government would be impoverished, and everyone would starve. The remedy for all of these specters was US annexation.[86]

Soon after McKinley took office, delegates from the Republic negotiated a treaty of annexation. In Honolulu, President Sanford Dole called a special session of the Senate to ratify the treaty, while the poʻe aloha ʻāina planned a massive anti-annexation petition. The September 10, 1897, front page of Poepoe's *Kuokoa* featured a report on the special Senate session, a drawing of Dole above the text of the treaty, and a story about the mass meeting of the poʻe aloha ʻāina.

The coverage of the mass meeting was sarcastic, ridiculing the size of the crowd. In subsequent weeks, *Kuokoa* was silent on the topic of the anti-annexation petition, except for occasional jabs at the arguments among the leaders of the two main hui, Hui Kālaiʻāina and Hui Aloha ʻĀina, about who might be best to deliver the petition to Washington, DC. When the four emissaries departed, however, the paper (maybe Poepoe himself) expresses affection and perhaps concern for them, ending a short report on their departure with "Aloha Kaulia! Aloha oukou apau"[87] (An affectionate goodbye, Kaulia! An affectionate goodbye to all of you). I read affection and concern in the word "aloha" here because so often Kānaka Hawaiʻi had traveled to the United States or Europe only to never return. In Poepoe's memory would have been the very recent journeys of Kalākaua and Nāwahī, both of whom died in San Francisco.

Those emissaries were successful in derailing the proposed treaty of annexation: the US Senate could not get enough votes to pass the treaty after the petition was presented and became publicized. When the four returned in March 1898, there was no mention in *Kuokoa* of the failure of the treaty or their return. During their travel home, the USS *Maine* suffered an explosion while docked in Havana, Cuba, and that provided a rationale for the Spanish-American War. It didn't take long for a joint resolution of the US Congress (called the Newlands after its author) to be drafted and passed that annexed Hawaiʻi based on the argument that the United States needed Hawaiʻi as a coaling station for its warships bound for the Philippines to fight the Spanish.

As the Newlands resolution was being voted on, Poepoe published an editorial about the Hawaiian flag. The Republic of Hawaiʻi legislature was

FIGURE 4.2

Ka Nupepa Kuokoa front page, September 10, 1897. Left headline (translation): "Special Session of the Senate, 1897." Center (translation): "Text of the Annexation Treaty." Right (translation): "Mass Meeting of the Royalists."

debating a resolution to use the national flag as its territorial flag after annexation. Poepoe argues, however,

> Ma ko makou manao ana, ma ka wa e make maoli ai ko Hawaii kulana Aupuni kuokoa nona iho, elike me ko na wa i kaa hope ae nei, a komo oia he Aupuni "panalaau" no Amerika, ua oi aku ka pono e haawi i ka hoomaha mau loa i kona hae Aupuni, e hiamoe pu me kona "kuokoa" i kapae ia a i omoia iloko o Amerika.[88]

> In our opinion, when Hawaiʻi's independent status truly dies, as in past times, and it becomes a "territory" of America, it would be more pono to give a permanent retirement to its National flag, to sleep together with its "independence" which has been set aside and swallowed up in America.

It is not difficult to detect Poepoe's sadness or regret at contemplating the permanent loss of Hawaiʻi's independence here. He argues that the flag should remain forever a symbol of Hawaiʻi as an independent country, not a symbol of Hawaiʻi as a colony. The flag would then represent Hawaiʻi's nonindependence, rather than its independence, just as the nation's motto celebrating its sovereignty ("ua mau ke ea o ka ʻāina i ka pono") was later appropriated by the State of Hawaiʻi. Poepoe, it seems, would rather see the flag put to sleep than to see that. He ends the short essay like this: "O ke aloha i ka hae, aole hiki ia mea ke holoiia mai ka puuwai aku o ke kanaka Hawaii i hanau i Hawaii nei. Aole—aole" (Love for the flag is not something that can be erased from the heart of the Kānaka Hawaiʻi born in Hawaiʻi nei. No—no).[89] Poepoe, the tireless advocate for annexation and defender of the Republic, still loved his country and the flag that symbolizes it. The annexation question was not simple or easy. It may have been for the best in his view, but the loss of the country and the flag were still very painful.

A week later, when news arrived that the Newlands resolution had passed, Poepoe's *Kuokoa* celebrated with a front-page story whose headline says, decorated in stars and stripes, "Hoohui Aina," meaning "annexation." The story of receiving the news—titled "Lanakila loa ka Hoohui Aina" (Annexation triumphs)—was dramatic: the ship *Coptic* was spotted flying US flags as it passed through the Kaiwi channel and came into Kalehuawehe, nearing Honolulu Harbor. Those flags clearly signaled that the US Senate had passed the Newlands resolution. The reactions to the news reflected the differing stakes that various groups in Hawai'i had in this outcome. Especially stark in contrast were those that worked for annexation versus the po'e aloha 'āina who worked so hard to keep their country independent. In Honolulu, supporters of annexation hoisted US flags up their own flagpoles, and crowds of people ran down to the wharf; others, greatly disturbed, ran helter-skelter in the streets. At 4:15, a hundred guns were fired from the armory in Kaka'ako and at 4:20 cheerful sirens resounded. In contrast, Edward Like and Emma Nāwahī's *Ke Aloha Aina* printed the following headline: "Lawe Lima Nui o Amerika i ka Paemoku o Hawaii—me ka Ae Ole o ka Poe Nona ka Aina"[90] (America takes the Hawaiian Islands by force—without the consent of the people to whom the land belongs).

Poepoe immediately expresses that he would like everyone to put the annexation fight behind them and work together for the good of the native people. He salutes the anti-annexation papers (except for *Ke Aloha Aina*) and says, to each one, "Ua hui kakou. Pau ae la keia" (We are together. This is over). The word "hui," "together," also means "annexed," however.[91] The following week his main editorial asks that the Kanaka leaders from all sides form a new political organization together to work for the pono of the lāhui. It reads, in part,

> Aole makou i ike iki, pehea la i hiki ole ai i na Hawaii naauao, elike me John L. Kaulukou, W. C. Achi, S. K. Ka-ne, A. Rosa, J. M. Kaneakua, E. Johnson, J. K. Kahookano, J. K. Kaulia, R. W. Wilikoki, S. M. Kaaukai, John F. Colburn, F. J. Testa, R. H. Baker, W. H. Tell, E. K. Like, Abraham Fernandez ame kekahi poe Hawaii e ae he nui o loko nei o ke kulanakauhale, ke hapai i Ahahui holomua o keia ano maloko nei o keia kulanakauhale?[92]

> We don't know at all, but why couldn't educated Hawaiians like John L. Kaulukou, W. C. Achi, S. K. Ka-ne, A. Rosa, J. M. Kaneakua, E. Johnson, J. K. Kahookano, J. K. Kaulia, R. W. Wilikoki, S. M. Kaaukai, John F. Colburn, F. J. Testa, R. H. Baker, W. H. Tell, E. K. Like, Abraham Fernandez, and many other Hawaiians in the city, take up a progressive Association of this kind, in this city?

Here, Poepoe calls on the leaders and newspaper editors from his own pro-annexation side to work with Kaulia, Wilikoki, Testa, Edward Like of *Ke Aloha Aina*, and so on. For some time, however, the po'e aloha 'āina did not accept the finality of the annexation. Wilikoki was sent to the United

FIGURE 4.3

Front page of *Ka Nupepa Kuokoa*, July 15, 1898.

States to see if he could get the Newlands resolution overturned. When he was fully persuaded that that was impossible, he returned to Hawaiʻi with the idea of establishing a Kanaka political party. The Hui Aloha ʻĀina under Kaulia and the Hui Kālaiʻāina under David Kalauokalani merged to form a new party called the Home Rule Party, or Ka ʻAoʻao Home Rula.[93] Poepoe's editorial foreshadows the poʻe aloha ʻāina and their Hawaiian political opponents coming back together in a political association.

Nupepa Kuokoa, the Organic Act, and the First Election of the Territory, 1900

On April 30, 1900, the US Congress approved *An Act to Provide a Government for the Territory of Hawaii*, commonly known as the Organic Act. It detailed the structure of the colonial government, specifying that the power would be held in Washington, DC, and exerted via the existing haole business and political oligarchy in Hawaiʻi. The governor and the Supreme Court justices of the new territory were to be appointed by the US president, and the territory would have no representation in the US Congress except for a nonvoting delegate to the House of Representatives.[94] A local territorial legislature was to be established, and the act specified that "all legislative proceedings shall be conducted in the English language."[95]

The government published this act in Honolulu through the Hawaiian Gazette Company but in English only, so confusion and misinformation circulated in the community for a while. A letter in *Kuokoa* from Moses Palau, for example, mistakenly bemoans that English literacy is required to vote, while the law actually said that voters needed to know either English or Hawaiian.[96] In May 1900, Poepoe stepped down from editing *Nupepa Kuokoa* and was replaced by William J. Coelho. In July 1900, Poepoe and Coelho announced in *Kuokoa* that together they were translating the Organic Act into Hawaiian and would make the translation available for purchase. The following month, they announced that the government had purchased their translation and would make copies available to the public at no charge.[97] The booklet was published, but without any preface and without the names of the translators anywhere in it.[98] At this same time, *Kuokoa* published this translation of the act under the title "Ke Kanawai Kumu o Hawaii," also without noting the names of the translators. Poepoe's translation of the Organic Act reflects his lifelong commitment to providing Hawaiians access to the law.

Also at this time, Poepoe took an active part in the coming first election that would establish the territorial legislature and send the first delegate to Congress. He wrote a series of articles interpreting the law concerning that election to be held in November, meant to assist the Hawaiian-speaking public in understanding their new law and political situation. Poepoe explained American citizenship and the new one-year residency requirement for voting.[99] He signed these articles as J. Mokuohai Poepoe, emphasizing his Hawaiian name for the first time in print.

Moses Palau and others suggested that Poepoe run for the territorial legislature and he agreed. Although his close associates, such as W. C. Achi and John Kaulukou, with whom he had coauthored the pro-annexation essay mentioned above, and William Coelho, who took over his position as editor of *Kuokoa* and with whom he translated the Organic Act, all ran for office as members of the Republican Party, Poepoe remained his own man and ran as an independent.

Despite *Kuokoa* definitely favoring the Republican Party, Coelho gave Poepoe the front page to publish his platform. The first points in the platform included the following:

> E AEIA KA HAE HAWAII I HAE AUPUNI NO KA PANALAAU A E AEIA KA OLELO HAWAII I OLELO KANAWAI A I OLELO OIHANA MA KA AHAOLELO KULOKO.[100]
>
> ———
>
> THE HAWAIIAN FLAG SHOULD BE ALLOWED TO BE THE FLAG OF THE TERRITORY AND THE HAWAIIAN LANGUAGE SHOULD BE ALLOWED TO BE A LANGUAGE OF THE LAW AND THE TERRITORIAL LEGISLATURE.

Here, Poepoe reversed his position on the flag, perhaps out of the same emotion that caused him to want it retired previously (i.e., his aloha for the ʻāina and his lāhui). More important, he wanted to work to change the law requiring everything be done in English. Although he pushed for annexation and was multilingual, Poepoe never wanted to see Hawaiian disappear, and it is clear here and throughout his writing life that he dearly loved Hawaiian language and literature.

The US government demand that everything be conducted in English was problematic in many ways. For example, leaders who didn't know English would not be able to serve in the legislature. Also, no one "who can not understandingly speak, read, and write the English language shall be a qualified juror or grand juror in the Territory of Hawaii."[101] These settler-colonial restrictions on participation in government confer power and privilege on members of the colonizing country and include only the educated elite among natives.

On September 7, Palau wrote a column recommending which men to vote for, and he wrote this about Poepoe:

> J. Mokuohai Poepoe. E kakoo kakou nona, no keia mau mahele nui, penei: (1) He oiwi no ka aina; (2) he loio piha naauao; (3) he Lunahooponopono no ka nupepa Kuokoa (mamua); (4) he ike i ka olelo Latina; (5) olelo Farani; (6) he oi aku ma ka olelo Beritania ame ka olelo makua.[102]

> J. Mokuohai Poepoe. Let's support him, for these important reasons: (1) He is a native of the land; (2) he is an attorney filled with wisdom; (3) he was the Editor of the Kuokoa (before); (4) he knows Latin; (5) French; (6) he is even better at English and the mother tongue.

In November voters elected Robert Wilcox to the nonvoting delegate seat in the US House of Representatives, and the Independent Home Rule Party swept the rest of the election also, dominating the seats in both houses of the territorial legislature.[103] Poepoe did not win a seat.

After the election, Poepoe wrote for *Kuokoa* for a time. He reported on the first legislature, as well as writing and translating moʻolelo for the paper. The new editor, Arthur W. Pearson, wrote that readers might wonder where their moʻolelo had gone and that Poepoe was busy covering the legislature. Pearson did not specify, however, which moʻolelo were Poepoe's.[104] After this legislative session, Poepoe disappears from the pages of *Kuokoa*.

Kuokoa Home Rula, Hawaii Aloha, and *Ka Naʻi Aupuni*, 1902–1908

The newspapers of the Independent Home Rule Party have not been preserved very well, but we do know that Poepoe was involved with both of them. The main paper starting in 1901 was the *Kuokoa Home Rula*. It is a terrible loss that issues from the first six years of its publication are nowhere to be found. It is likely that when Poepoe left the *Nupepa Kuokoa* he began to write for *Kuokoa Home Rula*, but so far there is no concrete evidence to support that. It is also not clear exactly when or why he decided to become a member of the Independent Home Rule Party. In April 1902, he reportedly spoke at a Home Rule Party meeting, stating at that time he was still not a member of any party.[105] Four months later, in August 1902, he was reported among the leadership at a meeting of the Home Rule Party.[106] Around this time he presented a resolution to a US Senate committee regarding Pacific Islands and Puerto Rico on behalf of the Home Rule Party. Unfortunately, the text of the resolution is not included within the report of that committee.[107] Because of this, however, we can fairly safely surmise that by the fall of 1902, Poepoe had thrown his support to the Independent Home Rule Party.

During this time Poepoe announced the publication of another book on law meant to assist the Hawaiian-speaking public. Unfortunately, no other mention of this book has been found in any library.[108] He was also among the Hawaiian intellectual stars enumerated by *Kuokoa*'s young editor, David Kanewanui, in an editorial, "Na Hawaii Kaulana" (Famous Hawaiians), that appeared in May 1902. Here is the first paragraph of that editorial:

> Eia i Hawaii nei kekahi mau hoku malamalama. Owai la keia mau hoku malamalama? O na kanaka naauao o ka aina. A owai lakou? He ninau keia i hiki ole ke pane ia me ka pololei loa, no ka mea, he nui na kanaka naauao i ike nui ole ia . . . aka, e helu aku ana makou i na malamalama a makou i ike [sic], a i lohe nui ia hoi i keia mau la.[109]

> Here in Hawaiʻi are some shining stars. Who are these shining stars? They are the educated Kānaka of the land. Who are they? This is a question that cannot be answered very precisely because there are many educated Kānaka who are not well-known. . . . However, we will recount the brilliant ones that we know, and who are greatly listened to these days.

This seems to indicate that Poepoe was prominent in the Hawaiian-speaking public's mind. Probably because we don't have the Home Rule Party's newspaper(s), however, it appears that Poepoe did not play a part in the election of 1902, the second election that sent a delegate to the US House of Representatives. In that election, Jonah Kūhiō Kalanianaʻole was elected as a Republican, ousting the Home Rule Party's Wilcox. According to Esther Mookini, in 1903 Poepoe took over editing the Home Rule Party's paper, *Kuokoa Home Rula*; however, nothing more is known about his editorship at that time.[110]

In 1905, Poepoe was a member of a group called Hui (or ʻAhahui) Hawaiʻi Lani Honua, and in July of that year they began to publish a weekly magazine, *Hawaii Aloha*. Poepoe was the editor as well as the Lunahoʻomalu o ka Papa Huli Kūʻauhau a Moʻolelo Hawaiʻi (chair or presiding officer of a board for researching genealogies and moʻolelo). Although this publication only lasted until November 1905, it is important because we can see that it was concerned with the perpetuation of Hawaiian literature, genealogies, and other fields of knowledge in the native language. The magazine published a new version of the Hiʻiakaikapoliopele moʻolelo, the first since 1893.[111] It ran a series called "Na Wahi Pana o ka Mokupuni o Kauai" (The legendary places of Kauaʻi) written by Joseph A. Akina (signed J. A. Akina), a similar series for Waikīkī by John Mika Sobe, and a genealogy of Kamehameha by the board that Poepoe chaired. Another series was called "Oihana Kilokilo Hawaii" (Hawaiian forecasting, or reading of signs and omens), which described how to read the signs and omens in clouds.[112] Besides these and other rich Hawaiian cultural offerings, the magazine also ran one story translated from a series in the *San Francisco Examiner* ("Masiliano Ke Koa"; Masiliano the warrior or soldier), and published the new laws of the territory. Most of these are written anonymously, but it is highly likely that Poepoe wrote many of them. Some were republished later in his paper *Ka Naʻi Aupuni*. "Na Mea Kaulana o ka Lipolipo o Kalihi-uka" (The famous places of the dark green [forest] of Upland Kalihi), for example, re-edited or revised, forms part of "Ka Moolelo Hawaii Kahiko" (see chapter 6). Sometime between the issues of October 20 and November 10, 1905, Poepoe stopped editing *Hawaii Aloha*.

On November 27, 1905, Poepoe and Charles Kahiliaulani Notley launched a new daily paper called *Ka Naʻi Aupuni*. Notley was the owner and Poepoe the editor. The paper was a daily companion to their weekly, *Kuokoa Home Rula*. The name *Ka Naʻi Aupuni* is an epithet for Kamehameha I (whose moʻolelo begins on the front page of the first issue of the paper) and is most often translated as "the conquerer of the nation." However, the words "naʻi" (conquerer) and "aupuni" (nation) can each be understood in multiple ways. As Leilani Basham has persuasively argued, a word in Hawaiian is best understood not by using the dictionary as a menu of options for single-word translation; rather, we must consider that a word such as "naʻi" represents a category that may require several words in English to describe, or it may overlap two or more English categories.¹¹³ In addition, as we have seen before, kaona is valued and expected in Hawaiian sayings, so we expect that the kupuna who coined the phrase to describe Kamehameha chose something that was multilayered in meaning. Consider Pukui and Elbert's dictionary entry for "naʻi":

> **naʻi** 1. nvt. To conquer, take by force; conqueror. ʻO Ka-mehameha ka naʻi aupuni, Ka-mehameha, the conqueror of the nation. (PCP ngaki).
> 2. vt. To strive to obtain, endeavor to examine or understand. Ua naʻi ʻoia i ka pono o nā keiki, he does all he can for the well-being of the children.¹¹⁴

Further, "aupuni" is commonly used for government as well as kingdom, nation, and so on; thus additional ways we could understand *Ka Naʻi Aupuni* are as striving for a government, which Kamehameha certainly did, and as an endeavor to examine or understand the nation or government. This is an apt description of Poepoe's intellectual and political efforts and accomplishments in this newspaper.

In *Ka Naʻi Aupuni*, Poepoe continuously promoted the perpetuation of the native language and published works of historical and cultural importance in Hawaiian, while using the daily as an organizing and public relations vehicle for the Independent Home Rule Party. Poepoe's advocacy for the Hawaiian language started in the first issue, in which he questioned why new county laws were being published in English only.¹¹⁵ In December 1905, an editorial called "Ka Ipu Alabata" (The alabaster cup [a possible reference to the Holy Grail]) bemoaned the lack of skill in the language and lack of knowledge of moʻolelo among Hawaiian youth, and Poepoe encouraged people to buy the paper so that they could read the Kamehameha story.¹¹⁶ Poepoe quickly followed this up on January 4, 1906, with "Mai Haalele i Kau Olelo Makuahine" (Do not abandon your mother language), in which he supports the acquisition of English but argues for the value of indigenous knowledge. He writes, "O ka oi aku nae, o ka Hawaii kanaka maoli, ke ike maopopo i ka olelo a kona mau kupuna" (What is best is that Native Hawaiians understand the language of their ancestors). He adds this warning: "E hoea mai ana ma keia mua aku e lilo ai ka hapanui loa o na huaolelo

Hawaii i kamaaina ia kakou i keia wa, i mau huaolelo pohihihi i na opio Hawaii o keia mau mua ae" (It will happen that most of the Hawaiian words familiar to us now will become mysteries to the Hawaiian youth of the future).[117] His editorial on the following day asks the legislature to make Hawaiian a required subject in the public schools: "Pehea e Mau ai ke Ola ana o ka Olelo Hawaii?" (How shall the life of the Hawaiian language be perpetuated?). He rightly points out in that essay that "ka olelo Hawaii oiaio ka olelo a ke kanawai o ka aina i hoomake loa ai" (the true Hawaiian language is the language that the law of the land has killed).[118]

The next day, January 6, Poepoe publishes an essay called "Ka Moolelo o Kou Aina Oiwi" (The moʻolelo of your native land), in which he argues that Kanaka must know their own history before they can make proper decisions. He continues this topic in the January 17, 1906, editorial "Ko Kakou Moolelo Hawaii Kahiko" (Our ancient Hawaiian moʻolelo). There he discusses the lack of Hawaiian moʻolelo in Hawaiian in books:

> He mea na makou i minamina nui i keia wa, ma ka hoomaopopo ana iho, he lahui kakou i nele maoli i ko kakou moolelo Hawaii kahiko; aole hoi i paa maloko o kekahi buke a mau buke paha i paiia ma ka kakou olelo makuahine maoli.
>
> ———
>
> Something we greatly regret is understanding that we are a people who lack our ancient Hawaiian moʻolelo; they are not preserved in any books published in our real mother language.

He goes on to say that Kamakau patiently researched and wrote his moʻolelo, which were published in newspapers now gone from most Hawaiian homes and that Davida Malo's manuscript was *translated* and published in a book (his emphasis) but not published in Hawaiian. He ends this essay and this whole series by saying that

> o ka loaa ana he moolelo Hawaii kahiko ia kakou ma ka kakou olelo ponoi, oia ka mea waiwai nui; a ke lana nei ko makou manao e haawi i na hoao ana e loaa he mau mahele o keia moolelo ma keia mua aku.
>
> ———
>
> to have a moʻolelo Hawaiʻi kahiko in our own language, that would be the most valuable thing; and we hope to give a try to obtain some parts of this moʻolelo in the future.

These essays show Poepoe's commitment to promoting the indigenous knowledge of the past for the youth of his day and into the future. While many people had to spend their time and energy learning English in order to survive, and most prevented their children from learning Hawaiian in an ultimately futile attempt to provide them with a better life, a few intellectuals like Poepoe saw what others didn't and were able to articulate and insist upon the value of our ancestral language, literature, and culture.

For the first seven months of the paper, instead of headlines on page 1, Poepoe ran a saying in Hawaiian in each issue that celebrates the language, geography, or literature. These were ʻōlelo noʻeau or lines from mele or moʻolelo. Mary Kawena Pukui may have used *Ka Naʻi Aupuni* as one of the sources for her collection of ʻōlelo noʻeau, since, except for her addition of diacriticals, several are identical and others are very similar. Pukui translated thousands of these sayings, offering both interpretations of the metaphors and possible usages.[119] The many that have not been published with her helpful interpretations remain in *Ka Naʻi Aupuni* for us to puzzle out and enjoy.

Poepoe's dedication to Hawaiian knowledge is also reflected in his calendars. Many newspapers included yearly or monthly calendars, but Poepoe added the names of Hawaiian moon nights to the calendar in *Ka Naʻi Aupuni*, and the paper published them nearly every day.[120]

The most important indicator of Poepoe's love for the language, history, culture, and literature is that the paper emphasized Hawaiian moʻolelo in proportions far beyond what he had published in *Nupepa Kuokoa*. Under his own name, he published "Ka Moolelo Hawaii Kahiko," and, using the pseudonym Hooulumahiehie (Hoʻoulumāhiehie) he published "Kamehameha I: Ka Naʻi Aupuni o Hawaii" and "Ka Moolelo o Hiiaka-i-ka-poli-o-Pele," both full-length books in serial form (more on Hoʻoulumāhiehie later in this chapter). In addition, a version of "Laieikawai," different from Haleʻole's version, was begun but never finished, as was a version of "Ka Moolelo Walohia o Hainakolo."[121] Only one non-Hawaiian moʻolelo, "He Moolelo no Alamira ka Uʻi Hapa Paniolo" (A story of Almira, the half-Spanish beauty) by Hoʻoulumāhiehie, ran in the paper. It is unclear whether that was a translation or an original composition.[122]

Hoʻoulumāhiehie

Hoʻoulumāhiehie is a pseudonym that Poepoe used when he made substantial contributions to and editing of manuscripts written by others. In "He Hoakaka Aku," a letter on his own editorial page in *Ka Naʻi Aupuni*, he explains a little about the provenance of the Hiʻiaka moʻolelo in that paper and his right to take the manuscript when he left the monthly *Hawaii Aloha* for *Ka Naʻi Aupuni*.[123] For "Kamehameha I," Poepoe as Hoʻoulumāhiehie consults Fornander's *Account of the Polynesian Race* and Kamakau's newspaper serial works.[124] He also credits Solomon Lehuanui Peleioholani, kekahi alii hanau o ka aina (an aliʻi born of the ʻāina), with a section of the story.[125] kuʻualoha hoʻomanawanui calls this type of assemblage "a weaving of strands or intertextuality" among various versions of moʻolelo.[126] In these cases when Poepoe does not sign a work with his own name, it is important not to credit him erroneously for full authorship, but rather to research the provenance of the moʻolelo in its pages, or at its start or end. A noticeable feature of Poepoe's works is his own crediting and citing of other sources.

Poepoe also used *Ka Naʻi Aupuni* to disseminate works translated for the Reorganized Church of Latter-Day Saints, including "Ka Buke a Aberahama" (The Book of Abraham) and "Ka Buke Hooakakaolelo o ka Buke a Moramona" (A dictionary of the Book of Mormon). And, especially in the first year of the paper, *Ka Naʻi Aupuni* featured opinion pieces debating the practice of Mormon polygamy.[127]

Finally, *Ka Naʻi Aupuni* was a platform for the Independent Home Rule Party. The party's leaders articulated and debated their politics in the paper and organized its meetings. During these years Hawaiians were trying to band together to forward Hawaiian interests while they were spread out over the three political parties. From 1905 to 1906, the Home Rule Party tried to collaborate with Democrats to run one candidate for US Congress against the popular Republican, Kalanianaʻole. Women were active in the Home Rule Party and sent reports on their membership and activities to the paper. The paper also contains protests of anti-Hawaiian racism that was rife in party politics in those years.[128] Analysis of these issues is beyond the scope of this chapter but it is notable that there is a wealth of material for future research on how American racism, women's suffrage, and other issues were debated within the Hawaiian-speaking community during these early years of formal US colonial rule.

Kuokoa Home Rula, a Profusion of Moʻolelo, and Advocacy for Kanaka and Our Language, 1907–1909

Issues from the first six years of *Kuokoa Home Rula*, an important medium for politics and literature, are not available to us. Thus we begin our review with the issues of the paper that we have, the first being the single issue of 1907. The paper overall runs a mix similar to that in *Ka Naʻi Aupuni* but with more editorials and more news. The front page typically has moʻolelo, either a translation like "He Moolelo no ka Hooilina o Rivela" (A story of the heir, Rivela) or moʻolelo kuʻuna like Poepoe's own "Ka Moolelo Kaao o Hiiaka-i-ka-Poli-o-Pele," or "Ka Moolelo Hiwahiwa o Kawelo" by Hooulumahiehie-i-ka-oni-malie-a-pua-lilia-lana-i-ka-wai (most likely a variation of Hooulumahiehie). These works of literature rotated among the first, third, and fourth pages of the paper.[129]

In the first issue preserved, we see on the front page a reprint of Poepoe's plea to his peers to perpetuate the Hawaiian language (originally published in *Ka Naʻi Aupuni* in 1906).[130] Poepoe also runs a story about March 17, the birthday of Kauikeaouli, Kamehameha III, the long-reigning Mōʻī. Kauikeaouli is said to have been stillborn, and the kahuna and seer Kapihe prayed and brought him back to life. This story contains the text of the prayer and an explanation of the name Kauikeaouli (Placed in a dark cloud).[131] The calendar in the paper includes the names of the monthly moon nights along with the haole names for the days of the week. These kinds of articles are common throughout Poepoe's time as editor; he was committed to using the native tongue, along with its literature, cultural practices, and native-centered historiography. One gem is Peleioholani's account of the ceremony to start training in moʻolelo and moʻokūʻauhau, which includes hints about how Kauikeaouli and Liholiho II (Kamehameha III and IV) cultivated intellectuals—an important part of our intellectual history that needs more research.[132]

Kuokoa Home Rula was also the weekly publication of the Independent Home Rule Party. Notley, the owner, was a perennial candidate for delegate to the US Congress and Poepoe himself ran for the territorial senate with the Home Rule Party in the 1908 election. Poepoe was called "Ko Hawaii Pohakuhauoli" (Hawaiʻi's Gladstone).[133] All the candidates made a point of using or emphasizing their Hawaiian names. Notley was always called Kahiliaulani; Poepoe's name was J. Mokuohai Poepoe; Geo. Beckley was Mooheau, the sole name that runs under his photo in the issue of October 26, 1908. They were proud of their Hawaiianness and Hawaiian names during this time when assimilationism was ramping up. Poepoe expressed political opinions every week and ran guest editorials by Home Rule Party politicians like David Kalauokalani.

The look and contents of the newspaper reflect the rise of English and the weakening of Hawaiian in the country. In November 1908, for example, Poepoe ran an editorial titled "E A'o i ka Olelo Beritania" (Learn English). While he hadn't given up his advocacy for the language or his love of mo'olelo, in this editorial he encouraged young people to learn to speak English well, for familiar reasons: to be able to get a better job, have a career, become famous perhaps. He notes that the Hale Lunamaka'āinana (House of Representatives) was the last place in government where Hawaiian was to be heard, and he wondered how long that would last. He also seems to blame voters who elected representatives that would do nothing to change the shift of everything to English. He ends the editorial with "Mai huhu i ka Home Rula, ea!" (Don't be angry with the Home Rule Party!).[134] In the same month, he began to publish articles and tidbits in English, some in a column on page 1 or 2, called "Our English Items." For seven weeks in 1909, Poepoe offers the Hawaiian text along with English translations of some of the chants from the Hi'iaka mo'olelo and one contemporary song.[135] He used the "English Items" column to explain terms in Hawaiian, like "poi" and to publish wahi pana, such as "The Legend of Kou Harbor" (Honolulu).[136] It was during this same time period that he ran "Hawaiian Astronomy" in English. All of these English items stopped when Poepoe left the paper, so it is safe to surmise that these were his translations and his own writing in English.

In this paper, as in the majority of Hawaiian-language papers, reporters kept in touch with the exiled Hansen's disease patients on Molokai. In 1908 Poepoe and *Kuokoa* brawled politically with the Board of Health about a physician who claimed he could cure the disease. The discursive battle went on in the pages of the papers for months. The Board of Health wouldn't allow the doctor to treat patients, while Poepoe and many others fought fiercely to let him give his treatments a chance. In this era, the quarantine settlement on Molokai was often called "ka 'āina o ka 'eha'eha" (the land of pain).[137] After this crisis passed, letters from patients living in the settlement were published frequently and concern for their welfare continued throughout the life of the paper. The idea that exiled Hansen's disease patients were forgotten is proven untrue in these pages.[138]

This newspaper kept readers informed of world events, some that seemed threatening to Hawaiians and other people of color in Hawaiʻi and in other colonies around Oceania. One example is the arrival of President Theodore Roosevelt's "Great White Fleet," an armada of sixteen or seventeen battleships accompanied by other ships. Marilyn Lake and Henry Reynolds quote Roosevelt saying,

> We have got to build up our western country with our white civilisation, and (very vehemently) we must retain the power to say who shall or who shall not come to our country. Now it may be that Japan will adopt a different attitude, will demand that her people be permitted to go where they think fit, so I thought it wise to send that fleet around to the Pacific to be ready to maintain our rights.[139]

Roosevelt's administration was intent on excluding further Japanese labor immigration, and that was nowhere more likely than in Hawaiʻi. Roosevelt was also keen to have the fleet visit Australia and New Zealand to "show England . . . that those colonies were white man's country."[140] The story in *Kuokoa Home Rula* reported that the fleet stopped in Hawaiʻi on its way to the Philippines and noted that it was meant as a warning to Japan. In the same edition a story ran about the impending arrival of Filipino workers on the plantations.

The July 30, 1909, issue was Poepoe's last as editor. The staff of the paper ran a paragraph showing their aloha for him and sadness about his departure:

> Ke haawi aku nei makou i ko makou aloha ame ko makou hoomaikai i ko makou makua a Luna Hooponopono nupepa Kuokoa Home Rula, ka ipu kukui a waha olelo nana i na'i Kauakukalahale nei a me na huli Koolau. Aloha kakou. O ke aloha o makou o kau mau keiki o ka na'i pu ana, hele pu ana i ka po a me ke ao, ka ua a me ka makani, aohe poka dainamaita nana e wawahi ko makou puuwai. O ke aloha, eia mau no ia i ka puuwai nou. O kau huaolelo auanei e Papa J. M. Poepoe ka makou e hoomau opuu rose ae ma ko makou umauma. "Mai hopohopo." So Good-bye kakou me ke aloha walania.[141]

We give our aloha and gratitude to our parent and editor of *Kuokoa Home Rula*, the lighthouse and spokesperson who conquered the Kūkalahale rain [Honolulu] and the two Koʻolau. Aloha among us. The love of the children who strove with you, going together night and day, in the rain and wind, no stick of dynamite could break our hearts' feeling for you. The aloha for you continues in the heart. Your word, Papa J. M. Poepoe, is our inspiration to continue like rosebuds blooming in our chests. "Don't worry." We say goodbye sadly.

The Switch to the Democratic Party: *Ke Aloha Aina*, Election to the Territorial Legislature, and the Passing of a Great Writer and Editor, 1909–1913

Just one week after Poepoe left *Kuokoa Home Rula* his name was listed as an editor in *Ke Aloha Aina*. *Ke Aloha Aina* had been founded in 1895 by Joseph Nāwahī as the Hui Aloha ʻĀina paper, and it was continued after his death the following year by his widow, Emma Aima Nāwahī, and her nephew, Edward Like. After annexation and the 1900 Organic Act, Nāwahī and Like sided with the Democratic Party, and thus the paper became a voice for that party. The paper was owned by a hui (company) with Nāwahī as president and Like as vice president and editor until January 2, 1909, when Lincoln McCandless became president and Nāwahī evidently retired. Like remained as an editor until Poepoe took over.

Poepoe's leaving *Kuokoa Home Rula* for *Ke Aloha Aina* was the result of his decision to leave the Home Rule Party and join the Democratic Party. His first editorial outlined his reasons for switching parties, extolling the virtues of the Democratic Party, including its support for labor and equal rights for all. He does not write anything negative about the party and paper that he just left.[142]

McCandless was a wealthy landowner involved in diverting water from the Koʻolau side of the island to the dry leeward side to irrigate sugar plantations. Jacqueline Lasky notes,

> Artesian well diggers Lincoln Loy McCandless and his brothers, James and John, were key developers of Hawaiʻi's sugar industry and participants in the 1893 overthrow of the Hawaiian Kingdom. By the early 20th century, "Link" was among the top ten landowners in Hawaiʻi, owning or controlling most of Waiāhole and Waikāne valleys among other large tracts of land.[143]

In the pages of *Ke Aloha Aina*, McCandless is most often referred to as "Linekona Eliwai," "ʻeliwai" meaning "digger for water." Although he was a large landowner and employer, he was a dedicated Democrat. The party in these years was aligned closely with the Hui Uniona, the labor unions, and the Socialist Party as well.

At this time, *Ka Nupepa Kuokoa* was still being published and was affiliated with the Republican Party, with a Kanaka, Solomon Hanohano, as editor. *Kuokoa Home Rula* also remained in print, with the owner (and perennial candidate) Charles Kahiliaulani Notley as the editor. In Hilo, Stephen Desha was publishing his long-lived paper, *Hoku o Hawaii*. John Wise was the editor of *Ke Au Hou*, which was published weekly from 1910 to 1912 and resembled a magazine more than a newspaper, both in length and content. The volume and vitality of these publications in Hawaiian affirm that politics was conducted in the Hawaiian language among a large portion of Hawaiʻi's people well into the twentieth century, across a wide political spectrum, and that many writers produced Hawaiian literature. With the exception of *Kuokoa Home Rula*, Poepoe engaged in debates and disputes with writers from each of these papers within the pages of *Ke Aloha Aina*. It is noteworthy that all of these papers were publishing moʻolelo and other works of literature in the Hawaiian language. They were all engaged in trying to prevent the death of the language and its many literary forms.

Ke Aloha Aina under Poepoe ran a familiar mix of world and local news, human interest stories, political stories and editorials, moʻolelo kuʻuna, and foreign moʻolelo translated into Hawaiian. Readers were clearly interested in both moʻolelo kuʻuna and translated moʻolelo. Hoʻoulumāhiehie, mentioned above, appears as the author of several moʻolelo in *Ke Aloha Aina*. In the four years of Poepoe's editorship, four long serialized moʻolelo kuʻuna were published, three of which form a trilogy. The first is the "Moolelo Hoonaue Puuwai no Kama-a-ka-Mahiai, Ka Hiʻapaiʻole o ka Ikaika o ke Kai Huki Hee Nehu o Kahului" (A heart-stirring story about Kamaakamahiai, the expert in strength of the sea of anchovy fishing of Kahului, Maui), which appears in the first issue of this paper that Poepoe edited.[144] The Kamaakamahiʻai moʻolelo runs until March 11, 1911, when Hoʻoulumāhiehie signs the moʻolelo, and he notes that the story is at an end, but that the story of Kamaakamahiʻai's child, Kahelekūlani, will continue under the same title. On December 2, 1911, this moʻolelo of Kahelekūlani ends and is signed with another pen name, Na-Hau-o-Maihi—Au Ana i ke Kai. The following February, the third story in the series, "Ka Moolelo Hooni Puuwai no Keakaoku, ka Moopuna Leo Ole a Kamaakamahiai, a o ke Koa Nana i Wehe i na Pu Kaula a Makalii," about the grandchild of Kamaakamahiʻai, begins, and is also signed by Na-Hau-o-Maihi—Au Ana i ke Kai.[145] It seems reasonable to infer that Na-Hau-o-Maihi is another pen name for Hoʻoulumāhiehie, itself the pen name for Poepoe and his colleagues who had been collecting and publishing moʻolelo kuʻuna since 1905.[146]

Another long and complete epic in these years is "Moolelo Nani o Kekalukaluokewa" (A beautiful Hawaiian story of Kekalukaluokewa), which ran from March 12, 1910, to November 18, 1911. Its preface describes it as somewhat like the story of Kamaakamahiʻai, a Maui story, but of Kauaʻi. Unfortunately, the author is unknown as the final installment is merely signed "Mea Kakau" (Author).

Translations of several European and American stories were published during Poepoe's tenure at *Ke Aloha Aina*. It is sometimes difficult to determine whether a story is a translation or the work of an author writing in Hawaiian but setting the story in Europe or the United States. For example, "He Moolelo no ka Naita Leopaki a i Ole he Nanea no ke Kaua Kerusade Ekolu ma Palesekina" (A story of the Knight Leopold, or a fascinating tale of the Third Crusade in Palestine) might seem like a translation, but Poepoe takes credit as its author.[147]

Ke Aloha Aina printed the Democratic Party's platform in the 1912 campaign leading up to the election for members of the territorial legislature as well as for the nonvoting delegate to the US Congress. In addition to the party platform, Poepoe promoted both statehood for Hawaiʻi and the cause of women's suffrage. His daughter, Cecilia Sharpe, served as the secretary for Hawaiʻi's association of women working for the vote, and she published the accounts of their meetings in *Ke Aloha Aina*. In ways reminiscent of the anti-annexation organizing, the women held mass meetings in Honolulu and traveled around Oʻahu (and presumably to other islands) assisting women in various communities to establish branches of the organization.[148] In addition to reporting on the women's hui, Sharpe published a long editorial in her father's paper advocating both statehood and the vote for women.[149] She writes well and colorfully in Hawaiian, taking after her father. Here is a portion of her account of a train ride that took the vote-seeking women around the western point of Oʻahu, from Honolulu to Kahuku on the north shore:

> Haalele ka liohao ia Kuwili Hale Hoolulu. He naueue mai hoi tau i ka lawe haaheo a ka liohao e u-hi-u-ha nei ma kona alahele. Ike ae la i ka Ua Poolipilipi o Kalihi; kapeke i Kahauiki; pahee pono i Moanalua;

ike ia Kinimakalehua; hama-hamau ka leo ia Ewauli; hoomanalo ka wai i Waimanalo; kaalo ana Puuohulu; ike ia Kanepuniu; he nani okoa no o Maunalahilahi; moe kokolo i na Keaau; ike i ke one opiopio o Makua, lei ana [K]oiahi i ka maile laulii, kau aheahe i Mokuleia, ani peahi ana o Kawaikumuole, kiei i ke kowa o Waimea, ike i na hala o Kahuku hoea i Keana (Hale Hoolulu Kaaʻhi) hora 12.[150]

The iron horse departed Kūwili Hale Hoʻolulu [Honolulu Rail Station]. There was a great movement of the iron horse puffing and blowing as it proudly took off on its tracks. We saw the Adze Head Rain of Kalihi; revealed Kahauiki; slid right through Moanalua; saw Kinimakalehua, the mountain rain called Countless Lehua Blossoms; the voices were silenced by ʻEwauli [a reference to oyster fishing in ʻEwa]; removed the saltiness of the water (mānalo) at Waimānalo; passed Puʻuohulu; saw Kānepūniu; Maunalahilahi was completely beautiful; crawled around the areas called Keaʻau; saw the young sands of Mākua; Koʻiahi was draped in maile lauliʻi [a reference to places in Mākua Valley and also the fragrant maile vine that grows there]; the breeze appeared at Mokulēʻia; Kawaikumuʻole was beckoning; we looked into the valley of Waimea; saw the hala trees of Kahuku; and arrived at Keana, the train station, at noon.

This description shows off Sharpe's knowledge of the winds, rains, place names, and lore of the places the train passed during their journey. It is perhaps also a testament to the linguistic and cultural knowledge of readers of Hawaiian in 1912.

Poepoe, previously an ever-hopeful candidate of both the Home Rule and Democratic parties, was finally elected to the territorial legislature. He took office on February 19, 1913. There are no issues of his paper *Ke Aloha Aina* accessible for this time, so we do not have a picture of his efforts at lawmaking on behalf of the lāhui from the perspective of a source close to him.

The last issue of *Ke Aloha Aina* that bears his name as an editor also bears his unmistakable hand in its content. On page 4 are two unsigned editorials worrying about the state of our native language and literature and advocating for instruction in Hawaiian, its literature, grammar, and other branches of knowledge.[151] Poepoe writes,

Ia makou i huli aku ai a nana he mea ehaeha no, no ka naau ka hoohemahemaia ana o ka moolelo o ko kakou aina i ke aʻo ole ia ma na kula a pela i lilo ai ka hanauna hou i poe ike a hoomaopopo ole i ke ano o ko lakou nohona lahui ana mai kinohi mai.[152]

When we look at it, it is very painful [to see] the neglect or ignorance of the hi/stories/literature of our ʻāina because they are not being taught in the schools, and that is how the younger generation become people who do not know or comprehend their culture from the beginning [of their history].

This seems like a sad prediction of what happened to the majority of Kānaka of those generations that followed him in the twentieth century: US policies of assimilation deprived them of their native language and their own histories and literature. With rare exceptions, they became people who did not fully comprehend their culture.

Joseph Mokuʻōhai Poepoe died on April 10, 1913, just a few months after these last acts of advocacy were published. Through all of the political twists and turns of his long writing career, his love of the Hawaiian language and its literature remained constant. His moʻokūʻauhau consciousness shines through these hundreds of pages, right through the dark age of the twentieth century to today. All of us who are able to read Hawaiian today owe him our gratitude. His moʻolelo and essays supporting our native language articulate what he, the others in his hui moʻolelo, and unknown others believed that led to a few kīpuka (enclaves) of people keeping Hawaiian alive in classrooms, churches, and family life.[153]

I think he would be amazed and very pleased to see, one hundred years later, today's younger generations embracing our native language and literature, not the least of which are many of the works from his own pen and newspapers. Chapters 5 and 6 provide an examination of two of those works, which further elaborate his firm foundation of moʻokūʻauhau consciousness.

5

Singing (to) the ʻĀina

This chapter is a study of mele about the ʻāina in Joseph Poepoe's moʻolelo of Hiʻiakaikapoliopele. The bulk of the moʻolelo concerns Hiʻiaka's epic journey across almost the entire archipelago from its easternmost point on Hawaiʻi to Kauaʻi in the west, and back again. Hiʻiaka is sent on this journey by her elder sister, the volcano (deity) Pele, to fetch Pele's lover on Kauaʻi and take him back to Kīlauea, Pele's home on Hawaiʻi. When Hiʻiaka agrees to undertake the journey, she also leaves her own lover,[1] the young woman Hōpoe, making Pele promise not to harm her. Hiʻiaka travels along the north side of the islands, stopping at Maui, Molokai, and Oʻahu along the way, then returns along the south side of these same islands on the way back. At each place that she stops, she and/or others sing or chant mele to or about the ʻāina, and ʻāina characters sing or chant back to her. This chapter examines selections of these mele for their artistry and what they tell us about the ʻāina and the worldviews or epistemologies and ontologies of our kūpuna. These mele serve as examples of our kūpuna's moʻokūʻauhau consciousness, which includes Poepoe's care to record the moʻolelo and explain some of its many mele for generations of Hawaiians in a future he foresaw.

Several versions of the moʻolelo were written and published in Hawaiian before Poepoe's (and there is one afterward). kuʻualoha hoʻomanawanui details and analyzes this body of literature in *Voices of Fire: Reweaving the Literary Lei of Pele and Hiʻiaka*. John Charlot notes Poepoe's contribution to this body of literature in this way:

Poepoe was a masterful stylist with an extensive vocabulary, which he used with great smoothness and precision. As seen in his book on King Kalākaua (1891), he was a student of classical Hawaiian rhetoric, which he deploys on appropriate occasions in his series. He shares many of Hoʻoulumāhiehie's late nineteenth-century characteristics as a writer, such as using an encyclopedic style to preserve vocabulary and customs, and explaining and interpreting his material; he even draws out the stages of a story to make it clearer and adds descriptions of the psychological and emotional factors involved.[2]

As Charlot explains, Poepoe often teaches readers various ways to interpret the mele, cluing us in to embedded kaona, foreshadowing, and other literary devices that we may miss without his kōkua, or what hoʻomanawanui calls authorial asides.[3] I interpret Poepoe's assistance as evidence of his moʻokūʻauhau consciousness, as he foresees our generations who grow up deprived of the knowledge of our kupuna that would allow us to interpret on our own. I see this as Poepoe taking opportunities to teach his descendants.

Poepoe's version of this moʻolelo is unique in other aspects as well. Each version is a separate literary work, based on some combination of the author or authors' home knowledge, manuscripts that were sought out, and previously published versions. Poepoe had been the owner and editor of the newspaper *Ka Naʻi Aupuni*, and he had published a version of the Hiʻiaka moʻolelo by Hoʻoulumāhiehie in that paper. In his introduction, Poepoe writes that his is a new publication of the moʻolelo:

> A ma keia hoomaka hou ana o ka Hiiaka, e ikeia ana he mau aui ana i ko kekahi mau mahelehele i puka mua ai maloko o ka nupepa *Ka Naʻi Aupuni* ma ka M. H. 1906. O keia mau aui hou e ikeia ana ma keia puka ana mamuli o ka loaa hou ana mai i ko makou mea kakau moolelo, he Hiiaka i kapaia o ko Maui Hiiaka ia. O ka mahele Hiiaka mua i puka ai ma *Ka Naʻi Aupuni* . . . ua oleloia o ko Hawaii Hiiaka ia.[4]

> In this new beginning of the Hiʻiaka [moʻolelo], it will be seen that there are variations from some of the sections that had been published previously in *Ka Naʻi Aupuni* in 1906. These new variations will be seen in this publication because our author [i.e., Poepoe himself] has newly obtained a Hiʻiaka [moʻolelo] that is called Maui's Hiʻiaka. The version of Hiʻiaka published before in *Ka Naʻi Aupuni* . . . is said to be Hawaiʻi [Island's] Hiʻiaka.

Poepoe also incorporated elements from the Hawai'i Island version, as is evident in the subtitle "I hooponopono hou ia elike me na maawe Moolelo Hiiaka a ko Hawaii ame Maui" (Newly edited in accordance with the Hi'iaka Mo'olelo strands of Hawai'i and Maui's people).

In addition, based on ho'omanawanui's careful charting of all the mele in all the known versions of the Pele and Hi'iaka literature, it appears that nearly one hundred mele appear in Poepoe's version only.[5] That is a tremendous wealth of literary production, which alone would justify a careful reading of this mo'olelo.

Poepoe's mo'olelo was published in weekly installments in *Kuokoa Home Rula* from January 1908 to January 1911. Its concentrated focus on the 'āina and its divine nature, as revealed by the many spiritual characters who interact with Hi'iaka, many of whom inhabit kino lau such as plants, animals, land features, forests, and so forth, can inspire us today to envision a more Hawaiian world. I imagine that Poepoe himself, faced with an increasingly foreign Hawai'i, inhabited by American fortune-seekers and the US military, sought, by writing this elaborate version, to inspire and perhaps provoke in the young people a desire for a more Hawaiian world. He was very concerned about young peoples' lack of knowledge of Hawaiian-language literature, which I interpret as part of this decolonial desire (see the introduction). For this chapter, I focus on the "people" of the 'āina who, if restored, would greatly contribute to this vision. It seems to me that as so-called development ravages more and more of our lands, more and more of our 'aumākua and akua in their kino lau are destroyed. As we work to undo such destruction, we also restore our divine kin, who are then returned to their rightful places in our physical world and who are then more able to play their parts in our mental, emotional, and spiritual lives. In the 1893 version of the Hi'iaka mo'olelo, John E. "Ailuene" Bush wrote,

> Aole he loihi o ka noho ana o ka lahui a nalo aku mai ke ao, ke hoomaloka a hoopoina lakou i ka hiipoi ana me na ohohia nui i na moolelo a ma na mele o na ano a pau, a kamailio mau imua o ka poe opio i kumu e mau ai na hooipo a me na li'a ana o ka naau o ke kanaka i ke aloha aina mamuli o ka hooni ana o na moolelo a me na mele e pili ana i kona one hanau, na wahi pana, a me na hana kaulana a kona mau kupuna.[6]

> It would not be long before a lāhui would disappear from the world should they disbelieve and forget to actively cherish the moʻolelo and mele of every kind, and continually discuss them in front of their young people as a way to perpetuate the romantic love and desire of the heart [gut] of the person for the love of the land. How stirring are the moʻolelo and mele about his/her birth sands, the storied places, and the famous deeds of his/her ancestors.

Bush, the great aloha ʻāina fighter for the independence of our nation, and an outspoken newspaper editor, here explicitly links remembering the moʻolelo and mele to the ideology of aloha ʻāina, and he argues that disparaging and forgetting the moʻolelo and mele will cause us to lose our identity as the lāhui Hawaiʻi. He argues that we must read, recite, and discuss the moʻolelo so that our young people love their own land and respect our ancestors. Just eleven days after this was published, a conspiracy of haole businessmen and the US minister to Hawaiʻi overthrew the native government. Fifteen years later, in his own introduction to his new version of the same moʻolelo, Poepoe writes (and, unfortunately, some words are illegible on the surviving copy),

> E hoomaopopoia, eia na poe naauao o kakou iho nei a me ko na aina e ke apu mai nei i na moolelo kahiko o Hawaii nei, [a o ka] kakou poe opio naau—[naaupo or naauao] hoi, ke hoohemahema nui nei i keia kumu waiwai nui o ka aina oiwi. Aohe huli, aohe imi, aohe no he makemake [i] ia mau mea. Aka, no makou iho, ke hoomau nei makou i keia hana no ka makemake maoli e hoouluia a hoomauia aku ka ikeia ana o na moolelo a kaao kahiko o Hawaii nei i hiki ai ke malamaia e kakou, ka lahui.[7]

> It should be understood that there are educated people of ours as well as others from foreign lands that are snatching up [and destroying] the ancient moʻolelo of Hawaiʻi, while our [un-/educated] young people are greatly neglecting this great treasure of the native land. There is no research or seeking out, nor any desire for these things. However, for ourselves, we are continuing this work out of a genuine desire to collect and to perpetuate the knowledge of the moʻolelo and kaʻao of Hawaiʻi so that they can be cared for [or preserved] by us, the lāhui.

I read Poepoe here as saying that, just fifteen years after the overthrow of the native government, because the United States had instituted its forms of education and vastly accelerated an almost complete shift to the English language, young Kānaka were not seeking out the moʻolelo of their own land and their own ancestors. No doubt this was generally true, as young people sought to make their way in the newly Americanizing world they found themselves in, and as their own parents and grandparents encouraged them to abandon the Hawaiian language and culture so that they could prosper in the colony. Around the same time, Nathaniel Emerson, Thomas Thrum, and W. D. Westervelt were writing distorted and destructive English-language versions of our moʻolelo and here Poepoe criticizes their actions. As hoʻomanawanui explains,

> Haole settlers such as Nathaniel B. Emerson, Abraham Fornander, William D. Westervelt, and Thomas G. Thrum also collected and published moʻolelo kuʻuna (under the rubric of folklore) with the aid of Native "informants." Publishing Hawaiian legends, myths, and folklore under their own names, they claimed an authority (kuleana) over the moʻolelo they did not have, and reframed the moʻolelo to forward settler agendas.[8]

This must have been sad and infuriating to Poepoe as he had been a witness and contributor in the decades when literature in Hawaiian flourished. At the time of this publication, he now witnessed an abandonment of integral parts of Kanaka identity: our language, literature, and aloha ʻāina. Like his predecessor Kānepuʻu, however, he foresaw the generations of the late twentieth century and beyond who are now embracing what our more recent kūpuna were denied. When he says at the end that we, the lāhui, should keep the moʻolelo, he is specifically talking to and about the lāhui Kanaka Hawaiʻi, because these moʻolelo are necessary parts of ourselves. Leilani Basham writes,

> ʻO ko kākou manaʻo nō ka mea nui, a he pono hoʻi ka hoʻomaopopo ʻana a me ka hahai ʻana i nā mea o ko kākou poʻe kūpuna i kuhi pono ai. Wahi a lākou, ʻaʻole nō ʻike ʻia ka Lāhui Hawaiʻi ma kona koko a me kona ʻili. ʻIke ʻia nō naʻe ka Lāhui Hawaiʻi ma nā ʻano like ʻole, e laʻa me ka moʻokūʻauhau, ʻoiai, he pili ko ka Lāhui i kona poʻe kūpuna a i ka ʻāina hoʻi.[9]

Our own ideas/beliefs are the important thing, and it is right that we strive to understand and follow the ways that our ancestors directed us to. According to them, the Lāhui Hawaiʻi is not known or recognized by its blood or skin. The Lāhui Hawaiʻi is known by its various features, including moʻokūʻauhau, since the Lāhui has a close relationship to our ancestors and our land.

Here we can follow the progression of the moʻokūʻauhau of indigenous Kanaka thought and belief from our ancient ancestors, to Poepoe of the early twentieth century, to Basham of the early twenty-first century. For both Basham and hoʻomanawanui, it is crucial that we study and understand the moʻolelo as written by native writers such as Poepoe—and specifically *not* in the distorted forms by the writers mentioned above or other shortened or Americanized forms—in order to understand ourselves and to thrive as a lāhui.

Mele as Maps in Poepoe's Hiʻiaka

Many mele in this moʻolelo can help us comprehend how our ancestors understood their relationships with ʻāina, including how they ordered places in mind and text. As is the case in Kānepuʻu's work, we can see the sensual nature of the poetry and thus how some of the mele can be thought of as performance cartography. In the way that they are ordered we can also view some of them as maps. The mele in the Hiʻiaka moʻolelo are some of the best examples of the Kanaka value of aloha ʻāina, because they portray the ʻāina as living relatives who chant and act in many different ways, and because the mele extol the beauty and other features of the ʻāina. Because land formations, plants, and other natural elements are kin and precede Kanaka in cosmogonical genealogies like the Kumulipo, they are also ancestors in our collective moʻokūʻauhau.

In an earlier study, I examined Pele's calling of the winds in this moʻolelo.[10] One of the many functions of her calling the hundreds of names of winds on the western islands of Nihoa, Lehua, Kaʻula, Niʻihau, and Kauaʻi, is what Poepoe himself termed its "kulana panoonoo," which I interpret as "remembering function," and which hoʻomanawanui glosses as "repetitive memory device."[11] The wind names are remembered by their specific places, and they are usually chanted in a relatively orderly way around each island, either clockwise or counterclockwise, as in this excerpt:

He Kiuwaiula ko Kikiaola,
He Waialae ko Koaie,
He Kumulipo-hooulualii ko Mokihana,
He Waikea ko Waiahulu.[12]

Kīkīaola has a wind named Kiuwaiʻula,
Koaiʻe has a Waiʻalae wind,
Mokihana has a Kumulipo-hoʻoulualiʻi wind,
Waiahulu has a Waikea wind.

The chant functions as a kind of a map in that one could follow the place names and make a circuit of the island. Poepoe was a bit concerned that his readers might find the lists of places and their winds tedious, but he was committed to recording them in the paper in order to pass this knowledge down to us and to the generations after us.

Here I interpret one other mele that functions similarly as a kind of map of the moku (district) of Puna. The mele is a love song that Hiʻiaka sings to her aikāne, the young woman Hōpoe. As they journey farther away from Hiʻiaka's home of Puna, she becomes more bereft at leaving Hōpoe. At Laupāhoehoe, she stops, weeps in sorrow, and then chants this mele.[13] I give a brief translation here with numbers in parentheses that correspond to areas within figure 5.1. I have also retained the numbers of the lines themselves from the original publication in order to make the interpretation easier to follow. The translation does not explain the mele, which is analyzed below, nor does it do it any justice, but I offer it as assistance for readers unable to read Hawaiian.

1. E kuu aikane i ke kai hee o Hoeu maloko
2. O Awili mawaho i kai popolo-hua o Kalaloa
3. A he kai heenalu ia me kuu aikane i ka ulu niu e—
4. O Makena i ka wai-akolea
5. I ka maunu opae ula a ka lawai[a] e—
6. I ka opule moe one o ke kai e—
7. I Kalapana maua me kuu aikane,
8. I ka niu kulakulai a na ʻlii ai ahupuaa
9. O Kupahua i Kalapana i Kaunaloa a—
10. A he aina—

11. Aia kuu aikane la i na hala o Halaaniani
12. I Kapaahu a p[a]e i kai o Kamilopaekanaka e—
13. I Kau e—
14. I Kahaualea e—
15. I Pahoehoe e—
16. A i Poupoukea a he aina,
17. Aia ke ola i ka lae laau—a—e—
18. Ike ia Kamoamoa i Pahoehoe,
19. Pali kuu aina,
20. I Poupou—
21. I Leapuki—
22. I Panau-iki—
23. I Panau-nui—
24. I ka Pāhoehoe—
25. I ka ulu ohia—
26. Kuu aikane i Kealakomo i Apua,
27. Okioki aho—
28. Pale o Puna, pale o Kau i Mawae e—
29. I kaawale o Hilo
30. Kuu aikane hoi e—
31. Aloha—e—o—e—o—e—

1. My aikāne in the surfing sea of Hōʻeu (3) inside [near shore perhaps]
2. ʻĀwili is outside in the purplish-blue sea of Kalaloa [Kanaloa]
3. This a sea to surf in with my aikāne near the coconut grove(s)
4. Mākena (5) in the ʻākōlea water, or the pond called Waiʻākōlea
5. The red shrimp bait of the fisher
6. The ʻōpule fish [a wrasse] of the sea who sleeps in the sand
7. My aikāne and I at Kalapana (6)
8. The pushed-over or bent-over coconut trees of the ahupuaʻa-ruling aliʻi
9. Kupahuʻa (7) in Kalapana, in Kaunaloa (9)
10. And it is an ʻāina
11. My aikāne is there in the hala trees of Halaaniani
12. At Kapaʻahu (10) and landing on shore at Kamilopaekanaka
13. At Kaʻū
14. At Kahaualeʻa (11)

15. At Pāhoehoe
16. And at Poupoukea (12), which is an ʻāina
17. Life is in the wooded/forested point or cape
18. Kamoamoa (14) at Pāhoehoe is seen
19. My ʻāina is clifflike
20. At Poupou
21. At Lēʻapuki (15)
22. At Pānauiki (16)
23. At Pānaunui (17)
24. In the Pāhoehoe
25. In the ʻōhiʻa grove
26. My aikāne at Kealakomo (18) at ʻĀpua (20)
27. Cutting off the breath [or cutting the line, cord, or lashing]
28. Separating Puna from Kaʻū at Māwae [the fissure]
29. So that Hilo [braided] will be separate
30. My aikāne
31. You are beloved

This song resembles a mourning song, a kanikau of an uē helu type, which recounts the activities the composer and the person who died did together, as well as the places they went. Here Hiʻiaka mourns not only her days of love and play, especially surfing, with Hōpoe, but also having to leave the ʻāina itself. She names the lands of the Kalapana region starting with Hōʻeu (in Kaimū, number 3 in the figure) in the east, and proceeding westward to ʻĀpua (number 20) on the border of Kaʻū in the west. If one follows the numbers in parentheses in the translation above when looking at the map below, it is clear that the names appear roughly in order from east to west.

In addition, the place names are chosen for their metaphoric or symbolic value (not every place name in the area is included). Several of the places are surfing spots and surfing recalls the romantic relationship between the two women. The first place name, Hōʻeu, is glossed in the Pukui and Elbert Hawaiian dictionary as "to stir up." The next, ʻĀwili, means to be intertwined and/or agitated, describing their entwinement with each other, as well as how they are both intertwined with the land itself. The poet had to borrow this place name from nearby Kaimū in order to get this sense into the chant. Mākena means "abundance," but spelled without the kahakō (macron) it evokes mourning, as "makena" glosses as "mourning, wailing, lamentation" and so forth.[14] The fish, ʻōpule moe one, or the ʻōpule who sleeps in the sand,

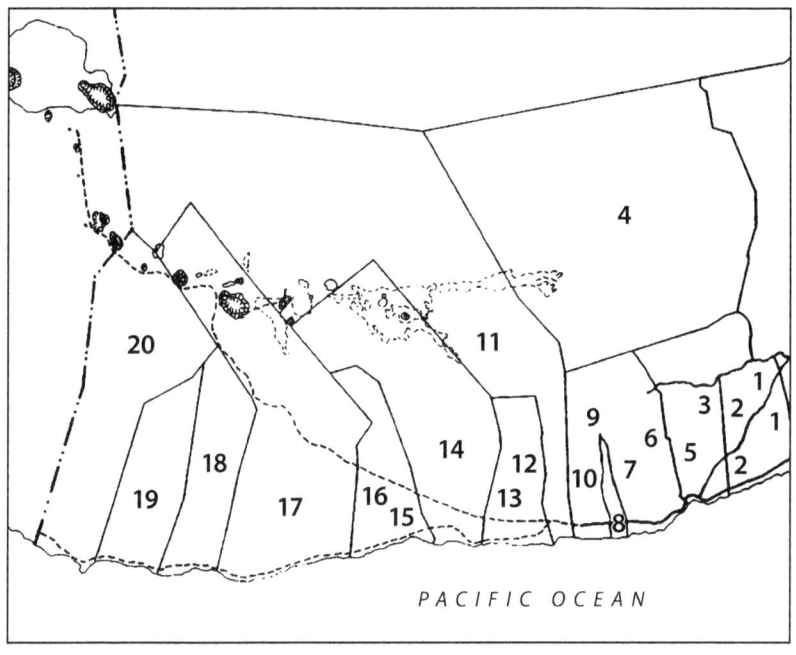

FIGURE 5.1

Map of the ahupuaʻa of the Kalapana region. The numbers on the map correspond to the numbers following the place names in the translation of the mele.

evokes prayer (pule), perhaps an appeal to Pele to spare Hōpoe, and the word "moe" (sleep) can refer to both death and sex. "Hilo," at the end of line 29, means "braided together," and thus the line "I kaawale o Hilo" refers to the separation of Hiʻiaka from Hōpoe and from Puna.

Some words and place names describe the trees and forest plants of the area. Kalapana is famous for its coconut trees made to bend low as if bowing in honor of visiting aliʻi (line 8).[15] The poet here, rather than use the much more common term "niu moe," or "sleeping or lying down coconut tree," has chosen "ka niu kulakulaʻi," a different saying that refers to aliʻi pushing over the trees, probably in acts of battle.[16] Kulakulaʻi is a reduplicated form of kulaʻi, meaning "to push over, knock down, overthrow, shove, push to one side; to brush off, as a horse switches flies with its tail; to dash to pieces . . . ; to hurl."[17] This more violent term is suggestive of Hōpoe's impending death from Pele's lava flow, as well as Hiʻiaka's turbulent emotions as she leaves the one she loves. It also reminds the reader of Kalapana's landscape, always ravaged by lava. The ʻōhiʻa (the tree that bears lehua flowers) is closely identified with both Hiʻiaka and Hōpoe; Hōpoe is named after the lehua in full blossom and the lehua grove that she frequents. The ʻōhiʻa is one of the first trees to grow after a fresh lava flow and is thus equated with Hiʻiaka, who represents the greening of the land after Pele creates it.[18] Line 11 refers to the region's hala (pandanus) trees, which provide lauhala for woven hats, mats, and sails. "Hala" also means "to pass by" and "to pass on," thus also expressing Hiʻiaka's sadness at leaving and foreshadowing Hōpoe's death.

At the end of the song are three lines further expressing the sadness Hiʻiaka feels at separating from Hōpoe and from the ʻāina of Kalapana, using the place name "Māwae," which, in addition to indicating separation, glosses as "cleft, fissure, crevice, crack, as in rocks; to crack, split, cleave."[19] This creates an image for us of the volcanic ʻāina and Pele's passionate nature, which bring about not just this separation of Hiʻiaka embarking on the journey, but the more permanent one away from Hōpoe.

Besides poetic land descriptions that function as maps as in the mele above, other mele in this moʻolelo express the identification of people, akua, ʻaumākua, kupua, and so on, with ʻāina, that is, specific landforms, plants, and other elements in the natural world. Pualani Kanahele teaches us about the chants in the Hiʻiaka epic:

> Chants describe forms and patterns in the natural world, including nature's endowment for life and destruction. These natural elements were visible, immediate, and constant for our ancestors, and the generic term accorded to these forebears is akua, or gods. These akua have specific names and designations based on their form, function, and characteristics.[20]

We can see that in the Hawaiian philosophy expressed in the moʻolelo, then, plants and all the elements in the world are considered to be animate beings capable of action. The concept of kino lau, discussed in the introduction, animates plants, animals, birds, clouds, and so on as deities, either the powerful akua nui like Kāne, Kū, Pele, and others, or less powerful but just as meaningful ʻaumākua, family spirits. In this world, one looks at a certain cloud form and sees the deity Lono; a breadfruit tree is Kāmehaʻikana, a kino lau of Haumea; and a sweet potato leaf is Kamapuaʻa. This world is divine and is the family of human beings. Kanahele explains, "The family line may include humans, elements of nature, sharks, or other forms of life."[21] In the genealogical chant Kanahele analyzes, Pelehonuamea "is the red-hot magma," and an eldest child (or brother), "Kamohoaliʻi, or Kānekamohoaliʻi, . . . [i]n the form of Kāne is the heat in the earth and in the sky."[22] Kamohoaliʻi also manifests in a shark kino lau. Hiʻiakaikapoliopele, the protagonist in this moʻolelo, is considered the growth of vegetation on the land that follows a lava flow. Kanahele writes,

> The abundance of growth seen growing out of lava land—such as herbs, weeds, trees and vines—takes root in kapoliopele, or the bosom of Pele. . . . Hiʻiakaikapoliopele is . . . translated as "causative of growth on or in lava." Hiʻiakaikapoliopele is considered a healer. She causes growth on the land.[23]

In the following examples taken from Hiʻiaka's trek across Koʻolaupoko and Koʻolauloa on the island of Oʻahu, we see Hiʻiaka interact with the people of the ʻāina in various ways from simple but necessary recognition through kau, "sacred chant[s], as Hiʻiaka's chants of affectionate greeting to persons, hills, and landmarks," to destruction of dangerous elements such as moʻo (Hawaiian reptilian water deities who embody the life-giving and death-dealing qualities of water) that are a menace to humans.[24] Because Hiʻiaka, her sister Pele, and her lover Hōpoe are actually ʻāina themselves, as well as acting as human characters and deities, all simultaneously, Hiʻiaka must always greet landforms and other deities with chants of affection; another, related reason is that they are part of the same ʻohana. The landforms are her sisters, brothers, cousins, parents, and grandparents. To treat them with respect and affection is her kuleana.[25] The mele often simultaneously function to express Hiʻiaka's thoughts and emotions.

An example is this kānaenae, a chant of affection that Hiʻiaka offers when she is standing atop Mahinui in Kailua observing the wahi pana and people around her. She looks at Heʻeia to the northwest and sees a group of women traveling to the uplands of ʻĀhuimanu to make lei from hala fruit.

> Ke pii ae la ka huakai wahine e
> Apahu lei hala i uka o Ahuimanu
> He manumanu au i ka lokoino e—
> Pau ke aho i ka loa o Auliilii
> Ke hele ae la ka ua kalepa e—
> Ka ua okioki koa o Heeia;
> Ke hehi la i ke kai o Luhi e—
> Luhi i ke kai ke koa o Heeia-kea.[26]

> The women's journey is climbing
> To cut hala for lei in the uplands of ʻĀhuimanu
> I am bruised by the malevolence [I've been experiencing]
> Exhausted by the length of Auliʻiliʻi
> The fluttering rain is traveling
> The coral-carving rain of Heʻeia
> (Is) stepping on the sea of Luhi [tired; worn]
> The coral of Heʻeia is worn down by the sea.

This kau, offered as a chant of affection to these storied places, describes the ʻāina for us—we hear that the women living in Heʻeia who want to make hala lei must travel a long way uphill to the mountain area of ʻĀhuimanu to do so. The poet has selected a choice word to describe the hala lei making; the mele doesn't say they go to gather (ʻohi) the hala, but uses "ʻāpahu," "to cut off squarely" instead. This gives us the visual image of how the hala keys are cut in preparation for lei.[27] The area is rainy and the rain feels heavy enough to break or carve the coral in the bay of Heʻeia. Four different places are named. That is all one level of the mele, but Poepoe teaches us to see another level, the thoughts and emotions of Hiʻiaka. He writes,

> Ua hapai ae o Hiiaka i ka hopunaolelo "manumanu au i ka lokoino," no kona ike ana iho, ua lilo oia i mea haika wale ia a manao ino wale ia, e na kupua manao lili iaia ma na wahi apau ana i hele mai ai me ke aikane. . . . He mea oiaio, ua ano paupauaho oia i nei hele ana e hele nei, a oia kana i hookanaaho ae ai: "Pau ke aho i ka loa o Au-liilii."[28]

Hiʻiaka sang this line "I am bruised by the malevolence," because she saw that she had become a figure of contempt and thought badly of by the kupua who were jealous of her everywhere she went with her aikāne. . . . It is true, she was rather exhausted by this journey they were on, and that was what she expressed with some relief: "Exhausted by the length of Auliʻiliʻi."

Other mele are songs of recognition. When Hiʻiaka and Wahineʻōmaʻo reach Kaliuwaʻa (called Sacred Falls in English) in the Hauʻula area of Oʻahu, Poepoe has Hiʻiaka explain to Wahineʻōmaʻo the necessity of recognizing the ʻāina:

Aia o Kaliuwaa ke waiho mai la i uka. He Kaliuwaa okoa no ko Puna, a he okoa nohoi ko onei. A i mea hoi no kela kamaaina e ohumu ole mai ai ia kaua, no ko kaua hele loa ma ke alanui, e paeaea ae au.[29]

———

Kaliuwaʻa lies inland here. Puna [their home on Hawaiʻi] has a different Kaliuwaʻa. And so that the native [Kaliuwaʻa] of this place doesn't complain to us about our traveling far on the road [and thus bypassing him/her], I offer this chant.

In this short explanation, we learn why Hiʻiaka always sings to the ʻāina as she goes along. Various places, which/who speak and act, will be insulted or hurt if she doesn't recognize them. She, in turn, demands recognition and hospitality from both these divine characters who are landforms and so forth, and humans. Mutual recognition and hospitality to travelers are central values of Hawaiian culture, as is often seen in the oral tradition.[30] The following is the chant Hiʻiaka offered to Kaliuwaʻa:

Aia oe, Kaliuwaa, i ka uka,
Noho no a lipo i ke anu,
Anuanu ka noho ana i ka wao,
I mehana i ke kapa lau-ki,
I ke kapa lau ahi a ka pii kuahiwi,
Ke hele nei no.

Kaliuwaʻa, you are there in the upland,
Living in the deep dark in the cold,
It is very cold living in the forest,
Warmed by a blanket of ti leaf,
The blanket of many fires of those climbing the mountain,
We are going.

Hiʻiaka's chant describes the ʻāina of Kaliuwaʻa: it is high in elevation, forested, and cold. She alludes to its sacred nature as the home of the pig god, Kamapuaʻa, and to the pilgrimages that people make to the valley. Kaliuwaʻa may be lonely in his/her isolation, expressed by the lines about cold, but is warmed by visitors and their fires. The mele also alludes to the Kumulipo in its use of the word "lipo" (dark). Kaliuwaʻa responds to this warm greeting with an invitation to Hiʻiaka and Wahineʻōmaʻo to come and eat, but they decline so that they can keep traveling. This exchange is mutually affectionate and fulfills the requirements of mutual recognition and hospitality.

How can we understand this Kanaka idea of the land feeling cold and lonely without humans? Basham, in analyzing the idea of "ea" in Hawaiian, a word used for sovereignty, breath, life, and to rise up, examined an 1871 article in Hawaiian that reads "1. Ke ea o na i-a, he wai. 2. Ke ea o ke kanaka, he makani. 3. O ke ea o ka honua, he kanaka"[31] (1. The ea of fish is water. 2. The ea of humans is wind (i.e., air). 3. The ea of the earth is humans). Basham explains,

> Wahi a ka helu ʻekolu, ʻo ke ea o ka honua, he kanaka nō ia. Maliʻa paha, ma muli o ko ke kanaka kanu ʻana i ka ʻāina, no kona noho ʻana ma ka ʻāina, no ka mea, ʻo ke kanaka, he mea ia e ola ai ka ʻāina. He pili ʻohana nō hoʻi ka ʻāina a me ke kanaka, a ʻo Wākea a me Papa nā mākua o ka ʻāina, no laila, ʻo ke kanaka nō ka mea e ea ai ka ʻāina.[32]

Number three in this list says the ea of the earth is humans. Perhaps it is because of humans planting the ʻāina for their sustenance on the ʻāina, since humans make the land live/grow. The ʻāina is also a close relative to humans, and Wākea and Papa are the parents of the land, so humans are the ones by which the land has ea.

Here we can see that aloha ʻāina is relational. The ʻāina can be seen to enjoy its productive interactions with Kānaka. Kānaka plant and shape the ʻāina to make it bloom and produce food, but they also chant, sing, and converse with the ʻāina. Kānaka have aloha for the ʻāina, and in this episode, we have one example of the ʻāina's reciprocal aloha for Kānaka.

Hiʻiaka offers similar chants all along the coast, including to Waiahilahila, who is described as a "pua ponoi a Haumea" (Haumea's own offspring) and a kupua. According to Lloyd Soehren's online database of place names, Puʻu Waiahilahila is a peak and a boundary marker in this same area. Her name means (roughly) "Water-of-shyness," and accordingly she never does show herself. Hiʻiaka also sings to Waialua (a "moku," or large district) and its four calm times of day, and to Kamae near Mokulēʻia, who chants back. As they travel to Kaʻena Point, Hiʻiaka speaks to her hoahānau (cousin or sibling) Kawaikumuʻole (the water without a source), explaining once again that they are on a journey and unable to stay for a visit. Hiʻiaka's kānaenae expresses aloha to Kawaikumuʻole, as well as her knowledge that Lohiʻau (Pele's lover whom they are going to fetch) is dead:

1. Ani peahi mai la ka ehu a ka wai,
2. Hoohauoli ana i ka manao, e lealea iho,

3. Lele maopu ka auhau a ka wai
4. Oia wai kumu ole i ka pali—e—
5. Aia ke kumu o ka wai i Kaala—
6. Manowai eha ai o Kaena,
7. He ena aloha keia nou, e ka hoa,
8. O ka hoa ipo i ka maka o ka opua,
9. Opua kau iluna o Haupu,
10. Haupu, hauli ka manao,
11. E——aohe a kakou ipo.³³

1. The spray of the sea waves to us,
2. Cheering the mind, to have fun,
3. The "stems" of the water leap without splashing
4. That is the water without source at the cliff
5. The source of the water is at Kaʻala
6. The source of the four streams of Kaʻena,
7. This is an affectionate greeting for you, my friend,
8. The lover companion in the presence/at the tip of the cloud bank
9. The cloud bank resting at the top of Hāʻupu,
10. The mind recalls, and is shocked/bruised
11. We have no lover [Lohiʻau].

In this chant to Kawaikumuʻole, Hiʻiaka sings about this singular place, Kaʻena Point on the extreme west end of Oʻahu. It is desertlike, seemingly without streams, but the knowledgeable kamaʻāina know there are actually four streams along the cape. Kawaikumuʻole is one of the streams that seems to have no source, but the closely observant natives of the area have determined the source of the water is atop Kaʻala. This mele has many examples of linked assonance, a common poetic feature in Hawaiian: lines 3, 4, and 5, for example, have "ka wai," "wai kumu ole," and then "ke kumu o ka wai." Lines 6 and 7 have Kaʻena followed by "He ena aloha." Lines 7 and 8 have "ka hoa" followed by "O ka hoa ipo." Line 8 is linked to 9 by the word "ʻōpua," and 9 to 10 by the place name and word "Hāʻupu." The final two lines are Hiʻiaka's recognition that Lohiʻau is dead and she will have to revive him when she arrives on Kauaʻi.

Shortly thereafter, Hiʻiaka greets Pōhakuokauaʻi, a large stone in the sea off of the western point of Kaʻena. He is their kupuna or grandfather whom Pele had threatened earlier in the moʻolelo when she thought he was the source of the drumming she was following. Here he exchanges affectionate chanting with Hiʻiaka and loans her a waʻa so that she and Wahineʻōmaʻo can sail to Kauaʻi.

DANGEROUS ELEMENTS OF THE ʻĀINA

Other people, moʻo, and beings with various kino lau are dangerous to humans or violate basic social laws, such as offering food, drink, and shelter to travelers. These Hiʻiaka must fight and defeat. I offer two examples here: Pueo of Waiāhole, and Mokoliʻi, the moʻo of the Kualoa area.

As Hiʻiaka and Wahineʻōmaʻo approach Waiāhole Valley, Hiʻiaka explains to Wahineʻōmaʻo,

> O keia wahi a kaua e hele aku nei la, o Pueo ke alii o ia wahi. He kupua. He alii puni hakaka. He kino pueo kona. Ua ike mai la oia ia kaua, aole auanei e liuliu, a ike aku ana no auanei kaua i ka lele mai a ka pueo me ke *kī* hele ana maluna o kaua.[34]

> This place we are traveling through, Pueo [Owl] is the aliʻi of this place. He is a kupua. He is an aliʻi who loves to fight. He has an owl body. He has seen us, and soon we will see an owl flying over, flying quickly above us.

The word "kī," which Poepoe italicizes to bring our attention to it, evokes both a sight and a sound: it means to fly very quickly and is also a spitting sound that Pueo makes. As Pueo flies over, Poepoe writes, "He *kī* ia o ka leo o ka Pueo, me ke keʻu keʻu ana nohoi" (There was a spitting of the voice as well as hooting). Without any provocation from Hiʻiaka, Pueo calls to them, saying,

> Hoopaa olua i ka hele mai imua nei . . . ahu Kauwawe a ka manu maluna o olua . . . O kahi kaikamahine hua haule a Pele. . . . He keu ka hoona-na. . . . Hele mai oe, e Hiiaka imua nei, make oe iaʻu. Eia o Pueo, he kino lau, he kino manamana, a he ikaika.[35]

> You two insist on going forward . . . the imu covering of the birds will pile up over you . . . the girl who is the fallen egg of Pele. . . . So very hostile. . . . If you come before me, Hiʻiaka, I will kill you. This is Pueo, a kino lau, a body with many branches, and strong.

Hiʻiaka replies that they have done nothing to cause offense, and she reminds him that he is a mature being, whereas she is a youth. She says, "Kuhi au i kou alii ana, e opu alii iho ka manao ame ka olelo, eia ka, elike no me ke ano o ka pueo, o ke *ki* no a me ke keʻu o ia no oe e Pueo"[36] (I thought because you are an aliʻi that your thoughts and words would be ʻōpū aliʻi, or kind and benevolent, but like the nature of the owl, who spits and hoots, that is you, Pueo). Pueo transforms himself into many, perhaps thousands of, owl bodies and proceeds to attack Hiʻiaka and Wahineʻōmaʻo. Hiʻiaka uses her pāʻū (skirt) to strike them all out of the sky. Pueo then stands as a Kanaka to fight with Hiʻiaka. She chants:

> Keʻu ana ua Pueo e—
> Ki ana ua Pueo e—
> He Pueo kane ka Pueo e—
> Hilahila ole ka Pueo e—
> I ka hakaka me aʻu nei e—
> He wahine,
> E hakaka wahine aku au e—[37]

> This Pueo is hooting
> This Pueo is spitting and flying
> The Pueo is a male Pueo
> The Pueo is unashamed
> To fight with me
> A woman
> I will fight like a woman.

Pueo is terrifying and Hiʻiaka tells Wahineʻōmaʻo that if she dies in the fight, Wahineʻōmaʻo is to retrieve her pāʻū and take care of it. Pueo then approaches her with a weapon called a mākini in each hand, and here Poepoe explains that it is a sword with eight spear points on it, and that the word "mākini" comes from "maka" (points) and "kinikini" (many). This is another example of Poepoe recording information so that it doesn't disappear in the shift to English. While Pueo appears here as a "kanaka maoli" or human being, "Ua kawiliwili no nae iloko ona ke ano kino papalua. No kona ikaika a me kona ano eepa, ua lilo oia he kupua no ia mau kaha" (Blended inside of him was a dual nature. Because of his strength and this supernatural nature, he had become the kupua of those shores).[38]

Despite all his strength and supernatural powers, Pueo brought warriors and all the other strong people of the area to the fight with him, so many that the place was crowded with people. When the warriors saw that their opponents were two young women, they wondered at Pueo's lack of shame. Hiʻiaka addresses them and advises them to move out of the way as she fights Pueo so that they don't get hurt, calling Pueo "pookoi" (poʻo koʻi) or "adze-head," "an insulting term for evil sorcerers."[39]

The fight begins with Pueo throwing the mākini at Hiʻiaka; she waves her pāʻū at the mākini, whereupon they each catch fire and are destroyed. Pueo tries again and again to no avail. Hiʻiaka destroys all of his weapons with fire. She then taunts him, saying, "Aohe au make o nei la. Naʻu ka make na ka wahine" (You have no power to kill today. It is I, the woman, who has the power to kill). Pueo then jumps toward her, trying to catch her in a hold, but Hiʻiaka strikes with her pāʻū and dismembers his body, turning him into a hill of dirt.[40] The people of the area are relieved that he is dead:

> I ka make ana o Pueo, hooho ae la na kanaka, ua pono no kona make ana, he alii hana ino oia. Ua hele lakou, a, [sic] aikena i kana mau hana hookaumaha he nui.[41]
>
> ———
>
> When Pueo died, the people shouted, his death was pono, he was an abusive aliʻi. They had become sick and tired of his many oppressive acts.

This episode is an excellent example of Hiʻiaka's mana wahine, or what Charlot calls specifically female power.[42] hoʻomanawanui expands this idea of mana wahine for us: "Within Oceania, mana wahine describes an indigenous, culturally based understanding of female power and empowerment that is rooted in traditional concepts such as moʻokūʻauhau, aloha ʻāina, and kuleana. It is the physical, intellectual, and spiritual (or intuitive) power of women."[43] She goes on to explain that "[Pele and Hiʻiaka's] mana wahine also demonstrates the power they have over kāne, both godly and human, over the ʻāina and the (re)shaping of it, as well as the ability to call on elements of the ʻāina (thunder, lightning, wind, rain, and various vegetation), which are also the kino lau of their large ʻohana."[44] Pueo misunderstands and misreads the situation because of his arrogance. He is accustomed to wielding his power in oppressive ways, which blinds him to Hiʻiaka's divine nature and mana wahine. His actions directly contradict the values of pono, which here include balance—recognizing both male and female power, and youth and maturity—reciprocity, hospitality, and aloha.

This episode is a cautionary tale about more than the consequences of failing to recognize the divine, or failing to credit the potential of youthful female power. Pueo is an example of an aliʻi who is not pono. The Hawaiian governing system depended on aloha among the aliʻi, makaʻāinana, kāhuna, akua, ʻaumākua, and ʻāina. The hierarchical or layered system of konohiki who managed or ruled various districts, from a tiny moʻo to an ahupuaʻa, to a large moku, to an entire island, was characterized by the power of not only the top aliʻi nui to appoint konohiki, but also the makaʻāinana who worked the land and fisheries, and the kāhuna who advised the aliʻi (among other professions they had). Konohiki who were good land managers and did not take more than their share or compel makaʻāinana to do things such as fight in wars to benefit themselves were loved and trusted. All aliʻi were expected to have ʻōpū aliʻi, or aliʻi insides—an internalized ethic that guided them to be considerate, kind, and generous in their dealings with others, as Hiʻiaka indicated. In many tales, konohiki who abuse or oppress makaʻāinana are stripped of their positions or killed by the makaʻāinana or kāhuna.[45] Hiʻiaka here assists the makaʻāinana of Waiāhole by killing the despotic aliʻi for them.

This practice of aloha among the various strata of Hawaiian society is one of the major ways that it differed from European feudal systems, to which it is often compared.[46] Jonathan Osorio has analyzed how the transformation of the land tenure system to private property not only allowed corporations and motivated individuals to dispossess Kānaka of their ʻāina, but also fundamentally destroyed the konohiki system based on aloha between the aliʻi and the makaʻāinana and dealt a serious blow to the ideology of aloha ʻāina. It is because of this that the title of his book is *Dismembering Lāhui*.

Finally, Pueo is identified with the ʻāina itself in Waiāhole today. One of the pali that defines the valley is noted by residents to look like a pueo, and below it on the ground is a pōhaku (large stone) with an owl image discernible on it as well. Kamaʻāina often see pueo flying in that spot. The moʻolelo as recorded in Poepoe's Hiʻiaka may not have survived orally in Waiāhole Valley, but Pueo is still there in other forms.[47]

Not long after the battle with Pueo, Hiʻiaka and Wahineʻōmaʻo arrive at the sacred district called Kualoa. The ridge called the Moʻo Kapu o Hāloa (Sacred Ridge of Hāloa), topped by the high peak Kānehoalani (in other versions said to be the father of Pele), forms the dividing line between the moku (large land divisions) of Koʻolaupoko and Koʻolauloa. The pali there is known as Palikū and is an ancestor of Haumea (see the moʻolelo in chapter 6). The Kualoa district is famed as being among the most valuable to aliʻi power, and the story of Kahahana, who made the fateful error of promising control over it to his hānai father, the aliʻi nui Kahekili of Maui, has been cited over and over again by Kanaka writers. Kamakau records the words of Kahahana's kahuna, Kaʻōpulupulu, upon hearing that the aliʻi was giving away Kualoa:

> E ke 'Lii, haawi no oe i keia mau aina, o ka lilo no ia o ke aupuni, aole o oe ke Alii.—O Kualoa, o na kanawai no ia o ko mau kupuna, o Kalumalumai a me Kekaihehee; o na pahu kapu o Kapahuulu me Kaahuulapunawai; o ka pali kapu o Kauakahiakahoowaha o Kualoa. O ka palaoa pae, aole oe e hai ana i ko akua, i na heana a me na kaua kuwaho, ua lilo ia Kahekili, aia ma Maui e hai ai, nolaila, ua lilo ke aupuni ia Kahekili, a o oe hoi, aole oe he alii.[48]
>
> ———
>
> O chief! If you give away these things your authority will be lost, and you will cease to be a ruler. To Kualoa belong the water courses[49] of your ancestors, Ka-lumalumaʻi and Ke-kai-heheʻe; the sacred drums of Ka-pahu-ulu, and the spring of Ka-ʻahu-ʻula; the sacred hill of Ka-ua-kahi son of Kahoʻowaha of Kualoa. Without the [whale tooth] ivory that drifts ashore you could not offer to the gods the first victim slain in battle; it would be for Kahekili to offer it on Maui, and the rule would become his. You would be no longer ruler.[50]

In our Hiʻiaka story, Kualoa is impassable on foot, as the sea reached the foot of the cliffs. Travelers had to paddle or sail by waʻa or climb the ridge to reach the other side. The area was dominated by a huge and dangerous moʻo named Mokoliʻi, who was hostile to the people and to Hiʻiaka. When Hiʻiaka sees him she chants:

1. Kiekie Kanehoalani
2. Hopuepue [sic] ana Mokolii i ke anu,
3. He keiki maka hiapo ia na Koolau,
4. Lau ena ke one a Kane,
5. Lau na koʻa maokioki o Heeia,
6. Eia au la, ua kena i ka ino.[51]

1. Kānehoalani rises high above,
2. Mokoliʻi crouches in the cold,
3. A firstborn child of the Koʻolau,
4. The burning sands of Kāne are many,
5. The broken-up reefs of Heʻeia are many,
6. Here I am, weary of evil/abuse.

Through this mele, we can visualize the land: the high peak of Kānehoalani far above, the small peak of Mokoliʻi sitting in the cold water of the ocean just off shore. Not far away are the many small reefs of Heʻeia Bay. Line 4 "recalls the name "Onelauʻena," the "legendary homeland of the god Kāne, a land of plenty," which reminds us that the peak Kānehoalani is a kino lau of the god Kāne.[52] It also links that "land of plenty" with Koʻolaupoko, a district replete with fresh water, good ʻāina for planting, and abundant fishing. Poepoe interjects teaching here too. He explains that Hiʻiaka uses line 5 as a metaphor for her many battles:

> Ma keia kau a Hiiaka, e hoomaopopo aku ana oia imua o Mokolii, ua aikena oia (Hiiaka) ia mea he hakaka, a e hoohalike ana hoi ia, ua like ka nui o na poe ana i hakaka pu ai me na koʻa maokioki o Heeia. Ua manao hoi o Hiiaka, e maliu mai ana la hoi o Mokolii i kana e noi aku nei, oia hoi, aohe pono e hakaka laua.[53]

In this kau of Hiʻiaka, she is telling Mokoliʻi that she is tired of fighting, and she is comparing the number of people she has had to fight with the many jagged reefs of Heʻeia. Hiʻiaka hoped that Mokoliʻi would heed her request, that is, that it was not pono that they should fight.

Mokoliʻi does not, however, heed Hiʻiaka's request. He comes out of the sea to fight her, whipping his long tail around the ʻāina like a giant whirlwind, destroying everything in its path. Trees and shrubs are cut down. Hiʻiaka strikes Mokoliʻi with her pāʻū and he turns into a hill of dirt. His head becomes the little islet off shore now called Mokoliʻi, and the rest of his body along with the debris from the destruction he caused becomes the solid land in front of the pali, the land area now called Kualoa. From that time on, people could walk between Koʻolaupoko and Koʻolauloa.[54]

In this episode, Hiʻiaka acts as a creator of ʻāina by transforming the dangerous moʻo into a portion of land that benefits Kanaka. In line 3 of the preceding mele and in a concluding explanation, Mokoliʻi is referred to as a keiki makahiapo na Koʻolau, or firstborn of the Koʻolau Mountains. Perhaps we can interpret this as the Koʻolau having been there for millenia before this episode, but after Hiʻiaka transforms him into new land, Mokoliʻi can be seen as a child of the mountain range.

Conclusion

We saw in this chapter the many ways in which characters in Poepoe's Hiʻiakaikapoliopele can act as divine beings, humans, animals, landforms, and natural elements or some combination thereof all at once. The mele that illustrate the moʻolelo poetically show us how and what our Kanaka ancestors thought about the ʻāina and their relationships with it and everything in, on, and around it. ʻĀina is our ancestor and our sibling; our human ancestors sang to and about the ʻāina, expressing their aloha and their concept of a reciprocal relationship with the ʻāina. Everything, including rains, winds, and stones, is imbued with life. Hiʻiaka herself is both a life-giving and death-dealing force, although she metes out death only when it is pono, or beneficial to humans. The dangerous owl/aliʻi Pueo and Mokoliʻi the moʻo are killed but also allowed to live on as landforms. When we travel across Koʻolaupoko and Koʻolauloa, we can perceive not just a mountain ridge and various beaches, but actors that are named Waiahilahila and Kaliuwaʻa, for example. We can remember that the seemingly inert islets like Pōhakuokauaʻi and Mokoliʻi are relatives or foes of Hiʻiaka with whom she exchanged chants, aloha, and perhaps battles. These islands we live on are a honua ola, a living world, as Pualani Kanahele puts it.[55] Everything around us that is native is a kino lau of someone divine: Kāne, Haumea, Kamapuaʻa, and so on.

When we work to restore native plants, when we ourselves sing to the ʻāina, dance hula for and on the ʻāina, we are like Hiʻiaka, regenerating the ʻāina, recognizing our mutual affinity and kinship, and expressing our aloha. This gives us new life as much as it gives the ʻāina new life.

This is but a short reading of some select elements in this epic moʻolelo. I hope that it has demonstrated at least in some part the magnificence of Poepoe's version of this moʻolelo. It is poetically extremely rich, containing hundreds of mele and poetic expositions in prose. Just as important, he filled its pages with his own insights and teachings on how to read and better understand and appreciate the mele. The moʻolelo is an expression of Poepoe's own unwavering aloha for the ʻāina and aloha for our ʻōlelo ʻōiwi (native language) and literature. As our kupuna in the moʻokūʻauhau of intellectual work, he created this moʻolelo full of poetry, riddles, and kaona for us to ponder, study, and enjoy. As his mamo (descendants), it is our kuleana to take up the work and play of reading this moʻolelo.

6

Moʻolelo Hawaiʻi Kahiko

O ka poe auanei e malama ana i na helu apau o keia nupepa mai ka wa i hoopukaia ai keia moolelo a . . . hoea i ka pau ana, ua loaa ia lakou he Moolelo Hawaii Kahiko waiwai nui.

―――――

The people who are saving all the issues of this newspaper from the start of the publication of this moʻolelo until the end, they have a very valuable Moʻolelo Hawaiʻi Kahiko.

―――――

JOSEPH MOKUʻŌHAI POEPOE

In this chapter I analyze one of Poepoe's most important works, "Ka Moolelo Hawaii Kahiko" (Ancient Hawaiian history), which was serialized over ten months in 1906 in a paper he edited, *Ka Naʻi Aupuni*. I situate this work within the genealogy of the genre, which begins in 1838 with the missionary-sponsored and -edited *Ka Mooolelo Hawaii*. One purpose of this chapter is to demonstrate Poepoe's commitment to teaching the younger generations of his own time as well as of our time. This is evident in his decisions on how to present the material, especially genealogies, so that they are more readily understandable than in the old chants themselves, and in his many interruptions to explain place names and the deeper meanings (kaona) of words, sayings, and so forth. Poepoe not only teaches us how to read the old genealogies, but also provides new information, new versions, and more elaborated versions of some important moʻolelo.

Further, I consider how Poepoe thinks of moʻokūʻauhau as a recurring way of connecting to ancestors (kupuna) and descendants (mamo, moʻopuna): moʻokūʻauhau as a way of approaching the world; a way of approaching study of our indigenous past; and a stance that supports the whole project of reconstructing Hawaiian political and intellectual history. In "Moolelo Hawaii Kahiko," Poepoe thus simultaneously examines works of moʻokūʻauhau and demonstrates his moʻokūʻauhau consciousness.

I argue as well that this work is important for us to study now. Poepoe published this series ten years after the oligarchic Republic of Hawaii outlawed Hawaiian as a medium in the schools, and six years after the Organic Act that made Hawaiʻi a colony of the United States and enshrined in the law the same ban on Hawaiian as a medium of learning. The young adults around him were increasingly becoming alienated from their own Kanaka traditions and being bombarded with American culture and language that denigrated their own native culture. Poepoe worries about haole misinterpretation and misrepresentation of Hawaiian texts and history, and he wishes to impart what he has learned through a lifetime of reading and study to coming generations of Kanaka. In this text he demonstrates what it is to be a native scholar who cites his sources and makes corrections. He wants to emphasize the intelligence and artistry of Kanaka in the generations before his own and to offer his interpretations for the coming generations.

In the early twentieth century, Poepoe could see the ongoing construction of what Ngũgĩ wa Thiongʻo calls the cultural bomb being built before his eyes.[1] The "psychological violence of the classroom" was in full view, and Poepoe was trying to defuse the bomb and mitigate the harms of the colonial, English-language, US hegemonic schooling.[2] He was but one officer in this bomb squad (if I may be indulged to extend the analogy) and he and his fellow anticolonial fighters were not able to completely stop the destruction. After all, the islands were overrun with the US military, sent from a country with a population of seventy million or so, to Hawaiʻi with but one hundred thousand. It seems to me that it is very important to see and appreciate that Poepoe's works assist us in reconstructing our own histories from our ancestral epistemologies, as our generations are now turning to creating indigenous resurgent futures.

Poepoe arranged this book in seven mokuna or chapters:

1. "Na Kuauhau Kahiko e Hoike ana i na Kumu i Loaa ai ka Pae Moku o Hawaii nei" (The ancient genealogies showing the sources

by which the Hawaiian Islands were obtained) (February 2, 1906–March 3, 1906)
2. "Ka Manao o ka Poe Kahiko no ke Kumu Mua o ko Hawaii nei Lahuikanaka" (The ideas of the ancients concerning the origins of Hawai'i's native people) (March 3, 1906–April 28, 1906)
3. "Hoomaka ka Moolelo Kuauhau mai a Wakea mai" and "Ka Moolelo o ko Wakea ma Noho ana ma Kalihi—Ka Loaa ana o ke Akua Ulu o Kameha'ikana" (The genealogy story begins at Wākea and the story of Wākea and others living at Kalihi—the acquisition of the breadfruit deity Kāmeha'ikana) (April 30, 1906–September 19, 1906)
4. "Ka Oihana Kilo Hoku Hawaii" (Hawaiian astronomy) (September 20, 1906–October 15, 1906)
5. "No ka Mahele o na Wa" (Concerning the division of time) (October 15, 1906–November 19, 1906)
6. "No ka Makahiki" (Concerning the Makahiki season and festival) (November 20, 1906–November 28, 1906)
7. "No na Heiau o ka Wa Kahiko o Hawaii Nei" (Concerning the heiau of ancient times of Hawai'i) (November 29, 1906)

The final installment published is not the end of the book, but merely the last chapter we have; unfortunately, the paper went out of business, and none of the scant issues after November 30, 1906, contain the conclusion.

Poepoe studied various sources in order to write this history, including John White's *The Ancient History of the Māori*.[3] We begin here with a description of the major works in the genre that Poepoe consulted and responded to.

Mo'olelo Hawai'i: "Moolelo Hawaii Kahiko"

To understand Poepoe's project in "Moolelo Hawaii Kahiko," it is helpful to recognize the genre that he was contributing to. The first written works in the genre were composed and published under the editing hands of two missionaries, after which our kūpuna produced their own works independently. Thus those works not only functioned as histories and cosmogonies but were also conscripted into important political contests in the nineteenth century: Christian evangelism worldwide, divine versus secular authority, and inherited (chiefly or monarchical) versus imagined democratic government. In other words, this is a genre of political speech and rhetorical art form that Poepoe enters. He is writing in a long Hawaiian tradition, but in his own time, having to work against strong and forceful US assimilationism as well.

Moʻolelo Hawaiʻi, or moʻolelo Hawaiʻi kahiko, is a genre that includes various works of Hawaiian history and/or autoethnographic accounts describing aspects of life in premissionary times. They generally include theories of the origin of the islands and/or the universe and the lāhui Hawaiʻi, and they often include genealogies. In this section I describe a selection of the works that Poepoe studied.

KA MOOOLELO HAWAII, 1838

Ka Mooolelo Hawaii is the first published work in the genre. It was written by students at Lahainaluna Seminary under the direction of the missionary Sheldon Dibble.[4] Established in 1831, just eleven years after the missionaries' arrival, Lahainaluna was the first secondary school in the islands, and its mission was to provide higher education and train promising Kanaka men in the Congregational denomination of Christianity. While the book itself does not reveal the names of either the student writers or the editor, in 1862 Jules Remy identified the principal author as Davida Malo.[5] As Samuel Kamakau was also a student at that time and became the preeminent historian of his day, it is assumed that he was among the participants as well. Perhaps as important as the identity of the student authors is Dibble's editing process, which is sure to have altered the content and tone of the work. Dibble prepared questions that students were to ask of knowledgeable elderly people and aliʻi. The students then wrote up their results and compared them in a seminar. Dibble described the process this way:

> At the time of meeting each scholar read what he had written—discrepancies were reconciled and corrections made by each other, and then all the compositions were handed to me, out of which I endeavored to make one connected and true account. Thus we proceeded from one question to another till a volume was prepared and printed in the Hawaiian language.[6]

What are the implications of this process? Some important distinctions and even events noted by women, the elderly, and aliʻi must certainly have been elided or smoothed over, and what these were we may never know.

Dibble's belief that a single truth was preferable and possible was prevalent at the time. A singular historical narrative, a singular truth, as is sought after here, so often serves political ends, such as the justification of often unjustifiable acts.[7] In this first *Mooolelo Hawaii* what is justified is the missionaries' project to convert Kānaka to their religion and political economic ways; the narrative of premissionary history is written to reflect their teleological belief that events in the islands were part of their god's plan to bring enlightenment to the Kanaka (that is, to save souls). This is most clear in the final sections of the moʻolelo, which mainly focus on the missionaries. The title of one of these is "No ka Hookaawale ana o ke Akua i ke Ala no na Misionari e Hiki mai ai" (Concerning God's clearance of the way for the arrival of the missionaries).[8]

The volume, as might be expected, expresses rather severe disdain for and condemnation of the beliefs and lifeways of the Kanaka. This is constituted by the belief in the superiority of missionary (haole, literate) beliefs and practices. The very first sentences of the book reflect this sense of the superiority of the missionary/literate:

> Aole paha i pololei loa na mea a pau i paiia iloko o keia buke. He pololei a he oiaio paha ka nui, aka, ma kau wahi ua kekee iki paha, no ka mea, o kekahi mau olelo, he mau olelo kahiko loa, a ma ka naau o na kanaka i paa ai, aole ma ka pepa, nolaila, ua paa kapekepeke, aole i pololei loa.[9]
>
> ———
>
> Probably not everything published in this book is completely correct. Most of it is probably correct and true, but in some places, it is slightly erroneous or distorted, because some of the stories or statements are very old, and were preserved in the minds of the people, not on paper, therefore, they were preserved incompletely, and not completely accurately.[10]

The assumption that written historical accounts are more truthful and correct is important to note because oral accounts may be equally or more reliable, and, of course, each is a selection from innumerable points of view, dependent on innumerable variables, and none can really be termed more objectively factual than another. Thus the assumption that written accounts are more truthful is a discursive ploy to denigrate native ways of keeping history. Noelani Arista comments on this same passage of Dibble's:

> Here orality is suspect, because it is thought to be a reflection simply of memory.... In this way of thinking, history was, in effect, writing. Dibble did not count the pedagogy that created trained genealogists, historians, *kahuna*, and other experts as historical training, and he was also not privy to the structures and rules that maintained the faithfulness and accuracy of traditions over time.[11]

Among other practices, Arista is alluding to the recitation of aliʻi genealogies (which contain moʻolelo also), which were subject to examination, disputation, and correction by other genealogists. This type of disputation and correction continued in practice in writing in the Hawaiian newspapers as well (witness the conflict between Kamakau and Unauna in 1842).[12]

This short text (116 pages), however, does recount a premissionary historical narrative. The first five pages cover the origin of the islands, the arrival of the native people in Hawaiʻi, and the arrival of the first foreign ships (thought by some Hawaiians to predate Captain Cook).[13] Cook arrives on page 6, and this is when history proper begins (for the missionary and all non-natives), as that is when Hawaiʻi becomes legible to Europe and the United States. The thousands of years of Kanaka life memorialized in moʻolelo and mele thus appear to be merely a prologue to the "real history" that begins with Cook. This set a precedent for the writing of a certain kind of Hawaiian history for the next two centuries. The book covers Cook's travels to Hawaiʻi and his death; some of the important European explorers that followed him, such as Vancouver; the rise of Kamehameha and his conquering of the archipelago; the sandalwood trade; and the arrival and first decade or so of missionary work.

After relating Kamehameha's deeds, death, and the hiding of his bones, the historical narrative is interrupted with a section called "Ke Ano o ka Noho Kahiko ana" (The nature of ancient life), which is a catalogue of the abuses of the aliʻi and the kahuna. These include holding land for themselves, burdening the common people with work, committing sinful and capricious kapu, instigating frequent wars, and encouraging a devotion to entertainments.[14] The final paragraph reads as follows:

> Auhea oe, e ka mea e heluhelu ana, ke ike nei oe i ke ano o ka noho kahiko ana o keia pae aina, ua paapu ka aina i ka poeleele, a me ka lapuwale, a me ka ino, a me ke kaumaha, a me ka eha, a me ka make. He lua meki, he lua pouli, he lua piha i na mea pelapela a pau, he lua

make, he lua ahi aa mau loa, malaila kahi i noho ai ko Hawaii a pau i ka wa kahiko! I keia manawa, ua puka mai ka malamalama, aka, ua makemake kekahi poe i ka pouli, no ka mea, ua hewa ka lakou hana ana. Mahea e huli nei ko kakou alo, mamua anei i ke ao? mahope paha i ka po?

You who are reading [this], you see/know the nature of the old way of life of this archipelago, the land was crowded with darkness, and foolishness, and evil, and burdens, and injury, and death. It was a deep pit, a dark pit, a pit filled with every kind of filth, a pit of death, a pit of eternally lit fire, and it was there that all Hawaiians lived in the past! Now, enlightenment has come, but some people want the darkness, because they do sinful things. Which way should we turn, forward to the light? backward into the dark?

This diatribe is meant to push natives to conversion and also meant to justify the missionization, that is, saving the natives from their own culture, here indistinguishable from hell. Further, the narrative overall is meant to disrupt the moʻokūʻauhau that leads to and legitimates the ascension of Kamehameha. Kamehameha was already a kind of heroic figure whose exploits were not only remembered by people living at the time, but also recorded in writing by explorers and other visitors. He was credited with uniting the islands under one government. Dibble (and perhaps some of the students too) wanted to sever—in text—the modern Kamehameha from his moʻokūʻauhau that reached back to Wākea and Papa. Kamehameha here becomes part of God's plan to clear a path for the mission, since his uniting of the islands made it easier for the missionaries to gain footholds on multiple islands; but he was a secular figure only, not one with a sacred or divine moʻokūʻauhau in a competing religious system.

John Fawcett Pogue (Pokuea in Hawaiian) followed this first *Mooolelo Hawaii* with a revised version in 1858. Most of the text follows Dibble's closely with some important revisions that made it more palatable to Kānaka. One striking difference is that he removed the footnotes attached to Kamehameha's moʻokūʻauhau.[15] Pokuea's text was reprinted in Joseph Nāwahī's *Ke Aloha Aina* in 1896, in the midst of the struggle to prevent annexation to the United States.[16] Poepoe refers to it many times throughout his "Moolelo Hawaii Kahiko."

SAMUEL MĀNAIAKALANI KAMAKAU'S VARIOUS MOʻOLELO, 1865–1871

Samuel Kamakau published historical, genealogical, cosmogonic, and autoethnographic works continuously in the Hawaiian papers between 1865 and 1871.[17] More of his works were translated and published in the twentieth century than those by any other Kanaka author. His moʻolelo are long and much more detailed than any other author's versions of ancient and (his) contemporary Hawaiian history in Hawaiian. Kamakau was a noted kūʻauhau (genealogist) who also apparently kept hundreds if not thousands of mele in his mind and enriched all of his narratives with them. This is a distinctly Kanaka way of recording histories and philosophies that, with the exception of Abraham Fornander, made/makes no sense to haole historians.

Kamakau published a series in 1865 called "Ka Moolelo o Hawaii nei," and another from January 1869 to February 1871 called "Ka Moolelo Hawaii."[18] The two series contain versions of cosmogonies that connect to Wākea and Papa. Kamakau interwove a great deal of autoethnography, including descriptions of the genealogical ranking system of aliʻi, kāhuna, and even makaʻāinana and kauā, and types of heiau. His work is and was in his time a constant and powerful antidote to the foreign narratives of our history and culture.

Like Poepoe after him, Kamakau pondered the various theories of the origin of the world and the islands. He asserted that the listener or reader of the koʻihonua, or cosmogonic chants, must expect kaona and not take any chant literally.[19] He followed this with an assertion of a true origin of the world—that of the trinity of akua who created the world. Poepoe later analyzed this as one of many possible theories of our ancestors.

ABRAHAM FORNANDER'S *ACCOUNT OF THE POLYNESIAN RACE*

Between 1878 and 1885, Fornander published three volumes in English of his study of moʻolelo Hawaiʻi kahiko. Fornander was born in Sweden, immigrated to Hawaiʻi in the 1830s, and married Pinao Alanakapu, an aliʻi of Molokai. According to his great-granddaughter, Helen Doty, Fornander "was ardently pro-Hawaiian and fearless in standing up for his opinions. Consequently, he was unpopular with many of the missionary descendants and many of the selfish merchants."[20]

Fornander imagined his audience to be the literati of Europe but he introduced himself with a protocol recognizable to us today as similar to indigenous ways: "It is meet and proper . . . on presenting myths and legends . . . which have never darkened a sheet of paper before, that I should state my right to present them, how I came by them, and also the lights which guided and the aids which assisted me on the journey."[21] Unlike other haole chroniclers of Hawaiian lore, he "gratefully acknowledge[d] [his] obligations" to Kānaka by name, including "the late David Malo," Samuel Kamakau, Naihe, S. N. Hakuole, and Kepelino.[22]

Fornander was Poepoe's source for Kepelino's theories of creation by the trinity of akua. Poepoe read and assessed these volumes, but they were inaccessible to most Kānaka, who read only Hawaiian. Part of Poepoe's project was to make Fornander's information available to Kānaka in Hawaiian.

HOIKE A KA PAPA KUAUHAU O NA ALII HAWAII

In the early 1880s, Mōʻī Kalākaua instituted the Papa Kūʻauhau o nā Aliʻi Hawaiʻi, or Board of Genealogy of Hawaiian Chiefs, who issued a report of its work in both Hawaiian and English. The English version of the report stated that

> the principal duties of the Board shall be, viz: 1.–To gather, revise, correct and record the Genealogy of Hawaiian Chiefs. 2.—To gather, revise, correct and record all published and unpublished Ancient Hawaiian History. 3.—To gather, revise, correct and record all published and unpublished Meles, and also to ascertain the object and the spirit of the Meles, the age and the History of the period when composed.[23]

In addition, the Papa set out to "arrive at a correct hypothesis to account for the existence of its prehistoric people." They obtained "maps and illustrations of the deep sea sounding . . . from the American continent to Honolulu, and from Honolulu to the Asian Continent," which they used in "solving many points and theories already advanced by writers of the history of the Polynesian Races."[24]

Poepoe responds to and corrects some of the information in this report. The Papa's attempt to reconcile native cosmogonies with nineteenth-century haole science was a fairly long-lasting trend. After the board was terminated by the Bayonet Constitution government in 1887, its work was continued by a private association, the Hale Nauā. The Hale Nauā also drew on oceanography of the day for the same reasons. Joseph Kukahi incorporated the debate into his 1902 study of the Kumulipo and so did Poepoe.[25]

EMERSON'S TRANSLATION OF MALO'S *MOʻOLELO HAWAII*, 1903

In 1903, Nathaniel B. Emerson's English translation of Davida Malo's *Moolelo Hawaii* was published by the Bishop Museum. This is the only access that people of the era had to Malo's work. Malo was venerated as a genealogist who studied under the esteemed ʻAuwae; he was a fairly early convert to the Congregational Church and served in various government positions until he organized a protest of land sales to foreigners, after which he was stripped of his positions.[26] As mentioned earlier, he was the principal author of the original *Mooolelo Hawaii*. His own *Moolelo Hawaii*, however, is much more autoethnography than cosmogony or history. Only the last nine of sixty-seven chapters are genealogical moʻolelo of Hawaiʻi's early history. It is most unfortunate that Malo's full knowledge of the genealogies was not written or published. Nevertheless, Poepoe considered this an important work, despite the questionable translation by Emerson. As with Fornander's work, Poepoe wished to make the Hawaiian-reading public aware of this work in English, and he endeavored to correct what he saw as errors in it.[27]

Finally, John Charlot, a student and professor of these moʻolelo Hawaiʻi kahiko for decades, suggests that Poepoe was responding to Joseph Liwai Kukahi's 1902 publication of the Kumulipo with his own commentary and framing.[28] This may be so but Poepoe, not one shy to debate or correct anyone, never mentions Kukahi's work in his own. That book was well known through advertisements at the time, so Poepoe was undoubtedly aware of it.

POEPOE'S "MOOLELO HAWAII KAHIKO"

By the time of the publication of his own "Moolelo Hawaii Kahiko," Poepoe had been reading the above works of moʻolelo Hawaiʻi kahiko, and he had been collecting, editing, and publishing works of moʻolelo, mele, and moʻokūʻauhau since at least 1883, when he had been the editor of *Ka Hoku o ke Kai*. As mentioned in chapter 4, in 1896, in the midst of the intense struggle over annexation, when he was in the unpopular position of editing the pro-annexation paper, *Nupepa Kuokoa*, he gave and then published two lectures about the origin and peopling of the islands.[29] After establishing his own newspaper, *Ka Naʻi Aupuni*, in 1905, he published moʻolelo that he thought were important, notably the moʻolelo of Kamehameha, for whom the paper was named, and the moʻolelo of Hiʻiakaikapoliopele.

Hoʻoulumāhiehie was credited as the author of those two, but Poepoe signed his own name to "Moolelo Hawaii Kahiko."

He gave his reasons for writing and publishing the series in the preface, which I reproduce at length here because of its importance in framing the whole text:

> Ke hoopuka aku nei makou ma keia wahi o KA NAʻI AUPUNI i ka Moolelo Kahiko o Hawaii nei, e like me ia i hoomakaukau ia a kakauia e ka luna hooponopono o keia nupepa, a ke lana nei ko makou manao e lilo ana keia mahele i mea e pulamaia e na Opio Hawaii. Ua pili keia Moolelo i ko Hawaii nei "Ancient History," e like me ia i hoikeia ma na mele ame na kuauhau a ka poe kahiko.
>
> Ua hoalaia ae keia hana e ka Mea Kakau no kona makee a minamina maoli i ka moolelo e pili ana i na hana, ka nohona, a me na manao o ko Hawaii nei poe kupuna i hala aku i ka po. A no ia kumu, ua hoakoakoaia, hoiliiliia, houluuluia a hoonohonohoia na mahele o keia Moolelo, mai loko mai o na mele, na kuauhau ame na moolelo i paa ma na buke o keia ano i loaa i ka mea kakau, a he nui aku na mea i koe. O ka mea i paa a i loaa i ka mea kakau, e paa ana ia; aka, o ka mea i loaa ole a i paa ole iaia, na ka nalowale aku ia. A he nui hoi ka minamina no ka nalowale aku o kekahi mau mea ano nui iloko o ka ole mau loa.
>
> E hoomaopopoia, he lahui kakou me ko kakou Moolelo Kahiko, i ano like loa aku me ka moolelo kahiko o ka lahui o Helene; a he mau mele kahiko hoi ka ko kakou mau kupuna i like aku a i oi aku nohoi ko lakou hiwahiwa ame ke kilakila i ko na mele kaulana loa o ua lahui Helene nei.
>
> Ua piha ko kakou mau mele me na hoonupanupa ana a ia mea he aloha; piha me na keha ana no na hana koa a wiwo ole a ko kakou poe ikaika o ka wa kahiko; ka lakou mau hana kaulana; ko lakou ola ana ame ko lakou make ana. Aia maloko o ko kakou Moolelo Kahiko na Mele ame na Pule Wanana, na mele haʻi-kupuna a kuauhau hoi. Aia hoi maloko o na hana maa i ko kakou mau kupuna, he mau mahele ike i komo nui iloko o ke kupaianaha a me ke kamahao; a ua kapaia aku hoi ia mau mea e ka poe e noho ana iloko o na olino ana a ka naauao, he mau hana pouli, hupo, hoomanamana a Pegana hoi. Aka nae, o ka mea oiaio; he mea pono ke malamaia kekahi oia mau ike o ke au kahiko o na kupuna o kakou, elike me ka ike kalaiwaa, kilo-hoku, ame na ike e ae he nui. A i ka hoakoakoa ana i keia mau

mea apau me ka hoomaopopo ana i na olelo e hoike ana i ko lakou ano, ka lakou hana ame ko lakou waiwai i'o e loaa ai he moolelo.

"A o ka Moolelo," wahi a Cicero, "oia ka mea e hoao ai i ka manawa; oia ka malamalama o ka oiaio; ke ola o ka hoomanao; ka rula o ka hoomanao; ka elele o ka wa kahiko."[30]

―――

We are publishing in this space of KA NA'I AUPUNI the Ancient History of Hawai'i, as has been prepared and written by the editor of this newspaper, and we hope this section [of the paper] (mahele) will become something cherished, saved, or treasured by the Hawaiian Youth. This Moʻolelo concerns Hawai'i's "Ancient History," as was expressed in the mele and the kūʻauhau of the ancient people.

This work was started up (hoalaia) by the Author because of his affection and true valuing of the moʻolelo about the deeds, the lives, and the ideas of Hawai'i's kūpuna who have passed into the pō. For this reason, the parts of this Moʻolelo have been gathered, collected, assembled, and arranged from the mele, the genealogies, and the moʻolelo recorded in the books of this type that the author has, and there is a great deal besides those. The collection held by the writer will be recorded; however, what he does not have will disappear. Great is the regret for the disappearance of some important things into the unrecoverable void.

It should be understood, we are a people with our own Ancient Moʻolelo, which is rather like the ancient history of the people of Greece and our ancestors had old mele, which were similar to and which were beloved and whose majesty is superior to the most famous songs of the Greeks.

Our mele are filled with the lushness of that thing, aloha; filled with boasts about the brave and fearless deeds of our strong people of the past; their famous acts; their lives and their deaths. In our Ancient Moʻolelo are Mele and Prophetic Prayers, ancestral and genealogical mele. Also in the actions customary to our kūpuna are some types of knowledge (mahele ike) that have entered into the fantastic and strange; these things were called by the people living in the brightness of enlightenment, acts of darkness, ignorance, superstition, and Paganism. However, the truth is, it is pono that some of this knowledge of the old times of our kūpuna should be preserved, like canoe-carving knowledge, astronomy, and many other branches of knowledge. It is in gathering together all of these things, understanding the language that speaks of their nature, their deeds and their true worth, that we obtain a moʻolelo [our own history].

"History," according to Cicero, "is what enlightens time; it is the light of truth; the life of memory; the rule of memory; the messenger of the past."[31]

Poepoe hoped that this moʻolelo would be treasured by the Kanaka youth of his time, being educated in schools where English was the only allowable medium; they were the first generation expected to live their lives without knowing or caring about the language, literature, and traditions of their parents and grandparents.[32] Unlike some early Hawaiian writers, Poepoe was not primarily concerned with explaining the old language and culture to foreigners, not even to defend them. Like a more modern-day Kamakau or Kānepuʻu, he wanted to teach the younger Kanaka generations about the genius and artistry of their own ancestors. He knew, whether or not *they* knew it, that they needed to know who they were through knowing our people's traditions. Like Kānepuʻu he anticipated our need for this knowledge.

In some ways, Poepoe's "Moolelo" is similar to Fornander's: he examined all the theories about the origin of the islands and the native people. Unlike Fornander, however, he was not intent on proving the provenance of the Hawaiians from any specific places in the so-called Old World.

Poepoe begins by locating Hawaiʻi in the world, according to Hawaiian concepts rather than longitude and latitude:

> O ka Pae Moku o Hawaii nei, e like me ia e ikeia nei a i hoomaopopoia e ko Hawaii nei poe kahiko, eia no ia ke ku nei ma kahi, he aneane 1200 mile mai ka Piko mai o Wakea; oia hoi ka Poai-Waena, ma ka olelo a ka haole. A ke ku nei hoi ia maloko ponoi o ke Alanui Polohiwa a Kane, oia hoi, ke ala poai o ka hoailona o ke Ala-La (Zodiaka), i kapaia o "Papai," oia hoi ke "Ku-kuau" ma ka helu Hawaii.[33]

> The row of islands of Hawaiʻi, as known and understood by Hawaiʻi's ancient people, stands in a place nearly 1,200 miles from the Piko of Wākea, that is, the Middle Circle [Equator], in the language of the haole. It also stands directly inside of the Dark Path of the deity Kāne, that is, the circular path of the sign of the Zodiac called "Crab," the Kūkūau in the Hawaiian accounting.

The Alanui Polohiwa, or "Dark Path," of Kāne is one of the divisions of the sky in Hawaiian astronomy, used in long-distance ocean travel through star navigation. According to Pukui and Elbert, it is the "northern limit of the sun, about the middle of the month Kaulua."[34] This immediately alerts us that Poepoe was doing his best to situate his moʻolelo within Hawaiian epistemology/ies, using native concepts of the division of space and time, and the geography of the earth. He wanted the youth of his day and ours to know that our kupuna have not only their own histories but also their own ways of conceiving and organizing the world, utterly independent of haole technologies and ideas assumed by them to be superior.

He then proceeds to the names of the islands and their origins, using as source material "Mele a Pākuʻi" (which he calls a mele inoa [name song] for Kūaliʻi) and "Mele a Kahakukamoana."[35] These are ancient mele koʻihonua 5cited by Kamakau, Fornander, and other authors. The parents of the islands in these two mele are different from each other.[36] After showing them to the reader, he asks, "A o ka ninau nui i kupono e hoouluia ae, ma keia wahi, oia keia: Heaha la na manao o ka poe kahiko no na kumu i loaa ai ka aina ma Hawaii nei?" (The important question that it is appropriate to raise here is this: What were the ideas of the people of ancient times about the sources by which land was gotten in Hawaiʻi? [i.e., the origin of the islands].)[37] There are several words that can be interpreted differently here. One is "kumu," which I translated as "sources," but other possible glosses include foundation, base, beginning, and origin. Another is "loaʻa," which I translated as "gotten" but could be glossed as found, obtained, acquired, even discovered. The last phrase, then, could also be interpreted as "the origins of how land was obtained or discovered in Hawaiʻi."

Poepoe explains that people, and specifically Pogue, foolishly and erroneously mixed together the very different accounts of the genealogies of the Kumulipo, the stories of Papa and Wākea having given birth to the islands, and Wākea having made them with his hands. He, perhaps like Kamakau, implies that these are metaphors: they are actually genealogies disguised as stories of Papa giving birth to her children.

> No ka mea hoi e pili ana i ka mookuauhau, a i ole, i ka moolelo o ka Papa hanau ana mai i keia pae moku, a i ole, o ko Wakea hana maoli ana i keia mau mokupuni me kona mau lima, he lehulehu wale na mele ame na moolelo-kaao e hoike mai ana i keia mau manao. A ua kuhihewa kekahi poe, oia mau hoike ana mai a na mele, no ko

Papa hanau maoli ana mai la i keia mau Pae Moku, oiai nae o ka mea pololei maoli he mau kuauhau ia e hoike ana i ko Papa hanau ana i kana mau keiki.[38]

Concerning the genealogy, or the story of Papa's birthing the islands, or Wākea having made them with his hands, there are many mele and moʻolelo showing/telling these ideas. Some people are mistaken that these things told in the mele are about Papa giving birth to these islands, because the really correct thing is that these are genealogies telling of Papa giving birth to her children.

Poepoe then examines an important genealogical mele called "Hanau-a-Hua-ka-Lani," a birth chant for Kauikeaouli (Kamehameha III). This mele had been published previously in a very long version beginning on March 17, 1866, in *Nupepa Kuokoa*, with additions composed by six aliʻi, including Liholiho (Kamehameha II) and ke aliʻi nui Kuakini.[39] At that time March 17 was celebrated as the late Kamehameha III's birthday.[40] In 1886, another long, slightly different version was published in the book of songs celebrating Kalākaua on the occasion of his Jubilee (fiftieth birthday), *Na Mele Aimoku*, without the additions of the aliʻi appended in 1866. Poepoe excerpted about 126 lines from the version in *Na Mele Aimoku*.[41]

Each paukū (verse; stanza) is about the birth of one of various elements: first, the Lani, or sky/heavens; second, Papa, the Earth; third, the Pō, as in the Kumulipo; fourth, the island(s), Hawaiʻi (probably the archipelago and not the sole island); fifth, the Ao, the visible world, daylight, and clouds; sixth, the Mountain of Wākea (Mauna Kea); seventh, the Sun, which includes allusions to Māui and his mother, Hina; and last, the Ocean, which includes the names of the deities Kū, Kāne, Lono, Kanaloa, Kaekae, and Maliu, and finally Kamehameha, Keōpūolani (mother of Kamehameha II and III), Liholiho, and Kauikeaouli (Kamehameha II and III).

Mary Kawena Pukui and Alfons Korn interpret the mele as a hula whose purpose "was to bring 'an enriching and empowering magic' to the ceremonial and sexual union of *aliʻi* . . . especially to the birth of a royal child destined to become a great leader."[42] They did not, however, attend to genealogy in their very brief introduction to the mele. They focus some attention on Kauikeaouli's birth; he had been stillborn and was "prayed into life" by the kahuna Kapihe, famous until today for the following prophecy:

> E iho ana ʻo luna,
> E piʻi ana ʻo lalo,
> E hui ana nā moku,
> E kū ana ka paia.
>
> What is above will come down,
> What is below will ascend,
> The islands will be joined,
> The walls will stand.

The prophecy seems to have foreshadowed events in Kauikeaouli's life, when the religion undergirding the aliʻi system was taken down and makaʻāinana could be elected to decision-making positions.

Kameʻeleihiwa excerpts the mele as an illustration of the familial relationships among the ʻāina, the aliʻi, and makaʻāinana. The aliʻi is Kauikeaouli, whose name contains the word(s) "ao uli" or "aouli." "Ao" is the word for "daylight" or "cloud"; "ao uli" could be a dark cloud; "aouli" as a single word refers to the "firmament, sky, blue vault of heaven."[43] The name aligns the aliʻi with the heavens while makaʻāinana are symbolically what is below, the land (the word "ʻāina" forms part of the word "makaʻāinana").[44]

For Poepoe this mele is an important part of our ancestral lore on the cosmos and genealogy. He notes it as "kekahi moolelo o ka lilo ana o Wakea a pela no me Papa i mau kumu e loaa ai he Lani, he Honua ame na mea apau i piha ai laua" (another moʻolelo about how Wākea and Papa become the sources of the Sky and Earth and everything that fills them).[45] He explains,

> Ke ike ae la no kakou i na hoike a ke mele i hoikeia ae la. He ano a he kulana mookuauhau maoli no ka hoike a ke mele a kakou e ike ae la. Ke hookolo nei ke mele i ka hoomailani ana i ko Kauikeaouli mookuauhau alii mai ia Wakea ma mai me na kikoo ana ae i na kikepakepa ana i ka Honua, ka Lani, ka Moana, ke Kai, ka La, a pela aku.
>
> No laila, ke ike maopopo nei kakou, he kahua, a he kaona maopopo ka ka poe haku mele i kukulu ai i ka lakou mau mele kuauhau alii i haku ai, aole no ko lakou manaoio ana ua hanau maoli ia mai e Wakea ame Papa ka Honua ame ka Lani ame ko laua mau mea i piha ai; aole.[46]

———

We see what the mele has shown. What it shows (ka hoike) takes the form and shape of an actual genealogy that we see. The mele tracks the exalting of Kauikeaouli's aliʻi genealogy from Wākea [and Papa, etc.], stretching the sides to the Earth, the Sky, the open Ocean, the Sea, the Sun, and so forth.

Therefore we understand there is a platform or foundation (kahua) and that composers had kaona they understood upon which to construct the genealogical chants that they composed, not because they believed that the Earth and Sky and all that is in them were born of Wākea and Papa, no.

In other words, the mele is a genealogical chant similar to the Kumulipo; it begins with the sky and the earth, moves through the deities, with specific attention to Māui from whom Kamehameha is descended, and finally to Kamehameha and his royal children. Papa and Wākea are also exalted ancestors whose importance is highlighted in the mele. Again, kaona must be expected as an integral part, a *foundation*, of any mele koʻihonua and the task of any listener or reader is to interpret the mele accordingly.

Here is an excerpt of one stanza (paukū 6) with a translation by Poepoe himself:

> O hanau ka mauna a Wakea
> O puu aʻe ka mauna a Wakea
> O Wakea ke kane, o Papa o Walinuu ka wahine
> Hanau Hoohoku he wahine
> Hanau Haloa he ʻlii
> Hanau ka Mauna he keiki mauna na Wakea
> O ka lili o Wakea o haʻi ka hala
> O ke kuku a ka manene
> I hoouka ai i iloko o Kahiki-ku
> Hee Wakea kalewa kona ohua
> Kuamu ia e Kane, kuawa ia e Kane
> Hoi mai o Kane a loko o Lanimoemoe,
> Moe Wakea moe ia Papa
> Hanau ka la na Wakea
> He keiki kapu na Wakea . . .[47]

> The mountain of Wakea arises,
> Wakea's mountain rises up into knolls,
> Wakea the husband, Papa, Walinuu the wife,
> Hoohoku, a woman, is born,

> Haloa, the king, is born,
> The mountain is born, the mountain child of Wakea,
> The anger of Wakea was caused by the telling of his fault [wrongdoing],
> The fault (his) was fighting with sticks,
> Which he fought at Kahiki-ku,
> Wakea was routed, he and his people swam in the ocean,
> He was laughed at by Kane, and derided by Kane,
> Kane returned to Lanimoemoe,
> Then Wakea cohabited with Papa,
> And she gave birth to the Sun, a son of Wakea
> A tabued child of Wakea . . .[48]

Here Poepoe teaches us a great deal. Although the mele does not look like a genealogical table of names of male and female parents, it is in the form of a genealogy. Genealogies of aliʻi nui here were "stretched" to attach to cosmogonies in order to exalt or legitimate the aliʻi. One mustn't think our kupuna kahiko actually took the moʻolelo of Wākea and Papa literally, far from it. Rather, these are ingeniously crafted metaphors. They are carrying substantial symbolic weight and are also indicative of a way of being in the world and of conceiving the world and our place in it—we are part of a family that includes the sun, stars, ocean, and everything else in the world.

Further, this is part of his teaching us how to read an ancient composition. In the Hawaiian, the first line reads "O hanau ka mauna a Wakea," which is virtually the same as the phrasing of the later lines "Hanau Hoohoku he wahine" and "Hanau Haloa he 'lii." In the latter two, he translates the word "hānau" as "was born" but in the first line, he uses "arises" instead. One lesson is not to be too literal in the reading and, in addition, to be careful with translation. He doesn't allow himself to be tied to one English word for one Hawaiian word, but instead he shows by example that there is no word-for-word simple correspondence between English and Hawaiian. It is ironic that his translation was labeled (by someone else) as a literal translation.[49]

Another lesson is to read this mele as the moʻolelo of Papa, Wākea, Hoʻohōkūkalani, and Hāloa. Hoʻohōkūkalani was a girl child of Papa and Wākea and, when she grew up, Wākea slept with her. The first child Wākea and Hoʻohōkūkalani produced was Hāloalaukapalili, or Hāloanaka, born as a cord and planted/buried (the concept "kanu" is two concepts in English, "plant" and "bury"). From the burial site grew the first kalo. The second child was also named Hāloa and said to be the first aliʻi. This moʻolelo is one of the most important and central to understanding aliʻi culture, and since Lilikalā Kameʻeleihiwa's groundbreaking interpretation in her doctoral dissertation and the book that followed, it became central to contemporary discourses of sovereignty and love for and protection of the land.[50] Hāloalaukapalili is the elder brother who represents the land, and Hāloa, the human being, is the younger brother who represents Kanaka ʻŌiwi. The sibling relationship explains, in part, the values of aloha ʻāina and mālama ʻaina (care for the land).

The final part of this stanza that strengthens the idea of the ʻāina as our family reads as follows:

Hanau ka Mauna
He makahiapo kapu na Wakea
Oia ho—i, o ka Mauna
Hanau ka Mauna
O ka mauna la hoi auanei ko lalo nei
Owai la hoi auanei ko luna la?
Owai la, o ka La,
Aia! Aia hoi ha.[51]

Then, it was the mountain,
The mountain was [Wākea's] firstborn son,
That is it, the Mountain,
The mountain is born,
The mountain is that which is below here.
And what is it like in the space above?
What is it? What? The Sun!
There! There you have it.[52]

He again interprets the word "hānau" differently in the identical lines "Hanau ka mauna," first as "it was the mountain," then as "The mountain is born." Mauna Kea here, the highest point in the Hawaiian archipelago, is the firstborn son of Wākea, and above this mountain is the sun. Here we are presented with Mauna Kea as the older sibling of both Hāloas and, thus, the sacred oldest sibling of all Kanaka Hawaiʻi as well. As powerfully as Hāloa, Mauna Kea is our family member, as is Wākea and the island-birthing mother, Papa. This explains why Kānaka Hawaiʻi are passionately defending this mountain against damage from ever more and ever larger telescopes.[53]

In the final section, paukū 8, the ocean also belongs to, was born, and is connected to Wākea, but while the ocean is said to be what is down below here, what is above, at the end, is not Wākea, but the deities Kū, Lono, Kāne, Kanaloa, Kaekae, and Maliu. The last two are names of stars, and Kamakau says they were the names of haole kāhuna.[54]

In sum, this mele is like another Kumulipo in a different poetic form and connected to a more recent aliʻi, Kauikeaouli. Poepoe's inclusion of it in this text and his explanations allow us to consider its importance and deepen our understanding of all our relations.

THE KUMULIPO

Poepoe now leaves off his explanations of what caused some people to believe that the islands were created through birth by Papa and Wākea, and he moves on to consider the theory expressed in the Kumulipo: the islands were not a creation by a god but a coming into being from the Pō. He first calls the Kumulipo "he mele kahiko loa," a very ancient mele, and describes its two main divisions: the Pō (the origins of the universe, earth, plants, animals, and deities) and the Ao (the eras of human beings). He then gives the known history of the mele: it was performed at a ceremony for Captain Cook in 1779 at Hikiau heiau in Kona, Hawaiʻi Island, but it was composed much earlier, in the time of Kūaliʻi, according to Kamakau.[55]

Poepoe defines the name "Kumulipo" as "he hookumu ana iloko o ka lipolipo hohonu o ka Po" (an establishing in the deep darkness of the Pō).[56] In the sections that follow he further divides the genealogical eras (wā) into three: the Pō until Laʻilaʻi the first woman is born, the Ao from Laʻilaʻi to Papa and Wākea, and from Papa and Wākea to Kamehameha I. The Kalākaua text, which is the only complete version of the Kumulipo known to us and probably to Poepoe, does not trace to Kamehameha but rather to Lonoikamakahiki, an ancestor of Kalākaua.[57] It is quite easy, however, to follow Hāloa's line through a different descendant and arrive at Kamehameha, as did Kepoʻokūlou in 1835 and Kamakau in 1842.[58]

Poepoe, unlike more recent scholars, was not fascinated with the first third of the Kumulipo that recites the names of plants, animals, stars, and deities. Rather he desired to impress upon us the importance of the second and third sections, pages and pages of which seem to be just lists of names. He begs the reader's patience in this section, "oiai, he ano panoonoo a ku ole i ka hoihoi na maawe o nei kuauhau, elike no me na mookuauhau Hawaii e ae"[59] (since, it is a type of memorization or recording (panoonoo) and the strands or paths of this genealogy are not interesting, like the other Hawaiian genealogies). He begins with a kūʻauhau that starts with Kumulipo and Pōʻele, the male and female pair of mysterious darkness or night, and ends at Kapōkini because "mai iaia mai i loaa mai ai o Lailai (w), ke kino kanaka mua loa i ikeia ma 'Hawaii' kahiko nei" (from him or her comes Laʻilaʻi [woman]. the first physical person known in ancient "Hawaiʻi"). He puts quotation marks around Hawaiʻi because it had not been named that yet. Although he constructed this genealogy from the different wā in the Kumulipo, it doesn't match the Kalākaua text exactly.[60] For the next five weeks, or thirty-four issues of the paper, lists of names of kūpuna appear, interrupted from time to time by corrections to the Papa Kūʻauhau Aliʻi's report, or very short moʻolelo.

Starting on April 1, 1906, he explains the separate kūʻauhau of Papa and Wākea. This is very instructive. Ololo is the older brother whose line leads to Wākea, and Palikū is the younger brother whose line leads to Papa. Poepoe notes that some versions have this order reversed.[61] He places the lines side-by-side so we can see how they run at the same time, whereas in the Kumulipo, they appear one after another and it is not clear without careful examination that they happen in the same period and eventually, separately, produce the pair, Wākea and Papa. In other words, wā 12 leads to Wākea via Kahikoluamea, his father. Wā 13 leads to Papa via her mother, Kahakauakoko. Then wā 14 gives the genealogy of both Wākea's mother, Kupulanakēhau, and Papa's father, Kūkalaniehu, who are siblings. Now the reader can see that wā 12, 13, and 14 all happen during the same period, as they all lead to Papa and Wākea through their different parents (see Table 6.1).[62]

In addition to showing us how to read the Kumulipo in this way, Poepoe directs our attention to important elements in the text. He notes where the man named Kumuhonua appears in the moʻokūʻauhau, which is important because some have posited this as "ke kumu . . . e nee mai ai ka lakou hahau kuauhau ana" (the source by which their genealogy building moves). He also notes that there are other "maawe mookuauhau" (genealogical tracks) that he will show later on. Although the text had been preserved in print by Kalākaua, Poepoe also believed that publishing these texts in the newspaper helped to preserve them:

TABLE 6.1. Excerpts from Poepoe's Moʻokūʻauhau Kumulipo in translation.

Wā 12: Wākea's Descent from Ololo Line	Wā 13: Papa's Descent from Palikū Line		Wā 14: Wākea's Brother Was Papa's Father
Born was Palikū Born was Ololo	Palikū, the man	Palihai, the woman	
…	…		…
WELAAHILANINUI, the man	Mohala, the man	Luukaualani, the woman	Maluapo Lawekeao
Owe, the woman			[Among the many children of these two was KUPULANAKĒHAU w. The twenty-three named siblings that follow are not shown here. The Kalākaua text of the Kumulipo does not make this at all clear.]
KAHIKOLUAMEA [son of Welaahilaninui, father of Wākea]	Kupulanakēhau [mother of Wākea]	Kahakaiawe- aukelekele	KUPULANAKĒHAU Kahikoluamea [mother of Wākea] [father of Wākea]
		Hinawainonolo	
WĀKEA Lihauʻula Makulu	Kahokukele-moana	Hinawaioki	KŪKALANIEHU k. [father of Papa, brother of Wākea]
	Kahakauakoko w.		
	Kūkalaniehu	KAHAKAUAKOKO	
	PAPA-NUI-HĀNAU-MOKU is born		

The table was created by Marie Alohalani Brown.

Ua hana ka mea kakau pela i mea e hoouluulu pono ia ai na mahele Kuauhau i ikeia o Hawaii nei i ole e nalowale mai ka Lahui Hawaii aku o kela [*sic*] wa ame ko muli aku nei hoi.⁶³

The writer has done this so that the parts of the genealogies of Hawaiʻi that are known will be compiled in full so that they will not disappear from the Lāhui Hawaiʻi of this time or that of those coming after.

To transition from this section, he notes that the time period between Laʻilaʻi and Papa is estimated at "7 mano, 5 lau, 2 kaau, 4 kauna ame 2 keu makahiki, oia hoi, he 30,090 makahiki ia ma ka helu o keia wa"⁶⁴ (7 four thousands, 5 four hundreds, 2 forties, 4 fours, and 2 years, which is 30,090 years in the counting system of today). He uses the Hawaiian counting system when most readers do not know it in order to show that it can and should be used. Like Kānepuʻu, who back in 1867 was already decrying the loss of the native counting system, Poepoe wanted to perpetuate this ancestral way of thinking and doing things.⁶⁵

Poepoe writes that the Kumulipo plus the Kumuhonua genealogies together constitute moʻolelo Hawaiʻi kahiko and that Wākea is the piko at which they come together.⁶⁶ Two of Pukui and Elbert's glosses for "piko" are "navel, navel string, umbilical cord" and "place where a stem is attached to the leaf, as of taro."⁶⁷ Poepoe emphasizes,

Mamuli o keia mookuauhau i hoikeia ae la, e hele ana mai a Lailai w mai a hoea ia WAKEA ame PAPA . . . e maopopo ai "ka manao o ko Hawaii nei Lahuikanaka."⁶⁸

It is through this moʻokūʻauhau just shown, running from Laʻilaʻi to WĀKEA and PAPA[,] . . . that the "thought of Hawaiʻi's native people" can be understood.

What is the native thought that we can understand from these cosmogonic genealogies? To begin with, Wākea and Papa are at once divine and natural elements (Wākea, the sky and sun; Papa, the earth) and human ancestors in the genealogies. This explains why the bulk of the work and the longest mokuna (III) focus on the moʻolelo of Wākea, Papa, and their descendants.

"KA MOOLELO O KO WAKEA MA NOHO ANA MA KALIHI—
KA LOAA ANA O KE AKUA ULU O KAMEHAʻIKANA"

This part of mokuna III (a story about Wākea and others' life in Kalihi and the acquisition of the breadfruit deity, Kāmehaʻikana) is the first long historical, legendary, and possibly religious narrative in the work. It is an excellent example of how moʻokūʻauhau carry moʻolelo along with them. This one is located within the genealogy that Poepoe says he is tracing from Wākea and Papa to Kamehameha I. It ran daily from May 2 to June 18, 1906, in this paper published six days a week, for about 19,500 words. It appears to be the longest extant account. Kamakau's version of this is comparatively short and only a portion of a single newspaper installment.[69]

Many elements in this narrative illustrate Poepoe's statement that it is through the moʻokūʻauhau that we can understand our kupuna's thought. One of the most important is how it shows the integral nature and centrality of mana wahine (female mana) in Hawaiian religious, political, and genealogical thought, as evident in the discussion that follows.

In the moʻolelo, Papa, in her form as Haumea, is living with Wākea in their mountain home in Kilohana, high in the uplands at the back of Kalihi Valley, Oʻahu. She goes shore fishing one day at Keʻalohi, Heʻeia, on the Koʻolau side. Wākea goes to gather in the forest for food to accompany the fish. He cuts down an "ahui maia a ka nui launa ole. Ua hele nohoi a oo pono"[70] (a very large bunch of bananas, which was completely ripe). Bananas were important not only for food, but also as a kino lau of Kanaloa and as offerings to both Kāne and Kanaloa.[71] Here they may also be symbolic of the people, since they are growing in an area claimed by the aliʻi Kumuhonua (also known as Kānekumuhonua), whom Wākea, Haumea, and their people will defeat. Wākea and his people then will control the area.

Kumuhonua's guards grab Wākea and take him prisoner for stealing the bananas. They take him to a breadfruit tree near the stream Pūehuehu in Nuʻuanu, now bordering the Liliʻuokalani Botanical Garden and Kuakini Medical Center in Honolulu. He is tied to the tree while messengers go to Waikīkī and report to Kumuhonua that the "mu ai maia" (banana-eating Mū) has been caught.[72] Kumuhonua orders the man to die by burning in an imu (an underground oven similar to that used for cooking). The imu is lit while Wākea is tied to the tree. In the meantime, Haumea sees signs in the sky (a storm) and returns home, then follows the smoke of the imu. She meets a man named Kaliʻu, who tells her what has happened, whereupon she delivers this soliloquy:

> He maia ulu wale ko ke kuahiwi, he maia ma ka nahelehele, he inai na ke kini a me ka pukuʻi o ka manu. No ke aha hoi i kapu ole ia ai ka manu i ka maia a kapu iho la hoi i ke kanaka? Hoouna ka hoi ua ʻlii nei o oukou i kona poe kanaka, e kiu i ke kanaka e kii ana i ka mea a kona lima i luhi ole ai; a hoouna ole ka hoi oia i na kau-kia-manu ana e pulehua a e ahele i ka ma[n]u ai maia? He aha la kana. Ola ka manu ai maia, ola nohoi ke kanaka ai maia. Noonoo ole nohoi ua ʻlii nei o oukou, he maia ke kanaka, a kona la nohoi e hua iho ai, hua no.[73]
>
> ———
>
> The mountains have bananas that grow by themselves; the forest has bananas, which are food for people and the assemblies of birds. Why is it that the banana is not kapu [forbidden] to the birds but only to people? Your aliʻi has sent his people to spy on a person getting something for which [your aliʻi's] hands did not labor; but he did not send his bird catchers to gum the trees and snare the banana-eating birds. What is his reason? The banana-eating birds live, and so do the banana-eating people [i.e., birds live on the bananas and so do people]. This aliʻi of yours has not considered [the ʻōlelo noʻeau] a person is a banana tree that in his/her day will fruit, and it will fruit.

Kawena Pukui included a version of this ʻōlelo noʻeau in her 1983 collection: "He maiʻa ke kanaka a ka lā e hua ai. A man is like a banana tree on the day it bears its fruit. One can tell what kind of man he is by his deeds. In olden days banana stalks were often likened to men."[74] Implicit here is that a person's character, whether pono or hewa, will eventually be known by the results of their actions. Haumea's speech expresses ideas of what is pono and hewa: the food is in the forest for people to gather. The aliʻi has overstepped his kuleana in claiming the food of the forest, which neither he nor his people had to expend labor on. The banana stand had likely been planted a long time before by a previous generation and intentionally "left to grow and propagate untended."[75] This aliʻi, therefore, can be seen to be behaving in a way that is not pono, but hewa. This serves as a justification for Haumea and Wākea to wage war against him and take over the rule of Oʻahu.

With Kaliʻu providing a bit of leftover ʻawa, Haumea prepares an ʻawa ceremony to ask their ancestors for assistance in freeing Wākea. The area is dry, however, without fresh water to mix the ʻawa to drink. Haumea sends up a prayer to her ancestors whose names begin with the word "Pali" (cliff) and to the deity Kāne, after which she is able to lift and throw a huge "pali pōhaku" (rock cliff or a rock large enough to be compared to a cliff) against the side of a dry streambed, filling it with water.[76] This stream now flows continuously and is called Pūehuehu (sprayed or dispersed) in honor of the event.[77] It also created a pool of the same name that people of the area used to dive and swim in.[78]

The ʻawa ceremony was successful, and from there Haumea went to the place where Wākea was tied up:

> Ike aku la no keia i ke kane, ua hauhoaia a paa i ke kumu ulu. A ua ike mai la nohoi o Wakea i ka wahine a kulu iho la kona mau waimaka, a kau pololei mai la kona mau maka i ka wahine, a na ka waimaka no e huʻe i ka lau o ka lihilihi.[79]
>
> ———
>
> She saw the man who was tied up to the breadfruit tree. Wākea also saw the woman and his tears fell; when his eyes were directly upon the woman, tears overflowed his eyelashes.

This is the first but not the last time that we see Wākea in a helpless position, able to do nothing but cry and get rescued by his wahine. This would seem unmasculine in a haole story so it brings up questions about how gender is conceived, as well as highlighting Haumea's mana wahine. Do concepts of masculine and feminine exist in this Hawaiian world? If so, what are they and how are they performed? Wākea is, in a sense, an archetypal male, the male progenitor of the lāhui, if not the whole human race, along with the islands and the sun. Being rescued by the powerful female progenitor does not diminish his own mana; weeping and getting rescued are not shameful or humiliating. He will have a role to play in which his mana kāne (male mana) is fully exercised. When he does so, that similarly does not seem to diminish Haumea's mana wahine. This is an indicator of the concept of balance (pono) in gender roles shared by our ancestors.

Haumea rescues Wākea by approaching to honi him goodbye (sharing breath through the nose) but instead striking the tree, which makes a huge noise and opens up like the mouth of a cave; the pair disappear into it, emerge on the other side of the tree, and proceed down to the shore, unseen by the guards. This action creates the deity called Kāmehaʻikana in the kino (physical body) of the ʻulu (breadfruit) tree; Kāmehaʻikana is thereafter one of Haumea's names and the ʻulu tree is one of her kino lau.[80] In this part of the moʻolelo, Haumea is the one who subsequently wages war in wondrous ways, while using the name Haumea rather than Kāmehaʻikana, but it was the latter name that was used by Kamehameha, and probably by other aliʻi, in her role as a war god.[81]

Poepoe calls attention to the ʻulu tree being a kino lau of Haumea, giving us "ke mele Koihonua a ka poe kahiko no Haumea ame kona kino kumu-ulu"[82] (the genealogical song of the ancestors about Haumea and her breadfruit-tree body). He observes,

> E kakoo ana keia mele i ka mea i hoikeia ma ka moolelo e pili ana i ko Haumea iho ana mai uka mai o Kalihi a hoea i Waikahalulu ae nei, kahi ona me Wakea, kana kane i komo ai iloko o ka ulu; a kapaia ai ka ulu o Kamehaikana; a oia hoi ke kino ulu o Haumea.
>
> ———
>
> This mele supports what has been said in the moʻolelo concerning Haumea's descent from the uplands of Kalihi and arrival in Waikahalulu, the place where she and Wākea her man entered into the breadfruit tree, which was called Kāmehaʻikana, and is the breadfruit body of Haumea.

This is an example of how Poepoe brings in ancient and genealogical mele to substantiate his observations and analyses, just as Kamakau did before him. It is also indicative of an epistemology firmly grounded in Hawaiian thought. While haole historians and others saw the absence of writing in the old world as a lack, Poepoe trusts the old mele as interpretable testimony, while appreciating its artistry. Poepoe refuses to see the oral ways of recording history and knowledge as lacking in sophistication or development; rather they are evidence of our kupuna's intelligence, competence, and talent. They are a different, but no less valuable, perhaps even more valuable, method of recording.

In a later section of the moʻolelo, Haumea directs Kaliʻu and his ʻohana to settle on the other side of the Koʻolau Mountains at Luluku. There the story takes a detour to show Haumea as the deity of childbirth. The aliʻi ʻOlopana's daughter is in labor but the child is unable to emerge. Haumea administers the lāʻau (medicine), flowers of a plant called Kalauokekahuli, also known as Kamaunaihalakaipo. In exchange she asks ʻOlopana for the child as hānai (adopted). The child is stillborn, born blue (uliuli), but she revives it by burning the still-attached placenta in a fire, and both mother and child live. ʻOlopana is a powerful aliʻi nui, and it is a political move for Haumea to ask for the child to hānai, as that brought the two aliʻi nui families together, lessening any chance of ʻOlopana turning against Haumea and Wākea when they take over the rule of the island. Haumea (sometime later) takes the lāʻau to Maui and Kauaʻi. On Kauaʻi the two flowers, also known as Kanikawī and Kanikawā, become deities of Lohiʻau and bring Pele to him.[83] Here Poepoe takes the opportunity to teach the various aspects of Papa/Haumea as deity and to point out the link to another series of moʻolelo, that of Hiʻiakaikapoliopele.

A salient aspect of Haumea/Kāmehaʻikana is that of a female deity of war. The first battle between Haumea-Wākea on the one side and Kumuhonua on the other takes place over the entrance to Kalihi Valley. The sides are evenly matched even though Kumuhonua has more people. Haumea does not intervene in this skirmish:

> O Haumea hoi, aole oia i hana mai i kahi hana ma kona ano kupua maluna o na kanaka o ko laua hoa paonioni, oiai ua aloha oia i na kanaka no ko lakou mauna maʻu wale ana i ko lakou mau kino e lilo i mau moe-puu mahope o Kumuhonua.[84]
>
> ———
>
> Haumea did not take any action through her magical powers on the people of their opponent, because she felt aloha for the people wasting their bodies to become death companions for Kumuhonua.

Haumea disapproves, apparently, of Kumuhonua using the makaʻāinana to fight the war. Later, however, when the battles move to the other side of the island, she mercilessly kills many of his men.

Eventually, when Kumuhonua's numbers overwhelm Wākea's side, Wākea asks Haumea what to do and she advises moving to the windward side, first to Luluku where she had settled Kaliʻu and his ʻohana, then to Palikū, the ridge at Kualoa that separates Koʻolaupoko from Koʻolauloa, who is Haumea's ancestor. (The sacredness of Kualoa and Palikū were discussed in chapter 5.) She gains strength and a tremendous advantage by conducting war at the place symbolic of her "pali" ancestors. The ʻāina itself here provides her strength and spiritual support. Haumea's knowledge of both her genealogy and the geography is necessary to access this strength and support. On another level, since she is also a manifestation of Papa, she is the land itself. This is in contrast to Kumuhonua's lack of knowledge of his geography that is revealed, when the kahuna Kamōʻawa felt compelled to tell him that he was living at ʻĀpuakēhau, the birthplace of Haumea.[85] Kumuhonua's ignorance foreshadows his defeat.

Once they move to Palikū, Haumea unleashes her powers against Kumuhonua's forces. She first hides Wākea and their companions in a cave inside Pohukaina, in the mountain of Palikū.[86] Between the spring in Kaʻaʻawa called Kaʻahuʻula and Kalaeokaʻōʻio (the seaward boundary line between Koʻolauloa and Koʻolaupoko), from the uplands to the shore, the land was filled with women holding kukui nuts in their hands:

> O keia poe wahine a nei poe kanaka e ike aku nei, oia na kino lehulehu o Haumea. A o ia no ke kumu o kona kapaia ana he wahine kino lehu, kino mano, a kino hoopahaohao hoi.[87]
>
> ⸻
>
> These women that the people saw were the many bodies of Haumea. This is the reason she was called a woman with 400,000 bodies, 4,000 bodies, and wondrous, mystifying, or transfigured bodies.

The warriors approach, not understanding that the women too are warriors, and ask Haumea where Wākea is. She advises them that the only way to get to Wākea is to fight the women, but they return to their leader for instructions as the women do not seem prepared for battle, because they hold only kukui nuts. When the warriors come back, the women throw the nuts at their foreheads and they are struck dead. The kukui is called in English the candlenut because Kanaka used to use the oil for lamps. It is thus a symbol of intelligence and enlightenment (as problematic as that term is). The forehead is also a symbol of intelligence. The striking of the foreheads by kukui nuts, then, is symbolic of Haumea's use of her superior intelligence against Kumuhonua's attempt at brute force. Poepoe says this event is remembered by an ʻōlelo noʻeau and in a mele honoring Kūaliʻi. He takes some time to point out the specific lines. This is a good example of the ways that he teaches us to read:

> Aia nohoi iloko o na lalani mele:
>
> "O kukui alii i ke alo o Papa
> I kumu-kukui la ka Papa"
>
> E loaa ai na hoomanao ana a ka mea haku mele alii no na hua o ke kumu-kukui a Haumea (Papa) kino pahaohao e luku ai i na kanaka o

Kane Kumuhonua, elike me ia i hoikeia ae la. A ke hoike nei ke mele, he "alii" ke "kukui" i ke alo o Papa; a o ua "kumu kukui" alii la, wahi no a ke mele he papa ia; oia hoi, he papa au-kai a heenalu paha no ua Haumea nei. He hohonu a he kuliu ke mele a ka poe kahiko, a he ano pohihihi no ke *Kuailo* ana i ka manao.[88]

In the lines of the mele:

"Aliʻi kukui in the presence of Papa
The kukui tree becomes a Papa [board]"

are found the composer's remembrance of the nuts of the kukui tree with which mystical-bodied Haumea destroyed Kumuhonua's people, as was said above. The mele says that the kukui is an "aliʻi" in the presence of Papa, and this aliʻi kukui tree, according to the mele, is a "papa," that is, a swimming or surf board for Haumea. The mele of the ancient people are profound and deep, and of a complex nature to challenge the mind (and perhaps make one give up).

Although this seems a bit like a riddle within a riddle, we must venture to interpret Poepoe's interpretation and try to understand what he wants to teach us. The kukui is Papa's aliʻi—an aliʻi is one who leads, governs, is surrounded with kapu, and whose genealogy connects to the deities. The kukui here then is a leader or ruler and possibly is divine.[89] The tree becomes a swim- or surfboard, a device that assists one to travel across the water with greater speed and less effort, a metaphor perhaps for the event of the kukui nuts killing Kumuhonua's warriors, which gets Haumea where her ancestors want them to go: deeper into a war with Kumuhonua and, in a step in that war, then swept out into the bay. Kukui is a type of tree that provides wood that is suitable for surfboards.[90] That "Papa" is the word that is used for all of these facilitates the multiplicity of meaning: it is a board; a name for Haumea, the female progenitor symbolizing the earth; the ʻāina itself; and a foundation from which to act.

Poepoe is teaching us that we have to read this in a certain way, keeping in mind that it is complex, and we may never fully understand it. In other words, we shouldn't think we understand a mele at first reading. It may be even more than that: is reading in this way part of our continually becoming the Lāhui Hawaiʻi? Are we to learn to read this way in order to transform ourselves, to recognize ourselves as Kanaka, to see ourselves as a specific lāhui? This kind of challenging mele and moʻolelo full of kaona and our obligation to interpret them are aspects of our kupuna's culture that characterize us as a people, an intellectual people. It is not just a characterization that belongs to the past but also to today. How do we keep becoming our lāhui? What is our kuleana in regard to learning our kupuna's language and ways of being, thinking, and doing? In our own actualizing of moʻokūʻauhau consciousness, it seems to me that it is our kuleana to learn to read and think this way, and we must teach this to the younger generations of Kanaka.

Haumea has won this battle but allows the next one to be won by Kumuhonua "i ko ai ka makemake o kona mau kupuna i ka po" (to satisfy the desire of her kūpuna in the pō). This is apparently so that a ceremony in the ocean can be performed. She requests that the "kai mimiki," a "roiling sea" or a sea that sucks things in, come onto shore and engulf them and sweep them into the ocean.[91]

Once they are swept out to the deep sea, we see Wākea again represented as rather helpless with his tears flowing. This time he asks Kamōʻawa the kahuna what to do, and the kahuna says that they will build a heiau, perform a ceremony, and then be assisted by the akua to reach land and escape drowning.[92] But how to build a heiau while treading water in the ocean? Wākea's hands serve as the walls of the heiau; they also catch a humuhumunukunukuapuaʻa fish to substitute for a pig (puaʻa) as an offering; and the kahuna gathers their people that are floating in the water to form the ʻaha, or assembly, for the ceremony. The word "ʻaha" simultaneously refers to the conduct of the ceremony and the result; if the ceremony is successful, an ʻaha has been reached.[93] This episode illustrates how the lack of any element for a ceremony need not be an obstacle because acceptable substitutions can always be made. It is notable that Haumea does not seem to have a part in this ceremony, although her actions made it happen. Until they were abolished, heiau ceremonies were primarily a male sphere of activity. When Wākea's ceremony is successful, they are all taken by a wave to an island near shore, which is called Kapapa in her honor.

Following this, Wākea and company successfully defeat Kumuhonua, who dies from a wound in the hip from a spear thrown by Wākea's war leader, Kaliʻu. Wākea then takes over the rule of the whole of Oʻahu. In that rather long narrative, we can see the tight identification of the divine—Wākea with the sky, Haumea of the wondrous bodies and deeds—with the ʻāina and natural elements. Haumea's ancestors are mountain cliffs, and she can manifest as a breadfruit tree; she is Papa, the earth. This close identification extends to the aliʻi as well; Wākea and Haumea become the aliʻi nui ruling Oʻahu, and the moʻolelo represents them as pono, and in opposition to Kumuhonua, who is seen as greedy and overreaching his kuleana. Kamōʻawa is an ideal kahuna who goes on a quest for the proper aliʻi to serve. He knows his religion and how to advise his aliʻi, both Wākea and Haumea. Kaliʻu and his ʻohana are archetypal makaʻāinana who farm, fish, and are happy to have aliʻi who are pono for leaders and land managers. The moʻolelo thus demonstrates our kupuna's ideas about the proper balance in society and politics, and it shows the two major paths to island rule, i.e., war, and diplomacy through marriage or other family relations.[94] When Haumea takes ʻOlopana's grandchild to hānai, she creates good diplomatic relations.

GENEALOGICAL MOʻOLELO

Poepoe follows this moʻolelo with "Ka Moolelo o ko Wakea pio ana ia Hoohokukalani, kana Kaikamahine" (The story of Wākea's "arching" to Hoʻohōkūkalani, his daughter). The word "piʻo" is glossed as "arch" or "to be bent or curved"; it is used to indicate the generation of offspring by close family members, often brother and sister. This was a practice among aliʻi to enhance and protect aliʻi genealogies.[95] The implications and connotations of the word "incest" are absent in the Hawaiian concept of piʻo; similarly, the word "marriage," though commonly used, is inappropriate to describe child-producing couplings in the Hawaiian world because of the many religious and societal assumptions that accompany it. Wākea conspires with the kahuna, Kamōʻawa, to deceive Papa so that Wākea can sleep with Hoʻohōkūkalani. Papa sees him, however, and they argue and then she leaves him for a while.[96]

When Papa returns, she also engages in a piʻo coupling with Hāloa, the son of Wākea and Hoʻohōkūkalani, and gives birth to Waia. This begins the sequence of Papa as Haumea, who couples with the male children for ten generations in the bodies of different women having different names. This is Haumea nui āiwaiwa, great Haumea, the marvelous and inexplicable. Here she is the archetypal childbearing woman, poetically celebrated in the Kumulipo in wā 15.[97]

Poepoe then follows the moʻokūʻauhau through the big figures of our ancient history: Puna and Hema, ʻUlu, Paumakua, Kahaʻi, and others. Many of these are the long-distance open ocean navigators who travel to Kahiki—Tahiti and other places—and back.

Poepoe ends his genealogical moʻolelo with the familiar story of Pāʻao that Malo, Kamakau, Fornander, and others had written about before he did. This is a story of migration to Hawai'i at a time when Hawai'i was said to be lacking in ali'i. Pā'ao, a kahuna, arrived with a talented kāula (prophet, seer) named Makuakaumana and a company of others. After seeing that Hawai'i was lacking ali'i, Pā'ao returned to Tahiti and brought back Pilika'aiea, who became an ali'i and powerful ancestor in Kamehameha's genealogy.[98] Pā'ao is famous for building heiau at Puna (Waha'ula) and Kohala (Mo'okini) and for being the ancestor of the most prestigious mo'okahuna, or genealogy of kahuna. Kamehameha's head kahuna, Hewahewa, himself famous for participating in the destruction of the 'ai kapu, was the last in this line.

Poepoe includes a whale-rider story. Makuakaumana, the kāula or seer, settled at Hau'ula on O'ahu as a farmer, telling Pā'ao to send a palaoa (sperm whale) messenger if he needed to return to Tahiti. One day an immense whale beached at Kaipapa'u at Hau'ula, with its middle and tail on shore and head in the water. (Whales who beach to die will place their heads on the sand.) People came from all over Ko'olauloa to celebrate the arrival of the whale, holding 'aha 'aina (feasts) and other entertainments for ten days. They climbed up on the whale and dove into the water, following a rule that a person must have a lei on before climbing and jumping. Makuakaumana had become an influential person in the area because of his skill and intelligence, so people sent a messenger to him in the far uplands, asking what to do, whether they should kill the whale or not. Makuakaumana told them the whale is not a real i'a (fish or sea mammal) but a person and they should not harm it. He conducted an 'awa ceremony, in which akua confirmed that the whale was the messenger from Pā'ao. Makuakaumana then bedecked himself in lei and went down to shore, and when people saw him dressed this way, they shouted in excitement. He climbed up onto the whale, who then swam away with him on top, taking him to Kohala to meet with Pā'ao. The place the whale landed was named Ka Lae o ka Palaoa (The cape of the whale) in commemoration of the event.[99] Variations of this tale of a whale landing and carrying a kahuna away are noted in *Sites of O'ahu* by Sterling and Summers,[100] but only Poepoe's version is explicit in naming Makuakaumana as the kahuna.

This provides the conclusion to the text that is devoted to cosmogonies and genealogies. The mo'olelo of Pā'ao who traversed the thousands of miles of open ocean spurred Poepoe to devote the following chapter (mokuna IV) to "Ka Oihana Kilo Hoku Hawaii" (Hawaiian astronomy), in order to explain the navigation by stars that our ancestors perfected. "O ka nana aku i na hoku ko Paao ma panana i holo mai ai a hiki i Hawaii nei" (Observation of the stars was Pā'ao and company's compass by which they sailed to Hawai'i).[101] Poepoe expresses deep regret "no ka loaa pau pono loa ole ana o na mea e pili ana i ka ike i ao ia ai e ko kakou mau kupuna kahiko ma keia oihana ano nui" (for not having acquired all there is concerning the knowledge taught and learned by our ancient ancestors on this very important profession).[102] He feels strongly that what he does have needed to be published:

> E aho ka paa ana o keia mau mea ma ke pai hua kepau maoli ia ana elike me keia e paiia nei i keia wa, mamua o ka nalowale loa ana 'ku apau.
>
> O ka poe auanei e malama ana i na helu apau o keia nupepa mai ka wa i hoopukaia ai keia moolelo a hiki mai nei i keia wa; a pela me na helu apau ma keia hope aku a hoea i ka pau ana, ua loaa ia lakou he Moolelo Hawaii Kahiko waiwai nui.[103]
>
> ———
>
> It is best that these things be recorded by publication in type as is being published now, before it completely disappears.
>
> The people who are saving all the issues of this newspaper from the time this mo'olelo has been published until now, and also all the issues in the future until the end, they [will] have a very valuable Mo'olelo Hawai'i Kahiko.

STAR NAVIGATION

Long before the promotion of the damaging and eventually discredited drift theory of the settlement of the Pacific by the likes of Thor Heyerdahl, Poepoe understood the importance of documenting intentional long-distance voyaging by star navigation. He divides the chapter into three large sections: (1) "Ke kulana kahiko ... o ka Oihana Kilo Hoku ma Hawaii nei," a description of Hawaiian astronomy; (2) "Ke Ao ana i ka Oihana Kilo Hoku," a description of how astronomy was taught; and (3) "Na Hoakaka no na Hoku i ikeia maloko o keia oihana," an explanation of the stars that were known in this branch of knowledge.

In the first section he again notes the many ancient kūpuna who sailed to and from Tahiti, even before Wākea and Papa, pointing out that Wākea's younger brother learned astronomy. He cites wā 14 of the Kumulipo (noted in the Kumulipo genealogy earlier), which recounts fifty lines of star and constellation names.[104]

In the section on the teaching of ʻoihana kilo hōkū, he observes that the teaching methods were like that of hula, lāʻau lapaʻau, and so forth, which were governed by kapu and ʻihiʻihi (to treat as sacred); the rules reinforced the sacredness and seriousness of such important knowledge. First, students had to memorize all the star names until they could say them from memory without prompts (walewaha). Then they did the same for the prayers that went with the star names. Poepoe here expresses regret at not having these prayers in any of the papers or books that he has. Once the prayers were also memorized, then the kahuna began teaching with pebbles on a square mat. The kahuna taught the constellations starting with Makaliʻi (Pleiades). The stars were taught in the order that they rose in the east and set in the west, which is one of the ways star navigators find their way to this day.[105] Mau Piailug, the Satawal master navigator who taught Nainoa Thompson star navigation in the 1970s and 1980s, used a similar teaching method.[106]

The kahuna taught the students "na kau o ka po," or the periods of the night when specific stars rose and then descended in the sky. The kumu (teacher) also used an ipu (gourd) or ʻumeke (bowl) to mark "Na Alanui o na hoku-hookele" (the paths of the navigation stars), the fixed stars (that do not change position in the sky during the night, like the North Star), and finally the stars that lead the way to Tahiti.[107]

For the last section on the known stars, Poepoe draws heavily from an article or series either by or about Kamohoʻula, a noted astronomer of the old school, which had been published in Poepoe's magazine, *Hoku o ke Kai*, in 1885.[108] He again expresses great regret at not being able to record everything that Kamohoʻula knew. Poepoe also draws upon the series "Ka Mookuauhau Elua o Hawaii" (also known as a history of Kanalu), which catalogued stars with some explanation.[109]

Poepoe's final chapters discuss how the ancients understood time, that is, how they calculated the year, the months, the number of nights in the months, and the names of the nights and the months. He also wrote about the makahiki (new year) time and festivals, and he began a chapter on heiau that was never finished because the newspaper went out of business.

Conclusion

Joseph Poepoe left us a unique elaboration on a familiar genre in Hawaiian studies. It is worthy of study not only because of his analytical approach to the subjects, considerable talent in prose writing, and understanding of Hawaiian poetic form and content, but also because he was probably the last of the intellectuals born into a Hawaiian-speaking world who produced a moʻolelo Hawaiʻi kahiko.

More perhaps than other authors of his generation, he invites us to think about the significance of the genealogical ordering of knowledge, the past, and historiography. Moʻokūʻauhau can teach us about places because place names are prominent in the mele and moʻolelo associated with moʻokūʻauhau. The mele koʻihonua reveal to us a particular way of understanding the world: that everything in the world is alive and we are related to everyone and everything. They teach us that our kupuna knew that women are as important as men, having distinct mana and areas of kuleana. They give us a sense of being and belonging to the past and future as well as the present, as our kupuna live on in us, and we live on in our descendants. Moreover, Poepoe teaches that moʻokūʻauhau can also be messy and politically constructed, although he does not emphasize that very much.

We can see and benefit from Poepoe's concern over the historiography of Hawaiʻi. He endeavors to correct errors in both Hawaiian and English texts, while also promoting Hawaiian versions of history. In doing these things, he is striking against the non-Hawaiian and ill-informed representations of Hawaiians that were being created at that time.

Poepoe directs our attention to the verbal artistry of our ancestors as well as their incredible achievement in sailing the length and breadth of Oceania by the stars. While he situates himself within Hawaiian epistemology/ies, he models modern scholarship for us in his comparisons with the haole science of his day and in his citation practices.

Furthermore, Poepoe demonstrates his commitment to the language, literature, epistemologies, and practices of our kupuna. He wrote "Moolelo Hawaii Kahiko" during a time when the United States and the haole oligarchy in Hawaiʻi were trying to replace Hawaiian with English, an even bigger cultural bomb than the denigration of the first generations of puritanical missionaries. Out of his admiration and respect for our ancestors, he produced a text that he anticipated would be of great value to us today. We do need knowledge of how our ancestors understood and acted in the world because we are forced to live in a capitalist, English-language, settler colonial world not of our making; we need our kupuna's knowledge to help us imagine and build a world we want to live in and that we want our moʻopuna to live and thrive in.

Poepoe is an important link in our own intellectual moʻokūʻauhau. His commitment to writing for us whom he foresaw can be inspiring to us to study and write for the generations in the future and in that way we can see ourselves as part of the past and the future. We can carry on his work by trying to understand the mele, moʻolelo, and moʻokūʻauhau of our ancestors, and by teaching and writing down our interpretations and analyses so that the great moʻo/ʻōlelo/kūʻauhau of ʻike Hawaiʻi lives on.

Conclusion

Ua lehulehu a manomano ka ʻikena a ka Hawaiʻi.

The knowledge of Hawaiians is extraordinarily vast. (translation mine)

MARY KAWENA PUKUI,
ʻŌlelo Noʻeau, 309, no. 2814

We live in a time when many indigenous peoples around the world are claiming our ancestors' languages, philosophies, and ways of life as worthy of our deepest attention. We are seeing anew how our connections to those ancestors and their/our lands provide bases not only for decolonizing our minds, but also for the resurgence of indigenous ways of life. In this book, I have offered examples of how sustained reading of the works of our intellectual predecessors, those before us in the unending genealogy of indigenous thought, can contribute to a fuller understanding of some of that ancestral world of native epistemology and ontology.

Perhaps at first observation, Joseph Kānepuʻu and Joseph Mokuʻōhai Poepoe do not seem to have all that much in common: the former went to school for only a few years, while the latter completed secondary school and law training, for example. One is from small but mighty Molokai and the other from the largest in land mass and in our national imagination, the island of Kamehameha and Pele.[1] Kānepuʻu was a primary school teacher, and Poepoe an attorney, editor, politician, and translator of religious and legal texts. What I hope to have demonstrated is not how they each are exceptional in their time and talents but rather are exemplars from *multitudes* of our kupuna who saw the necessity of perpetuating our ancestral thought in the midst of increasing colonialism. That enduring colonialism took several forms: it deployed discourses that became hegemonic to economically justify the move to plantation capitalism, which wrought mass dispossession of our ʻāina; its concurrent Christian missionizing despised and destroyed many native ways of life; it attacked our kinship and social systems; and it caused the loss of ancestral wisdom via the shift to English. Kānepuʻu and Poepoe are but two who worked tirelessly to keep the kahua (foundation) of indigenous intellectualism and knowledge in place so that succeeding generations could build on it.

It seems to me useful to articulate and contribute to a sense of intellectual genealogy. Prior to the dismantling of the aliʻi socio-religious-political system (gradually from Kamehameha's death in 1819 to the first constitutional government in 1840), many intellectual individuals and pursuits developed in the group known as kahuna: they were not only the conductors of religious rituals but also advisors to the aliʻi ʻai moku (island or district rulers) and konohiki (land managers at lower levels). They were engineers of irrigation systems and fishponds, architects of buildings and places of religious ceremonies (heiau), and so on. They kept our histories in moʻokūʻauhau, moʻolelo, and mele. Many were composers (and many aliʻi and others were also).

As the aliʻi system changed, individuals with these talents were taken into aliʻi circles as advisors, as in the case of Davida Malo, or other informal members of aliʻi households. Those with sufficiently valued genealogies, like John Papa ʻĪʻī, had careers of tremendous responsibility as kahu (caretakers or guardians) for aliʻi, as well as political advisors.[2] Those without that standing eventually found their way to contributing to the well-being of the lāhui by writing down the moʻokūʻauhau, moʻolelo, mele, and other orature and publishing them in the newspapers. They were there in print from the first issue to the last of the Hawaiian-language newspapers. From those vantage points they were able to act as kahu of our ancestral intellectual treasures, as well as advise aliʻi and other politicians and government officials.

I hope this work will encourage other, similar studies recovering and analyzing our remarkable intellectuals. Kānepuʻu's era has so far been almost entirely overshadowed by Samuel Kamakau's extensive accomplishments. But Kamakau was only one of hundreds of Kanaka writers, only one Kanaka among many in the native legislature, and only one Kanaka judge among others in the judiciary. We need to know who all the others were, their political theories, their works of moʻolelo, and their commentary on, and debates with, other Kanaka intellectuals. In Poepoe's time (post-annexation), two other names are fairly well known: Emma Nakuina and her accomplished writer husband, Moses Nakuina.[3] I have shown that there are many more writers and political actors who need to be researched. Their works deserve to be compiled in bibliographies and then read together. Right now, we have many moʻolelo printed from the microfilm or digitized pages of the newspapers, bound in flimsy plastic at copy shops. Each volume is a single moʻolelo or part of a moʻolelo; they fall over on each other on the shelf because of their thin bindings.[4] Eventually, as the number of our lāhui literate in Hawaiian expands, and our commitment and resources grow, we could—and we should—have shelves of books of the collected works of these kūpuna. Then study of our kūpuna's thought worlds can really begin: we will be able to see who influenced whom and understand so many more references and where they came from.

Since the late 1970s a small (but always increasing) number of Kānaka worked undaunted to educate as many Kānaka as possible in the Hawaiian language and in Hawaiian studies, which also includes knowledge of the language. Thousands have now received that education. Each generation that studies our language accumulates more understanding than the generation that precedes it, knowing better how to read what our ancestors wrote. One welcome result of this intellectual resurgence is that it should be undeniably clear by now that it is unacceptable to continue writing histories of our people without attending to this archive, or otherwise having kuleana to do so. I am one of a collective that accepts the kuleana to produce works that bring us closer to understanding the complex philosophies of our kupuna that are expressed in poetic, sometimes deeply puzzling language. Those of us able to write and publish books now are but a few, but we are ever increasing, and there is a surge of new Kanaka intellectuals right behind us.

Appendix A. Kānepuʻu Selected Bibliography

Note: "Ka," "ke," "nā," and "he" are articles, and "e," "i," and "ua" are verb markers; these have thus been ignored in alphabetizing the bibliography entries.

———

J. H. K. [J. H. Kānepuʻu]. "Makaikai ia Kauai." *Ka Nupepa Kuokoa*, 2, 9, and 16 September 1871.

———. "Ka Moeuhane a Moi." *Ka Hae Hawaii*, 19 September 1860, 106.

———. "He Wahi Moolelo No Kaohele." *Ka Elele Poakolu*, 9 February 1881, 3.

Kanepuu, Joseph H. "Ahe! He Nupepa Hou ka!!" *Ko Hawaii Pae Aina*, 2 February 1878, 1.

———. "Ke Ano o ka Wa Ui o ke Kanaka a me na Mea a Pau e Hiki mai ana ia Ia mahope Ona." *Ka Hae Hawaii*, 15, 22, and 29 October; 5 November 1856.

———. "Ke Awawa o Palolo." *Ke Au Okoa*, 17 September 1866, 3.

———. "Ke Emi ana o na Kanaka." *Ka Hoku o ka Pakipika*, 1 May 1862, 2.

———. "Ka Hana Kupono e Ao aku ai na Makua i ka Lakou Poe Keiki." *Ka Hae Hawaii*, 24, 31 December 1856; 14, 21 January 1857.

———. "Ka Helu Hawaii." *Ke Au Okoa*, 21 January 1867, 3.

———. "Na Hoalohaloha i ka Pokii Benj. W. K. Kawainui." *Ko Hawaii Pae Aina*, 11 July 1885, 4.

———. "Ka Honua Nei: A me na Mea a Pau maluna iho." *Ka Lahui Hawaii*, 21 June–13 December 1877.

———. "Ka Iniki Poaeae a R. P. Kanealii i Hapala mai nei, e Kuhi ana Paha he Pau Loa ke Kamaa i ka Palakiia." *Ke Au Okoa*, 30 April 1866, 2.

———. "Kaahele ma Molokai." *Ke Au Okoa*. 5 and 26 September, 17 October, 1867.

———. "Ke Kumukanawai, a me na Kanawai." *Ke Au Okoa* 10 December 1866, 1.

———. "Ka La Ho[i]hoi Ea o ke Aupuni Hawaii." *Ke Au Okoa*, 24 July 1865, 3.

———. "Ka Makahiki 1864 ma Hawaii Nei." *Ka Nupepa Kuokoa*, 12 January 1865, 1.

———. "E Malama i ka Nupepa." *Ka Hae Hawaii*, 1 October 1856, 122.

———. "Mea Minamina i Pau Ole i ka Hoolahaia mai e A. Bihopa." *Ka Hoku o ka Pakipika*, 21 November 1861, 4.

———. "He Mele no ke Kauo ana i na Waa o Kana ia Kauwelieli ma." *Ka Hae Hawaii*, 9 May 1860, 26.

———. "He Moolelo no Hamanalau, Hanai a Hawea: I Laweia mailoko mai o na Kaao Kahiko o Hawaii nei." *Ka Nupepa Kuokoa,* 28 December 1867–29 August 1868.

———. "Mooolelo no ka Hookumu ana o Ka Hoku o ka Pakipika." *Ka Hoku o ka Pakipika,* 14, 21, 28 November 1861.

———. "He Moolelo no Kana, ka Hanai a Uli i Unuhi ia mailoko mai o na Kaao Kahiko o Hawaii nei." *Ke Au Okoa,* 19 December 1867–13 February 1868.

———. "He Moolelo no Kanewailani, ke Keiki a Maoloha. I Unuhi ia mailoko mai o na Moolelo Kahiko o Hawaii Nei." *Ke Au Okoa,* 20 February–2 April 1868.

———. "He Moolelo no Pakaa." *Ke Au Okoa,* 24 October; 7, 14, 21, 28 November 1867.

———. "No Ke Kuhihewa Iwaena o kekahi Poe o Kakou e Noho nei, a me A'u no hoi kekahi." *Ka Hoku o ka Pakipika,* 5, 12, 19 December 1861.

———. "Pane i ka Poe Loiloi i ka Moolelo o Hamanalau." *Ka Nupepa Kuokoa,* 18 April 1868, 1.

———. "Pau Ole ke Ano Pouli o Hawaii nei." *Ka Hae Hawaii,* 19 June 1861, 48.

———. "Ka Poe Kakau Moolelo a Kaao Paha." *Ka Hoku o ka Pakipika,* 30 October 1862, 1.

———. "Ka Poe nana i Unuhi mua ka Baibala." *Ka Elele Poakolu,* 9 February 1881, 6.

Appendix B. Poepoe Selected Bibliography

Note: "Ka," "ke," "nā," and "he" are articles, and "e," "i," and "ua" are verb markers; these have thus been ignored in alphabetizing the bibliography entries.

Achi, William C., C. L. Hopkins, John Lot Kaulukou, and Joseph M. Poepoe. "Ke Ola ame ka Palekana o ka Lahui Hawaii." *Ka Nupepa Kuokoa*, 12 February 1897, 2.

Mokuohai, J. P. "Ke Kumu o ka Hoohui Aina." *Kuokoa Home Rula*, 12 June–3 July 1908.

Poepoe, Joseph M. *Ke Alakai o ke Kanaka Hawaii: He Buke no na Olelo Hooholo o ka Aha Kiekie i Kuhikuhiia ma ka Buke Kanawai Kivila Hou i Hooponoponoia ai e ka Hon. L. McCully a me Kekahi Mau Olelo Hooholo e ae he Nui; Na Rula Aha Hookolokolo o Ko Hawaii Pae Aina i Hooponopono Hou ia; a me na Hoakaka Kanawai i Kakau Mua ia e ka Hon. A. Francis Judd, Lunakanawai Kiekie a Kaulike o ke Aupuni a i Hooponopono ia a Hoomahuahua Hou ia Hoi.* Honolulu: Hawaiian Gazette, 1891.

———. "Ke Alakai Koho Balota." *Ka Nupepa Kuokoa*, 14 and 28 September 1900, 2.

———. "Ka Haiolelo Akea imua o ka Lahui Hawaii: Ke Kumu o na Paeaina ma Hawaii Nei." *Ka Nupepa Kuokoa*, 3 April 1896, 2.

———. "The Hawaiian Astronomy." *Kuokoa Home Rula*, 2 April–4 June 1909.

———. "He Hoakaka Aku." *Ka Na'i Aupuni*, 18 December 1905, 2.

———. "E Hoomaopopo ka Lehulehu." *Hawaii Holomua*, 1 February 1893, 4.

———. "Joseph Mokuohai Poepoe." *Ke Aloha Aina*, 26 October 1912, 1.

———. "Na Kumuhana a ka Moho Lunamakaainana Kuokoa." *Ka Nupepa Kuokoa*, 26 October 1900, 1.

———. "Ka Moolelo Hawaii Kahiko." *Ka Na'i Aupuni*, 1 February–29 November 1906.

———. "Ka Moolelo Kaao o Hiiaka-i-ka-Poli-o-Pele." *Kuokoa Home Rula*, 10 January 1908–20 January 1911.

———. "He Moolelo Kaao no ke Keiki Alii Otto! Ka Naita Opio o Geremania." *Ko Hawaii Pae Aina*, 17 January 1880–23 October 1880.

———, trans. "He Moolelo Kaao no ka Naita Rokekila Hinedu! Ke Koa Pukani o na Au Pouliuli." *Hoku o ke Kai*, December 1883–June 1884.

———. *Ka Moolelo o ka Moi Kalakaua I: Ka Hanau Ana, ke Kaapuni Honua, ka Moolelo Piha o Kona Mau La Hope ma Kaleponi, Amerika Huipuia, na Hoike a Adimarala Baraunu me na Kauka, etc., etc., etc.: Hoohiwahiwaia me na Kii*. Honolulu: s.n, 1891.

———. "He Moolelo no ka Naita Leopaki a i Ole he Nanea no ke Kaua Kerusade Ekolu ma Palesekina." *Ke Aloha Aina*, 23 September 1911–5 April 1913.

———. "Na Paemoku o Hawaii." *Ka Nupepa Kuokoa*, 24 and 31 July 1896.

———. "Ka'u Papa Iliili Imua o ka Lehulehu." *Ke Aloha Aina*, 7 August 1909, 2.

Poepoe, Joseph M., and W[illiam] J[oseph] Coelho. "Ke Kanawai o ka Panalaau." *Ka Nupepa Kuokoa*, 17 August 1900, 2.

———. "Ke Kanawai Teritori." *Ka Nupepa Kuokoa*, 2 July 1900, 2.

SELECTED UNSIGNED EDITORIALS AND ARTICLES

"Ahi Wela." *Kuokoa Home Rula*, 21 May 1909, 1.
"Alemanaka no 1906." *Ka Na'i Aupuni*, 27 January 1906, 3.
"E A'o i ka Olelo Beritania." *Kuokoa Home Rula*, 20 November 1908, 2.
"Ka Buke a Aberahama." *Ka Na'i Aupuni*, 4 December 1905–20 January 1906 (not in every issue).
"He Buke Moolelo Maikai." *Ka Nupepa Kuokoa*, 14 February 1902, 5.
"He Buke Mele Lahui." *Ka Nupepa Kuokoa*, 10 January 1896, 2.
"Ka Hae Hawaii." *Ka Nupepa Kuokoa*, 8 July 1898, 2.
"E Hapai koke ka Lahui Hawaii Maoli i Ahahui Kalaiaina Ponoi no Lakou iho." *Ka Nupepa Kuokoa*, 22 July 1898, 2.
"Halawai a na Wahine Na'i Pono Koho Balota." *Ke Aloha Aina*, 4 May 1912, 1.
"A Hiiaka Chant." *Kuokoa Home Rula*, 23, 30 April; 7, 14, 28 May; 4 June 1909, 1 or 2.
"Hookahi Wai o ka Like." *Kuokoa Home Rula*, 16 October 1908, 1.
"Ka Ipu Alabata." *Ka Na'i Aupuni*, 21 December 1905, 2.
"Ke Kanawai." *Hoku o ke Kai*, August and October 1883; March, April, June, and July 1884.
"Ke Keiki Hoopapa." *Ka Hoku o ke Kai*, August and September 1883.
"Na Komisina 'Roialiti' no Wasinetona." *Ka Nupepa Kuokoa*, 26 November 1897, 3.
"E Kukulu ke Aupuni i Kula Nui Olelo Hawaii ma ke Kula Kahunapule." *Ka Nupepa Kuokoa*, 17 January 1896, 2.
"Ke Kumukanawai Hou." *Hawaii Holomua*, 30 January 1892, 2.
"Na Kumu Mua o ke Kanawai." *Hoku o ke Kai*, January, March, June, and July 1883.
"Ka La Hoomanao o ka Moi Kauikeaouli." *Kuokoa Home Rula*, 22 March 1907, 4.
E Nalowale ana Paha ka Olelo Hawaii." *Ka Hoku o ke Kai*, June 1883, 133.
"E Nalowale loa anei ko Kakou Moolelo Kumu." *Ke Aloha Aina*, 18 January 1913, 4.
"Ka Papa Hoonohonoho Hana o ka Hui a na Opio Hawaii no 1896." *Ka Nupepa Kuokoa*, 10 January 1896, 3.
"Ko Makou Kulana i keia Kau Koho Balota." *Hawaii Holomua*, 23 January 1892, 2.
"Kuamuamuia na Hawaii he Keko e Robikana." *Ka Na'i Aupuni*, 2 October 1906, 2.
"The Legend of Kou Harbor." *Kuokoa Home Rula*, 18 December 1908, 1.

"Lele ke Aho ma ka Aina Malihini! Joseph Nawahi—ua Hala!" *Ka Nupepa Kuokoa*, 25 September 1896, 3.

"Na Lunamakaainana a me kekahi mau Hana Kupono no ke Kau Ahaolelo M. H. 1884." *Hoku o ke Kai*, January 1884, 313.

"Mai Haalele i ka Olelo Makuahine." *Kuokoa Home Rula*, 22 March 1907, 1.

"Mai Haalele i Kau Olelo Makuahine." *Ka Naʻi Aupuni*, 4 January 1906, 2.

"Na Maʻi Lepera i Waeia no ka Lapaau ia ana e J. Lor Wallach!" *Kuokoa Home Rula*, 24 January 1908, 1.

"Mare Lehulehu." *Ka Naʻi Aupuni*, 27 November 1905–19 March 1906.

"No ka Ona Miliona Claus Spreckels." *Hoku o ke Kai*, February 1884, 335.

"No Keaha e Hoolaha Akea Ole ia ai ma ka Olelo Hawaii." *Ka Naʻi Aupuni*, 27 November 1905, 2.

"O Ka Olelo Hea Ka Ol[e]lo Kanawai e Hiki ai ke Hilinaiia ka Pono." *Hoku o ke Kai*, June 1884, 441.

"Na Olelo Hooholo o ka Aha Kiekie." *Hoku o ke Kai*, December 1883, 463.

"Pehea e Mau ai ke Ola ana o ka Olelo Hawaii?" *Ka Naʻi Aupuni*, 5 January 1906, 2.

"Pehea Kakou i ka Kakou [O]lelo Ponoi." *Ke Aloha Aina*, 18 January 1913, 4.

"What Is Poi?" *Kuokoa Home Rula*, 1 January 1909, 1.

HOʻOULUMĀHIEHIE

Hoooulumahiehie. "Kamehameha I: Ka Naʻi Aupuni o Hawaii." *Ka Naʻi Aupuni*, 27 November 1905–16 November 1906.

———. "He Moolelo no Alamira Ka Uʻi Hapa Paniolo." *Ka Naʻi Aupuni*, 27 November 1905–30 November 1906.

———. "Ka Moolelo o Hiiaka-i-ka-poli-o-Pele." *Hawaii Aloha*, 15 July–24 November 1905.

———. "Ka Moolelo o Hiiaka-i-ka-poli-o-Pele." *Ka Naʻi Aupuni*, 1 December 1905–30 November 1906.

———. "Moolelo Hoonaue Puuwai no Kama.A.Ka.Mahiai [*sic*], Ka Hiʻapaʻiole o ka Ikaika o ke Kai Huki Hee Nehu o Kahului." *Ke Aloha Aina*, 7 August 1909–11 March 1911.

Hooulumahiehie-i-ka-oni-malie-a-pua-lilia-lana-i-ka-wai. "Ka Moolelo Hiwahiwa o Kawelo." *Kuokoa Home Rula*, 1 January 1909–1 April 1910.

Notes

INTRODUCTION

1. Alfred, *Wasáse*, 19.
2. Kikiloi, "Rebirth of an Archipelago," 75.
3. Kuleana is described as "right, privilege, concern, responsibility, title, business, property, estate, portion, jurisdiction, authority, liability, interest, claim, ownership, tenure, affair, province; reason, cause, function, justification; small piece of property, as within an ahupuaʻa; blood relative through whom a relationship to less close relatives is traced, as to in-laws." Pukui and Elbert, *Hawaiian Dictionary*, s.v., "kuleana."
4. Bush, "Olelo Hoakaka," Jan. 6, 1893, 1.
5. Oliveira, "Wahi a Kahiko," 101.
6. Oliveira, "Wahi a Kahiko," 102.
7. Kameʻeleihiwa, *Native Land and Foreign Desires*.
8. hoʻomanawanui, *Voices of Fire*.
9. Oliveira, *Ancestral Places*, 1.
10. P. Kanahele, *Ka Honua Ola*, 1.
11. Brown, *Facing the Spears*, 27.
12. Perkins, "Kuleana," 14–27.
13. Kimura, "Ke Au Hawaiʻi."
14. Kanepuu, "Ka Poe Kakau Moolelo."
15. Alfred, *Wasáse*.
16. Warrior, *Tribal Secrets*, 87.
17. Warrior, *Tribal Secrets*, 97–98.
18. Warrior, *Tribal Secrets*, 88.
19. Warrior, *Tribal Secrets*, 90.
20. Kanepuu, "He Moolelo no Kanewailani," Feb. 20, 1868, 4.
21. Holt, *Waimea Summer*, 172.
22. Meyer, *Hoʻoulu*, 166. Meyer interviewed kūpuna with whom she established affectionate relationships; thus she calls them mentors rather than the more distancing and inappropriate term "informant" (141).
23. Kikiloi, "Rebirth of an Archipelago," 74.

24 P. Kanahele, *Ka Honua Ola*, xiii–xiv.
25 Pukui, "Songs (Meles) of Old Ka'u, Hawaii."
26 McDougall, *Finding Meaning*.
27 McDougall and Nordstrom, "Ma Ka Hana Ka 'Ike," 101.
28 W. Homestead in Solis, "Ma Ka Wahi Wali," 98.
29 Pukui and Elbert, *Hawaiian Dictionary*, s.v., "pua," "pu'a," and "pū'ā."
30 Pukui, Elbert, and Mookini, *Place Names of Hawaii*, x.
31 Pukui, Elbert, and Mookini, *Place Names of Hawaii*, 266–267.
32 G. Kanahele, *Kū Kanaka*, 184.
33 Oliveira, *Ancestral Places*.
34 Charlot, *Classical Hawaiian Education*.
35 See http://manoa.hawaii.edu/hshk/kawaihuelani/courses-oh/courses-op/, accessed May 27, 2015.
36 Ho'oulumāhiehie, *Epic Tale of Hi'iakaikapoliopele*. A translation of Ho'oulumāhiehie's biography of Kamehameha I is forthcoming from University of Hawai'i Press.
37 Schütz, *Voices of Eden*, 98–133.
38 Kamakau, *Ruling Chiefs of Hawaii*, 270–271 (a translation).
39 Quoted in Mookini, *Hawaiian Newspapers*, iv.
40 For more on the above papers, see Silva, "Early Hawaiian Newspapers."

CHAPTER ONE: JOSEPH HOʻONAʻAUAO KĀNEPUʻU

1 J. H. K. [J. H. Kānepu'u], "He Wahi Moolelo No Kaohele."
2 Kanepuu, "Ka Iniki Poaeae."
3 Kanepuu, "Ka Iniki Poaeae."
4 Kanepuu, "Pau Ole ke Ano Pouli."
5 Kanepuu, "E Malama."
6 For more on this idea, see ho'omanawanui, *Voices of Fire*.
7 See appendix A for a selected bibliography.
8 For the serialized essays, see Kanepuu's "Ke Ano o ka Wa Ui" and "Ka Hana Kupono." On history, see, for example, "Mooolelo no ka Hookumu Ana" and "Ahe! He Nupepa Hou Ka!!" On geography, see "Ka Honua Nei," "Kaahele ma Molokai," "Ke Awawa o Palolo," and "Makaikai ia Kauai." For his short essays, see, for example, "Ka Helu Hawaii."
9 Benham and Heck, *Culture and Educational Policy in Hawai'i*.
10 Chapin, *Newspapers of Hawaii 1834 to 1903*, 52.
11 When the American Board of Commissioners for Foreign Missions withdrew their support, the missionaries formed the 'Ahahui 'Euanelio Hawai'i. See Williams, "Claiming Christianity," 6. Fuller's name appears only as J. or as Mr. Fuller in most documents; however, his name was given as Jas. Fuller in an account in the *Polynesian*, Mar. 10, 1860, 2.
12 Kalaiohauola, "He Wahi Kaao"; Hauola, "He Wahi Kaao."
13 Kuapuu, "He Wahi Mooolelo," Mar. 20, 1861; Mar. 27, 1861; Apr. 10, 1861. Kuapu'u's full name is given in the unpublished commonplace book of Kānepu'u.

14 Kuapuu, "He Wahi Moolelo [He Moolelo No Pakaa a Me Kuapakaa]"; Nakuina, *Moolelo Hawaii O Pakaa*; Nakuina, *Wind Gourd of Laʻamaomao*. Kānepuʻu also wrote a version of this moʻolelo, discussed later, as did Kamakau.
15 Kahiolo, "He Moolelo No Kamapuaa."
16 Limaikaika, "Na Mele no ka Wa Kahiko."
17 Silva, *Aloha Betrayed*, 45–86.
18 Kaelemakule, "No ka Halawai Kumu ma Hilo."
19 Kanepuu, "He Mele no ke Kauo ana"; J. H. K. [J. H. Kānepuʻu], "Ka Moeuhane a Moi."
20 I feel fairly confident that no previous versions exist in print because I reviewed all available issues of the previous newspapers, although it is possible that one may surface from some currently unknown source. Keawekolohe, "No Kana."
21 Pukui, "How Legends Were Taught."
22 Fornander, *Fornander Collection*, iv:436–449, vi:489–491.
23 Kanepuu, "He Mele no ke Kauo ana."
24 The spelling of "Kūpaʻaikeʻe" is courtesy of Marie Alohalani Brown, personal communication, Jun. 23, 2015.
25 Kanepuu, "He Mele no ke Kauo ana." For example, "This chant, shared by Pua Kanakaʻole is from David Malo's *Hawaiian Antiquities* and was sung when the great logs for canoes and/or heiau idols were hauled. The spirit of the chant calls for the joining together of people for a single purpose. This was used in the protest march against the Bishop Estate Trustees, May 1997 and the vigils at the State Capitol against the Gathering Rights and Autonomy Bills, Jan/Feb 1998." See http://www.huapala.org/Chants/I_Ku_Mau_Mau.html, accessed Sep. 30, 2013.
26 Fornander, *Fornander Collection*, iv:436–449.
27 Fornander, *Fornander Collection*, iv:438–439.
28 Kanepuu, "He Mele no ke Kauo ana." "The waʻa that Kapipimaia carved" could also be interpreted as "Ka waʻa a Kapipi mā ia lā i kālai" (The voyaging vessel that Kapipi and his folks carved that day), although this is less satisfactory.
29 Fornander, *Fornander Collection*, iv:440–441.
30 Kanepuu, "He Mele no ke Kauo ana."
31 J. H. K. [J. H. Kānepuʻu], "Ka Moeuhane a Moi."
32 Pukui, *ʻŌlelo Noʻeau*, 11, no. 79.
33 "He kuli au i ka moana" does not seem to make sense, but it could be a typo for "He huli au i ka moana," which suggests a current in the ocean that may be turning. At the same time, it suggests some wordplay, because "huliau" means a time of change, which this dream foretells.
34 Keawekolohe, "No Kana."
35 Dibble, *Ka Mooolelo Hawaii* (2005), xxvii.
36 Kamakau, "Ka Moolelo Hawaii," Oct. 27, 1870, 1; Kamakau, *Ka Poʻe Kahiko*, 4.
37 Mignolo, *Darker Side of the Renaissance*, 45.
38 N. Arista, "Foreword," x–xi, xiii.
39 I documented this previously in Silva, *Aloha Betrayed*, 45–86.

40 Kawailiula, "Mooolelo no Kawelo," Sep. 26, 1861, 1.
41 I am grateful to kuʻualoha hoʻomanawanui for sharing her list of moʻolelo published in this newspaper.
42 Kapihenui, "He Mooolelo no Hiiakaikapoliopele."
43 Kaai, "He Mooolelo no Aladana"; Kalimahauna, "Ke Au ia Kamehameha"; Kealoha, "No na Kaua i Koe o Kamehameha"; Timoteo, "No ke Kaua ana o Kamehameha"; Keolanui, "He Mooolelo no Esetera."
44 Kanepuu, "No ke Kuhihewa."
45 Kanepuu, "Mea Minamina."
46 Kuykendall, *Hawaiian Kingdom: Vol. 2*, 86.
47 Kuykendall, *Hawaiian Kingdom: Vol. 2*, 86.
48 Beamer, *No Mākou ka Mana*.
49 Schmitt and Nordyke, "Death in Hawaiʻi." It is also possible that, in some cases, infertility was caused by infectious diseases.
50 Kanepuu, "Ke Emi ana o na Kanaka."
51 Osorio, *Dismembering Lāhui*, 115–136.
52 Kānepuʻu summarized these events in Kanepuu, "Ka Makahiki 1864 ma Hawaii nei."
53 Untitled, *Nupepa Kuokoa*, Jun. 4, 1864, 2.
54 Dowsett et al., "Na Elele Makaainana."
55 Chapin, *Shaping History*, 61.
56 Chapin, *Shaping History*, 54.
57 Chapin, *Shaping History*, 57.
58 Kanepuu, "Ahe! He Nupepa Hou Ka!!"
59 Hulikahiko, "Na Mea Kahiko o Hawaii nei."
60 Wini (Whitney), "Olelo Hoolaha!"; Kulika (Gulick), "E na Makamaka."
61 Hawaiian Mission Children's Society, *Missionary Album*, 106, 110.
62 Parker's parents were missionaries in Nuʻuhiwa, as well, which is where he was born. Hawaiian Mission Children's Society, *Missionary Album*, 154–156.
63 I am indebted to Ronald C. Williams, Jr. for pointing out that the name of the organization was officially ʻAhahui ʻEuanelio Hawaiʻi and not the translation Hawaiian Evangelical Association. See Williams, "Claiming Christianity," 6.
64 Kupakee.
65 Kahiamoe, "Ke Au Okoa."
66 Kahoohalahala, "Manao Hoohalahala."
67 Mookini, *Hawaiian Newspapers*, viii.
68 Untitled, *Ke Au Okoa*, Apr. 24, 1865, 2.
69 Koko, "He Moolelo no Lonoikamakahiki."
70 Readers may wonder why Arabic tales were translated, but I do not have a definite answer.
71 Haleole, "Ka Nupepa Hou."
72 Note that the last two numbers are so high they are called "poina" (forget/forgotten) and "nalowale" (disappear/ed).

73 The issues of *Ke Au Okoa* of Dec. 5 and 12, 1867, have not been preserved, and the Nov. 28 issue is not the end, so it is not possible at this time to determine when the moʻolelo ended.
74 *Nupepa Kuokoa*, Jan. 4, 1868, 2. Only the first and middle initials of Lyons and Andrews were in the paper; I took the full names from Hawaiian Mission Children's Society, *Missionary Album*, 145, 22.
75 Kanepuu, "He Moolelo no Hamanalau."
76 Another translator might use the word "husband" for "kāne hoʻāo," but the word carries too many foreign connotations that I do not wish to impart to the story.
77 Kulanakauhalealii, "He Mau Ninau."
78 Kanepuu, "Pane i ka Poe Loiloi."
79 Kamakau, "He Mau Mea i Hoohalahala ia."
80 J. H. K. [J. H. Kānepuʻu], "Makaikai ia Kauai."
81 Manu, "He Moolelo Kaao no Keaomelemele."
82 Kanepuu, "He Moolelo no Kanewailani," Feb. 20, 1868, 4.
83 Molokainuiahina, "No Ka Moolelo o Kanewailani."
84 Kanepuu, "He Moolelo no Kanewailani," Feb. 20, 1868.
85 Chapin, *Guide to Newspapers of Hawaiʻi*, 65.
86 Osorio, *Dismembering Lāhui*, 151–157.
87 For a full explanation of these issues, see Osorio, *Dismembering Lāhui*, 145–180.
88 Silva, *Aloha Betrayed*, 87–122.
89 For more on Gibson, see Osorio, *Dismembering Lāhui*.
90 Kanepuu, "Ahe! He Nupepa Hou Ka!!"
91 This can be interpreted as either "the warrior-strategist named Kaohele" or Kaohele's warrior-strategist. J. H. K. [J. H. Kānepuʻu], "He Wahi Moolelo No Kaohele."
92 Poomaikelani, *Hoike a ka Papa Kuauhau*, 26–27.
93 Hawaii, *Rex v. William Auld*. See also Silva, *Aloha Betrayed*, 109–111.
94 Kanepuu, "Na Hoalohaloha."

CHAPTER TWO: SELECTED LITERARY WORKS OF JOSEPH KĀNEPUʻU

1 For more detail, please see chapter 1.
2 "Na Luna."
3 See, for example, Kahekili-wahine and Kailinaoa, "He Mele Koihonua."
4 [J. H. Kanepuu], "He Moolelo No Pakaa," Nov. 14, 1867, 4.
5 [J. H. Kanepuu], "He Moolelo No Pakaa," Oct. 24, 1867, 4.
6 Kamakau, *Ruling Chiefs*, 219–228, 275.
7 "Ka Moolelo o Pakaa."
8 Kalakaua, *Legends and Myths*, 67–94.
9 Rice, *Hawaiian Legends*, 93–105.
10 kuʻualoha hoʻomanawanui, personal communication, Oct. 9, 2013. For more of this analysis, see hoʻomanawanui, *Voices of Fire*.
11 Kanepuu, "He Moolelo no Kana," Dec. 19, 1867, 4.
12 Charlot, *Classical Hawaiian Education*, 223; ibid., 226.

13 Kanepuu, "He Moolelo no Kana," Jan. 16, 1868, 4.
14 Kanepuu, "He Moolelo no Kana," Jan. 9, 1868, 4.
15 Kanepuu, "He Moolelo no Kana," Jan. 2, 1868, 4.
16 Kanepuu, "He Moolelo no Kana," Dec. 26, 1867, 4.
17 Kanepuu, "He Moolelo no Kana," Jan. 16, 1868, 4.
18 Kanepuu, "He Moolelo no Kana," Jan. 23, 1868, 4.
19 Hāwea is also the name of the pahu (drum) brought to Hawaiʻi by Laʻamaikahiki (Pukui, Elbert, and Mookini, *Place Names of Hawaii*, 43). Mahalo to Noelani Arista for reminding me of this.
20 Kanepuu, "He Moolelo no Hamanalau," Dec. 28, 1867, 1.
21 Kanepuu, "He Moolelo no Hamanalau," Jan. 11, 1868, 1.
22 Kanepuu, "He Moolelo no Hamanalau," Jan. 18, Jan. 25, Feb. 1, 1868, 1.
23 Kanepuu, "He Moolelo no Hamanalau," Feb. 8, 1868, 1.
24 Kanepuu, "He Moolelo no Hamanalau," Feb. 8, Feb. 22, Feb. 29, 1868, 1.
25 Kanepuu, "He Moolelo no Hamanalau," Mar. 7, 1868, 1.
26 This name could be Kaili, Kaʻili, or Kāʻili, so I have not guessed but left it spelled without diacriticals.
27 Kanepuu, "He Moolelo no Hamanalau," Mar. 14, 1868, 1–2.
28 Kanepuu, "He Moolelo no Hamanalau," Feb. 8, Feb. 22, Feb. 29, 1868, 1.
29 Kanepuu, "He Moolelo no Hamanalau," Jul. 11, 1868, 1.
30 Kanepuu, "He Moolelo no Hamanalau," Jul. 25, 1868, 1.
31 Kanepuu, "He Moolelo no Hamanalau," Aug. 1, Aug. 8, 1868, 1.
32 Kikiloi, "Rebirth of an Archipelago," 87, 95.
33 Kanepuu, "He Moolelo no Hamanalau," Aug. 22, 1868, 1.
34 Kanepuu, "He Moolelo no Hamanalau," Aug. 29, 1868, 1.
35 hoʻomanawanui, *Voices of Fire*; Hooulumahiehie-i-ka-oni-malie-a-pua-lilia-lana-i-ka-wai, "Ka Moolelo Hiwahiwa o Kawelo."
36 Kanepuu, "He Moolelo no Hamanalau," Dec. 28, 1867, 1.
37 Kanepuu, "He Moolelo no Hamanalau," Jan. 18, 1868, 1.
38 A kauhale is the collection of buildings that constitutes an ʻohana's residence. I have translated kauhale as "houses" for lack of an equivalent term in English.
39 Pūʻulīʻulī are "a variety of small gourd, as used for making feather gourd rattles . . . medicine cups . . . and individual poi containers." Pukui and Elbert, *Hawaiian Dictionary*, s.v., "pūʻulīʻulī".
40 Kanepuu, "He Moolelo no Hamanalau," Feb. 1, 1868, 1.
41 Pukui and Elbert, *Hawaiian Dictionary*, s.v., "ʻū" and "ʻūʻū."
42 Kanepuu, "He Moolelo no Hamanalau," Feb. 1, 1868, 1.
43 Pukui and Elbert, *Hawaiian Dictionary*, s.v., "mākena" and "makena."
44 Kanepuu, "He Moolelo no Hamanalau," Feb. 22, 1868, 1.
45 Pukui and Elbert, *Hawaiian Dictionary*, s.v., "makapā."
46 Kanepuu, "He Moolelo no Hamanalau," Feb. 29, 1868, 1.
47 Pukui and Elbert, *Hawaiian Dictionary*, s.v., "nene," nēnē," and "nenene." "Nenene" is the root word and hoʻo is a causative or simulative prefix. See Pukui and Elbert, *Hawaiian Dictionary*, s.v., "hoʻo-".

48 Kanepuu, "He Moolelo no Hamanalau," Feb. 29, 1868, 1.
49 Kanepuu, "He Moolelo no Hamanalau," Jul. 11, 1868, 1, and Jul. 18, 1868, 1.
50 Pukui and Elbert, *Hawaiian Dictionary*, s.v., "ʻiwa." They also note that the ʻiwa is figuratively used for "thief," because it steals its food from other birds. I don't think that is as relevant here.
51 Kanepuu, "He Moolelo no Hamanalau," Aug. 1, 1868, 1.
52 Pukui, *ʻŌlelo Noʻeau*, 23, no. 189.
53 Kanepuu, "He Moolelo no Hamanalau," Aug. 8, 1868, 1.
54 Holt, *Art of Featherwork in Old Hawaiʻi*.
55 Holt, *Art of Featherwork in Old Hawaiʻi*, 24, 21.
56 Kameʻeleihiwa, *He Moʻolelo Kaʻao o Kamapuaʻa*, x.
57 Pukui, *ʻŌlelo Noʻeau*, xi–xix.
58 See Wong, "Kuhi Aku"; McDougall, *Finding Meaning*.
59 Solis, "Ma Ka Wahi Wali," 98. The translation is mine.
60 Pukui, "Songs (Meles) of Old Kaʻu, Hawaii."
61 Solis, "Ma Ka Wahi Wali," 79.
62 Solis, "Ma Ka Wahi Wali," 80.
63 Pukui, *ʻŌlelo Noʻeau*, 126–127, no. 1162.
64 Kanepuu, "He Moolelo no Hamanalau," Aug. 29, 1868, 1.
65 Kanepuu, "He Moolelo no Hamanalau," Mar. 28, 1868, 1.
66 "Mele maʻi, song in honor of genitals, as of a chief, as composed on his or her birth, rarely if ever composed for adults; usually gay and fast." Pukui and Elbert, *Hawaiian Dictionary*, s.v., "maʻi." For the text of the mele see http://www.kalena.com/huapala/Liliu_E.html, accessed August 12, 2016.
67 "The substantial part of a thing; that which gives character or adds ornament; the upper naked person of a well built man." Andrews, *Dictionary of the Hawaiian Language*, 75.
68 Kanepuu, "He Moolelo no Hamanalau," Aug. 1, 1868, 1.
69 Pukui, *ʻŌlelo Noʻeau*, 285, no. 2595.
70 Kanepuu, "He Moolelo no Hamanalau," Aug. 1, 1868, 1.
71 Hawaiian lyrics from http://www.huapala.org/Li/Liliu_E.html, accessed Mar. 15, 2013; my translation, modified from other sources, including this one.
72 http://www.huapala.org/Li/Liliu_E.html, accessed August 12, 2016.
73 Kanepuu, "He Moolelo no Hamanalau," Aug. 1, 1868, 1.
74 Kahiolo, "He Moolelo No Kamapuaa," Jul. 10, 1861, 60.
75 Fornander, *Fornander Collection*, v. 5, 320.
76 Pukui, *ʻŌlelo Noʻeau*, 12, no. 86; 263, no. 2405.
77 Kanepuu, "He Moolelo no Hamanalau," Aug. 1, 1868, 1.
78 http://www.kingjamesbibleonline.org/Revelation-9–11/. Accessed Mar. 25, 2013.
79 Kanepuu, "He Moolelo no Hamanalau," Aug. 1, 1868, 1.
80 Pukui and Elbert, *Hawaiian Dictionary*: s.v., "pē," and "lomia."
81 Kanepuu, "He Moolelo no Hamanalau," Jul. 18, 1868, 1.

82 Kanepuu, "He Moolelo no Hamanalau," Aug. 15, 1868, 1.
83 Pukui and Elbert, *Hawaiian Dictionary*, s.v., "ʻōmale" and "uhu."
84 Kanepuu, "He Moolelo no Hamanalau," Feb. 15, 1868, 1.
85 Kanepuu, "He Moolelo no Hamanalau," Mar. 28, 1868, 1.
86 Kanepuu, "He Moolelo no Hamanalau," Mar. 14, 1868, 1–2.
87 Charlot, "Application of Form."
88 Kanepuu, "He Moolelo no Hamanalau," Mar. 14, 1868, 1.
89 Clark, *Hawaiʻi Place Names*, 223.
90 Kanepuu, "He Moolelo no Hamanalau," Mar. 28, 1868, 1.
91 Kanepuu, "He Moolelo no Hamanalau," Jan. 11, 1868, probably page 1. This issue is not available on microfilm or online; Kalani Makekau-Whittaker was kind enough to share a handwritten copy with me. Unfortunately, I do not have the page number.
92 Kanepuu, "He Moolelo no Hamanalau," Jan. 11, 1868. See footnote 79.
93 Kanepuu, "He Moolelo no Hamanalau," Aug. 22, 1868, 1.
94 Sterling and Summers, *Sites of Oahu*, 119; Pukui, Elbert, and Mookini, *Place Names of Hawaii*, 214.
95 Soehren, "Hawaiian Place Names," accessed Mar. 31, 2013; Pukui, Elbert, and Mookini, *Place Names of Hawaii*, 133.
96 Kanepuu, "He Moolelo no Hamanalau," Dec. 28, 1867, 2.

CHAPTER THREE: KANAKA GEOGRAPHY AND ALOHA ʻĀINA

1 De Silva, "Liner Notes."
2 Wolfe writes, "settler colonizers come to stay: invasion is a structure, not an event." "Settler Colonialism," 388.
3 This book was based on her 1986 PhD dissertation.
4 Kameʻeleihiwa, *Native Land and Foreign Desires*, 25.
5 Andrade, *Hāʻena*; Oliveira, *Ancestral Places*; Louis, *Kanaka Hawaiʻi Cartography*.
6 Andrade, *Hāʻena*.
7 Andrade, *Hāʻena*, xv.
8 Andrade, *Hāʻena*, 3.
9 Oliveira, *Ancestral Places*, 1.
10 Oliveira, *Ancestral Places*, 94.
11 Louis, "Hawaiian Storied Place Names," 169.
12 Louis, "Hawaiian Storied Place Names," 168.
13 Louis, "Hawaiian Storied Place Names," 168.
14 Moreton-Robinson, "ʻI Still Call Australia Home,ʻ" 31.
15 Moreton-Robinson, "ʻI Still Call Australia Home,ʻ" 32.
16 J. H. K. [J. H. Kānepuʻu], "He Wahi Moolelo No Kaohele."
17 Kanepuu, "Kaahele ma Molokai," Sep. 26, 1867, 2.
18 Pukui, *ʻŌlelo Noʻeau*, 146–147, no. 1346.
19 Kanepuu, "Kaahele ma Molokai," Sep. 26, 1867, 2.
20 Kameʻeleihiwa, *Native Land and Foreign Desires*, 185; Liliuokalani, *Hawaii's Story*, 4.

21 Kanepuu, "Kaahele ma Molokai," Oct. 17, 1867, 4.
22 Pukui and Elbert, *Hawaiian Dictionary*, s.v., "lawekeō."
23 Pukui, *ʻŌlelo Noʻeau*, 253, no. 2327.
24 Oliveira, *Ancestral Places*, 91.
25 Silva, "E Lawe," 241.
26 Kanepuu, "Kaahele ma Molokai," Oct. 17, 1867, 4.
27 Kanepuu, "Kaahele ma Molokai," Oct. 17, 1867, 4.
28 Woodbridge, *He Hoikehonua*. Mahalo nui David Chang to bringing this to my attention. See Chang, *World and All the Things upon It*.
29 Kameʻeleihiwa, *Native Land and Foreign Desires*; Beamer, *No Mākou Ka Mana*; Perkins, "Kuleana."
30 Kanepuu, "Ka Honua Nei," Jul. 12, 1877, 1.
31 Kanepuu, "Ka Honua Nei," Jul. 19, 1877, 1.
32 Kanepuu, "Ka Honua Nei," Jul. 26, 1877, 1.
33 Kanepuu, "Ka Honua Nei," Jul. 26, 1877, 1.
34 Hawaii, *Compiled Laws*, 328, §1129.
35 Kanepuu, "Ka Honua Nei," Jul. 26, 1877, 1.
36 Kanepuu, "Ka Honua Nei," Jul. 26, 1877, 1.
37 Kanepuu, "Ka Honua Nei," Jul. 26, 1877, 1.
38 Kanepuu, "Ka Honua Nei," Jul. 26, 1877, 1
39 Kanepuu, "Ka Honua Nei," Jul. 26, 1877, 1.
40 "Pau Ole no hoi ke Kuhihewa."
41 For a fuller discussion of the enduring white supremacist ideas of the missionaries, see Williams, "Claiming Christianity."
42 The use of this title "Moe uhane a Kanepuu," recalls the text within Kānepuʻu's moʻolelo of Kana called "Moe a Moi," wherein the kahuna Moi receives knowledge from the spirit world via his dream. The words "moe ʻuhane" can be glossed as "spirit sleep."
43 Kanepuu, "Ka Honua Nei," Aug. 23, 1877, 1.
44 Kānepuʻu quoted from the Bible in Hawaiian; this translation is from the King James version, http://www.kingjamesbibleonline.org/Psalms-41-9/, accessed Nov. 5, 2013.
45 Goodyear-Kaʻōpua, *Seeds We Planted*, 64.
46 Goodyear-Kaʻōpua, *Seeds We Planted*, 65.
47 Foucault, *Fearless Speech*, 15–16.
48 Kanepuu, "Na Hoalohaloha i ka Pokii."
49 Kanepuu, "Ka Honua Nei," Sep. 20, 1877, 1.
50 Kanepuu, "Ka Honua Nei," Sep. 20, 1877, 1.

CHAPTER FOUR: JOSEPH MOKUʻŌHAI POEPOE

1 Poepoe, "Joseph Mokuohai Poepoe."
2 "Ua Haalele mai"; Kahiolo, "He Moolelo no Kamapuaa." It is likely that his mother's first initial was E. A notice in *Ka Hae Hawaii* says that Kahiolo and E.

Keawehiku had a child who died, and a kanikau was published, stanzas of which were signed by E. Keawehiku and G. W. Kahiolo. "Hanau"; Kahiolo, "He Kanikau no Moenahele."

3   McKinzie, *Hawaiian Genealogies*, 2:108. Parker Ranch was the first cattle ranch in Hawai'i; its founder married into Kamehameha I's family, and thus the ranch and its owners became influential throughout the nineteenth and twentieth centuries in Hawai'i. See http://parkerranch.com/legacy/history-of/. Accessed September 4, 2016.
4   Kamakau, *Ke Kumu Aupuni*, 74.
5   Poepoe, "Joseph Mokuohai Poepoe"; Brown, *Facing the Spears of Change*, 85–88.
6   Poepoe, "Joseph Mokuohai Poepoe."
7   "Heart Disease."
8   Poepoe, "Joseph Mokuohai Poepoe."
9   Osorio, *Dismembering Lāhui*.
10 "Ka Moi Ata . . ." (King Arthur) ran in *Ka Makaainana* in 1888, but so many issues of that paper are missing that a full citation is impossible. The May 3, 1888, issue is noted as "Buke IV" (Volume 4). The translator's name is not given.
11 It was continued in Poepoe's *Hoku o ke Kai* from December 1883 to June 1884.
12 Montalba, *Fairy Tales from All Nations*.
13 Montalba, *Fairy Tales from All Nations*, 174.
14 Pukui and Elbert, *Hawaiian Dictionary*, s.v., "kalukalu."
15 Pukui and Elbert, *Hawaiian Dictionary*, s.v., "kēwā."
16 Poepoe, "He Moolelo Kaao no ke Keiki Alii Otto!," Jan. 17, 1880, 1.
17 La Motte-Fouqué, *Magic Ring*.
18 Poepoe, ""He Moolelo Kaao no ke Keiki Alii Otto!," Jan. 17, 1880, 1. La Motte-Fouqué, *Magic Ring*, 3.
19 Poepoe, "He Moolelo Kaao no ka Naita Rokekila Hinedu!"; "Ka Moolelo o Kalausele Kopala" among others; Verne, "He Moolelo no Kapena Nimo"; Kaiaikawaha, "Ka Moolelo o ka Elemakule Haze."
20 Hipa, "Ka Moolelo no ke Kiai Puka"; Hipa, "He Moolelo Kaao no Keaka Manu"; Kaeo, "He Moolelo Kaao no ka Hakaka Pahikaua"; Kaeo, "Ka Helu Ekahi"; Kaiaikawaha, "Ka Moolelo o ka Elemakule Haze"; Tao Se, "He Nanea Kamahao."
21 "Ke Keiki Hoopapa."
22 "E Nalowale ana."
23 "O Ka Olelo Hea."
24 "Ke Kanawai"; "Na Kumu Mua"; Poepoe, *Ke Alakai o ke Kanaka Hawaii*.
25 "Na Lunamakaainana"; "No ka Ona Miliona Claus Spreckels."
26 Osorio, *Dismembering Lāhui*, 243.
27 Osorio, *Dismembering Lāhui*, 245.
28 Williams Jr., "Claiming Christianity," 119.
29 "Meeting of Hawaiians."
30 Osorio, *Dismembering Lāhui*, 246.
31 Kuykendall, *Hawaiian Kingdom: Vol. 3*, 410.
32 "Na Kahua i Kukuluia ai."

33. Issues of the paper between October 1887 and January 1888 have not been preserved on microfilm or electronically. Mookini, *Hawaiian Newspapers*, 52.
34. Kekoa, "E Hoomau i ke Kupaa" (1900), 2. This is the first of a post-annexation six-part series urging people to continue to fight for their country. Readers may find a translation of one installment in the *ʻōiwi* journal: Kekoa, "E Hoomau i ke Kupaa" (2002). See also Kuykendall, *Hawaiian Kingdom: Vol. 3*, 417.
35. See the issues of Jun. 16, Jun. 30, Jul. 7, and so on of *Ke Alakai o Hawaii* of 1888. They are available on nupepa.org.
36. It is also possible that this and other moʻolelo set in foreign lands are original works of fiction rather than translations. Mahalo to Craig Howes for pointing this out.
37. Nakanaela, *Ka Buke Moʻolelo o Honorable Robert William Wilikoki* 48, 58.
38. "Kipi Kuloko." On Aug. 10, *Ko Hawaii Pae Aina* reported that Poepoe was in custody, held at a place called Kuapapanui. "Nu Hou Hawaii."
39. Hawaii, First Circuit Court, Criminal Cases, nos. 1369 and 1376.
40. See chapters 4 and 5 in Silva, *Aloha Betrayed*.
41. Kuykendall, *Hawaiian Kingdom: Vol. 3*, 429.
42. Nakanaela, *Ka Buke Moʻolelo o Honorable Robert William Wilikoki*, 37.
43. Nakanaela, *Ka Buke Moʻolelo o Honorable Robert William Wilikoki*, i–xx; Basham, "He Puke Mele Lāhui," 53–59.
44. Poepoe, *Ka Moolelo o ka Moi Kalakaua I*, 33–34; Kuykendall, *Hawaiian Kingdom: Vol. 3*, 470.
45. Poepoe, *Ka Moolelo o ka Moi Kalakaua I*, 42.
46. Poepoe, *Ka Moolelo o ka Moi Kalakaua I*, 44. The word "kahanahana" is likely a typographical error for "kahakahana," "markings" or "narrow strips of cloth." Pukui and Elbert, *Hawaiian Dictionary*, s.v., "kāhanahana" and "kahakahana." Kuykendall reports that "the hull and spars of the ship [were] draped in black." *Hawaiian Kingdom: Vol. 3*, 473.
47. Poepoe, *Ka Moolelo o ka Moi Kalakaua I*, [ii].
48. Thanks to Craig Howes for suggesting this descriptor.
49. Poepoe, *Ka Moolelo o ka Moi Kalakaua I*, 33.
50. Poepoe, *Ke Alakai o ke Kanaka Hawaii*, vi.
51. Lucas, "E Ola Mau Kākou," 4.
52. Poepoe, *Ke Alakai o ke Kanaka Hawaii*, viii.
53. Poepoe, *Ke Alakai o ke Kanaka Hawaii*, 291–304.
54. Poepoe, *Ke Alakai o ke Kanaka Hawaii*, Mahele II n.p.
55. Poepoe, *Ke Alakai o ke Kanaka Hawaii*, Mahele II, 5.
56. Kuykendall, *Hawaiian Kingdom: Vol. 3*, 514–521, 519.
57. Liliuokalani, *Hawaii's Story by Hawaii's Queen*, 228–229.
58. Liliuokalani, *Hawaii's Story by Hawaii's Queen*, 229–231.
59. "Ko Makou Kulana i keia Kau Koho Balota."
60. "Ke Kumukanawai Hou."
61. Malo, "Ke Aupuni Moi." There is no indication whether or not this David Malo is related to the famous writer of a previous era who has the same name.

62. "He Moolelo no Pakaa a me Kuapakaa"; Dumas, "Ka Moolelo Walohia."
63. Poepoe, "E Hoomaopopo Ka Lehulehu"; "Nuhou Kuloko."
64. See chapters 4 and 5 in Silva, *Aloha Betrayed*.
65. See Liliuokalani, *Hawaii's Story by Hawaii's Queen*, 267–294.
66. "Hawaiians Want Annexation."
67. "Court Proceedings."
68. The Ua Kanilehua is the famous rain of Hilo, referenced in countless mele and ʻōlelo noʻeau. See, for example, Pukui, *ʻŌlelo Noʻeau*, 107, no. 1000.
69. Kanilehua, "He Lolelua Maopopo Io no," 3.
70. Kanilehua, "He Lolelua Maopopo Io no," 6.
71. Kanilehua, "He Lolelua Maopopo Io no," 6.
72. Kanilehua, "He Lolelua Maopopo Io no," 6.
73. Kanilehua, "He Lolelua Maopopo Io no," 6.
74. Mokuohai, "Ke Kumu o ka Hoohui Aina."
75. Mokuohai, "Ke Kumu o ka Hoohui Aina."
76. Warner, "Movement to Revitalize," 133; Lucas, "E Ola Mau Kākou," 8–9.
77. Mahalo to Marie Alohalani Brown for her insights into this article.
78. "E Kukulu ke Aupuni."
79. "He Buke Mele Lahui"; Basham analyzes this book in Basham, *I Mau Ke Ea*.
80. "Ka Papa Hoonohonoho."
81. Poepoe, "Na Paemoku o Hawaii." On Apr. 3, the same lecture was begun but seems to have been expanded and revised from the beginning on Jul. 24. Poepoe, "Ka Haiolelo Akea."
82. Kamakau, *Ke Kumu Aupuni*; Kamakau, *Ke Aupuni Mōʻī*.
83. Poepoe, "Na Paemoku o Hawaii," Jul. 24, 4.
84. "Lele ke Aho."
85. Kaulukou, Kaunamano, Kaaukai, and Kanealii appear in the photograph of the men of Hui Aloha ʻĀina who delivered the documents and testimony to James Blount in 1893.
86. Achi et al., "Ke Ola ame ka Palekana."
87. "Na Komisina 'Roialiti' no Wasinetona."
88. "Ka Hae Hawaii."
89. "Ka Hae Hawaii."
90. "Lawe Lima Nui."
91. *Nupepa Kuokoa*, Jul. 15, 1898, 8.
92. "E Hapai koke ka Lahui Hawaii Maoli."
93. Silva, "I Kū Mau Mau."
94. United States, *Act to Provide a Government*, 23, 30, 31–32.
95. United States, *Act to Provide a Government*, 14.
96. Palau, "Ua Like no a Like."
97. Poepoe and Coelho, "Ke Kanawai Teritori"; Poepoe and Coelho, "Ke Kanawai o ka Panalaau."
98. United States, *He Kanawai e Hoonoho*.
99. Poepoe, "Ke Alakai Koho Balota."

100. Poepoe, "Na Kumuhana."
101. United States, *Act to Provide a Government*, 2, Sec. 44; 14.
102. Palau, "Oia Maoli no ke Kaulike."
103. "Wilcox Is It." For a fuller story, see Williams, "Race, Power, and the Dilemma of Democracy."
104. Untitled editorial column, *Nupepa Kuokoa*, Apr. 26, 1901, 2. I studied the moʻolelo being published before, during, and shortly after this legislative season to see if I could determine which moʻolelo were Poepoe's but could not determine that precisely.
105. "Will Get Out Votes."
106. "Wilcox Has Some Brand New Fakes."
107. US Congress, *Hawaiian Investigation*, 597.
108. "He Buke Maikai."
109. "Na Hawaii Kaulana."
110. Mookini, *Hawaiian Newspapers*, 23.
111. Hooulumahiehie, "Ka Moolelo o Hiiaka-i-ka-poli-o-Pele."
112. "Oihana Kilokilo Hawaii."
113. Basham, "Ka Lāhui Hawaiʻi and Peoplehood," 4–5.
114. Pukui and Elbert, *Hawaiian Dictionary*, s.v., "naʻi."
115. "No Keaha."
116. "Ka Ipu Alabata."
117. "Mai Haalele i Kau."
118. "Pehea e Mau ai ke Ola."
119. Pukui, *ʻŌlelo Noʻeau*.
120. "Alemanaka no 1906."
121. "He Moolelo no Laieikawai"; "Ka Moolelo Walohia o Hainakolo."
122. Hooulumahiehie, "He Moolelo No Alamira."
123. Poepoe, "He Hoakaka Aku."
124. Mea Kakau Moolelo o Kamehameha (Hoʻoulumāhiehie), "Alamira," Nov. 30, 1906, 3; Fornander, *Account of the Polynesian Race*.
125. Probably Peleiōhōlani.
126. hoʻomanawanui, *Voices of Fire*, 52.
127. See "Mare Lehulehu"; Kinney, "He Pane Akea ia J. Mahuka"; and others.
128. One example is "Kuamuamuia na Hawaii."
129. "He Moolelo no ka Hooilina o Rivela"; Poepoe, "Ka Moolelo Kaao o Hiiaka-i-ka-Poli-o-Pele"; Hooulumahiehie-i-ka-oni-malie-a-pua-lilia-lana-i-ka-wai, "Ka Moolelo Hiwahiwa o Kawelo."
130. "Mai Haalele i ka Olelo Makuahine."
131. "Ka La Hoomanao o ka Moi Kauikeaouli." A partial translation of this story may be found at http://nupepa-hawaii.com/tag/kalanikupuapaikalaninui/, accessed Dec. 22, 2014. The prayer differs from the one Kamakau that records.
132. Peleioholani, "He Hoakaka."
133. "Hookahi Wai o ka Like."
134. "E Aʻo i ka Olelo Beritania."

135 Most of these are titled "A Hiiaka Chant." The song is "Ahi Wela."
136 "What Is Poi?"; "Legend of Kou Harbor."
137 Support for J. Wallach began with "Na Ma'i Lepera," and remained prominent in the paper until Mar. 8.
138 See also Inglis, *Maʻi Lepera*.
139 Lake and Reynolds, *Drawing the Global Colour Line*, 192.
140 Lake and Reynolds, *Drawing the Global Colour Line*, 197.
141 *Kuokoa Home Rula*, Jul. 30, 1909, 2. Mookini lists Poepoe as the editor until 1912, but that appears to be in error.
142 Poepoe, "Kaʻu Papa Iliili."
143 Lasky, "Community Struggles, Struggling Communities," 81.
144 Hooulumahiehie, "Moolelo Hoonaue Puuwai no Kama.A.Ka.Mahiai [*sic*]." In the first installments of this moʻolelo, the title appears as "He Moolelo Onini Puuwai. . . ." Also, note that Pukui and Elbert have the word "hiʻapaiʻole" spelled as "hiapaʻiʻole." Many issues of *Ke Aloha Aina* in 1911 and 1912 were never microfilmed and thus not digitized either. I am grateful to Marie Alohalani Brown for photographing the originals at the Hawaiian Historical Society and sharing the images with me.
145 Na-Hau-o-Maihi, Ka Moolelo Hooni Puuwai no Keakaoku," Feb. 3, 1912, 3.
146 Mahalo nui to Marie Alohalani Brown for alerting me to Hoʻoulumāhiehie's authorship of these moʻolelo and for photographing the installments not previously microfilmed.
147 Poepoe, "Moolelo no ka Naita Leopaki," Jan. 18, 1913, 3.
148 "Halawai a na Wahine"; Sharpe, "Ka Huakai Kukulu Kalapu."
149 Sharpe, "Ka Nanehai o ka Manawa."
150 Sharpe, "Ka Huakai Kukulu Kalapu."
151 "Pehea Kakou"; "E Nalowale Loa anei."
152 "E Nalowale Loa anei."
153 See McGregor, *Nā Kuaʻāina*.

CHAPTER FIVE: SINGING (TO) THE ʻĀINA

1 The term used often in the moʻolelo is "aikāne," not always translatable as lover. In this moʻolelo their romantic and sexual relationship is clear, especially the description of their surfing on the same board. Hiʻiaka's kau (sacred chant) of both delight in their romance and grief because Hōpoe will soon be consumed by Pele's volcanic fires includes these lines: "He ena aloha keia ia oe/Ke kau nei ka haili/kau ka haili moe i ke ahiahi/He hele ko ke kakahiaka" (This is a loving heat, an intense affection for you/A premonition is appearing/A dream in the evening/Morning will bring a departure). "Haili"—a premonition, a dream—is very close to "hāliʻi," and "hāliʻi moe" is a covering for a bed. Poepoe, "Ka Moolelo Kaao o Hiiaka-i-ka-poli-pele," Jun. 12, 1908, 1.
2 Charlot, "Pele and Hiʻiaka," 64.
3 hoʻomanawanui, *Voices of Fire*, 76, 179.

4   Poepoe, "Ka Moolelo Kaao o Hiiaka-i-ka-poli-pele," Jan. 10, 1908, 1.
5   Hoʻomanawanui, "Pele's Appeal," 439–494.
6   Bush and Paaluhi, "Ka Moolelo o Hiiakaikapoliopele," Jan. 6, 1893, 1.
7   Poepoe, "Ka Moolelo Kaao o Hiiaka-i-ka-poli-pele," Jan. 10, 1908, 1.
8   hoʻomanawanui, *Voices of Fire*, 45. I might quibble and say that Fornander is arguably not in the same category as the other writers, because he collected moʻolelo in the native language for the purpose of studying the migrations across the Pacific. It wasn't until after his death that the bulk of his collection was purchased by the Bishop Museum, which then hired Thomas Thrum and W. D. Alexander to produce the translations. Fornander, *Fornander Collection* IV:1.
9   Basham, "Ka Lāhui Hawaiʻi," 62.
10 Silva, "E Lawe i ke Ō."
11 hoʻomanawanui, *Voices of Fire*, 43.
12 Poepoe, "Ka Moolelo Kaao o Hiiaka-i-ka-poli-pele," Apr. 24, 1908. 1.
13 Poepoe, "Ka Moolelo Kaao o Hiiaka-i-ka-poli-pele," Jul. 31, 1908, 1.
14 Pukui and Elbert, *Hawaiian Dictionary*, s.v., "kulaʻi."
15 "In ancient times it was a custom in Kalapana, Puna, to force a young coconut tree to grow in a reclining position in commemoration of a chiefly visit." Pukui, *ʻŌlelo Noʻeau*, 249, no. 2280.
16 Pukui, *ʻŌlelo Noʻeau*, 249, no. 2279.
17 Pukui and Elbert, *Hawaiian Dictionary*, s.v., "makena."
18 Kanahele, *Ka Honua Ola*, 75, 115, 123.
19 Pukui and Elbert, *Hawaiian Dictionary*, s.v., "māwae."
20 Kanahele, *Ka Honua Ola*, xv.
21 Kanahele, *Ka Honua Ola*, 1.
22 Kanahele, *Ka Honua Ola*, 4, 5.
23 Kanahele, *Ka Honua Ola*, 33.
24 The definition of "kau" is from Pukui and Elbert, *Hawaiian Dictionary*, s.v., "kau." The definition of "moʻo" is from Marie Alohalani Brown, personal communication, June 28, 2015. Readers of Hawaiian may refer to Brown's master's thesis, "Ka Poʻe Moʻo Akua."
25 This contrasts with Pele, however, since as hoʻomanawanui and Charlot both point out, "Noho Pele i ka ʻāhiu" (Pele stays [lives] in the wild). Pele is the volcano, so she is unpredictable, fiery, intemperate, and always potentially destructive; her role is to overturn and remake the world. Where Hiʻiaka chants a kau to their kupuna, Pōhakuokauaʻi, Pele threatens him. hoʻomanawanui, *Voices of Fire*, xl; Charlot, "Pele and Hiʻiaka," 57.
26 Poepoe, "Ka Moolelo Kaao o Hiiaka-i-ka-poli-pele," Jul. 16, 1909, 4.
27 For a photo of the hala being cut for lei, see https://www.pinterest.com/pin/43347215140952028/. Accessed September 4, 2016.
28 Poepoe, "Ka Moolelo Kaao o Hiiaka-i-ka-poli-pele," Jul. 16, 1909, 4.
29 Poepoe, "Ka Moolelo Kaao o Hiiaka-i-ka-poli-pele," Aug. 13, 1909, 4.
30 See, for example, the story of Pele asking girls for food and water. Pukui, *Folktales of Hawaiʻi He Mau Kaʻao Hawaiʻi*, 23.

31 D. K. Kahalemaile, in Basham, "Ka Lāhui Hawai'i," 60.
32 Basham, "Ka Lāhui Hawai'i," 60.
33 Poepoe, "Ka Moolelo Kaao o Hiiaka-i-ka-poli-pele," Aug. 27, 1909, 4.
34 Poepoe, "Ka Moolelo Kaao o Hiiaka-i-ka-poli-pele," Jul. 23, 1909, 4.
35 Poepoe, "Ka Moolelo Kaao o Hiiaka-i-ka-poli-pele," Jul. 23, 1909, 4.
36 Poepoe, "Ka Moolelo Kaao o Hiiaka-i-ka-poli-pele," Jul. 23, 1909, 4.
37 Poepoe, "Ka Moolelo Kaao o Hiiaka-i-ka-poli-pele," Jul. 23, 1909, 4.
38 Poepoe, "Ka Moolelo Kaao o Hiiaka-i-ka-poli-pele," Jul. 23, 1909, 4.
39 Pukui and Elbert, *Hawaiian Dictionary*, s.v., "po'o ko'i."; Poepoe, "Ka Moolelo Kaao o Hiiaka-i-ka-poli-pele," Jul. 23, 1909, 4.
40 Poepoe, "Ka Moolelo Kaao o Hiiaka-i-ka-poli-pele," Jul. 30, 1909, 4.
41 Poepoe, "Ka Moolelo Kaao o Hiiaka-i-ka-poli-pele," Jul. 30, 1909, 4.
42 Charlot, "Pele and Hi'iaka," 57.
43 ho'omanawanui, *Voices of Fire*, 132.
44 ho'omanawanui, *Voices of Fire*, 133.
45 Pukui, *Folktales of Hawai'i He Mau Ka'ao Hawai'i*, 74–76, 131–133.
46 See the Hawaiian Kingdom website, for example, which reproduces an 1891 article by W. D Alexander. The first sentence of that article reads, "The ancient system of land titles in the Hawaiian Islands was entirely different from that of tribal ownership prevailing in New Zealand, and from the village or communal system of Samoa, but bore a remarkable resemblance to the feudal system that prevailed in Europe during the Middle Ages." http://www.hawaiiankingdom.org/land-system.shtml, accessed Jan. 4, 2014.
47 John Charlot, longtime resident of Waiāhole, personal communication, Dec. 26, 2013.
48 Kamakau, "Ka Moolelo o Kamehameha I," Mar. 16, 1867, 1.
49 The word "kānāwai," here translated as "water courses," also means "law."
50 Kamakau, *Ruling Chiefs of Hawaii*, 129. This is a translation by Mary Kawena Pukui and others.
51 Poepoe, "Ka Moolelo Kaao o Hiiaka-i-ka-poli-pele," Jul. 30, 1909, 4.
52 Pukui and Elbert, *Hawaiian Dictionary*, s.v., "Onelau'ena."
53 Poepoe, "Ka Moolelo Kaao o Hiiaka-i-ka-poli-pele," Jul. 30, 1909, 4.
54 Poepoe, "Ka Moolelo Kaao o Hiiaka-i-ka-poli-pele," Jul. 30, 1909, 4.
55 Kanahele, *Ka Honua Ola*.

CHAPTER SIX: MO'OLELO HAWAI'I KAHIKO

1 Ngūgī, *Decolonising the Mind*, 3.
2 Ngūgī, *Decolonising the Mind*; See also Goodyear-Ka'ōpua, *Seeds We Planted*.
3 Dibble, *Ka Mooolelo Hawaii* (1838); Pokuea, *Ka Mooolelo Hawaii*; Kamakau, "Ka Moolelo o Hawaii Nei"; Kamakau, "Ka Moolelo Hawaii"; Fornander, *Account of the Polynesian Race*; Poomaikelani, *Hoike a ka Papa Kuauhau*; *Na Mele Aimoku*; White, *Ancient History of the Māori*.
4 Dibble, *Ka Mooolelo Hawaii* (1838).

5. Malo, *Ka Moʻolelo Hawaii*, 11.
6. Dibble, *History of the Sandwich Islands*, iv.
7. Orwell, "Politics and the English Language."
8. Dibble, *Ka Mooolelo Hawaii* (1984), 112; translation by Kahananui, 230.
9. Dibble, *Ka Mooolelo Hawaii* (2005), 1.
10. All translations are mine unless noted otherwise.
11. N. Arista, "Foreword," x, n 22.
12. Silva, "Early Hawaiian Newspapers," 119–123.
13. See Silva, *Aloha Betrayed*, 17–20.
14. Dibble, *Ka Mooolelo Hawaii* (2005), 42–44.
15. Pokuea, *Ka Mooolelo Hawaii*, 34–36; Pokuea, "Mooolelo Hawaii," Aug. 4, 1858, 69–70.
16. Pokuea, "He Moolelo No Ka Hookumuia."
17. For a comprehensive listing of Kamakau's newspaper articles, see the bibliography in Nogelmeier, *Mai Paʻa I Ka Leo*. I use the term "autoethnography" in the sense introduced by Mary Louise Pratt in *Imperial Eyes* (i.e., as a cultural description by a member of the culture).
18. Kamakau, "Ka Moolelo o Hawaii Nei"; Kamakau, "Ka Moolelo Hawaii."
19. Kamakau, "Ka Moolelo Hawaii," Oct. 14, 1869, 1; Kamakau, *Tales and Traditions*, 125–126.
20. Helen Doty, in Fornander, *Account of the Polynesian Race* (1969), x.
21. Fornander, *Account of the Polynesian Race*, iii.
22. Fornander, *Account of the Polynesian Race*, v–vi. It is possible that the name "Hakuole" should be "Haleole." The well-known author Haleʻole had the same first and middle initials. Searches of newspaper databases turn up no instances of this name with these initials, although the family name, Hakuole, is there.
23. Poomaikelani, *Hoike a ka Papa Kuauhau*, 3.
24. Poomaikelani, *Hoike a ka Papa Kuauhau*, 11.
25. Kukahi, *Ke Kumulipo*.
26. D. Arista, "Davida Malo, Ke Kanaka O Ka Huliau," 128–129.
27. Recent work by Jeffrey (Kapali) Lyon illuminates the serious problems with Emerson's translation, which include a lack of understanding of the text because of his rusty Hawaiian-language skills, his "pigeonhol[ing] [of] Malo as an unreasoning Christian zealot who despised his own culture," and his failure to "[grasp] its essential purpose," "Davida Malo, Nathaniel Emerson," 122–123. With Charles Langlas, Lyon is now preparing a new transcription and translation of Malo's *Moʻolelo Hawaii*.
28. John Charlot, personal communication, Mar. 2015.
29. Poepoe, "Na Paemoku o Hawaii"; Poepoe, "Ka Haiolelo Akea imua o ka Lahui Hawaii."
30. A translation into English from the Latin reads as follows: "the witness of the times, the light of truth, the life-force of memory, life's teacher, and the messenger of the past." Livy, *History of Rome*, viii.
31. "Ka Moolelo Hawaii Kahiko," Feb. 1, 1906, 1.

32 "No Keaha."
33 Poepoe, "Ka Moolelo Hawaii Kahiko," Feb. 2, 1906, 1.
34 Pukui and Elbert, *Hawaiian Dictionary*, s.v. "alanui."
35 Elsewhere this name appears as Kahakuikamoana. Fornander, *Fornander Collection* IV, 2–3.
36 Poepoe, "Ka Moolelo Hawaii Kahiko," Feb. 2–Feb. 5, 1906, 1.
37 Poepoe, "Ka Moolelo Hawaii Kahiko," Feb. 6, 1906, 1.
38 Poepoe, "Ka Moolelo Hawaii Kahiko," Feb. 7, 1906, 1.
39 Kuakini et al., "No Kalani 'Kauikeaouli Kamehameha III.'"
40 Some explanation, different from what is given in the text, and translation of the parts of the mele are found in Peleioholani, "Ancient History of Hookumu-ka-Lani."
41 Titled "He Kanaenae no ka Hanau Ana" and "Kanaenae no ka Hanau ana o Kauikeaouli" in *Na Mele Aimoku, Na Mele Kupuna*, 290–304.
42 Pukui and Korn, *Echo of Our Song*, 12.
43 Pukui and Elbert, *Hawaiian Dictionary*, s.v. "aouli."
44 Kameʻeleihiwa, *Native Land and Foreign Desires*, 31–32.
45 Poepoe, "Ka Moolelo Hawaii Kahiko," Feb. 9, 1906, 1.
46 Poepoe, "Ka Moolelo Hawaii Kahiko," Feb. 13, 1906, 1.
47 Poepoe, "Ka Moolelo Hawaii Kahiko," Feb. 10, 12, 1906, 1.
48 Peleioholani, "Ancient History of Hookumu-ka-Lani," 22–23.
49 Peleioholani, "Ancient History of Hookumu-ka-Lani."
50 Kameʻeleihiwa, *Native Land and Foreign Desires*, 23–33.
51 Poepoe, "Ka Moolelo Hawaii Kahiko," Feb. 12, 1906, 1.
52 Peleioholani, "Ancient History of Hookumu-ka-Lani," 23.
53 Salazar, "Multicultural Settler Colonialism"; Peralto, "Portrait."
54 Pukui and Elbert, *Hawaiian Dictionary*, s.v., "kaekae" and "maliu"; Kamakau, *Tales and Traditions*, 113 and "Ka Moolelo o Kamehameha," Jan. 19, 1867, 1.
55 Poepoe, "Ka Moolelo Hawaii Kahiko," Feb. 14, 1906, 1.
56 Poepoe, "Ka Moolelo Hawaii Kahiko," Feb. 15, 1906, 1.
57 John Charlot analyzes a manuscript copy of the Kumulipo, also associated with Mōʻī Kalākaua. Charlot, *Kumulipo of Hawaiʻi*, 2.
58 Kamakau, "Ke Kuauhau o na Kupuna"; Kepookulou, "No Na Alii o Na Moku." Although Poepoe is interested in Kamehameha's moʻokūʻauhau, he doesn't pursue it in this text. Running alongside this in the paper, however, is the moʻolelo of Kamehameha I. Hooulumahiehie, "Kamehameha I."
59 Poepoe, "Ka Moolelo Hawaii Kahiko," Mar. 15, 1906, 1.
60 Poepoe, "Ka Moolelo Hawaii Kahiko," Mar. 16–17, 1906, 1.
61 Poepoe, "Ka Moolelo Hawaii Kahiko," Apr. 21, 23, 1906, 1.
62 Poepoe, "Ka Moolelo Hawaii Kahiko," Apr. 23–27, 1906, 1.
63 Poepoe, "Ka Moolelo Hawaii Kahiko," Apr. 24, 1906, 1.
64 Poepoe, "Ka Moolelo Hawaii Kahiko," Apr. 25, 1906, 1.
65 Kanepuu, "Ka Helu Hawaii."
66 Poepoe, "Ka Moolelo Hawaii Kahiko," Apr. 30, 1906, 1.

67 Pukui and Elbert, *Hawaiian Dictionary*, s.v., "piko."
68 Poepoe, "Ka Moolelo Hawaii Kahiko," Apr. 26, 1906, 1.
69 Kamakau, "Ka Moolelo o Hawaii Nei," Jun. 29, 1865, 1.
70 Poepoe, "Ka Moolelo Hawaii Kahiko," May 3, 1906, 1.
71 Handy et al., *Native Planters*, 156–157.
72 For an explanation of the banana-eating Mū, see Handy et al., *Native Planters*, 157–158.
73 Poepoe, "Ka Moolelo Hawaii Kahiko," May 9, 1906, 1.
74 Pukui, *ʻŌlelo Noʻeau*, 86, no. 779.
75 Abbott, *Lāʻau Hawaii*, 37.
76 The prayer to Kāne is "E Kane-i-ka-pohakaa—e! E ala! / E Kane-lu-honua—e! E ala! E Pohaku-o-Kane—e! E ala!" (Kāne of the rolling rock, Wake up! / Earth-scattering Kāne! Wake up! / Rock of Kāne! Wake up!). Kāne is the god of fresh water. Poepoe, "Ka Moolelo Hawaii Kahiko," May 12, 1906, 1.
77 Poepoe, "Ka Moolelo Hawaii Kahiko," May 10–12, 1906, 1.
78 Pukui, Elbert, and Mookini, *Place Names of Hawaii*, 192. The Pūehuehu pool is still there, but all freshwater streams in Hawaiʻi are now polluted with leptospirosis, so people can no longer swim there.
79 Poepoe, "Ka Moolelo Hawaii Kahiko," May 17, 1906, 1.
80 Poepoe, "Ka Moolelo Hawaii Kahiko," May 18, 1906, 1.
81 Kamakau, "Ka Moolelo o Hawaii nei," 29 June 1865, 1. Pukui's translation of Kamakau reads as follows: "The breadfruit tree became the goddess Kāmehaʻikana . . . famed from Hawaiʻi to Kauaʻi for mana and for seizing governments. . . . She became a goddess for Kamehameha during his reign." Kamakau, *Tales and Traditions*, 13.
82 Poepoe, "Ka Moolelo Hawaii Kahiko," May 22, 1906, 1. The mele is a part of the Kumulipo wā 15 as well.
83 Poepoe, "Ka Moolelo Hawaii Kahiko," May 31, 1, and Jun. 1–4, 1906, 1.
84 Poepoe, "Ka Moolelo Hawaii Kahiko," Jun. 5, 1906, 1.
85 Poepoe, "Ka Moolelo Hawaii Kahiko," May 26, 1906.
86 See http://www.pacificworlds.com/nuuanu/native/native3.cfm, accessed Feb. 5, 2014, for an explanation of the Pohukaina cave system.
87 Poepoe, "Ka Moolelo Hawaii Kahiko," Jun. 7, 1906. The numbers 400,000 and 4,000 are figurative ways of saying "very many" or "innumerable."
88 Poepoe, "Ka Moolelo Hawaii Kahiko," Jun. 9, 1906, 1.
89 The kukui is also the kino lau of Kamapuaʻa, and thus also Lono, as Kamapuaʻa is one of Lono's kino. Handy, "Traces of Totemism," 46.
90 Clark, *Hawaiian Surfing*, 25.
91 Poepoe, "Ka Moolelo Hawaii Kahiko," Jun. 13, 1906, 1.
92 Poepoe, "Ka Moolelo Hawaii Kahiko," Jun. 13, 1906, 1.
93 Pukui and Elbert, *Hawaiian Dictionary*, s.v. "ʻaha."
94 For an excellent analysis of these two paths to mana, see Kameʻeleihiwa, *Native Land and Foreign Desires*, 44–49.
95 Kameʻeleihiwa, *Native Land and Foreign Desires*, 40–44.

96 Unlike the powerful Haumea, Hoʻohōkūkalani never seems to have a story of her own; she has no discernible mana in the moʻolelo. Why is it that we do not hear either her consent or refusal in any of the accounts of this story of the origin of the kalo and the first aliʻi? This event is also said to be the origin of the ʻai kapu, the separation of men and women in eating, and the prohibition of certain foods to each. See Kameʻeleihiwa, *Native Land and Foreign Desires*, 23–25.
97 Poepoe, "Ka Moolelo Hawaii Kahiko," Jun. 25, 1906, 1.
98 Poepoe, "Ka Moolelo Hawaii Kahiko," Sep. 6, 1906, 1.
99 Poepoe, "Ka Moolelo Hawaii Kahiko," Sep. 13–18, 1906, 1.
100 Sterling and Summers, *Sites of Oahu*, 161.
101 Poepoe, "Ka Moolelo Hawaii Kahiko," Sep. 20, 1906, 1.
102 Poepoe, "Ka Moolelo Hawaii Kahiko," Sep. 20, 1906, 1.
103 Poepoe, "Ka Moolelo Hawaii Kahiko," Sep. 20, 1906, 1.
104 Poepoe, "Ka Moolelo Hawaii Kahiko," Sep. 22, 1906, 1.
105 Poepoe, "Ka Moolelo Hawaii Kahiko," Sep. 25, 1906, 1.
106 Low, *Hawaiki Rising*, 53–58.
107 Poepoe, "Ka Moolelo Hawaii Kahiko," Sep. 26–28, 1906, 1.
108 Poepoe, "Hawaiian Astronomy." See also Makemson, *Morning Star Rises*, 140. While Poepoe himself gives this citation, it appears that *Hoku o ke Kai* ended in 1884, so an error of some sort occurred. A review of all of the content of *Hoku o ke Kai* (twice) does not turn up this article.
109 "Ka Mookuauhau Elua o Hawaii."

CONCLUSION

1 Molokai is a comparatively sparsely populated island, also known as Molokai Pule Oʻo, Molokaʻi of the potent prayers. Pukui and Elbert, *Hawaiian Dictionary*, s.v., "oʻo."
2 Brown, *Facing the Spears of Change*.
3 Emma Nakuina's works are discussed at some length in Bacchilega, *Legendary Hawaiʻi*, and Moses Nakuina's are analyzed in Charlot, "Moses Kuaea Nākuina: Hawaiian Novelist," in *Classical Hawaiian Education*.
4 We also have a few books reprinted from their originals. See the Hawaiian Language Reprint Series at https://www.hawaiianhistory.org/publications/books/, and the Bishop Museum Classical Reprints in Hawaiian Language, http://www2.bishopmuseum.org/press/web/searchresults2.asp?search=language, both accessed Dec. 10, 2015. What we are missing is the great number of major works that were never published in book form.

Glossary

Readers should keep in mind that Hawaiian terms describe categories that sometimes correspond to multiple categories in English. It is best not to think of multiple glosses, therefore, as a menu of choices, but rather to try to imagine all of them as a single category (see Basham, "Ka Lāhui Hawai'i and Peoplehood"). Most of the glosses here are drawn from the Pukui and Elbert *Hawaiian Dictionary* (1986), and I have put quotation marks around those entries. Other glosses have been developed as a result of my own and others' research. Plurals such as Kānaka and wāhine refer to countable numbers; the singular is used when referring to everything in that category.

Words that begin with the 'okina (') appear at the end.

———

ahupua'a. "Land division usually extending from the uplands to the sea, so called because the boundary was marked by a heap (ahu) of stones surmounted by an image of a pig (pua'a), or because a pig or other tribute was laid on the altar as tax to the chief."

aikāne. Friend or lover of the same sex.

ali'i. Of the ruling segment of society. Usually translated as chief.

ali'i nui. Highest ranking ali'i; district, island, and archipelago rulers.

aloha 'āina. Love for the land; a pro-Kanaka, pro-independence politics; individual who practices aloha 'āina.

ao. Forms the complementary pair with pō. The realm of human life; daylight; the world; clouds.

aupuni. "Government, kingdom, dominion, nation, people under a ruler; national."

———

hala. "The pandanus or screw pine (*Pandanus odoratissimus*), native from southern Asia east to Hawai'i, growing at low altitudes, both cultivated and wild. . . . Many uses: leaves (lau hala) for mats, baskets, hats; the yellow to red fruit sections for leis, brushes; male flowers to scent tapa, their leaflike bracts to plait mats."

hānai. Adopt; to feed; to raise for an ali'i nui. To be so adopted or raised. Such a parent or child.

haole. Foreign; now specifically white American or European; corresponds with "Western."

heiau. "Pre-Christian place of worship, shrine; some heiau were elaborately constructed stone platforms, others simple earth terraces. Many are preserved today."

hewa. "Mistake, fault, error . . . blunder, defect, offense, guilt, crime." The opposite of pono. Used in Christianity to mean sin.

hōʻailona. Signs.

hoʻāo. Joining of a couple; usually translated as marriage, which is misleading, as hoʻāo did not require monogamy.

hoʻomana. Religion.

hui. Group; association; company.

———

imu. Underground oven.

———

kaʻao. Legend; tale; moʻolelo with fabulous elements.

kahiko. Ancient; old.

kāhili. "Feather standard, symbolic of royalty."

kahua. "Foundation, base, site, location, ground, background, platform, as of a house . . . declaration of principles or policy, doctrine, platform."

kahuna; kāhuna (plural). Expert; priestly class.

kalo. Taro.

Kanaka; Kānaka (plural). Hawaiian; person; people.

kāne. Man; male.

kanikau. Mourning and condolence mele.

kaona. "Hidden meaning, as in Hawaiian poetry; concealed reference, as to a person, thing, or place; words with double meanings that might bring good or bad fortune."

kapa. "Tapa, as made from wauke [paper mulberry (Broussonetia papyrifera)] or māmaki [Pipturus spp.] bark; formerly clothes of any kind or bedclothes; quilt."

kapu. Restricted; sacred; forbidden.

kau.like. "Equality, equation, equity, justice; equal, impartial, just, mutual, parallel; to balance evenly, make alike, be in a similar situation, treat fairly and impartially, dispense justice; to arrive at the same time."

kau.papa.loʻi. "Molokai term for taro patch." See loʻi.

kauā. Segment of society thought of as outcast; they served aliʻi; drawn upon for human sacrifice. Often mistranslated as "slave."

kilokilo. The art of reading signs and omens.

kino lau. Many physical forms taken by akua (deities) or ʻaumakua (family deities).

koʻihonua, mele koʻihonua. "Genealogical chant; to sing such chants." Includes cosmogonical mele like the Kumulipo.

kōkua. Help; assistance.

kōlea. "Pacific golden plover (Pluvialis dominica), a migratory bird which comes to Hawaiʻi about the end of August and leaves early in May for Siberia and Alaska. . . . to repeat, boast." The kōlea is frequently used as a "scornful reference to foreigners," but that may not relevant to the passages analyzed here.

konohiki. Ruler or supervisor of moku (large districts), ahupuaʻa, or smaller land divisions.

kuhina. Cabinet minister.

kuhina nui. "Powerful officer in the days of the monarchy. Ka-ʻahu-manu was the first to have this title; the position is usually translated as 'prime minister' or 'premier.'" With rare, and short-lived exceptions, this office was held by women.

kukui. Candlenut tree (*Aleurites moluccana*), "a large tree in the spurge family bearing nuts containing white, oily kernels that were formerly used for lights; hence the tree is a symbol of enlightenment."

kuleana. "Right, privilege, concern, responsibility, title, business, property, estate, portion, jurisdiction, authority, liability, interest, claim, ownership, tenure, affair, province; reason, cause, function, justification . . . blood relative through whom a relationship to less close relatives is traced."

kumu hula. Hula master.

kumukānāwai. Constitution.

kupua. "Demigod or culture hero, especially a supernatural being possessing several forms . . . ; one possessing mana."

kupuna; kūpuna (plural). "Grandparent, ancestor, relative or close friend of the grandparent's generation, grandaunt, granduncle." Elder.

———

lāʻau. Plant; tree; stick; branch; medicine.

lāʻau lapaʻau. Plant-based medicine.

lāhui. "Nation, race, tribe, people, nationality; great company of people; species, as of animal or fish, breed; national, racial."

lehua. "The flower of the ʻōhiʻa tree (*Metrosideros macropus, M. collina* subsp. *polymorpha*); also the tree itself. . . . a warrior, beloved friend or relative, sweetheart, expert."

loʻi. "Irrigated terrace, especially for taro . . . ; paddy."

lūʻau. Young taro leaves.

———

makaʻāinana. The common people of society.

makahiki. Winter season of rest and recreation; the ceremony and celebration of the same; year.

mākini. "Group of spears tied together, used as a battering ram in war (from maka kini, many points)."

mālama ʻāina. To care for the land; to carry out the kuleana of the familial relationship with the ʻāina.

malihini. Newcomers; visitors.

mea kākau. Writer; author.

mele. "Song, anthem, or chant of any kind; poem, poetry; to sing, chant."

mele maʻi. "*Mele maʻi*, song in honor of genitals, as of a chief, as composed on his or her birth, rarely if ever composed for adults; usually gay and fast."

mohoea. "Hawaiian rail (*Pennula sandwichensis*), an extinct flightless bird."

mōʻī. Highest ranking aliʻi who occupy positions as island or archipelago rulers.

mōʻīwahine. Female mōʻī; used as a gloss for queen. In Hawaiian, however, it is not necessary to denote gender for such titles.

mokuna. Chapter.

moʻo. "Lizard, reptile of any kind, dragon, serpent; water spirit."

moʻokūʻauhau. Genealogy. "Genealogical succession."

moʻolelo. "Story, tale, myth, history, tradition, literature, legend, journal, log, yarn, fable, essay, chronicle, record, article; minutes, as of a meeting." Any narrative, in other words.

moʻolelo kuʻuna. Hereditary moʻolelo; moʻolelo passed down in the oral tradition.

moʻopuna. "Grandchild; great-niece or -nephew; relatives two generations later, whether blood or adopted; descendant; posterity."

---

pae ʻāina. Archipelago. The name of our country was Ko Hawaiʻi Pae ʻĀina, the Hawaiian Archipelago or Hawaiian Islands.

pali. Cliff.

paukū. Verse, stanza, or paragraph.

piko. "Navel, navel string, umbilical cord . . . place where a stem is attached to the leaf, as of taro."

piʻo. "Arch, arc; bent, arched, curved; to arch, of a rainbow. . . . Marriage of full brother and sister of *nīʻaupiʻo* rank, presumably the highest possible rank." In Poepoe, "piʻo" is used for parent-child coupling.

pō. The realm of the ancestors, and to which we return at death; darkness, night; far distant past. In the Kumulipo, the first 8 wā where and when the universe originated.

poʻe aloha ʻāina. Those who take aloha ʻāina political positions.

pono. "Goodness, uprightness, morality, moral qualities, correct or proper procedure, excellence, well-being, prosperity, welfare, benefit, behalf, equity, sake, true condition or nature, duty; moral, fitting, proper, righteous, right, upright, just, virtuous, fair, beneficial, successful, in perfect order, accurate, correct, eased, relieved."

pouli. "Dark; darkness, dark night."

pule. Prayer.

---

waʻa. Sailing vessels, including double-hulled and long-distance voyaging vessels. Commonly (mis)translated as "canoe."

wahine; wāhine (plural). Woman; female.

wahi pana. Storied places.

ʻahahui ʻelele. Convention.

ʻai kapu. Restricted eating system. See Kameʻeleihiwa, *Native Land and Foreign Desires*.

ʻāina. "Land, earth."

ʻākōlea. "A native fern (*Athyrium microphyllum* syn. *A. poiretianum*) with beautiful, large, lacy fronds."

ʻauwai. Canal; irrigation canal for loʻi.

ʻawa. Kava; kava kava. "(*Piper methysticum*), a shrub 1.2 to 3.5 m tall with green jointed stems and heart-shaped leaves, native to Pacific islands, the root being the source of a narcotic drink of the same name used in ceremonies . . . , prepared formerly by chewing, later by pounding. The comminuted particles were mixed with water and strained. When drunk to excess it caused drowsiness and, rarely, scaliness of the skin and bloodshot eyes. Kava was also used medicinally."

ʻelele. Messenger; delegate; representative.

ʻihiʻihi. "Sacred, holy, majestic, dignified; treated with reverence or respect."

ʻike. To see, to know. Knowledge.

ʻiwa. "Frigate or man-of-war bird (*Fregata minor palmerstoni*); it has a wing span of 12 [ft.]."

ʻohana. Family; extended family.

ʻōhiʻa. ʻŌhiʻa lehua (*Metrosideros macropus, M. collina* subsp. *polymorpha*).

ʻōiwi. Native. "Physique, appearance; to appear . . . , the upper naked person of a well built man" (Andrews, *Dictionary of the Hawaiian Language*).

ʻōlelo. Language, talk.

ʻōlelo Hawaiʻi. Hawaiian language.

ʻōlelo noʻeau. Proverbs; poetical sayings.

ʻōpū aliʻi. Aliʻi stomach, a metaphor: "Kind, thoughtful, forgiving, loving, possessed of *aloha*, beneficent, benevolent, loving heart."

ʻulu. Breadfruit; breadfruit tree.

Bibliography

Note: "Ka," "ke," "nā," and "he" are articles, and "e," "i," and "ua" are verb markers; these have thus been ignored in alphabetizing the bibliography entries.

Abbott, Isabella Aiona. *Lāʻau Hawaii: Traditional Hawaiian Uses of Plants.* Honolulu: Bishop Museum Press, 1992.
Achi, William C., C. L. Hopkins, John Lot Kaulukou, and Joseph M. Poepoe. "Ke Ola ame ka Palekana o ka Lahui Hawaii." *Ka Nupepa Kuokoa,* 12 February 1897, 2.
"Ahi Wela." *Kuokoa Home Rula,* 21 May 1909, 1.
"Alemanaka no 1906." *Ka Naʻi Aupuni,* 27 January 1906, 3.
Alfred, Taiaiake. *Wasáse: Indigenous Pathways of Action and Freedom.* Orchard Park, N.Y. : Broadview Press, 2005.
Andrade, Carlos. *Hāʻena: Through the Eyes of the Ancestors.* Honolulu: University of Hawaiʻi Press, 2008.
Andrews, Lorrin. *A Dictionary of the Hawaiian Language.* Waipahu, HI: Island Heritage, [1865] 2003.
"E Aʻo i ka Olelo Beritania." *Kuokoa Home Rula,* 20 November 1908, 2.
Arista, Denise Noelani Manuela. "Davida Malo, Ke Kanaka o ka Huliau—David Malo, a Hawaiian of the Time of Change." Master's thesis, University of Hawaiʻi, 1998.
Arista, Noelani. "Foreword." In *Kepelino's Traditions of Hawaii,* edited by Martha Warren Beckwith, rev. ed., iv–xiv. Bernice P. Bishop Museum Bulletin 95. Honolulu: Bishop Museum Press, 2007.
Bacchilega, Cristina. *Legendary Hawaiʻi and the Politics of Place: Tradition, Translation, and Tourism.* Philadelphia: University of Pennsylvania Press, 2007.
Basham, J. J. Leilani. "Ka Lāhui Hawaiʻi: He Moʻolelo, He ʻĀina, He Loina, A He Ea Kākou." *Hūlili: Multidisciplinary Research on Hawaiian Well-Being* 6 (2010): 37–72.
———. Ka Lāhui Hawaiʻi and Peoplehood: Native Hawaiian Identity as Genealogy, Cultural Practice, and Political Independence. Unpublished paper. Courtesy of the author.
———. "I Mau Ke Ea O Ka ʻāina I Ka Pono: He Puke Mele Lāhui No Ka Lāhui Hawaiʻi." PhD dissertation, University of Hawaiʻi, 2007.

———. "He Puke Mele Lāhui: Nā Mele Kūpaʻa, Nā Mele Kūʻē a Me Nā Mele Aloha O Nā Kānaka Maoli." Master's thesis, University of Hawaiʻi, 2002.
Beamer, Kamanamaikalani. *No Mākou Ka Mana: Liberating the Nation*. Honolulu: Kamehameha Schools Press, 2014.
Beckwith, Martha Warren. *Hawaiian Mythology*. Honolulu: University of Hawaiʻi Press, 1970.
Benham, Maenette K. P. Ah Nee, and Ronald H. Heck. *Culture and Educational Policy in Hawaiʻi: The Silencing of Native Voices*. Sociocultural, Political, and Historical Studies in Education. Mahwah, NJ: Lawrence Erlbaum, 1998.
Brown, Marie Alohalani. *Facing the Spears of Change: The Life and Legacy of Ioane Kaneiakama Papa ʻĪʻī*. Honolulu: University of Hawaiʻi Press, 2016.
———. "Ka Poʻe Moʻo Akua." Master's thesis, University of Hawaiʻi, 2010.
"Ka Buke a Aberahama." *Ka Naʻi Aupuni*, 4 December 1905–20 January 1906 (not in every issue).
"He Buke Mele Lahui." *Ka Nupepa Kuokoa*, 10 January 1896, 2.
"He Buke Moolelo Maikai." *Ka Nupepa Kuokoa*, 14 February 1902, 5.
Bush, John E. "Olelo Hoakaka." In "Ka Moolelo o Hiiakaikapoliopele," John E. Bush and S. Paʻaluhi. *Ka Leo o ka Lahui*, 6 January 1893, 1.
Bush, John E., and S. Paaluhi. "Ka Moolelo o Hiiakaikapoliopele." *Ka Leo o ka Lahui*, 5 January–12 July 1893.
Chang, David A. *The World and All the Things upon It: Native Hawaiian Geographies of Exploration*. Minneapolis: University of Minnesota Press, 2016.
Chapin, Helen Geracimos. *Guide to Newspapers of Hawaiʻi: 1834–2000*. Honolulu: Hawaiian Historical Society, 2000.
———. "Newspapers of Hawaii 1834 to 1903: From 'He Liona' to the Pacific Cable," *Hawaiian Journal of History* 18 (1984): 47–86.
———. *Shaping History: The Role of Newspapers in Hawaiʻi*. Honolulu: University of Hawaiʻi Press, 1996.
Charlot, John. "The Application of Form and Redaction Criticism to Hawaiian Literature." *Journal of the Polynesian Society* 86, no. 4 (Dec. 1977): 479–501.
———. *Classical Hawaiian Education: Generations of Hawaiian Culture*. Lāʻie: Pacific Institute, Brigham Young University–Hawaiʻi, 2005. CD-ROM. www.johncharlot.me/BOOKS/CHE%20post/index.html Accessed 27 August 2016.
———. *A Kumulipo of Hawaiʻi: Comments on Lines 1 to 615 of the Origin Chant*. Sankt Augustin, Germany: Academia Verlag, 2014.
———. "Pele and Hiʻiaka: The Hawaiian Language Newspaper Series." *Anthropos* 93 (1998): 55–75.
Clark, John R. K. *Hawaiʻi Place Names: Shores, Beaches, and Surf Sites*. Honolulu: University of Hawaiʻi Press, 2002.
———. *Hawaiian Surfing: Traditions from the Past*. Honolulu: University of Hawaiʻi Press, 2011.
"Court Proceedings: Bush and Nawahi, the Alleged Conspirators, on Trial." *Daily Bulletin*, 7 May 1895, 1.
de Silva, Kīhei. "Liner Notes for 'O Kaʻōhao Kuʻu ʻĀina Nani.'" Honolulu: n.p., 1993.

Deloria, Vine, Jr. *The World We Used to Live In: Remembering the Powers of the Medicine Men*. Golden, CO: Fulcrum, 2006.

Dibble, Sheldon. *History of the Sandwich Islands*. Lahainaluna, HI: Press of the Mission Seminary, 1843.

———, ed. *Ka Mooolelo Hawaii: Hawaiian Language Reader*. Translated by Dorothy M. Kahananui. Honolulu: University of Hawaiʻi, Committee for the Preservation and Study of Hawaiian Language, Art and Culture, 1984.

———, ed. *Ka Mooolelo Hawaii: The History of Hawaii*. Hawaiian Language Reprint Series. Hawaiian Historical Society, 2005.

———, ed. *Ka Mooolelo Hawaii. I Kakauia e Kekahi mau Haumana o ke Kulanui, a i Hooponoponoia e Kekahi Kumu o ia Kula*. Lahainaluna, HI: Mea Pai Palapala no ke Kulanui, 1838.

Dowsett, J. I. (Kimo Pelekane), T. Metcalf (Meka), G. P. Judd (Kauka), and W. N. Pualewa. "Na Elele Makaainana." *Ka Nupepa Kuokoa*, 21 May 1864, 2.

Dumas, Alexandre. "Ka Moolelo Walohia o ka Haku Moneka Karisto." *Hawaii Holomua*, 2 May 1891, 1.

Fornander, Abraham. *An Account of the Polynesian Race; Its Origins and Migrations, and the Ancient History of the Hawaiian People to the Times of Kamehameha I*. Vol. 3. London: Trübner, 1885.

———. *An Account of the Polynesian Race; Its Origins and Migrations, and the Ancient History of the Hawaiian People to the Times of Kamehameha I*. Rutland, VT: C. E. Tuttle, 1969.

———. *Fornander Collection of Hawaiian Antiquities and Folk-Lore: The Hawaiian Account of the Formation of Their Islands and Origin of Their Race, with the Traditions of Their Migrations, Etc., as Gathered from Original Sources*. Facsimile edition. Vol. IV, *Memoirs of Bernice Pauahi Bishop Museum*. Honolulu: Bishop Museum Press, 2004.

———. *Fornander Collection of Hawaiian Antiquities and Folk-Lore: The Hawaiian Account of the Formation of Their Islands and Origin of Their Race, with the Traditions of Their Migrations, Etc., as Gathered from Original Sources*. Facsimile ed. Vol. V, *Memoirs of Bernice Pauahi Bishop Museum*. Honolulu: Bishop Museum Press, 2004.

———. *Fornander Collection of Hawaiian Antiquities and Folk-Lore: The Hawaiian Account of the Formation of Their Islands and Origin of Their Race, with the Traditions of Their Migrations, Etc., as Gathered from Original Sources*. Facsimile ed. Vol. VI, *Memoirs of Bernice Pauahi Bishop Museum*. Honolulu: Bishop Museum Press, 2004.

Foucault, Michel. *Fearless Speech*. Edited by Joseph Pearson. Los Angeles: Semiotext(e), 2001.

Goodyear-Kaʻōpua, Noelani. *The Seeds We Planted: Portraits of a Native Hawaiian Charter School*. Minneapolis: University of Minnesota Press, 2013.

"Ua Haalele mai o Beniamina Kaiminaauao Poepoe i Keia Ola Ana." *Kuokoa Home Rula*, 16 July 1909, 3.

"Ka Hae Hawaii." *Ka Nupepa Kuokoa*, 8 July 1898, 2.

"Halawai a na Wahine Na'i Pono Koho Balota." *Ke Aloha Aina*, 4 May 1912, 1.

Haleole, S. N. "Ka Nupepa Hou." *Ke Au Okoa*, 24 April 1865, 4.

Hall, Mary L. *Ka Honua Nei: Oia ka Buke Mua o ka Hoike Honua, no na Kamalii o na Kula Maoli o ke Aupuni*. Translated by H. R. Hitchcock. Honolulu: Papa Hoonaauao, 1873.

"Hanau." *Ka Hae Hawaii*, 24 April 1861, 15.

Handy, E. S. Craighill. "Traces of Totemism in Polynesia: Theories of Embodiment of Tutelary Spirits in Animate and Inanimate Forms." *Journal of the Polynesian Society* 77, no. 1 (1968): 43–56.

Handy, E. S. Craighill, Elizabeth Green Handy, and Mary Kawena Pukui. *Native Planters in Old Hawaii: Their Life, Lore, and Environment*. Bernice P. Bishop Museum Bulletin no. 223. Rev. ed. Honolulu: Bishop Museum Press, 1991.

"E Hapai koke ka Lahui Hawaii Maoli i Ahahui Kalaiaina Ponoi no Lakou iho." *Ka Nupepa Kuokoa*, 22 July 1898, 2.

Hauola, B. K. "He Wahi Kaao a me ke Mele Pu. Helu 2." *Ka Hae Hawaii*, 15 August 1860, 81.

Hawaii. *Compiled Laws of the Hawaiian Kingdom*, 1884.

———. First Circuit Court. Criminal Cases, 1889.

———. *Rex v. William Auld*. First District Court, 1883.

"Na Hawaii Kaulana." *Ka Nupepa Kuokoa*, 9 May 1902, 2.

Hawaiian Mission Children's Society. *Missionary Album; Portraits and Biographical Sketches of the American Protestant Missionaries to the Hawaiian Islands*. Enl. ed. Honolulu, 1969.

"Hawaiians Want Annexation." *Pacific Commercial Advertiser*, 8 February 1895, 2.

"Heart Disease Causes Death of Lawmaker: Hon. J. M. Poepoe Is Stricken at His Home." *Honolulu Advertiser*, 11 April 1913, 1.

"A Hiiaka Chant." *Kuokoa Home Rula*, 23, 30 April; 7, 14, 28 May; 4 June 1909, 1 or 2.

Hipa, L. J. N[ahora]. "He Moolelo Kaao no Keaka Manu." *Hoku o ke Kai*, August 1884, 493.

———. "Ka Moolelo no ke Kiai Puka." *Hoku o ke Kai*, August and September 1884, 474 and 498, respectively.

He Hoikehonua: He Mea ia e Hoakaka'i i ke Ano o ka Honua Nei, a me na Mea Maluna iho. Oahu: Na na Misionari i Pai, 1832.

Holt, John Dominis. *The Art of Featherwork in Old Hawai'i*. 2nd ed. Honolulu: Ku Pa'a, 1997.

———. *Waimea Summer*. Honolulu: Topgallant, 1976.

"Hookahi Wai o ka Like." *Kuokoa Home Rula*, 16 October 1908, 1.

"Ka Hoomana Kahiko." *Ka Nupepa Kuokoa*, 5 January 1865.

ho'omanawanui, ku'ualoha. *Voices of Fire: Reweaving the Literary Lei of Pele and Hi'iaka*. Minneapolis: University of Minnesota Press, 2014.

———. "Pele's Appeal: Mo'olelo, Kaona, and Hulihia in 'Pele and Hi'iaka' Literature (1860–1928)." PhD dissertation, University of Hawai'i at Mānoa, 2007.

Ho'oulumāhiehie. *The Epic Tale of Hi'iakaikapoliopele: Woman of the Sunrise, Lightning-Skirted Beauty of Halema'uma'u*. Translated by M. Puakea Nogelmeier. Honolulu: Awaiaulu Press, 2006.

Hooulumahiehie. "Kamehameha I: Ka Na'i Aupuni o Hawaii." *Ka Na'i Aupuni*, 27 November 1905–16 November 1906.

———. "Moolelo Hoonaue Puuwai no Kama.A.Ka.Mahiai [*sic*], Ka Hi'apa'iole o ka Ikaika o ke Kai Huki Hee Nehu o Kahului." *Ke Aloha Aina*, 7 August 1909–11 March 1911.

———. "He Moolelo no Alamira ka U'i Hapa Paniolo." *Ka Na'i Aupuni*, 27 November 1905–30 November 1906.

———. "Ka Moolelo o Hiiaka-i-ka-poli-o-Pele." *Hawaii Aloha*, 15 July–24 November 1905.

———. "Ka Moolelo o Hiiaka-i-ka-poli-o-Pele." *Ka Na'i Aupuni*, 1 December 1905–30 November 1906.

Hooulumahiehie-i-ka-oni-malie-a-pua-lilia-lana-i-ka-wai. "Ka Moolelo Hiwahiwa o Kawelo." *Kuokoa Home Rula*, 1 January 1909–1 April 1910.

Hulikahiko. "Na Mea Kahiko o Hawaii nei." *Ka Nupepa Kuokoa*, 3 December 1864, 3.

Inglis, Kerri A. *Ma'i Lepera: Disease and Displacement in Nineteenth-Century Hawai'i*. Honolulu: University of Hawai'i Press, 2013.

"Ka Ipu Alabata." *Ka Na'i Aupuni*, 21 December 1905, 2.

"Ka Moolelo o Pakaa." Archives, Bishop Museum, Honolulu.

J. H. K. [J. H. Kānepu'u]. "Makaikai ia Kauai." *Ka Nupepa Kuokoa*, 2, 9, and 16 September 1871.

———. "Ka Moeuhane a Moi." *Ka Hae Hawaii*, 19 September 1860, 106.

———. "He Wahi Moolelo No Kaohele." *Ka Elele Poakolu*, 9 February 1881, 3.

Ka'ai, S. K. [Simona], trans. "He Mooolelo No Aladana," *Ka Hoku o ka Pakipika*, 1, 8, 15, and 22 May; 5, 12, and 26 June 1862.

Kaelemakule, J. "No ka Halawai Kumu ma Hilo." *Ka Hae Hawaii*, 10 July 1861, 57.

Kaeo, Sam. "Ka Helu Ekahi o ka Pupuka: He Kaao Hunegaria." *Hoku o ke Kai*, February, March, and April 1884, 324, 351, and 384, respectively.

———. "He Moolelo Nanea no ka Hakaka Pahikaua." *Hoku o ke Kai*, June and July 1883.

Kahekili-wahine, and Kailinaoa. "He Mele Koihonua No Ahukai Kauukualii." *Ka Nupepa Kuokoa*, 20 June 1868, 4.

Kahiamoe, J. W. "Ke Au Okoa o ke Aupuni Hawaii," *Ke Au Okoa*, 29 May 1865, 1.

Kahiolo, G. W. "He Kanikau no Moenahele." *Ka Nupepa Kuokoa*, 5 July 1862, 4.

———. "He Moolelo no Kamapuaa." *Ka Hae Hawaii*, 26 June–25 September 1861.

Kahoohalahala, D. K. "Manao Hoohalahala." *Ke Au Okoa*, 1 May 1865, 3.

"Na Kahua i Kukulu ia ai ka Nupepa 'Ke Alakai o Hawaii.'" *Ke Alakai o Hawaii*, 31 August 1887, 4.

Kaiaikawaha, Thos. N., trans. "Ka Moolelo o ka Elemakule Haze: Ka Makai Kiu Kaulana o Nu Ioka." *Hoku o ke Kai*, December 1883, 272.

Kalaiohauola, B. "He Wahi Kaao a Me Kekahi Mele Pu." *Ka Hae Hawaii*, 4 July 1860, 60.

Kalakaua, David. *The Legends and Myths of Hawaii: The Fables and Folk-Lore of a Strange People*. Honolulu: Mutual, 1990.

Kalana, Ben. "He Moolelo Kaao no Roumiana Ho! Ka Mea i Kapaia Ka Lima Hei i na Mea Kani a o ka Wahine Hiu Ia o Lae Makapana." *Ke Alakai o Hawaii*, 7 January–24 November 1888.

Kalimahauna, J. M. "Ke Au ia Kamehameha," *Ka Hoku o ka Pakipika*, 27 March 1862, 1.

Kamakau, Samuel Manaiakalani. *Ke Aupuni Mōʻī: Ka Moʻolelo Hawaiʻi no Kauikeaouli, Keiki Hoʻoilina a Kamehameha a me ke Aupuni āna i Noho Mōʻī ai*. Honolulu: Kamehameha Schools Press, 2001.

———. "Ke Kuauhau o na Kupuna Kahiko Loa mai o Hawaii nei, a Hiki mai ia Wakea. Mai ia Wakea mai i keia Manawa a Kakou e Noho nei, i Mea e Maopopo ai i keia Hanauna; a ia Hanauna aku ia Hanauna aku." *Ka Nonanona*, 25 October 1842, 49–52.

———. *Ke Kumu Aupuni: Ka Moʻolelo Hawaiʻi no Kamehameha Ka Naʻi Aupuni a me Kāna Aupuni i Hoʻokumu ai*. Honolulu: ʻAhahui Olelo Hawaiʻi, 1996.

———. "He mau Mea i Hoohalahala ia no na Mea iloko o na Kaao Hawaii." *Ka Nupepa Kuokoa*, 15 February 1868, 3.

———. "Ka Moolelo Hawaii." *Ke Au Okoa*, 7 January 1869–2 February 1871.

———. "Ka Moolelo o Hawaii nei." *Ka Nupepa Kuokoa*, 22 June–7 October 1865 [Begins under title "No ke Kaapuni Makaikai i na Wahi Kaulana a me na Kupua a me na ʻLii Kahiko mai Hawaii a Niihau" on 15 June 1865].

———. "Ka Moolelo o Kamehameha I." *Ka Nupepa Kuokoa*, 20 October 1866–12 October 1867.

———. "Ka Moolelo o na Kamehameha." *Ka Nupepa Kuokoa*, 2 November 1867–24 October 1868.

———. *Ka Poʻe Kahiko: The People of Old*. Translated by Mary Kawena Pukui. Paperback ed. Bernice P. Bishop Museum Special Publication no. 51. Honolulu: Bishop Museum Press, 1992.

———. *Ruling Chiefs of Hawaii*. Rev. ed. Honolulu: Kamehameha Schools Press, 1992.

———. *Tales and Traditions of the People of Old: Nā Moʻolelo o ka Poʻe Kahiko*. Edited by Dorothy B. Barrère. Translated by Mary Kawena Pukui. Honolulu: Bishop Museum Press, 1991.

Kameʻeleihiwa, Lilikalā, trans. *He Moʻolelo Kaʻao o Kamapuaʻa (A Legendary Tradition of Kamapuaʻa, the Hawaiian Pig-God): An Annotated Translation of a Hawaiian Epic from Ka Leo o ka Lāhui, June 22, 1891–July 23, 1891*. Bishop Museum Special Publication 89. Honolulu: Bishop Museum Press, 1996.

———. *Native Land and Foreign Desires: How Shall We Live in Harmony (Ko Hawaiʻi ʻĀina a Me Nā Koi Puʻumake a Ka Poʻe Haole: Pehea Lā E Pono Ai?)*. Honolulu: Bishop Museum Press, 1992.

Kanahele, George S. *Kū Kanaka, Stand Tall: A Search for Hawaiian Values*. Kolowalu Book. Honolulu: University of Hawaiʻi Press, 1992.

Kanahele, Pualani Kanakaʻole. *Ka Honua Ola: ʻEliʻeli Kau Mai (The Living Earth: Descend, Deepen the Revelation)*. Honolulu: Kamehameha, 2011.

"Ke Kanawai." *Hoku o ke Kai*, August and October 1883; March, April, June, and July 1884.

Kānepuʻu [published as Kanepuu], Joseph H. "Ahe! He Nupepa Hou Ka!!" *Ko Hawaii Pae Aina*, 2 February 1878, 1.

———. "Ke Ano o ka Wa Ui o ke Kanaka a me na Mea a Pau e Hiki mai ana ia Ia mahope Ona." *Ka Hae Hawaii*, 15, 22, 29 October; 5 November 1856.

———. "Ke Awawa o Palolo." *Ke Au Okoa*, 17 September 1866, 3.

———. Commonplace book of Kanepuu, ca. 1881. Liliuokalani Collection, Archives, Bishop Museum, Honolulu.

———. "Ke Emi ana o na Kanaka." *Ka Hoku o ka Pakipika*, 1 May 1862, 2.

———. "Ka Hana Kupono e Ao aku ai na Makua i ka Lakou Poe Keiki." *Ka Hae Hawaii*, 24, 31 December 1856; 14, 21 January 1857.

———. "Ka Helu Hawaii." *Ke Au Okoa*, 21 January 1867, 3.

———. "Na Hoalohaloha i ka Pokii Benj. W. K. Kawainui." *Ko Hawaii Pae Aina*, 11 July 1885, 4.

———. "Ka Honua Nei: A me na Mea a Pau maluna iho." *Ka Lahui Hawaii*, 1 June–13 December 1877.

———. "Ka Iniki Poaeae a R. P. Kanealii i Hapala mai nei, e Kuhi ana Paha he Pau Loa ke Kamaa i ka Palakiia." *Ke Au Okoa*, 30 April 1866, 2.

———. "Kaahele ma Molokai." *Ke Au Okoa*, 5 and 26 September, 17 October 1867.

———. "He Kaao." *Ka Hae Hawaii*, 12 December 1860, 155.

———. "Ke Kumukanawai, a me na Kanawai." *Ke Au Okoa*, 10 December 1866, 1.

———. "Ka La Ho[i]hoi Ea o ke Aupuni Hawaii." *Ke Au Okoa*, 24 July 1865, 3.

———. "Ka Makahiki 1864 ma Hawaii Nei." *Ka Nupepa Kuokoa*, 12 January 1865, 1.

———. "E Malama i ka Nupepa." *Ka Hae Hawaii*, 1 October 1856, 122.

———. "Mea Minamina i Pau Ole i ka Hoolahaia mai e A. Bihopa." *Ka Hoku o ka Pakipika*, 21 November 1861, 4.

———. "He Mele no ke Kauo ana i na Waa o Kana ia Kauwelieli ma." *Ka Hae Hawaii*, 9 May 1860, 26.

———. "He Moolelo no Hamanalau, Hanai a Hawea: I Laweia mailoko mai o na Kaao Kahiko o Hawaii nei." *Ka Nupepa Kuokoa*, 28 December 1867–29 August 1868.

———. "He Moolelo no Kana, ka Hanai a Uli i Unuhi ia mailoko mai o na Kaao Kahiko o Hawaii Nei." *Ke Au Okoa*, 19 December 1867–13 February 1868.

———. "He Moolelo no Kanewailani, ke Keiki a Maoloha. I Unuhi ia mailoko mai o na Moolelo Kahiko o Hawaii Nei." *Ke Au Okoa*, 20 February–2 April 1868.

———. "He Moolelo no Pakaa." *Ke Au Okoa*, 24 October, 4; 7, 14, 21, and 28 November 1867, 4.

———. "Mooolelo no ka Hookumu ana o ka Hoku o ka Pakipika." *Ka Hoku o ka Pakipika*, 14, 21, 28 November 1861.

———. "He Moolelo no Pakaa." *Ke Au Okoa*, 24 October; 7, 14, 21, 28 November 1867.

———. "No ke Kuhihewa iwaena o kekahi Poe o Kakou e Noho nei, a me Aʻu no hoi kekahi." *Ka Hoku o ka Pakipika*, 5, 12, 19 December 1861.

———. "Pane i ka Poe Loiloi i ka Moolelo o Hamanalau." *Ka Nupepa Kuokoa*, 18 April 1868, 1.

———. "Pau Ole ke Ano Pouli o Hawaii nei." *Ka Hae Hawaii*, 19 June 1861, 48.

———. "Ka Poe Kakau Moolelo a Kaao Paha." *Ka Hoku o ka Pakipika*, 30 October 1862, 1.

———. "Ka Poe nana i Unuhi mua ka Baibala." *Ka Elele Poakolu*, 9 February 1881, 6.

Kanilehua. "He Lolelua Maopopo Io no." *Ke Aloha Aina*, 6 June 1896, 3, 6.

Kapihenui, M. J. "He Mooolelo no Hiiakaikapoliopele." *Ka Hoku o ka Pakipika*, 26 December 1861–17 July 1862.

Kawailiula, S. K. "Mooolelo No Kawelo." *Ka Hoku o ka Pakipika*, 26 September–5 December 1861.

Kealoha, J. M. "No na Kaua i Koe o Kamehameha—Kaua Elua," *Ka Hoku o ka Pakipika*, 3 April 1862, 1.

Keawekolohe. "No Kana." *Ka Hae Hawaii*, 12 December 1860, 156.

"Ke Keiki Hoopapa." *Ka Hoku o ke Kai*, August and September 1883.

Kekoa, Edward. "E Hoomau i ke Kupaa no ke Aloha i ka Aina." *Ke Aloha Aina*, 20 January 1900, 2.

———. "E Hoomau i ke Kupaa no ke Aloha i ka Aina." Translated by Noenoe K. Silva. *ʻōiwi: a native hawaiian journal* 2 (2002): 121–124.

Keolanui, S. D. "He Mooolelo No Esetera," *Ka Hoku o ka Pakipika,* 21 November 1861, 1.

Kepookulou, "No na Alii o na Moku o Hawaii: Ke Kuauhau No na Alii o Hawaii," *Ke Kumu Hawaii*, 19 August 1835, 133.

Kikiloi, Kekuewa. "Rebirth of an Archipelago: Sustaining a Hawaiian Cultural Identity for People and Homeland." *Hūlili: Multidisciplinary Research on Hawaiian Well-Being* 6 (2010): 73–115.

Kimura, Larry Kauanoe. "Ke Au Hawaiʻi." Introduction to "Kaulana Nā Pua" on *Tropical Storm* by the Peter Moon Band. Honolulu: Panini Records, 1979.

Kinney, C. W. "He Pane Akea ia J. Mahuka." *Ka Naʻi Aupuni*, 28, 29, and 30 November, 2; 1 December 1905, 4.

"Kipi Kuloko ma Honolulu! Wilikoki a me kona Poe Kipi! Na Koa Kumau Puuwai Koa!" *Ko Hawaii Pae Aina*, 3 August 1889, 2.

Koko, B. L. "He Moolelo no Lonoikamakahiki," *Ke Au Okoa*, 4, 11, 18, and 25 September; 2, 9, 16, and 23 October, 1865.

"Ko Makou Kulana i keia Kau Koho Balota." *Hawaii Holomua*, 23 January 1892, 2.

"Na Komisina 'Roialiti' no Wasinetona." *Ka Nupepa Kuokoa*, 26 November 1897, 3.

Kuakini, John Adams, Iouli Kamehameha II, Aua, Hauna, and Piopio. "No Kalani 'Kauikeaouli Kamehameha III.'" *Ka Nupepa Kuokoa*, 17, 24, 31 March; 7, 21 April; 19 May 1866.

"Kuamuamuia na Hawaii he Keko e Robikana." *Ka Naʻi Aupuni*, 2 October 1906, 2.

Kuapuu, S. K. "He Wahi Mooolelo." *Ka Hae Hawaii*, 20 March 1861, n.p. [4].

———. "He Wahi Mooolelo." *Ka Hae Hawaii*, 27 March 1861, n.p. [4].

———. "He Wahi Mooolelo." *Ka Hae Hawaii*, 10 April 1861, 8.

———. "He Wahi Moolelo [He Moolelo no Pakaa a me Kuapakaa]." *Ka Hae Hawaii*, 17 April–19 June 1861.

Kukahi, Joseph L. *Ke Kumulipo: He Moolelo Hawaii*. 2 vols. Honolulu: n.p., 1902.

"E Kukulu ke Aupuni i Kula Nui Olelo Hawaii ma ke Kula Kahunapule." *Ka Nupepa Kuokoa*, 17 January 1896, 2.

Kulanakauhalealii, J. D. "He Mau Ninau no ke Kaao o Hamanalau." *Ka Nupepa Kuokoa*, 25 January 1868, 2.
Kulika (Gulick), L. H. "E na Makamaka hoi o ke Aupuni Hawaii." *Ka Nupepa Kuokoa*, 3 December 1864, 2.
"Na Kumu Mua o ke Kanawai." *Hoku o ke Kai*, January, March, June, and July 1883.
"Ke Kumukanawai Hou." *Hawaii Holomua*, 30 January 1892, 2.
Kupakee, J. W. *Ka Nupepa Kuokoa*, 24 December 1864, 5.
Kuykendall, Ralph. *The Hawaiian Kingdom Vol. 2: 1854–1874: Twenty Critical Years*. Honolulu: University of Hawai'i Press, 1953.
———. *The Hawaiian Kingdom: Vol. 3: 1874–1892 The Kalakaua Dynasty*. Honolulu: University of Hawai'i Press, 1967.
"Ka La Hoomanao o ka Moi Kauikeaouli." *Kuokoa Home Rula*, 22 March 1907, 4.
La Motte-Fouqué, Friedrich Heinrich Karl. *The Magic Ring, a Knightly Romance*. London: George Routledge, 1876. http://archive.org/details/cu31924026193981.
Lake, Marilyn, and Henry Reynolds. *Drawing the Global Colour Line: White Men's Countries and the International Challenge of Racial Equality*. Critical Perspectives on Empire. Cambridge: Cambridge University Press, 2008.
Langlas, Charles. *The People of Kalapana, 1823–1950: A Report of the Kalapana Oral History Project*. Honolulu: C. Langlas, 1990.
Lasky, Jacqueline Bella. "Community Struggles, Struggling Communities: Land, Water and Self-Determination in Waiāhole-Waikāne, Hawai'i." PhD dissertation, University of Hawai'i, 2010.
"Lawe Lima Nui o Amerika i ka Paemoku o Hawaii me ka Ae Ole o ka Poe Nona ka Aina." *Ke Aloha Aina*, 16 July 1898, 2.
"The Legend of Kou Harbor." *Kuokoa Home Rula*, 18 December 1908, 1.
"Lele ke Aho ma ka Aina Malihini! Joseph Nawahi—ua Hala!" *Ka Nupepa Kuokoa*, 25 September 1896, 3.
Liliuokalani. *Hawaii's Story by Hawaii's Queen*. Rutland, VT: C. E. Tuttle, 1964.
Limaikaika, S. C. "Na Mele no ka Wa Kahiko." *Ka Hae Hawaii*, 25 July 1860, 71.
Livy. *The History of Rome*. Cambridge, MA: Hackett, 2006.
Louis, Renee Pualani. "Hawaiian Place Names: Storied Symbols in Hawaiian Performance Cartographies." PhD dissertation, University of Hawai'i, 2008. http://scholarspace.manoa.hawaii.edu/handle/10125/20610.
———. "Hawaiian Storied Place Names: Re-Placing Cultural Meaning." In *Landscape in Language: Transdisciplinary Perspectives*, edited by David M. Mark, Andrew G. Turk, Niclas Burenhult, and David Stea, 167–186. Philadelphia: John Benjamins, 2011.
———. *Kanaka Hawai'i Cartography: Navigation, and Oratory, and Hula*. Corvallis: Oregon State University Press, forthcoming.
Low, Sam. *Hawaiki Rising: Hōkūle'a, Nainoa Thompson, and the Hawaiian Renaissance*. Waipahu, HI: Island Heritage, 2013.
Lucas, Paul F. Nahoa. "E Ola Mau Kākou i ka 'Ōlelo Makuahine: Hawaiian Language Policy and the Courts." *Hawaiian Journal of History* 34 (2000): 1–28.
"Na Luna o ke Kuokoa no 1868 no Kona, Oahu." *Ka Nupepa Kuokoa*, 4 January 1868, 2.

"Na Lunamakaainana a me kekahi mau Hana Kupono no ke Kau Ahaolelo M. H. 1884." *Hoku o ke Kai*, January 1884, 313.

"Na Lunamakaainana o ka Aha Kiekie." *Hoku o ke Kai*, December 1883, 463.

Lyon, Jeffrey (Kapali). "Davida Malo, Nathaniel Emerson, and the 'Sins' of Hawaiians: An Analysis of Emerson's *Hawaiian Antiquities* as a Guide to Malo's *Moʻolelo Hawaiʻi*." *Hūlili: Multidisciplinary Research on Hawaiian Well-Being* 7 (2011): 91–132.

"Mai Haalele i ka Olelo Makuahine." *Kuokoa Home Rula*, 22 March 1907, 1.

"Mai Haalele i Kau Olelo Makuahine." *Ka Naʻi Aupuni*, 4 January 1906, 2.

"Na Maʻi Lepera i Waeia no ka Lapaau ia ana e J. Lor Wallach!" *Kuokoa Home Rula*, 24 January 1908, 1.

Makemson, Maud W. *The Morning Star Rises, an Account of Polynesian Astronomy*. New Haven, CT: Yale University Press, 1941.

Malo, David. "Ke Aupuni Moi." *Hawaii Holomua*, 30 January 1892, 2–3.

Malo, Davida. *Ka Moʻolelo Hawaii* [Hawaiian antiquities]. Edited by Malcolm Nāea Chun. Honolulu: Folk Press, Kapiʻolani Community College, 1987.

Manu, Mose. "He Moolelo Kaao no Keaomelemele." *Ka Nupepa Kuokoa*, 6 September 1884–27 June 1885.

"Mare Lehulehu." *Ka Naʻi Aupuni*, 27 November 1905–19 March 1906.

McDougall, Brandy Nālani. *Finding Meaning: Kaona and Contemporary Hawaiian Literature*. Tucson: University of Arizona Press, 2016.

McDougall, Brandy Nālani, and Georganne Nordstrom. "Ma ka Hana ka ʻIke (In the Work Is the Knowledge): Kaona as Rhetorical Action." *College Composition and Communication* 63, no. 1 (September 2011): 98–121.

McGregor, Davianna Pōmaikaʻi. *Nā Kuaʻāina: Living Hawaiian Culture*. Honolulu: University of Hawaiʻi Press, 2007.

McKinzie, Edith Kawelohea. *Hawaiian Genealogies: Extracted from Hawaiian Language Newspapers*. Edited by Ishmael W. Stagner, II. Vol. 2. Lāʻie: Institute for Polynesian Studies, Brigham Young University, Hawaiʻi, 1986.

Mea Kakau Moolelo o Kamehameha (Hooulumahiehie). "Kamehameha I: Ka Na-i Aupuni o Hawaii." *Ka Naʻi Aupuni*, 27 November 1905–16 November 1906.

"Meeting of Hawaiians: Held Last Evening at Kaumakapili Church—Ticket for Representatives Nominated." *Pacific Commercial Advertiser*, 20 August 1887, 3.

Na Mele Aimoku, Na Mele Kupuna, a Me Na Mele Ponoi o ka Moi Kalakaua I: Dynastic Chants, Ancestral Chants, and Personal Chants of King Kalākaua I. Hawaiian Language Reprint Series, buke 1. Honolulu: Hawaiian Historical Society, 2001.

Meyer, Manulani Aluli. *Hoʻoulu: Our Time of Becoming: Collected Early Writings of Manulani Meyer*. Honolulu: ʻAi Pōhaku, 2003.

Mignolo, Walter D. *The Darker Side of the Renaissance: Literacy, Territoriality, and Colonization*. Ann Arbor: University of Michigan Press, 1995.

"Ka Moi Ata a me Kona mau Naita o ke Pakaukau Poepoe." *Ka Makaainana*, 3 May 1888, 1.

Mokuohai, J. P. "Ke Kumu o ka Hoohui Aina." *Kuokoa Home Rula*, 12 June–3 July 1908.

Molokainuiahina. "No Ka Moolelo o Kanewailani." *Ke Au Okoa*, 2 April 1868, 1.

Montalba, Anthony R. *Fairy Tales from All Nations*. London: Chapman and Hall, 1849. https://archive.org/stream/fairytalesfromaloomontiala#page/4/mode/thumb. Accessed September 5, 2016.

Mookini, Esther. *The Hawaiian Newspapers*. Honolulu: Topgallant, 1974.

"Ka Mookuauhau Elua o Hawaii." *Ka Nupepa Kuokoa*, 8 June 1900–14 June 1901.

"Moolelo Nani o Kekalukaluokewa (He Moolelo Hawaii Nani no Kekalukaluokewa)", *Ke Aloha Aina*, 12 March 1910–18 November 1911.

"He Moolelo no ka Hooilina o Rivela." *Kuokoa Home Rula*, 22 March 1907–30 December 1910.

"He Moolelo no Laieikawai." *Ka Naʻi Aupuni*, 2 January 1906, 1–22 January 1906, 3.

"He Moolelo no Pakaa a me Kuapakaa." *Hawaii Holomua*, 2 May 1891, 4.

"Ka Moolelo o Kalausele Kopala: Ke Keiki a ka Humu Kamaa." *Hoku o ke Kai*, February–April 1884.

"Ka Moolelo Walohia o Hainakolo." *Ka Naʻi Aupuni*, 4 January 1907–24 April 1908.

Moreton-Robinson, Aileen. "'I Still Call Australia Home': Indigenous Belonging and Place in a White Postcolonizing Society." In *Uprootings/Regroundings: Questions of Home and Migration*, edited by Sara Ahmed, Claudia Castañeda, Anne-Marie Fortie, and Mimi Sheller, 23–40, New York: Bloomsbury Academic, 2004.

Na-Hau-o-Maihi—Au ana i ke Kai. "Ka Moolelo Hooni Puuwai no Keakaoku." *Ke Aloha Aina*, 3 February 1912–18 May 1912.

"E Nalowale ana Paha ka Olelo Hawaii." *Ka Hoku o ke Kai*, June 1883, 133.

"E Nalowale loa anei ko Kakou Moolelo Kumu." *Ke Aloha Aina*, 18 January 1913, 4.

Nakanaela, Thomas K. *Ka Buke Moʻolelo o Honorable Robert William Wilikoki (The Biography of the Honorable Robert William Wilcox)*. Bishop Museum Classical Reprints in Hawaiian Language. Honolulu: Bishop Museum Press, 1999.

Nakuina, Moses K. *Moolelo Hawaii o Pakaa a Me Ku-a-Pakaa, na Kahu Iwikuamoo o Keawenuiaumi, ke Alii o Hawaii, a o na Moopuna Hoi a Laamaomao!: Ke Kamaeu nana i Hoolakalaka na Makani a Pau o na Mokupuni o Hawaii nei, a Uhao iloko o kana Ipu Kaulana i Kapaia o ka Ipumakani a Laamaomao!* Honolulu: Kalamakū, 1991.

———. *The Wind Gourd of Laʻamaomao: The Hawaiian Story of Pākaʻa and Kūapākaʻa: Personal Attendants of Keawenuiaʻumi, Ruling Chief of Hawaii and Descendants of Laʻamaomao*. Translated by Esther T. Mookini and Sarah Nākoa. Rev. ed. Honolulu: Kalamakū, 2005.

Ngũgĩ wa Thiongʼo. *Decolonising the Mind: The Politics of Language in African Literature*. London: J. Currey, 1986.

"No ka Ona Miliona Claus Spreckels." *Hoku o ke Kai*, February 1884, 335.

"No Keaha e Hoolaha Akea Ole ia ai ma ka Olelo Hawaii." *Ka Naʻi Aupuni*, 27 November 1905, 2.

Nogelmeier, M. Puakea. *Mai Paʻa i Ka Leo: Historical Voice in Hawaiian Primary Materials: Looking Forward and Listening Back*. Honolulu: Bishop Museum Press, 2010.

"Nu Hou Hawaii." *Ko Hawaii Pae Aina*, 10 August 1889, 2.

"Nuhou Kuloko." *Hawaii Holomua*, 2 February 1893, 2.

"Oihana Kilokilo Hawaii." *Hawaii Aloha*, 15 July–20 October 1905.
"O Ka Olelo Hea ka Ol[e]lo Kanawai e Hiki ai ke Hilinaiia ka Pono." *Hoku o ke Kai*, June 1884, 441.
"Na Olelo Hooholo o ka Aha Kiekie." *Hoku o ke Kai*, December 1883, 463.
Oliveira, Katrina-Ann R. [Rose-Marie] Kapāʻanaokalāokeola Nākoa. *Ancestral Places: Understanding Kanaka Geographies*. Corvallis: Oregon State University Press, 2014.
———. "Wahi a Kahiko: Place Names as Vehicles of Ancestral Memory." *AlterNative: An International Journal of Indigenous Peoples* 5, no. 2 (2009): 100–115, http://www.content.alternative.ac.nz/index.php/alternative/article/view/38.
Orwell, George. "Politics and the English Language." In *Shooting an Elephant and Other Essays*, 77–92. New York: Harcourt, Brace and World, 1950.
Osorio, Jonathan Kay Kamakawiwoʻole. *Dismembering Lāhui: A History of the Hawaiian Nation to 1887*. Honolulu: University of Hawaiʻi Press, 2002.
Palau, Moses. "Ua Like no a Like." *Ka Nupepa Kuokoa*, 24 August 1900, 3.
———. "Oia Maoli no ke Kaulike." *Ka Nupepa Kuokoa*, 7 September 1900, 5.
"Ka Papa Hoonohonoho Hana o ka Hui a na Opio Hawaii no 1896." *Ka Nupepa Kuokoa*, 10 January 1896, 3.
"Pau Ole no hoi ke Kuhihewa." *Ka Lahui Hawaii*, 2 August 1877, 2.
"Pehea e Mau ai ke Ola ana o ka Olelo Hawaii?" *Ka Naʻi Aupuni*, 5 January 1906, 2.
"Pehea Kakou i ka Kakou [O]lelo Ponoi." *Ke Aloha Aina*, 18 January 1913, 4.
Peleioholani, S. L. "The Ancient History of Hookumu-ka-Lani Hookumu-ka-Honua (The Creation)." Translated by J. M. Poepoe. Bernice Pauahi Bishop Museum, n.d. Collection H1 L.1.3.
———. "He Hoakaka Mai ke Alii S. L. Peleioholani—Ao Kuauhau Maoli." *Ka Naʻi Aupuni*, 2 April 1906, 2.
Peralto, Leon Noʻeau. "Portrait. Mauna a Wākea: Hānau Ka Mauna, the Piko of Our Ea." In *A Nation Rising: Hawaiian Movements for Life, Land, and Sovereignty*, edited by Noelani Goodyear-Kaʻōpua, Ikaika Hussey, and Erin Kahunawaikaʻala Wright, 232–243. Durham: Duke University Press, 2014.
Perkins, Mark ʻUmi. "Kuleana: A Genealogy of Native Tenant Rights." PhD dissertation, University of Hawaiʻi, 2013.
Poepoe, Joseph M. "Ke Alakai Koho Balota." *Ka Nupepa Kuokoa*, 14 and 28 September 1900, 2.
———. *Ke Alakai o ke Kanaka Hawaii: He Buke no na Olelo Hooholo o ka Aha Kiekie i Kuhikuhiia ma ka Buke Kanawai Kivila Hou i Hooponoponoia ai e ka Hon. L. McCully a me Kekahi Mau Olelo Hooholo e ae he Nui; Na Rula Aha Hookolokolo o Ko Hawaii Pae Aina i Hooponopono Hou ia; a me na Hoakaka Kanawai i Kakau Mua ia e ka Hon. A. Francis Judd, Lunakanawai Kiekie a Kaulike o ke Aupuni a i Hooponopono ia a Hoomahuahua Hou ia hoi*. Honolulu: Hawaiian Gazette, 1891.
———. "Ka Haiolelo Akea imua o ka Lahui Hawaii: Ke Kumu o na Paeaina ma Hawaii nei." *Ka Nupepa Kuokoa*, 3 April 1896, 2.
———. "The Hawaiian Astronomy." *Kuokoa Home Rula*, 2 April–4 June 1909.
———. "He Hoakaka Aku." *Ka Naʻi Aupuni*, 18 December 1905, 2.
———. "E Hoomaopopo ka Lehulehu." *Hawaii Holomua*, 1 February 1893, 4.

———. "Joseph Mokuohai Poepoe." *Ke Aloha Aina*, 26 October 1912, 1.

———. "Na Kumuhana a ka Moho Lunamakaainana Kuokoa." *Ka Nupepa Kuokoa*, 26 October 1900, 1.

———. "Ka Moolelo Hawaii Kahiko." *Ka Naʻi Aupuni*, 1 February–29 November 1906.

———. "He Moolelo Kaao no ke Keiki Alii Otto! Ka Naita Opio o Geremania." *Ko Hawaii Pae Aina*, 17 January 1880–23 October 1880.

———, trans. "He Moolelo Kaao no ka Naita Rokekila Hinedu. *Ko Hawaii Pae Aina*, 15 June 1878–31 December 1881.

———, trans. "He Moolelo Kaao no ka Naita Rokekila Hinedu! Ke Koa Pukani o na Au Pouliuli." *Hoku o ke Kai*, December 1883–June 1884.

———. "Ka Moolelo Kaao o Hiiaka-i-ka-Poli-o-Pele." *Kuokoa Home Rula*, 10 January 1908–20 January 1911.

———. "He Moolelo no ka Naita Leopaki a i Ole he Nanea no ke Kaua Kerusade Ekolu ma Palesekina." *Ke Aloha Aina*, 23 September 1911–5 April 1913.

———. *Ka Moolelo o ka Moi Kalakaua I: Ka Hanau Ana, ke Kaapuni Honua, ka Moolelo Piha o Kona Mau La Hope ma Kaleponi, Amerika Huipuia, na Hoike a Adimarala Baraunu me na Kauka, etc., etc., etc.: Hoohiwahiwaia me na Kii*. Honolulu: s.n, 1891. http://www.ulukau.org/elib/cgi-bin/library?e=d-okalakaua-000Sec--11en-50-20-frameset-book--1-010escapewin&a=d&d=D0&toc=0. Accessed 5 September 2016.

———. "Na Paemoku o Hawaii." *Ka Nupepa Kuokoa*, 24 and 31 July 1896.

———. "Kaʻu Papa Iliili Imua o ka Lehulehu." *Ke Aloha Aina*, 7 August 1909, 2

Poepoe, Joseph M., and W[illiam] J[oseph] Coelho. "Ke Kanawai o ka Panalaau." *Ka Nupepa Kuokoa*, 17 August 1900, 2.

———. "Ke Kanawai Teritori." *Ka Nupepa Kuokoa*, 6 July 1900, 2.

Pokuea, J. F. [Pogue, John Fawcett]. "He Moolelo no ka Hookumuia Ana o Hawaii." *Ke Aloha Aina*, 4 April 1896–20 February 1897.

———. "Mooolelo Hawaii." *Ka Hae Hawaii*, 7 April 1858–6 April 1859.

———. *Ka Mooolelo Hawaii*. Honolulu: Hale Paipalapala Aupuni, 1858.

Poomaikelani. *Hoike a ka Papa Kuauhau o na Alii Hawaii—Report of the Board of Genealogy of Hawaiian Chiefs*. Ka Papa Kuauhau Alii o na Alii Hawaii, 1884.

Pukui, Mary Kawena. *Folktales of Hawaiʻi He Mau Kaʻao Hawaiʻi*. Bishop Museum Special Publication 87. Honolulu: Bishop Museum Press, 1995.

———. "How Legends Were Taught," n.d. HEN I: 1602–1606. Bishop Museum.

———. *ʻŌlelo Noʻeau: Hawaiian Proverbs and Poetical Sayings*. Honolulu: Bishop Museum Press, 1983.

———. "Songs (Meles) of Old Kaʻu, Hawaii." *Journal of American Folklore* 62, no. 245 (July–September 1949): 247–258.

Pukui, Mary Kawena, and Samuel H. Elbert. *Hawaiian Dictionary: Hawaiian-English, English-Hawaiian*. Rev. and enl. ed. Honolulu: University of Hawaiʻi Press, 1986.

Pukui, Mary Kawena, Samuel H. Elbert, and Esther T. Mookini. *Place Names of Hawaii*. Rev. and enl. ed. Honolulu: University of Hawaiʻi Press, 1976.

Pukui, Mary Kawena, and Alfons L. Korn, trans. and eds. *The Echo of Our Song: Chants and Poems of the Hawaiians*. Honolulu: University of Hawai'i Press, 1973.

Reynolds, George. "Ka Buke Hooakakaolelo o ka Buke a Moramona [Translation of a Dictionary of the Book of Mormon]." *Ka Na'i Aupuni*, 14–24 July 1906.

Rice, William Hyde. *Hawaiian Legends*. Bernice P. Bishop Museum Bulletin 3. Honolulu: Bishop Museum, 1923.

Rohrer, Judy. *Haoles in Hawai'i*. Race and Ethnicity in Hawai'i. Honolulu: University of Hawai'i Press, 2010.

Salazar, Joseph A. "Multicultural Settler Colonialism and Indigenous Struggle in Hawai'i: The Politics of Astronomy on Mauna a Wakea." PhD dissertation, University of Hawai'i at Manoa, 2014.

Schmitt, Robert C., and Eleanor C. Nordyke. "Death in Hawai'i: The Epidemics of 1848–1849," *Hawaiian Journal of History* 35 (2001): 1–13.

Schütz, Albert J. *The Voices of Eden: A History of Hawaiian Language Studies*. Honolulu: University of Hawai'i Press, 1994.

Sharpe, Cecilia K. "Ka Huakai Kukulu Kalapu o ka Hui Imi Pono Koho Balota o na Wahine Kupa Amerika." *Ke Aloha Aina*, 6 July 1912, 4 (page number misprinted as 2).

———. "Ka Nanehai o ka Manawa, Mokuaina no Hawaii nei a i Pono Koho Balota no na Wahine Kupa Amerika." *Ke Aloha Aina*, 1 June 1912, 2.

Silva, Noenoe K. *Aloha Betrayed: Native Hawaiian Resistance to American Colonialism*. Durham: Duke University Press, 2004.

———. "Early Hawaiian Newspapers and Kanaka Maoli Intellectual History, 1834–1855." *Hawaiian Journal of History* 42 (2008): 105–134.

———. "I Kū Mau Mau: How Kānaka Maoli Tried to Sustain National Identity within the United States Political System." *American Studies* 45, no. 3 (Fall 2004): 9–31.

———. "E Lawe i ke Ō: An Analysis of Joseph Mokuohai Poepoe's Account of Pele Calling the Winds." *Hūlili: Multidisciplinary Research on Hawaiian Well-Being* 6 (2010): 237–266.

Soehren, Lloyd J. "Hawaiian Place Names." Ulukau: The Hawaiian Electronic Library. ulukau.org/cgi-bin/hpn?. Accessed through March 2016.

Solis, R. Kekeha. "Ma ka Wah[a] Wali (a ke Kino Lahilahi. Ma ke Kino Lahilahi) a ka Wah[a] Wali." PhD dissertation, University of Hawai'i, 2010.

Sterling, Elspeth P., and Catherine C. Summers. *Sites of Oahu*. Rev. ed. Honolulu: Bernice P. Bishop Museum, 1978.

Tao Se, trans. "He Nanea Kamahao no Ro Reina Huda: ka Olali, ke Kupua, ka Niuhi o na Kai, ka Ahikanana Nana i Hapapa ka Moana Iniana." *Hoku o ke Kai*, June and July 1883.

Timoteo, J. W. "No Ke Kaua Ana o Kamehameha, a me ka Hui ana o na Aupuni o keia Pae Aina malalo o na [ona]," *Ka Hoku o ka Pakipika* 12 December 1861, 1.

United States. *An Act to Provide a Government for the Territory of Hawaii*. Washington, DC: US Government Printing Office, 1900.

———. *He Kanawai e Hoonoho Ana i Aupuni no ka Panalaau o Hawaii*. Honolulu: Hawaiian Gazette, 1900.

US Congress. Senate Committee on Pacific Islands and Porto Rico [sic]. *Hawaiian Investigation: Report of Subcommittee on Pacific Islands and Porto Rico on General Conditions in Hawaii* . . . Washington, DC: US Government Printing Office, 1903.

Verne, Jules. "He Moolelo no Kapena Nimo: Ka Ahikanana Nona ka Moku Kupanaha Loa o ka Nautilo, a o ka Olali noi o na Papa-ku o ka Moana." *Hoku o ke Kai*, January 1883–September 1884.

Warner, Sam L. Noʻeau. "The Movement to Revitalize Hawaiian Language and Culture." In *The Green Book of Language Revitalization in Practice*, edited by Leanne Hinton and Ken Hale, 133–144. San Diego: Academic Press, 2001.

Warrior, Robert Allen. *Tribal Secrets: Recovering American Indian Intellectual Traditions*. Minneapolis: University of Minnesota Press, 1995.

"What Is Poi?" *Kuokoa Home Rula*, 1 January 1909, 1.

White, John. *The Ancient History of the Maori: His Mythology and Traditions*. Hamilton, New Zealand: University of Waikato Library, 2001 [1887–1890] CD-ROM.

"Wilcox Has Some Brand New Fakes." *Pacific Commercial Advertiser*, 12 August 1902, 1.

"Wilcox Is It." *Pacific Commercial Advertiser*, 10 November 1900, 1.

"Will Get Out Votes." *Pacific Commercial Advertiser*, 7 April 1902, 5.

Williams, Ronald C., Jr. "Claiming Christianity: The Struggle over God and Nation in Hawaiʻi, 1880–1900." PhD dissertation, University of Hawaiʻi, 2013.

———. "Race, Power, and the Dilemma of Democracy: Hawaiʻi's First Territorial Legislature, 1901." *Hawaiian Journal of History* 49 (2015): 1–45.

Wini [Whitney], H. M. "Olelo Hoolaha! I na Luna a me na Poe e Lawe Ana i ke Kuokoa." *Ka Nupepa Kuokoa*, 26 November 1864, 2.

Wolfe, Patrick. "Settler Colonialism and the Elimination of the Native," *Journal of Genocide Research* 8, no. 4 (December 2006): 387–409.

Wong, K. Laiana. "Kuhi Aku, Kuhi Mai, Kuhi Hewa Ē: He Mau Loina Kuhikuhi ʻākena No Ka ʻōlelo Hawaiʻi." PhD dissertation, University of Hawaiʻi at Mānoa, 2006.

Woodbridge, William C. *He Hoikehonua: He Mea Ia a Hoakakaʻi i ke Ano o ka Honua nei, a me na Mea maluna iho*. Translated by Samuel Whitney and William Richards. Honolulu: Na na Misionari i Pai, 1832.

Index

Note: The ʻokina (ʻ) are alphabetized as following the letter Z; the articles (he, ka, ke, na) in newspaper and moʻolelo names are ignored in the alphabetization.

Achi, William C., 127, 131, 134
AEH (ʻAhahui ʻEuanelio Hawaiʻi), 24, 38, 39, 43, 48
"Ahe! He Nupepa Hou Ka!!," 49–50
Akina, Joseph A., 137
akua, 4, 6, 30, 68, 152, 160, 169, 170, 182, 204, 206; Kāmehaʻikana, 199–201
Ke Alakai o Hawaii, 111–13
Ke Alakai o ke Kanaka, 116–18
Alexander, William De Witt, 28–29, 93
aliʻi, 8, 35, 36, 41, 59, 61, 67, 68, 72, 84, 92, 93, 94, 95, 107, 126, 159, 170, 201, 205–6, 212; abusive, 166–69; moʻokūʻauhau and, 6, 32, 45, 48, 51, 54, 180, 181, 182, 188–96; newspapers and, 15; Papa and, 202–3; wahine, 35, 55
allusion, 12, 64, 67–68, 71–74
aloha ʻāina, 4–6, 16, 164, 169; Kānepuʻu and, 77–80, 82–83, 89; mele and, 155, 192; moʻokūʻauhau consciousness and, 23; moʻolelo and, 153; place names and, 12, 89
Ke Aloha Aina, 120, 121, 126, 145–49, 180
ancestral knowledge, 3, 6, 8–9, 105
Andrade, Carlos, 84–85
Anglican Church, 34, 107
annexation, 120–21, 123, 127–31
Ao, 188, 189, 193
Arista, Noelani, 32–33, 178–79
Armstrong, Richard (Limaikaika), 15, 24, 42
Ke Au Hou, 146
Auld, William, 51

Auliʻiliʻi, Oʻahu, 161, 162
Ke Au Okoa, 40–43, 46, 47, 49, 54, 87
Auwana, Bila, 38

bananas, 62, 65, 79, 88, 197, 198
Bishop, Artemas, 34
Boki, 73
"Ka Buke a Aberahama," 141
"Buke Hoakakaolelo o ka Buke a Moramona," 141
Buke Mele Lahui, 124
Bush, John E. "Ailuene," 5, 113, 118, 120, 121, 152–53

canoe. See waʻa
Castle, William R., 107
ceremony, 62–63, 67, 71–73, 142, 193, 198–99, 204, 206
chant. See mele
Chapin, Helen Geracimos, 37, 40
Charlot, John, 13, 58, 76, 150–51, 168, 183
Church of Latter Day Saints, Reorganized, 141
Coelho, William, 133, 134
Constitution, Bayonet, 110–14, 117, 118, 119, 120, 182
constitution, of Kamehameha V, 35–37
Cook, Captain James, 179, 193
countercoup (Wilcox Rebellion 1895), 120–21
counting system, Hawaiian, 41–42, 196

Democratic Party, 145–46
Desha, Stephen L., Sr., 146
de Silva, Kīhei, 82
Dibble, Sheldon, 32, 177–80
Dole, Sanford, 107, 128

"E Liliʻu ē" (mele), 71–72
Ka Elele Hawaii, 15, 21
Ka Elele Poakolu, 48, 50
Ka Elele Poaono, 48
Emerson, Nathaniel B., 154, 183
Emma (Queen), 34, 48, 107
English language, 83, 134–35, 143
epidemics, 94–96
epistemology, 9–10, 53, 87, 93, 187, 200, 209
evangelism, 15, 24, 38, 43, 97, 176

farming methods, 88
fearless speech, 98–99
featherwork, 68
flag, Hawaiian, 105, 128, 130, 134
Fornander, Abraham, 27, 28, 29, 154, 181–82, 186

gender, 199
genealogy. *See* moʻokūʻauhau
geography, 6, 23, 41, 48, 82–101, 186–87, 201–2
Gibson, Walter Murray, 48
"Great White Fleet," 144
Gulick, Luther Halsey, 38–39, 43, 54

Ka Hae Hawaii, 21, 24–33
Haili, Hawaiʻi, 30
Hakalanileo, 27–28, 31, 59
hala (pandanus), 160, 161–62
Halaaniani, Hawaiʻi, 157
Hālawa, Molokai, 21, 62, 76, 77, 88
Hale Nauā, 48, 50–51, 182
Haleʻole, S. N., 33, 41
Hāloa, 4, 84, 190–92, 205
Hāmanalau: bird behavior, 62, 64–66; bird imagery, 64–68; hoʻāo ceremony, 63; literary features, 64–80; moʻolelo of, 59–80; purification bath, 63
hānai, 59, 61, 89, 170, 201, 205
Hanalei, Kauaʻi, 76
"Hanau-a-Hua-ka-Lani," 188–93

Hanohano, Solomon, 146
Hansen's disease, 94, 96–97, 143
Haumea, 160, 164, 170, 197–205. *See also* Papa
Hauola, B. K., 24–25
Haupoiakane (place name), 30
Hauʻula, Oʻahu, 77–78, 206
Hawaii Aloha, 137
Hawaii Holomua, 118–20
"Hawaiian Astronomy" (series), 143
Hawaiian language, 2–3, 83, 204, 213; courts and, 116–18; defense of, 7, 10, 48, 105, 110, 134, 137–40, 142–43, 146, 148–49, 154, 186; figurative aspects, 11–13, 64–77, 90; Kānepuʻu and, 22, 23, 42, 57; Organic Act and, 133–34; orthography of, 14; schools of, 124
Hāwea, 59, 61–62, 64–65, 67, 68
Hāʻena, Kauaʻi, 85
Hāʻupu (Hāʻupukele), Molokai, 27, 29, 165
Heʻeia, Oʻahu, 161–62, 171, 197
"Ka Helu Hawaii" (Hawaiian counting), 41–42
Hewahewanui (Hewahewa), 106, 206
Hīhīmanu, Kauaʻi, 75–76
Hikiau heiau, 193
Hikiaupea, Molokai, 77
Hilo, Hawaiʻi, 25, 121, 146, 157–59
hilu (fish), 77–78
Hinahelelani, 63, 67, 71–75
Hinalealua, 27
Hīnalenale (Molokai), 77
Hiʻiakaikapoliopele (Hiʻiaka), 5, 7, 14, 24, 33, 137, 141, 150–73, 201; Poepoe's mele translations, 143
Hikauhi, 70
Hipa, L. J. Nahora, 109
historiography, 178–79, 200, 209
Ka Hoku o ka Pakipika, 13, 15, 22, 33–34, 37–38, 41, 43, 48, 54; Kānepuʻu's history of, 49–50
Ka Hoku o ke Kai, 109–10, 208
Home Rule Party, 133, 135–38, 141–43
Honomakaʻu, Kohala, Hawaiʻi, 106
"Ka Honua nei: A me na Mea a Pau maluna iho," 48, 92–100
"Ka Hoomana Kahiko," 38
Hōpoe, 156, 159–61

Hopoikeau (ʻōlelo noʻeau), 70
hōʻailona (signs and omens), 9, 59, 62–63
hoʻāo ceremony, 62–63, 67, 70, 71–73, 75
Hōʻeu, Hawaiʻi, 156–58
Hoʻohōkūkalani, 84, 191, 205
hoʻomanawanui, kuʻualoha, 6, 57, 141, 150, 151, 154, 168
Hoʻoulumāhiehie (Hooulumahiehie,), 14, 140–41, 142, 146–47, 151, 184
Hooulumahiehie-i-ka-oni-malie-a-pua-lilia-lana-i-ka-wai, 142
Hui Aloha ʻĀina, 120, 121, 133, 145
Hui Kālaiʻāina, 119, 120, 128, 133
hula, 5, 10, 48, 51, 76, 172, 188

"I Kū Mau Mau" (mele), 28
indigenous resurgence, 2–3, 9, 211
intellectual sovereignty, 8–10, 16
"Ka Ipu Alabata," 138

Johnson, Enoka, 112
Judd, Albert Francis, 116–18
Judd, Gerrit (Kauka), 37

Kaeo, Sam, 109
Kahahana, 170
Kahakauakoko, 194, 195
Kahana, Oʻahu, 99–100
Kahaualeʻa, Hawaiʻi, 157
Kahauiki, Oʻahu, 147–48
Kahēhuna school, 107
Kahekili, 170
Kahiamoe, J. W., 39
Kahiki, 73, 190–91, 205
Kahikoluamea, 194, 195
Kahilipali, Kona, Hawaiʻi, 31
Kahiolo, G. W. (G. W. Poepoe), 25, 106
Kahoʻohalahala, D. K., 39
Kahuku, Oʻahu, 148
kahuna, 28, 29, 57, 59, 62, 67, 96, 106, 126, 142, 179, 181, 193, 208, 212; Kamōʻawa, 202, 204–5; Kapihe, 142, 188–89; Kaʻōpulupulu, 170
Kaiaka, 61
Kaiaikawaha, Thomas N., 109
Kaihuʻauwaʻalua, 61–62, 66, 75, 79, 80
Kaipapaʻu, Oʻahu, 206
Ka Lae o ka Palaoa, Oʻahu, 206

Kalaeokaʻōʻio, Oʻahu, 202
Kalaihauola, B., 24–25
Kalākaua, 33, 48, 51, 57, 92, 95, 107, 109, 110, 113, 117, 119; death, 114–15; Kumulipo, text of, 193–94; Ka Papa Kuauhau o na Alii Hawaii and, 182; Poepoe's biography of, 115–16
Kalama, B. R., 24
Kalama, L. S., 24
Kalana, Ben, 113
Kalanikaapau, 106
Kalapana, Hawaiʻi, 156–60
Kalapana, moʻolelo of, 109
Kalauao, Oʻahu, 107
Kalauokekahuli, 200
Kalaupapa, Molokai, 21, 88
Kalawao, Molokai, 1, 21, 46, 88
Kalihi, Oʻahu, 107, 137, 147–48, 197, 200, 201
Kaliuwaʻa, Oʻahu, 73, 162–63
Kaliʻu, 198, 200, 201, 204–5
kalo, 2, 4, 49, 79, 83, 84, 88, 94–95, 192
Kaluanou, 76–77
Kaluaʻaha, Molokai, 13, 21
ke kalukalu o kēwā (saying), 108
Kamae, Oʻahu, 164
Kamakaia, P, 107
Kamakau, Samuel M., 13, 24, 27, 139, 170, 177, 179, 193; Fornander and, 182; historical series, 181; Kānepuʻu, critique of, 44–46; literacy, 14; Poepoe, influence on, 186–87, 200
Ka-Mākaula, 62
Kamapuaʻa, 25, 44, 53, 73, 106, 162
Kamaunaihalakaipo, 200
Kamāʻalaea, Molokai, 77
Kamehameha I, 33, 55, 138, 179, 180, 188, 190, 193, 197, 200; moʻolelo of, 43, 137, 140, 141, 183
Kamehameha II, 188
Kamehameha III, 142, 188–89
Kamehameha IV, 34–35, 48, 107, 142
Kamehameha V, 35, 48
Kamehamehanui, 88, 89
Kāmehaʻikana, 160, 197, 199–200
Kameʻeleihiwa, Lilikalā, 6, 68, 83–84, 189
Kamilopaekanaka, Hawaiʻi, 157
Kamoamoa, Hawaiʻi, 157–58
Kamohoaliʻi (deity), 161

Kamohoʻula, 208
Kamōʻawa, 202, 204–5
Kana, mele of, 26–33; moʻolelo of, 25, 26, 44, 56–59, 89, 100
Kanahele, Pualani Kanakaʻole, 1, 6–7, 160, 172
Kanaloa (deity), 29, 157, 188, 193, 197
Kāne (deity), 28, 47, 160–61, 171, 188, 190–91, 193, 197, 199; Alanui Polohiwa a, 186–87; stones of, 92
Kāne, S. K., 111, 127, 131
Kanealuka, 28
Kānehoalani, 99–100, 169–71
Kānehunamoku, 47
Kanehunapegana, 47
Kānepūniu, Oʻahu, 148
Kānepuʻu, Joseph H.: birth, 21; criticism by Kamakau, 44–46; critique of Kalākaua, 97; critique of sugar plantations, 94–95; education, 21; Hawaiian language advocacy, 41–42; Hawaiian newspapers advocacy, 33, 49–50
Kanewanui, David, 136
Kanikawī and Kanikawā, 201
Kanilehua, 121–22
Kaohele, 50, 88, 89
kaona, 90, 108, 138, 151, 174, 181, 204; described, 10–13; Hāmanalau, in moʻolelo of, 64–66, 69, 73, 74–75; Poepoe on, 189–90
Kapapa, Oʻahu, 204
Kapaʻahu, Hawaiʻi, 157
Kapena, John Makini, 40
Kapepeʻekauila, 27, 29, 31
Kapihe, 142, 188–89
Kapihenui, M. J., 7–8, 33
Kau (mother of Kapihenui), 7–8
Kauhuhu (shark), 76–77
Kauikeaouli, 142, 188–90
Kaukanapōkiʻi, 62–63, 65, 67, 70, 75–76, 78
Kaulia, James Keauiluna, 121, 124–25, 128, 131, 133
Kaulukou, John Lota, 127, 131, 134
Kaunakakai, Molokai, 70, 88, 90
Kaunaloa, Hawaiʻi, 156–57
Kaunamano, John K., 113, 127
kaupapaloʻi. See loʻi
Kauwelieli, 26, 28

kava (kavakava). See ʻawa
Kawaikumuʻole, Oʻahu, 148, 164–65
Kawailiʻulā, S. K., 24, 33
Kawainui, Benjamin W. Kekapa, 51, 99
Kawainui, Joseph U., 38, 51; Ko Hawaii Pae Aina, editor of, 49, 108; Kuokoa, assistant editor of, 43, 54
Kawela, Molokai, 88
Kawelo, moʻolelo of, 14, 33, 63, 142
Kaʻahumanu, 55–56, 73
Kaʻahuʻula spring, Oʻahu, 202
Kaʻai, Simeona K., 33
Kaʻala, Oʻahu, 59, 61, 64, 66–67, 78–79, 165
"Kaʻahele ma Molokai," 87–92
Kaʻalihi, Aberahama, 21, 50
Kaʻawili, Molokai, 77
Kaʻaʻawa, Oʻahu, 99, 202
Kaʻelemakule, J., 25
Kaʻena Point, Oʻahu, 164–65
Kaʻōpulupulu, 170
Kaʻū, Hawaiʻi, 10, 30, 157–58
Kealakomo, Hawaiʻi, 157–58
Keawanui, Molokai, 88
Keawehiku, 106
Keawekolohe, 31–32, 58
Keawenuiaʻumi, 56
Keaʻau, Oʻahu, 148
"Ke Keiki Hoopapa," 109
Kelekona, Kahikina, 113, 115, 120
Keolewa (Keoloewa), 27–31, 59
Kepelino, 182
Keʻanae, Maui, 62
kilokilo, 9, 59, 62, 137
Kīnaʻu (son of Keʻelikōlani), 71
kino lau, 4, 68, 152, 160–61, 166, 168, 171, 172, 197; of Haumea, 199–200
Kohala, Hawaiʻi, 106, 107, 206
Ko Hawaii Pae Aina, 13, 49–50, 108–9
"Ko Kakou Moolelo Hawaii Kahiko," 139
Koko, B. L., 41
kōlea, 67, 73
Kona, Hawaiʻi, 31, 39, 84, 193
konohiki system, 93, 169
Ke Koo o Hawaii, 48
Koʻiahi, Oʻahu, 148
koʻokoʻolau, 79
Kū (deity), 28, 160, 188, 193
Kuaea, Moses, 43

Kuaihelani (place name), 63
Kualele, 62
Kūaliʻi (mele), 45
Kualoa, Oʻahu, 99–100, 166, 169–71, 201
Kuapuʻu, S. K., 24, 43, 55, 56
Kuhina Nui, 35, 55
Kukahi, Joseph Liwai, 183
Kūkalaniehu, 194, 195
Kūkona, 61–62, 63, 70
kukui, 68, 202–3
kuleana, 59, 168, 198, 204, 205, 213; defined, 4; interpretation and, 12, 204; Kānepuʻu's, 53, 98; Poepoe's, 105, 118; ʻāina and, 84–85, 161
Kuleana Act, 93
Kūmokuhāliʻi (deity), 28
Ke Kumu Hawaii, 15
Kumuhonua, 194, 196, 197, 201, 203, 204–5
Kumulipo, 84, 85, 110, 155, 163, 182, 187, 188, 205, 207–8; Poepoe's analysis of, 193–96
Kuokoa Home Rula, 123, 135–37, 142–45, 152
Kūolonowao (deity), 28
Kupahuʻa, Hawaiʻi, 157
Kupakee, J. W., 39
Kūpaʻaikeʻe, 28
Kūpepeiaoloa, 28
kupua, 28, 30, 58, 66, 76, 100, 160, 162, 164, 166–67, 201
Kupulanakēhau, 194, 195
Kūpulupulu (deity), 28
kūpuna o ka pō, 61, 64
Kuykendall, Ralph, 34, 113–14
kūʻauhau. *See* moʻokūʻauhau

Lahainaluna school, 21–22, 27, 32, 45, 177
Ka Lahui Hawaii, 48, 97, 99
Ka Lama Hawaii, 15
Lānaʻi, 89
land dispossession, 92–94, 169, 212
law, 110, 114, 116, 123, 133–34, 136; banning Hawaiian in schools, 124; Poepoe's book on, 116–18
Laʻamaomao, 24, 56
lāʻau lapaʻau, 200–201
Laʻilaʻi, 193, 194, 196
Lea (Laea, deity), 28
lehua. *See* ʻōhiʻa lehua
leprosy. *See* Hansen's disease

Lēʻapuki, Hawaiʻi, 157–58
Liholiho (Kamehameha II), 188
Liholiho (Alexander, Kamehameha IV), 34–35, 48, 107, 142
Like, Edward, 131, 145
Liliʻuokalani, 71–72, 118–21, 123
Limaikaika (Richard Armstrong), 15, 24, 42
lists, 58, 156; names in Kumulipo, 193–94
literary devices, 5, 57, 64–77, 151, 158–60, 162–63, 165, 171, 181, 203; lists as, 58. *See also* allusion; kaona; metaphor
Lohiʻau, 164–65, 201
Lokoea, 79–80
Lono (deity), 160, 188, 193
Lota Kapuāiwa (Kamehameha V), 35, 48
Louis, Renee Pualani, 84, 86–87, 91
loʻi, 2, 3, 88, 89, 94, 100
Luanuʻu, 71
Luhi, Oʻahu, 161–62
Luluku, Oʻahu, 200, 201
Lunalilo, 48
Luʻukia (sister of Kānepuʻu), 47
Luʻukia (Luʻukiakaʻahalanalana), 62, 75

Māhele, 93
Mahinui, Oʻahu, 161
"Mai Haalele i Kau Olelo Makuahine," 138
maile, 79, 148
Makakalo, Hawaiʻi, 30
Makaua, Oʻahu, 99–100
Mākena, Hawaiʻi, 156–58
Mākua, Oʻahu, 148
Makuakaumana, 206
male (for marry), 75
Malo, David, 43
Malo, Davida, 177, 182–83, 205, 212
mana wahine, 166–68, 199
Manu, Mose (Moses), 46
Marquesas Islands, 24, 30
Maui (island), 40, 55, 62, 84, 88, 89, 91, 146, 147, 150, 151, 170, 201
Māui (deity), 25, 188, 190
Mauna a Wākea, Hawaiʻi, 5
Mauna Kea, Hawaiʻi, 5, 188, 192
Maunalahilahi, Oʻahu, 148
Maunalua, Oʻahu, 22, 35
Māwae, Hawaiʻi, 157–58, 160
McCandless, Lincoln Loy, 145–46

mele, 10, 24, 39; aloha ʻāina and, 5, 12, 89, 124, 150; Armstrong and, 25; Kalākaua and, 48; Kānepuʻu and, 26–33, 55, 57, 58, 71–72, 89; kaona in, 11, 69; koʻihonua, 4, 6, 187–96, 200, 209; maps as, 99–100, 155–60; maʻi, 71–72; Poepoe and, 125, 126, 140, 150–73, 184–85, 187, 202–3; Wilikoki (Wilcox), 114; wind, 90–91

Na Mele Aimoku, 188

"Mele a Kahakukamoana," 187

"Mele a Pākuʻi," 187

"He Mele no ke Kauo ana i na Waa o Kana," 26, 27–29

memorization, 12, 26, 31, 58, 86, 91, 155, 179, 194, 208

metaphor, 84, 140, 162, 191, 203

Micronesia, 24

Mika Sobe, John, 137

missionaries, 13, 23; literacy and, 14; moʻolelo, effect on, 55–56, 176–80; newspapers and, 15, 24–25, 38, 54, 99

Moanalua, Oʻahu, 147–48

Moaʻula (waterfall, Molokai), 77

"Ka Moeuhane a Moi" (mele), 26, 29–31

mohoea, 67

Moi (in Kana moʻolelo), 26, 29–30, 57, 58–59

Mokoliʻi, Oʻahu, 170–71

Mokulēʻia, Oʻahu, 44, 148, 164

Molokai, 13, 21, 24, 25, 46, 47, 55, 56, 150; geography of, 87–92; Hāmanalau, moʻolelo of, 62, 76–77; Hansen's disease settlement, 143; Kana, moʻolelo and mele, 27, 31, 46; Kaohele, story of, 50; Pinao Alanakapu (wife of Fornander), 181

Molokainuiahina, 47

Mooaiku, 29

moon night names, 10, 23, 25, 57, 140, 142

Moreton-Robinson, Aileen, 87

moʻo, 161, 170–72

Moʻo Kapu o Hāloa, Oʻahu, 169

moʻokūʻauhau, 4, 6–7, 32, 142, 209, 212; Kamehameha's, 180, 188–93; Kānepuʻu and, 45–46, 50–51; Papa and Wākea, 194–97; Poepoe and, 174–75, 194–97, 205–6; ʻāina and, 83–87

moʻokūʻauhau consciousness, 4, 6–8, 204; Kānepuʻu's, 22–23, 53, 96; Poepoe's, 105, 126, 149–51, 155, 174–75

moʻolelo, importance of, 7–8, 44–46, 55–56, 81, 85–86, 89, 99, 138, 139, 149, 152–54, 173, 174, 177, 184–86, 204, 207

moʻolelo Hawaiʻi kahiko, as genre, 176–77

"Moolelo Hoonaue Puuwai no Kama-a-ka-Mahiai," 146

"Ka Moolelo Hooni Puuwai no Keakaoku," 146–47

"He Moolelo Kaao no ke Keiki Alii Otto!," 108–9

"He Moolelo Kaao no Roumiana Ho!," 113

"Moolelo Nani no Kekalukaluokewa," 147

"He Moolelo no Hamanalau, Hanai a Hawea," 43–46, 59–80

"He Moolelo no Kana, Hanai a Uli," 56–59

"He Moolelo no ka Naita Leopaki," 147

"He Moolelo no Kanewailani, ke Keiki a Maoloha," 45, 47, 53, 54

"He Moolelo no Lonoikamakahiki," 41

"He Moolelo no Pakaa," 24, 43, 44, 53, 54, 55–56, 89, 120

"He Moolelo no Rokekila Hinedu," 108

"Ka Moolelo o ko Wakea ma Noho ana ma Kalihi," 197–205

"Ka Moolelo o ko Wakea pio ana ia Hoohokukalani," 205

"Ka Moolelo o Kou Aina Oiwi," 139

Ka Mooolelo Hawaii 1838, 177–80

Ka Mooolelo Hawaii 1858, 180

Na-Hau-o-Maihi, 146–47

Nakanaela, Thomas, 114, 120

Nakuina, Emma, 213

Nakuina, Moses, 24, 56, 109, 213

Nāwahī, Joseph, 118, 120, 121, 126–27

Ka Naʻi Aupuni, 135–41, 151, 174, 183

Newlands Resolution, 128, 130, 133

newspapers, 1–2, 3, 13, 14–15, 212; importance of, 49–50; Kalākaua and, 48; Kānepuʻu and, 22, 23, 24, 33–34, 38–40, 43–44, 54, 89, 91; Poepoe and, 108, 112, 118–20, 121, 124–33, 135–48, 174, 194, 196

Nīheu, 26–28, 31, 59

Nīheukawa, Molokai, 50, 89

Ka Nonanona, 15

Notley, Charles Kahiliaulani, 137, 142, 146

Nukuhiva, 24, 30

Ka Nupepa Kuokoa, 49, 54, 60, 136, 146, 188; Kānepuʻu and, 34–39, 43–46; Poepoe, editor of, 121–35, 183
Nuʻo (place name), 30
Nuʻuhiwa (place name), 30

"Ka Oihana Kilo Hoku Hawaii," 206–8
Oliveira, Katrina-Ann Kapāʻanaokalāokeola, 6, 13, 85–86, 90–91
Ololo, 194, 195
ontology, 3, 9, 10, 87, 93, 101
Oo (place name), 30
orality, 178–79, 200
Organic Act, 133–34
origin theories, 125, 179, 181, 183, 186, 187, 193
overthrow of government, 120

Pacific Commercial Advertiser, 33, 37, 111, 121
Pāhoehoe, Hawaiʻi, 157–58
Pakaa (Pākaʻa), moʻolelo of, 24, 43, 44, 53, 54, 55–56, 89, 120
Pākaikai, Molokai, 88
Pākī, Abner, 88–89
Palau, Moses, 133, 134, 135
Pālāʻau, Molokai, 88
Palikū, Oʻahu, 170
Palikū, ancestor of Papa, 194, 195, 201, 202
Pālolo, Oʻahu, 41, 43, 54
Pānauiki, Hawaiʻi, 157–58
Pānaunui, Hawaiʻi, 157–58
Papa (Papahānaumoku), 4, 25, 84, 164, 187–92, 203, 205; Kumulipo, 193–96
Ka Papa Kuauhau o na Alii (Papa Kūʻauhau Aliʻi), 48, 51, 182, 194
Parker, Henry Hodges, 38, 48, 54, 99
Parker, Samuel, 107
parrhesia, 98–99
parties, political, 118, 119, 133, 136, 141, 145–47, 148
Pāʻao, 205–6
Pearl Harbor, 48
Pele, 150, 159–61, 165, 168; calling the winds, 155–56
Peleiōhōlani, 50
Peleioholani, Solomon Lehuanui, 141
performance cartography, 86
petition, anti-annexation, 128–29
Piʻipiʻi, 106

place names, 4, 86, 89, 99, 148; aloha ʻāina and, 77, 82–83, 85; kaona and, 11–12; as literary device, 5–6; mele map and, 156–59; moʻokūʻauhau consciousness and, 23
Pō, 9, 61, 64, 188, 193
Poepoe, G. W., 106 *See also* Kahiolo, G. W.
Poepoe, Joseph M.: annexation, support of, 120–24; arrest and imprisonment, 113; attorney training, 107; birth, 106; death, 149; education, 107; genealogy, 106; legislature, elected to, 148; political criticism of, 121–22
Pogue, John Fawcett (Pokuea), 180
Pōhakuokauaʻi, 165–66, 172
poi, 79–80, 95, 143
polygamy, Mormon, 141
Pōniuohua, Molokai, 88
Poupou, Hawaiʻi, 157–58
Poupoukea, Hawaiʻi, 157–58
poʻe aloha ʻāina, 124–31
Puaʻena, 61
Pūehuehu, Oʻahu, 199
Pueo, 166–69
Pukui, Mary Kawena, 12, 188; on kaona, 10–11; moʻolelo teaching method, 26–27; ʻiwa, figurative use of, 66–67; ʻōlelo noʻeau, 68, 70, 140, 198
Puna, Hawaiʻi, 30, 156–60, 163, 206
Punaluʻu, Oʻahu, 100
Puʻuohulu, Oʻahu, 148
Puʻupā, Molokai, 77

racism, 111, 141, 144
rain names, 25, 77, 144, 148, 162
Reciprocity Treaty, 127–28
redaction, 57, 76–77
resurgence, 2–3, 9, 211
Rice, William Hyde, 57

sandalwood, 73, 179
Savagery, representation of, 32, 37, 97
settler colonialism, 2, 83, 135, 154, 210
Sharpe, Cecilia, 147–48
Sheldon, John (Kahikina Kelekona), 113, 115, 120
Solis, Kekeha, 11, 13, 69, 81
Spencer, Thomas P., 113

star navigation, 207–8
sugar, 79, 88
sugar plantations, 48, 92, 94–95, 97, 98, 107, 128 144, 145, 212
Supreme Court decisions, 41, 110, 116–17

Tao Se, 109
taro. *See* kalo
teachers, 6, 14, 22, 32, 53, 82, 91–92, 98, 106, 107; moʻolelo kuʻuna and, 25; star navigation, 208
Testa, Francisco Joseph, 124, 127, 131
Thrum, Thomas, 29
Thiongʻo, Ngũgĩ wa, ix–x, 175
translation: issues, 28–29, 137–38, 140, 147, 183, 190–91; works into Hawaiian, 108–9, 110, 113, 120, 133–34, 142; works into English, 143
treaty of annexation, 128

uhu, 75
Uli, 27–28, 57, 59

wahi pana, 5, 77–80, 92, 137, 143, 152–53, 161; defined, 89
Puʻu Waiahilahila, Oʻahu, 164
Waiāhole, Oʻahu, 145, 166–69
Waiakeakua (Waiakeʻkua, place name), 30
Waialua, Oʻahu, 44, 61, 67, 76, 79, 80, 164
Waikahalulu, Oʻahu, 200
Waimānalo, ʻEwa, Oʻahu, 148
Waimea, Oʻahu, 148
Waipapa (place name), 30
Waipiʻo, Hawaiʻi, 61, 62, 64, 66
Waiʻākōlea, Hawaiʻi, 156–57
Wākea, 4, 84, 164, 186–93; Kumulipo, in, 193–96; Kāmehaʻikana moʻolelo, in, 197, 199–202, 204–5

war, 27, 59, 200–205
waʻa, 2, 61, 73, 166; Kana's, 26–31, 57, 59
whale rider, 206
Whitney, Henry (Wini), 33, 35, 36, 38, 39
Wilcox, Robert. *See* Wilikoki
Wilcox Rebellion 1889, 113
Wilikoki (Robert Wilcox), 112–13, 117, 118, 120, 127, 131, 135, 137; mele for, 114
winds, 24, 25, 55, 56, 148, 155–56; Hāmanalau, in moʻolelo of, 66–67, 74, 75, 77, 80; geography, in, 90–92; Inuwai, 75; Kiuwaiʻula, 156; Kumulipo-hoʻoululiʻi, 156; Pākaʻa, in moʻolelo of, 89; Waikea, 156; Waikōloa, 80; Waiʻalae, 156
Wini. *See* Whitney, Henry
Wise, John, 146
Wolfe, Patrick, 83
women, as sources of knowledge, 59
women's suffrage, 147–48

ʻAhahui ʻElele of Kamehameha V, 35–37
ʻAhahui ʻEuanelio Hawaiʻi. *See* AEH
ʻĀhuimanu, Oʻahu, 161–62; school, 107
ʻaumakua, 4, 9, 68, 152, 160, 169
ʻawa, 79, 198–99, 206
ʻĀwili, Hawaiʻi, 156–58
ʻEwa, Oʻahu, 107, 148
ʻiwa, 66–67, 68
ʻĪʻī, John Papa, 212
ʻiʻiwi, 62, 65, 68
ʻōhiʻa lehua, 64, 78–79, 148, 159–60
ʻōlelo noʻeau, 6, 73, 88, 90, 198; Kānepuʻu's use of, 68–71; Poepoe's use of, 108, 140, 202; ʻāina and, 5, 12–13, 25
ʻOlopana, 200–201, 205
ʻōpū aliʻi, 169
ʻUkoʻa, 80
ʻulu, 199–200